OXFORD HISTORICAL MONOGRAPHS

Literature and the Irish Famine 1845-1919

MELISSA FEGAN

CLARENDON PRESS · OXFORD

OXFORD
UNIVERSITY PRESS

Great Clarendon Street, Oxford OX2 6DP

Oxford University Press is a department of the University of Oxford.
It furthers the University's objective of excellence in research, scholarship,
and education by publishing worldwide in

Oxford New York

Auckland Bangkok Buenos Aires Cape Town Chennai
Dar es Salaam Delhi Hong Kong Istanbul Karachi Kolkata
Kuala Lumpur Madrid Melbourne Mexico City Mumbai Nairobi
São Paulo Shanghai Singapore Taipei Tokyo Toronto
with an associated company in Berlin

Oxford is a registered trade mark of Oxford University Press
in the UK and in certain other countries

Published in the United States
by Oxford University Press Inc., New York

© Melissa Fegan 2002

The moral rights of the author have been asserted
Database right Oxford University Press (maker)

First published 2002

British Library Cataloguing in Publication Data
Data available

Library of Congress Cataloging in Publication Data
Data Avaliable
ISBN 0–19–925464–8

1 3 5 7 9 10 8 6 4 2

Typeset by Hope Services (Abingdon) Ltd.
Printed in Great Britain
on acid-free paper by
Biddles Ltd.,
Guildford and King's Lynn

Look about you, and say what is it you see that doesn't foretell famine—famine—famine! . . . Isn't the airth a page of prophecy, an' the sky a page of prophecy, where every man may read of famine, pestilence and death?

(William Carleton, *The Black Prophet: A Tale of Irish Famine* (London and Belfast: Simms & M'Intyre, 1847), 15)

ACKNOWLEDGEMENTS

First, I would like to express my sincere thanks to Roy Foster, for his interest and participation in my research, and the positive example set by his own interdisciplinarity, which I have attempted to reflect in my own work. I would also like to thank Isabel Rivers for her support over the years. I owe a great debt of gratitude to my colleagues and students in the English and History Departments of Chester College for their patience, good-humour, and friendship—in particular Katharine Armstrong, Graham Atkin, Josie Billington, Arthur Bradley, Diana Dunn, Bill Hughes, Maggie Jackson, Jen Mawson, Emma Rees, Jeremy Smith, Will Stephenson, Beth Swan, Glyn Turton, Chris Walsh, Yvonne Siddle, Roger Swift, Jackie Turton, Angela Piatt. Thanks to Kate Flint, John Kelly, and Tom Dunne for advice and comments on the thesis from which this work grew. I appreciate the help of the staff at the Bodleian and English Faculty Libraries, Oxford, the British Library, Chester College and Liverpool University Libraries, St Deiniol's Residential Library in Hawarden, and Queen's University Library, Belfast. I gratefully acknowledge the financial support of the British Academy, which funded my doctoral research.

Friends and family have been tremendously supportive through the years; in particular, I'd like to mention Agnes Corrigan, Brian, Kelly, Tony and Glen Fegan, Lily and John Purcell, Maureen and Russell Blair, Tom Casement, Sara Haslam, Andrew Tate, Margaret Hughes, Angela Walsh, Sally Atkin, Paul Clark, Richard Wilson, Laura Johnson, Martin Dowling, Graham Kay, Siri Ellis, but, above all, my mother, Marie Fegan, who has been a constant source of encouragement and inspiration. Finally, thanks to Peter Blair, without whom, as the cliché goes, none of this would have been possible.

Some of the material in Chapter 3 first appeared in 'The Travellers Experience of Famine Ireland', *Irish Studies Review* 9/3 (Dec. 2001), 361–71.

CONTENTS

LIST OF PLATES

Introduction: Not So Ambiguous

> A history beset with such distracting problems, bristling with such thorny controversies, a history, above all, which has so much bearing upon that portion of history which has still to be born, ought, it may be said, to be approached in the gravest and most authoritative fashion possible, or else not approached at all.
>
> (Emily Lawless, *The Story of the Nations: Ireland* (London and New York: T. Fisher Unwin; G. P. Putnam's Sons, 1887), Preface.)

> I know not whether the time has even yet arrived when that theme can be fairly treated, and when a calm and just apportionment of blame and merit may be attempted. To-day, full thirty years after the event, I tremble to contemplate it.
>
> (A. M. Sullivan, *New Ireland: Political Sketches and Personal Reminiscences of Thirty Years of Irish Public Life* (Glasgow and London: Cameron & Ferguson; Fleet Street, 1877), 58.)

More than one hundred years after these expressions of trepidation, it is still a daunting experience to write about the Great Famine. For more than a decade, historians have been puzzled and concerned about the lack of recent research into the Famine, especially by Irish historians. But in the wake of the 150th anniversary of Black '47, such concerns have been assuaged by a flood of exciting new work on the local and national implications of this immense tragedy. Such is the hunger for these works that some historians and economists—notably Cormac Ó Gráda and Christine Kinealy—have published several books each on the subject. It is widely accepted that the Great Famine was a defining moment in Irish history; but can the same be claimed for Irish literature? The fact that the Famine made an impact on literature may seem commonplace, but it is not at all accepted. Terry Eagleton recently complained: 'There is a handful of novels and a body of poems, but few truly distinguished works. Where is the Famine in the literature of the Revival? Where is it in Joyce?'[1] It has been assumed that the proper medium for the Famine was silence, as it has been argued that the proper medium for the Holocaust—with which the Famine is too easily superficially identified—is silence. But, as Michael Bernstein has argued, even silence is a productive topic:

[1] Terry Eagleton, *Heathcliff and the Great Hunger: Studies in Irish Culture* (London and New York: Verso, 1995), 13.

As well as being simultaneously unimaginable and inevitable, at once unique and paradigmatic, the Shoah is also invoked as both unspeakable and as the single, decisive, twentieth-century event that must be talked about. Indeed, its radical unspeakableness, the inability of language or of any other medium to engage it adequately, is precisely what constitutes much of the conversation about the Shoah.[2]

There are notable silences in the literature of the Famine: as Cathal Póirtéir has noted: 'While there is a vast amount of written evidence, little or none of it comes from the perspective of the ordinary people.'[3] But other sections of the community were not silenced. In fact, the Famine proved a source of painful inspiration for literature from its inception until the present day. The poets of *The Nation*—such as James Clarence Mangan, Richard D'Alton Williams, Thomas D'Arcy McGee, and Jane Francesca Elgee (future mother of Oscar Wilde)—the novelist William Carleton and short-story writer Mrs Hoare and many others reacted by writing about the tragedy *in medias res*. Others, like Anthony Trollope, were so disturbed that it took many years before they were ready to acknowledge the true extent of the catastrophe. In the twentieth century, when a famine in Ireland would seem unthinkable, the Famine emerges as a powerful metaphor of social and spiritual degradation, as in the poetry of Patrick Kavanagh, or a manifestation of race memory, as in the work of Seamus Heaney and Eavan Boland. The Famine was a devastating historical event, leading to the deaths of approximately one and a half million Irish people, accelerating emigration and the loss of the Irish language; but it was also a major literary event, crushing the literary revival that had led William Carleton to boast that he would never publish in London, and decimating the Irish publishing industry. It claimed the lives of promising Irish writers like James Clarence Mangan, contributed towards outlawing John Mitchel and Thomas D'Arcy McGee, and alienated Charles Gavan Duffy and William Carleton from the people they had written and planned for. The impression that very little has been written about the Famine, or that it had very little impact on the country's literature, is clearly misguided and needs to be revised.

Perhaps one of the reasons why the literature of the Famine has been overlooked or dismissed as 'minor' is the tendency to ignore its interdisciplinarity. It is true that much of the poetry of the Famine is polemical, and many of the novels of the late nineteenth century that explore the Famine are written with a political or sectarian agenda, and this often

---

[2] Michael A. Bernstein, 'Homage to the Extreme: The Shoah and the Rhetoric of Catastrophe', *Times Literary Supplement* (6 Mar. 1998), 6–8, at 8.
[3] Cathal Póirtéir, *Famine Echoes* (Dublin: Gill & Macmillan, 1995), 3.

damages them as art. But Famine literature is much wider than this, encompassing a range of genres—histories, autobiographies and biographies, travel narratives, letters, diaries, journalism, must all be accommodated alongside novels, poems, short stories, and plays. Each genre does make certain demands of writer and reader: this can be traced in the curious homogeneity of works on the Famine. History is expected to be factual and objective, and so historians tend to argue less over facts and more over the conclusions to be drawn from those facts. Travel narratives are expected to be informative and entertaining, but in Ireland they become social documents, purporting to reveal the truth about the troubled sistercountry: travellers follow in each other's footsteps, quote each other, and come up with much the same conclusions—including a universal distaste for emigration, even among those travellers who, as adherents of political economy, might be expected to be in favour of it. Many of the Famine poets were also political activists; but while their poetry is often apocalyptic or religious, resigned to revenge by a 'spectral army', the poets themselves were mostly committed to political violence. The genre seems to impose restrictions and conclusions the authors would not necessarily have entertained outside literature. The strain of attempting to negotiate a genre can be seen in the disjunction between Anthony Trollope's *Six Letters to the Examiner*, in which he praises the government for its handling of the Famine and denies it was a major catastrophe, and his novel *Castle Richmond*, which exposes the mishandling of a government too closely wedded to political economy, and subtly explores the violence of the tragedy.[4] The boundaries are, however, not fixed: this can be seen most clearly in the debate over which medium is most appropriate for the representation of the Famine: 'revisionist' historians have been criticized for their scrupulous objectivity, and urged to reinvest Famine historiography with emotion, while 'traditional' historians have been dismissed as hysterical: 'Surely if we want moral and emotional registers as badly as [Brendan] Bradshaw suggests we do, we will not look to historians: we will read novels and poems, listen to ballads, stick close to our grandmothers and say our prayers.'[5] Similarly, Trollope and Carleton were both criticized for portraying the Famine as what it essentially was—not an isolated event, but part of the social, political, economic, religious, and cultural web of Ireland. Their texts acknowledge the historicity of the Famine

---

[4] This disjunction is also related to the passage of time: *Six Letters* were written between 1849 and 1850, while *Castle Richmond* was written in 1859, when Trollope was about to leave Ireland for England, and wanted to set the record straight.

[5] Colm Tóibín, *The Irish Famine* (London: Profile, 1999), 24.

while at the same time resisting it: Carleton links the Great Famine of
1845–52 with the many previous famines Ireland had endured, and stated
that his novel *The Black Prophet*, written in the midst of the calamity, was
not about that particular famine, or about famines in general, so much as
about the universal 'workings of those passions and feelings which usually
agitate human life'.[6] While novelists are expected to be historians, historians are transformed into novelists: Tóibín, who agrees with Eagleton that
the volume of literature on the Famine is insignificant, feels the need to co-
opt historians to flesh out the literature, comparing Cecil Woodham-
Smith, author of *The Great Hunger*, to A. S. Byatt, describing Joel
Mokyr's *Why Ireland Starved* as 'the historians' equivalent of *The Waste
Land*, and claiming David Fitzpatrick's *Oceans of Consolation* 'has the
depth and narrative range of a novel'.[7]

But it is not simply a question of medium, but a question of representation: how can one adequately represent the magnitude of the Great
Famine and the impact it made on individuals as well as on Ireland?
Tóibín has recently suggested that 'the problem may be endemic—wider
certainly than the personalities and backgrounds of a few academics. It
may lie in the relationship between catastrophe and analytic narrative.
How do you write about the Famine? What tone do you use?'[8] Tone would
appear to be central. Paul Bew's recent comment on Famine documents,
'the relevant papers are not so unambiguous', emphasizes in both style and
content the uncertainty felt by Famine historiographers.[9] Ambiguity and
obfuscation are keynotes, essentially because there are few disputes about
facts and figures, but huge, largely mythic, ideological polarities to be
maintained. It is surprising and enlightening to find on a close reading of
Famine literature that *The Times* can sound like *The Nation*, Charles
Trevelyan can sound like John Mitchel, Cecil Woodham-Smith can sound
like R. Dudley Edwards. Providentialism has become a topic of great
interest in Famine historiography, as embodying the crux of the difference
between the various groups who commented on the Famine: *The Times*—
the organ of British public opinion—and principal members of the government, including the secretary to the Treasury, Charles Trevelyan,
believed the Famine was the work of God, and were therefore reluctant to
intercede, while *The Nation* and Young Ireland were convinced the
Famine was the work of a genocidal agenda by government designed to

6 William Carleton, *The Black Prophet: A Tale of Irish Famine* (London and Belfast:
Simms & M'Intyre, 1847), p. iv.
7 Tóibín, *The Irish Famine*, 69, 70, 78.   8 Ibid., 22.
9 Paul Bew, 'A Case of Compassion Fatigue', *Spectator* (13 Mar. 1999), 37–8, at 38.

wipe out the Irish by starvation and emigration. In fact, as will be seen, it is not that clear-cut: *The Times* did not advocate providentialism as avidly as *The Nation* did, and, as Bew's article in the *Spectator* shows, Trevelyan was often less convinced of the divine nature of the Famine than members of the Roman Catholic clergy in Ireland, and indeed than some Young Ireland leaders—'the relevant papers are not so unambiguous'.

Just as many of these writers break the bounds in terms of our expectations of medium and message, the first chapter of the book breaks the bounds of its own chronology by taking Famine literature past 1919 and to the present day, eighty years later. The terminal date 1919 was a convenient break-off point as the beginning of the Anglo-Irish War, a new phase of Irish history, but also as the last time anyone could really claim to be writing using eyewitness evidence, as Louis J. Walsh did in his novel *The Next Time: A Story of 'Forty-Eight* (1919). However, given the renewed interest in the Famine in the wake of the 150th anniversary of Black '47, and the fact that much of the historiography written since 1919 casts light not only on the events, but on the texts and documents of the Famine period, it seemed illogical to exclude these later studies. This chapter explores the sense of a self-created polarity between 'traditional' and 'revisionist' historians writing on the Famine, and asks if there is really clear blue water between them on the essentials. Why is there so much emphasis on the emotion inspired by the Famine in late-twentieth-century historiography, when early Famine historians such as John Mitchel and Michael Davitt, who certainly raged against the impact of the Famine on their own lives, were curiously impassive in the face of the suffering of those who actually perished? The idea that we need to recapture the grief and anger of the past is a misconception. The chapter also views the way in which historians seek to make connections between the Famine and other historical events, notably the Holocaust, Ethiopia, and Bosnia, using emotive terms such as genocide, ethnic cleansing, race memory, and trauma. What role do mythology and oral history have to play in the creation of Famine history?

The second chapter examines the representation of the Famine in two ideologically opposed newspapers, *The Times* and *The Nation*. The Famine was a major event in journalism both in England and in Ireland: journalists and artists were sent to the ravaged areas as to a war-zone, to report back on conditions that seemed impossible in a part of the most powerful country on earth. Due to their efforts, famine-stricken towns like Skibbereen and Schull were publicized and relieved; those towns that missed out on the media-frenzy had to rely on often non-existent public support. The chapter charts the change in opinion manifested in some of the most popular newspapers of the day, from near universal sympathy in 1845, to compassion fatigue and suspicion in 1846 and 1847, to horror and outrage at murder and armed rebellion in 1848, and near-indifference in the final years of the Famine. *The Times*, regarded as the organ of public opinion, had a leader on Ireland and an Ireland column almost every day during the Famine; its decision not to support a Queen's Letter and Fast Day for the Irish in 1847 undoubtedly contributed towards the poor returns manifested by the public. Pitted against *The Times* is *The Nation*, the organ of Young Ireland. Many of *The Nation* journalists—including Charles Gavan Duffy, John Mitchel, Richard D'Alton Williams, and Kevin Izod O'Doherty—were prosecuted for sedition or treason during the Famine for their writings in support of an armed rebellion, so they were not disinterested commentators—Mitchel and O'Doherty were transported. Yet *The Times* and *The Nation*, always perceived as extremes, are in fact at times remarkably similar in tone, especially at the beginning of the Famine when all newspapers were united in condemning exportation from a starving country, and towards the end, when a disillusioned and bitter Duffy took to castigating his countrymen in the revived *Nation*. The providentialism of *The Times* has been misrepresented, and this chapter seeks to reinvest Famine journalism with its shifts of opinion and complexity. Famine journalists were aware that they were negotiating a relationship between England and Ireland: they used metaphors of disease, patronage, and kinship at various stages to represent the various connections they were prepared to make at the time. They were also highly aware that they were making history, either textually in their writings or physically by their presence in stricken areas or in their rebellion. Famine journalism is a rich and largely untapped source of information on the nuances of public opinion during this period.

Staying with supposedly non-fictional sources, the focus then moves onto travel literature. This is a movement away from the public voice of history and journalism towards the private voice of the tourist, recounting his own experiences and anecdotes. Yet travellers in Ireland during the Famine were still highly aware of their duties and responsibilities: unable to believe the wild stories of starvation and destitution being peddled by Irish scaremongers, they claimed to be visiting in order to discover the truth about Ireland with their own eyes. In most cases, they found that the stories they heard had not, could not, have been exaggerated. Travellers in Ireland during the Famine were extremely important in overturning the determined myopia of those who had no interest in believing in the

Famine, for instance those who were campaigning against the Repeal of the Corn Laws. Travellers to remote areas such as Belmullet and Erris undoubtedly saved lives by drawing much-needed subscriptions to areas which might otherwise have been left to their own limited devices. On the other hand, they were often granted positions of unofficial authority—as when Henry Inglis was quoted in parliament, or when Thomas Campell Foster was accorded the title '*Times*' Commissioner'—and may sometimes have done more harm than good. Their texts betray a fundamental uneasiness: first at the proximity of this medieval distress to the shores of the most industrialized nation on earth; secondly at the idea of shared nationhood; finally at the impact the sight of such suffering had on the viewer: at times, they demand more sympathy for themselves than for the poor wretches they gaze on. Their separation from the disaster—and indeed that of virtually every other writer on the Famine—deserves comment: how can relatively affluent, middle-class, educated men and women adequately represent what is essentially alien to them—death by starvation and disease? Even those travellers who were Irish—such as Samuel and Anna Maria Hall or Charles Gavan Duffy—register this feeling of alterity, and this panic when faced by something they cannot understand.

Anthony Trollope is perhaps the ultimate example of someone who tried to make connections between his own alterity and his recognition of Ireland as his spiritual homeland. Trollope had arrived in Ireland relatively poor, completely unknown, without hopes and prospects; he left Ireland as a published author, on the threshold of the great success of *Framley Parsonage*. Chapter 4 deals with Trollope's Irish experience: his first and last novels were Irish novels, he wrote several other novels and short stories either set in Ireland or with Irish protagonists, and would probably have written more had it not been for contemporary rejection of Irish stories, and his claim to be an Irish writer is recognized by his inclusion in the *Oxford Companion to Irish Literature*. But the Great Famine was the ultimate test to Trollope's Irishness, and he fell down at the first hurdle. Unable to cope with the misery he must have witnessed as a travelling post office inspector and resident in Ireland, he denied the severity of the Famine in his *Six Letters to the Examiner*, and praised government relief measures. This chapter argues that Trollope in his fiction employs subtextual strategies to deal with a famine that as an Englishman and a government employee he could not acknowledge. It may have been guilt that led him to deny it in the *Six Letters*, or simply political expediency; either way, by the time he left Ireland in 1859, he was ready to subtly undermine his own argument in *Castle Richmond*.

The next chapter deals with a writer who had no need to prove his nationality or claim an interest in Ireland—William Carleton. The son of a peasant farmer and an Irish-speaking songstress, Carleton was able to rely on his authenticity and connection with Gaelic Ireland to win an audience. Carleton was a key figure in the Literary Revival of the 1830s and 1840s, publishing—in Dublin—novels and short stories about the Irish peasantry. His claims to authenticity did not go unchallenged: as a convert to Protestantism, he was often viewed with suspicion, as a pen-for-hire. But one of the most interesting features of his writing is its frequent reference to famine—not just the Great Famine, but the many other famines that punctuated Irish history, in particular the famines of 1817 and 1822, of which Carleton had personal experience. Famine was not just a historical or literary event for Carleton: it formed one of his earliest childhood memories, and it was to crush the literary revival Carleton had sacrificed so much to. In the end, he was even forced to resort to publishing in England, something he had boasted he would not do. Carleton's work is fascinating because it captures the consciousness of a transition time; even before the Famine, Carleton knew that Gaelic Ireland was dying, and that he was its chronicler. In a sense, his work seems prophetic: for example, *The Black Prophet* was written in 1845, when the Famine had barely begun. But this was merely a manifestation of his authenticity, as his experience of previous famines feeds into this great tragedy. This chapter examines the famine narratives of a writer caught in a transition time between the peasant world he had rejected and the ascendancy world that would not accept him.

Chapter 6 deals with the poetry of the Famine. As already mentioned, the poetry, like so many of the genres employed in the representation of the Famine, is remarkably homogeneous in tone and style: much of it is exhortatory, apocalyptic, or infused with religious quietism. The chapter explores the disjunction between these poets' Famine poetry and their reaction to the Famine in daily life: for example, Aubrey De Vere in his poetry reads the Famine as part of Ireland's spiritual destiny, a purgation sent by God to purify the country; but in his prose writings, such as *English Misrule and Irish Misdeeds*, he clearly blames the English government. As a landowner, it is arguable that De Vere should not have had anything to say about the Famine, as he did not suffer personally, and could be held at least partly responsible for his tenants' sufferings. But this could be said of most of the poets who were inspired by the macabre scenes of the Famine: many were middle-class professionals writing about things they had no first-hand knowledge of, as is clear from the fact that so few use first-person narrators in their poetry. A few, such as James Clarence Mangan, John De Jean Frazer, and John Keegan, were in more precarious social positions—all three died in penury from starvation or disease during the Famine. But the middle-class professionals who wrote Famine poetry had been utterly transformed by it: Samuel Ferguson became a Protestant Repealer, De Vere ceased to be a dreamer and sprang into action to save his tenants, Jane Francesca Elgee rejected her unionist background to write fiercely nationalist poetry as 'Speranza'. Famine was metamorphic: differences of background, tradition, class, gender, and even style fell away, and these poets embraced an epic, exhortatory, apocalyptic tone which represented an idealistic escape from the harsh choices they were faced with in reality.

The final chapter examines late-nineteenth-century novels about the Famine. Earlier novels, such as those by William Carleton and Anthony Trollope, had sought to set the Famine in its historical context, and to see it as just one of many issues assailing Ireland at the time. But as the century progressed, the Famine as literary subject became loaded with political issues. There was always an agenda at stake: emigration, conversion, the Irish language, the Land League—the Famine was a political tool, a complex metaphor which became a shorthand for violence and oppression. Several evangelical Protestant texts even sought to claim the Famine for Protestant converts, arguing that they suffered most during the Famine. Ironically, as the novels became more critically acclaimed, the material stopped being controversial: in 1910 the *Times Literary Supplement* praised Mildred Darby's *The Hunger* without even seeking to challenge its claim that two million people died of starvation and disease during the Famine due to government incompetence.[10] The Famine had ceased to be historical, and begun to be literature.

Far from being an absence, there is a plethora of literature about the Famine, from 1845 to the present day. The repetition of the 'silence' of the Famine may mask an anxiety about its representation: what right do the survivors have to speak of the Famine? And are these narratives simply strategies to deal with the Famine, rather than a reliable source of information? In the end, reliability is not the remit of this book: it sets out to prove that the Famine had an impact on literature in Ireland and elsewhere, and that while much of the literature of the Famine is 'insignificant' because it is poor art, it is not 'insignificant' in quantity and certainly not in interest. In effect, it attempts to recuperate Famine literature from silence and ignorance.

[10] *Times Literary Supplement* (14 Apr. 1910), 135.

I

Faction: The Historiography of the Great Famine

Since the late 1980s, the Irish historical establishment, no doubt spurred by the impending 150th anniversary of the Great Famine, has been beating its collective breast about its apparent neglect of the tragic episode. Cormac Ó Gráda, who spearheaded this historiographical revival, noted the paradox and irony of this lacuna:

> Given the Irish propensity to be maudlin about the past, a continuous rush of research on the Irish Famine might be expected. It is, after all, the main event in modern Irish history, as important to Ireland as, say, the French Revolution to France or the First Industrial Revolution to England. Yet secondary references to the Famine are out of all proportion to the amount of fresh research published.[1]

More recently, Joseph Lee has described Famine historiography as 'abnormal', suggesting that obsession would have been a much more understandable reaction than relative silence, while Patrick O'Sullivan has gone so far as to infer that it was as if there was a world-wide academic conspiracy to ignore the Irish Famine.[2] These statements seem melodramatic: the Famine has never been far from the surface of Irish history-writing since 1847, and a study such as Liam de Paor's *Milestones of Irish History*, cited by Ó Gráda for ignoring the Famine completely, is an anomaly. Yet the comparative dearth of studies is odd, and stranger still in light of the obvious public interest that has kept Cecil Woodham-Smith's *The Great Hunger* in print since 1962, and made it the best-selling Irish history book of all time. The establishment has atoned with a vengeance since 1988, and Ó Gráda's disappointment has been assuaged by the deluge of books, articles, local studies, and collections of essays that have been published since then. Indeed, the response has been such that in his most recent work, Ó Gráda almost seems to regret the fertility of the field: 'In more recent years, though, such has been the outpouring of works on

---

[1] Cormac Ó Gráda, ' "For Irishmen to Forget?" Recent Research on the Great Irish Famine' (Dublin: Centre for Economic Research, University College Dublin, 1988), 1–2.

[2] Joseph Lee, 'The Famine as History', in Cormac Ó Gráda (ed.), *Famine 150: Commemorative Lecture Series* (Dublin: Teagasc: University College Dublin, 1997), 159; Patrick O'Sullivan, 'Introduction' to *The Irish World Wide: History, Heritage, Identity*, Vol 6: *The Meaning of the Famine* (London and Washington, DC: Leicester University Press, 1997), 1.

the Irish famine that fresh titles are at a premium. My own earlier choice of *The Great Irish Famine* for a booklet published in 1989 has been recycled at least three times since.'[3] There are so many Famine historians now that they have even been granted their own collective noun—'Faminists'.[4] The dam appears to have burst, and silence is no longer a problem or an option.

And yet suspicions remain that historians are still holding back. Irish historians have been castigated for being too conservative and reticent, allowing American and British historians, and even economists, to take the initiative and infringe on their territory. On the one hand, historians are accused of misguided political correctness, or self-censorship, due to fears that any examination of the Famine critical of Britain's conduct would inevitably fuel IRA violence (as if that organization did not have efficient propagandists of its own). On the other hand, they are attacked as 'revisionists', a term used pejoratively in the Irish context to describe those believed to be wilfully and gleefully debunking tradition, for the sake of deliberately giving pain to those whose ancestors suffered and died during the Famine. Christine Kinealy asserts: 'Suffering, emotion and the sense of catastrophe, have been removed from revisionist interpretations of the Famine with clinical precision. The obscenity and degradation of starvation and Famine have been marginalised.'[5] However, those who try to reinsert the suffering, emotion, and sense of catastrophe are accused of 'famine-pornography' and sensationalism.[6] In 1847 the future Home Rule leader Isaac Butt declared that the Famine had been made a party issue: 'To profess belief in the fact of the existence of a formidable potato blight, was as sure a method of being branded as a radical, as to propose to destroy the Church.'[7] One hundred and fifty years later, little seems to have changed: there is no surer way of being branded a revisionist than to suggest that the Famine was not causative of all subsequent Irish history; no surer way of being relegated to traditional nationalism than to accuse the government of culpability. One is either a traditionalist or a revisionist: as

---

[3] Cormac Ó Gráda, *Black '47 and Beyond: The Great Irish Famine in History, Economy and Memory* (Princeton: Princeton University Press, 1999), 3.

[4] See Christine Kinealy, 'Beyond Revisionism: Reassessing the Great Irish Famine', *History Ireland*, 3/4 (Winter 1995), 28–34, at 34; Donald Harman Akenson, 'A Midrash on "Galut", "Exile" and "Diaspora" Rhetoric', in E. Margaret Crawford (ed.), *The Hungry Stream: Essays on Emigration and Famine* (Belfast: Institute of Irish Studies, Queen's University Belfast, 1997), 5.

[5] Kinealy, 'Beyond Revisionism', 31.

[6] Akenson, 'A Midrash on "Galut", "Exile" and "Diaspora" Rhetoric', 5.

[7] Isaac Butt, 'The Famine in the Land. What Has Been Done, And What Is To Be Done', *Dublin University Magazine*, 29/172 (Apr. 1847), 501–40, at 502.

Kinealy states: 'Irish historiography—particularly Famine historiography—has been polarised within the confines of a concentric and narrow historical discourse.'[8] This would seem as good a reason as any to avoid the argument altogether. Yet this tradition–revision polarization seems largely self-generated, as much a myth as those that revisionists are supposed to be debunking. As James S. Donnelly Jr. points out, almost all the academic histories of the Famine, and films involving professional historians produced since 1989, have been on the traditional nationalist axis.[9] If there is a polarity, gravity appears to be working in only one direction, and those who care to suggest that the Famine was not the only historical event that shaped modern Ireland, as Raymond Crotty and Roy Foster have done, are left very much out in the cold.

This siege-mentality about the Famine is not, of course, a post-1989 phenomenon: as early as 1947, the year of the virtually unacknowledged 100th anniversary of 'Black '47', Timothy O'Herlihy warned in his study of the Famine of 'a tendency to-day to minimise the ancient ills of Ireland'.[10] The establishment of the journal *Irish Historical Studies* with its advocacy of what amounted to 'value-free history', and the publication in 1956 of R. Dudley Edwards and T. Desmond Williams's *The Great Famine*, have been pointed to ever since as the beginning of a divisive, reductive revisionism. Edwards seems to have anticipated the dangers: in his diary-entry for 11 September 1952, he noted: 'The Famine: danger of dehydrated history'; a few days earlier he had accepted the right of novelists such as William Carleton and Liam O'Flaherty, or even the arch-nationalists Archbishop MacHale and John Mitchel, to be taken seriously in their pronouncements about the Famine.[11] But for all Edwards's uncertainty, anti-revisionist attacks on *The Great Famine* can seem overstated and unfair. It is true, as many critics have pointed out, that there is no unifying vision—indeed Edwards and Williams themselves had no direct input at all, even their introduction being ghost-written by Kevin Nowlan. But many of the most interesting and productive Famine studies of the 1990s are similarly divided—Cathal Póirtéir's edition of *The Great Irish Famine* (1995), Ó Gráda's *Famine 150* (1997), O'Sullivan's *The Irish World Wide* (1997), Christine Kinealy and Trevor Parkhill's *The Famine in Ulster*

---

[8] Kinealy, 'Beyond Revisionism', 31.

[9] James S. Donnelly, Jr., 'The Construction of the Memory of the Famine in Ireland and the Irish Diaspora, 1850–1900', *Éire-Ireland*, 31 (Spring/Summer 1996), 26–61, at 26.

[10] Timothy O'Herlihy, *The Famine 1845–1847: A Survey of its Ravages and Causes* (Drogheda: Drogheda Independent Co., 1947), 5.

[11] Quoted in Cormac Ó Gráda, 'Making History in Ireland in the 1940s and 1950s: The Saga of the Great Famine', *Irish Review*, 12 (Spring/Summer 1992), 87–107, at 101.

(1997), and E. Margaret Crawford's *The Hungry Stream* (1997), to name but a few. The main charge, that *The Great Famine* sanitized the suffering and became an apologia for the government, also seems unjust. The introduction states outright: 'There was no conspiracy to destroy the Irish nation', striking right at the heart of nationalist mythology about the Famine.[12] However, even non-revisionists accept this. Cecil Woodham-Smith, whose book *The Great Hunger* is so often pitted against *The Great Famine*, categorically stated:

These misfortunes were not part of a plan to destroy the Irish nation; they fell on the people because the government of Lord John Russell was afflicted with an extraordinary inability to foresee consequences . . . parsimony was certainly carried to remarkable lengths; but obtuseness, short-sightedness and ignorance probably contributed more.[13]

Parsimony, obtuseness, short-sightedness and ignorance are formidable failings in a government, but they do not constitute genocide.

The Great Famine did its best to take the suffering of the people seriously, even including a chapter on oral tradition, an unusual step at the time; and although the introduction seems to dodge the important issue of famine mortality—'Perhaps all that matters is the certainty that many, very many died'—individual essays contain all the emotion and pain even a traditional nationalist could desire. Chapter 4 of the collection, Thomas P. O'Neill's 'The Organisation and Administration of Relief, 1845–52', repeats many key arguments of the nationalist mythology of the Famine. Of the exportation of food during a famine O'Neill says: 'the stock of food in the country, which could have bridged the gap until the new year, was allowed to be exported'. On the inadequacy of government resources for famine relief he comments, echoing Isaac Butt: 'If the political union of 1800 were complete, the rate-in-aid should have been levied not on Ireland alone but on England, Scotland and Wales as well.' He does not seek to hide the fact that people receiving rations died of starvation, that people were driven to eat horse and donkey flesh, that dogs ate corpses. And despite a qualificatory 'perhaps', he justifies Irish bitterness towards a perceived genocidal agenda: 'Perhaps it was natural that the Irish who survived should remember those who died and that they felt that the resources of the British empire were not used for the benefit of

---

[12] R. Dudley Edwards and T. Desmond Williams (eds.), *The Great Famine: Studies in Irish History 1845–52* (Dublin: Browne & Nolan, 1956), p. xi.
[13] Cecil Woodham-Smith, *The Great Hunger: Ireland 1845–9* (London: Hamish Hamilton, 1962), 410.

Ireland.'[14] The facts are the same, but the emotion is unobtrusive, so the authors of *The Great Famine* are dismissed as cautious, insensitive, establishmentarian.

Despite the apparently irresistible myth of Famine historiography as riven by an ideological polarity that consists in disputing facts as much as their interpretation, Famine historiographers, be they traditional or revisionist, are to a remarkable extent in agreement as to the facts—if differing as to the construction that should be placed on these facts, and, perhaps above all, the tenor of their expression. It may be true, as Joseph Lee has argued, that we cannot know if the Famine was a watershed because we do not really know what happened, but this does not really seem to concern Famine historiographers.[15] Facts are rarely at issue: there are disputes about chronology (whether it was the Famine of 1847, or of 1845–9, or 1846–52), or about the death-toll (estimates range from 500,000 to 1.5 million, some even including a figure for averted births). But historians are largely in uneasy consensus about the facts, no matter what they believe those facts prove. Interpretation and tone are all. One man's Providence is another man's act of nature, is another man's unfortunate policy, is another man's genocide. Even accepting these emotive inflections, things are not clear-cut, as ambiguity infiltrates even the most extreme outlooks. Consider the following statements about the much-criticized Relief Works:

> there were other multitudes behind, including often the most helpless portion of the community, for whom no work could be found. The Relief Works did not always furnish a subsistence even for those who were employed on them ... melancholy proof of which was afforded by daily instances of starvation in connexion with the Relief Works.[16]

> the poor people, delving macadamised roads with spades and turf-cutters, could not earn as much as would keep them alive, though, luckily, they were thereby disabled from destroying so much good road.[17]

Both are in agreement on the essential fact: the provision of relief was wholly inadequate. But it is surprising that the first extract, from Treasury apologist Charles Trevelyan—the man who above all others has been at

[14] Thomas P. O'Neill, 'Organisation and Administration of Relief, 1845–52', in Edwards and Williams (eds.), *The Great Famine*, 225, 248, 255.

[15] Joseph Lee, 'Irish Economic History Since 1500', in Joseph Lee (ed.), *Irish Historiography 1970–79* (Cork: Cork University Press, 1981), 182.

[16] Charles Trevelyan, *The Irish Crisis* (London: Longman, Brown, Green, & Longmans, 1848), 62–3.

[17] John Mitchel, *The Last Conquest of Ireland (Perhaps)* (1861; Glasgow and London: Cameron & Ferguson; Stationer's Hall Court, 1876), 123.

the centre of genocide allegations—is the one that expresses at least a sense of loss, if not remorse. The second statement, by self-professed champion of the starving John Mitchel, seems heartless and flippant by comparison. Similarly, we are not prepared to hear the Young Ireland leader Charles Gavan Duffy defend food exportation by landlords on the grounds that they had 'sometimes little choice between becoming an oppressor or becoming a beggar'; though by the time he made this admission he was an Australian elder statesman, with little to gain by abusing Irish landlords.[18] On the other side of the political divide, we are no more prepared to find that Lord John Russell, the *laissez-faire* Prime Minister, 'actually agreed with MacHale [the outspoken Roman Catholic Archbishop of Tuam] on the urgent need to curb ejectment and privately used language about evicting Irish landlords which sounded like that of a Whiteboy or a Rockite'.[19] It appears that no one can be trusted to be wholly consistent, to maintain the purity of polarity, even in the post-1989 revolutionary era of Famine historiography. How, for instance, is the reader to react to the uncritical adoption by Christine Kinealy, one of the most vociferous and eloquent of Trevelyan's critics, of 'this great calamity', a phrase taken from Trevelyan, as the title of her history of the period?[20] Perhaps Famine historiographers have much more in common than they like to believe. Where we might expect to find the extreme polarity of traditional nationalism and pre-revisionist sanitization, we are confronted instead by an uneasy consensus about the facts, and a curious disturbance about the feelings.

One of the most striking aspects of Famine historiography is its emphasis on emotion. The language of psychology is constantly invoked: suppression, trauma, abnormality, obsession, conspiracy theory, race memory. Facts are not enough; Famine historians may be absolutely accurate in their information, but those who fail to graphically portray the sufferings of the starving are seen to have failed in their duty. It is not difficult to see why the Famine should arouse such outrage; but it is disconcerting that it has been channelled into historiography, a medium that seems unsuited to it. As Austin Bourke has pointed out: 'It is difficult for an Irishman, even after the lapse of more than a century, to discuss the famine years with unemotional

---

[18] Sir Charles Gavan Duffy, *Four Years of Irish History 1845–1849* (London, Paris, and New York: Cassell, Petter, Galpin & Co., 1883), 46.

[19] James S. Donnelly, Jr., 'Mass Eviction and the Great Famine: The Clearances Revisited', in Cathal Póirtéir (ed.), *The Great Irish Famine* (Cork and Dublin: Mercier Press, 1995), 163.

[20] Trevelyan, *Irish Crisis*, 79; quoted in Christine Kinealy, *This Great Calamity: The Irish Famine 1845–52* (Dublin: Gill & Macmillan, 1994), 137–8.

objectivity, but an effort should be made.'[21] Ironically, it seems easier to reach emotional detachment in fields where subjectivity is expected. Roger McHugh notes that oral history of the Famine is paradoxically less subjective than written history: 'it has an objectivity and a detachment which perhaps seems strange, until one reflects that the history of the famine was indelibly printed upon the lives of our forefathers, that to them it was an accepted fact and might be recalled as a great and ruinous storm might be recalled.'[22] Even fiction seems to let the reader down when it comes to outrage: several authors, including Anthony Trollope and William Carleton, were criticized for making the Famine a backdrop to other concerns. More recently, the Mayo novelist Michael Mullen has unwittingly enacted this division, putting all his outrage and emotion into his amateur history of the Famine, the title of which is the very unhistorical sounding *The Darkest Years—A Famine Story*, while his Famine novel, *The Hungry Land*, is much more concerned with stock themes such as the wild Irish girl, the failed rebel, and the lowly but well-educated Irish woman who steals the heart of the local English lord.[23] But the emphasis on emotion in Famine historiography is all the more disconcerting for the detachment some of its first historians and propagandists exhibited. Obviously, those who survived to write histories were not usually those who suffered directly, just as those who promoted rebellion were not the starving but the middle classes. Still, the judgement of the Land League leader Michael Davitt on the passivity of the starving seems savage in its refusal to credit suffering. There is no doubt that the Famine had a major impact on Davitt and his family. As T. W. Moody says:

That Michael was born a peasant's son in 1846, at the height of the great famine, is profoundly significant; for, in cooperation with Parnell, it was to be his greatest achievement to arouse the sense of solidarity, inspire the will to resist disaster, and provide the leadership that the Irish peasantry so conspicuously lacked during the famine years.[24]

[21] Austin Bourke, *'The Visitation of God'? The Potato and the Great Irish Famine* (Dublin: Lilliput Press, 1993), 178.

[22] Roger McHugh, 'The Famine in Irish Oral Tradition', in Edwards and Williams (eds.), *The Great Famine*, 436.

[23] Michael Mullen, *The Hungry Land* (New York, London, Toronto, Sydney, and Auckland: Bantam, 1986); Michael Mullen, *The Darkest Years—A Famine Story* (Castlebar: Cavendish House, 1997).

[24] T. W. Moody, *Davitt and Irish Revolution 1846–82* (Oxford: Clarendon Press, 1982), 7–8. Parnell was born three months after Davitt.

Davitt, whose parents were ejected from Straide, County Mayo in 1852, when he was 5, dated his sense of outrage and the development of his political convictions from this time:

That eviction and the privations of the preceding famine years, the story of the starving peasantry of Mayo, of the deaths from hunger and the coffinless graves on the roadside—everywhere a hole could be dug for the slaves who died because of 'God's providence'—all this was the political food seasoned with a mother's tears which had fed my mind in another land . . .[25]

Although the emotion is sincere, it has become a personal history, detached from the common suffering. Davitt's family were forced to leave for Lancashire, but they are not subject to the condemnation he levels at those who stayed and starved: 'But, as the peasants had chosen to die like sheep rather than retain that food in a fight for life, to live or die like men, their loss to the Irish nation need not occasion many pangs of racial regret.'[26] Davitt obviously has an agenda—the desire to keep tenant farmers on their guard lest they too should be branded cowards—but his pronouncements seem unnecessarily callous in their failure to recognize trauma—which is what revisionists, not traditional nationalists, are supposed to do.

Like Davitt, other traditional nationalists, such as Mitchel and O'Rourke, mourned the fact that so many died of starvation when they could have died more profitably on a battlefield. And, like Davitt, Mitchel made it personal. This was not a localized phenomenon: Roy Foster has noted that 'the frequent personification of "Ireland" in nationalist writing is matched by the personal identification on the part of a long line of Irish activists of their country's history with their own identity'.[27] Mitchel's *Jail Journal* eschews its status as history in order to proclaim history the preface to the journal of a convict: 'The general history of a nation may fitly preface the personal memoranda of a solitary captive; for it was strictly and logically a *consequence* of the dreary story here epitomized, that I came to be a prisoner, and to sit writing and musing so many months in a lonely cell.'[28] The Famine he describes is not the 'last conquest' of a

[25] Michael Davitt, *The Fall of Feudalism in Ireland; or The Story of The Land League Revolution* (London and New York: Harper & Brothers, 1904), 222; ironically, when Davitt's grandson's Dublin home went on the market two generations later, the impressive mansion was also named Straide.

[26] Ibid., 66.

[27] Roy Foster, *Paddy and Mr Punch: Connections in Irish and English History* (London: Penguin, 1993), 1.

[28] John Mitchel, *Jail Journal; or, Five Years in British Prisons* (1854) (Washington: Woodstock Books, 1996), 20.

terrorist government on an unarmed and helpless people, but the preface to a personal attack on himself, leading to his trial and transportation for treason-felony. Despite his fulminations and his 'sacred wrath' that he should have been exposed to the sight of his countrymen dying, Mitchel, like Davitt, is detached and impersonal in his discussion of the 'preface' to the main event, his transportation. Modern Irish historians are encouraged to use their skills to foreground the suffering of the starving individual, but there is no such sentiment in *Jail Journal*, where Mitchel dramatizes his exploration of Famine within the intellectual confines of his 'Ego' and 'Doppelgänger'. Neither are sympathetic to the victims. Ego points out that Nature has laws, suggesting, as nationalists are not supposed to, that the Famine was providential: 'Because they would not fight, they have been made to rot off the face of the earth, that so they might learn at last how deadly a sin is patience and perseverance under a stranger's yoke.' Doppelgänger objects that in fact the Irish have drawn the opposite lesson, and become more moral and constitutional.[29] Late twentieth-century Famine historiographers are being urged to become more emotional about the Famine, as if there were some golden-age holistic Famine historiography, when in fact its first historians were often more concerned with intellectual abstractions like Mitchel's.

Famine historiography betrays a profound anxiety about the role and status of the historian. When facts are hardly contested and debate centres on interpretation, tone, and the right of the historian to make moral judgements, the façade of impartiality is fractured, and the spectre of mythology, history's mortal enemy, looms. Theodore Moody voiced their eternal opposition: 'History is a matter of facing the facts of the Irish past, however painful some of them may be; mythology is a way of refusing to face the historical facts.'[30] Famine historiography, however, blurs the line, assimilating and reclaiming mythology. This may be in part a reaction to the scepticism Famine historians have to confront: as Anna Kinsella discovered when she began researching her history of the Famine in Wexford, the first reaction of the people she approached was denial: 'there was no famine in Wexford'.[31] Cormac Ó Gráda has revised the perception that Dublin somehow escaped the fall-out, quoting Patrick Lynch and

---

[29] Mitchel, *Jail Journal*, 95.

[30] T. W. Moody, 'Irish History and Irish Mythology', reprinted in Ciaran Brady (ed.), *Interpreting Irish History: The Debate on Historical Revisionism 1938–1994* (Dublin: Irish Academic Press, 1994), 86.

[31] Anna Kinsella, *County Wexford in the Famine Years 1845–1849* (Enniscorthy: Duffry Press, 1995), 10.

John Vaizey's history of Arthur Guinness's brewery as typical of the myopia surrounding the subject: 'The Great Famine had taken place as though it were a war in a neighbouring country, while Dublin was a brightly lit, comparatively well fed, slightly anxious neutral country.'[32] Historians working on the Famine in Ulster, traditionally accepted to have been protected from the excesses of starvation by its linen industry, have faced even greater obstacles. The invocation of central nationalist myths about the Famine—such as the exportation of food that could have saved the people, or the genocidal agenda of the British government—at least emphasizes that the Famine made its impact on the national psychology, validating further historical research. In an atmosphere of denial, many 'myths' need to be re-examined:

The term *myth* as used here does not necessarily imply that the account is untrue. Rather, the myth comprises a combination of fact, fiction and the unknowable in a narrative of such power that, for the people who accept it, the myth provides a guide to future understanding and action. In this respect, Irish mythology about the English and the Famine is rooted in facts . . .[33]

Mythology can no longer be understood in Moody's terms, as a way of refusing to face historical facts. In light of perceived historiographical evasions, relegating the Famine to the hinterland of Irish history, and the acknowledged trauma and shame that led many survivors to remain silent about their Famine experiences, mythology may be the only way to face up to the truth, and must be accorded special status. Irish historians are now calling for the inclusion of the mythic narrative: 'Such myths and dreams need to be explained and deconstructed, not denied, destroyed or omitted, to suit a present convenience.'[34] This raises the question of whether mythology should be incorporated into the received body of fact, or whether a 'scientific' history, purged of all doubt, is even possible: 'the biases, the myths, and the silences of popular memory are history too, and they offer new insights into Ireland's famine'.[35] Where the line between history and mythology becomes so blurred, it is unsurprising that historians should become unsure of their status; in their ambiguity, their obsession with tone and nuance, their examination of myth, and their tendency to discuss *The Great Famine* as often as the Great Famine, Famine historiographers verge on the creation of a new branch of literary studies— the Story of Ireland during the Famine.

[32] Quoted in Ó Gráda, *Black '47 and Beyond*, 157.
[33] George L. Bernstein, 'Liberals, the Irish Famine and the Role of the State', *Irish Historical Studies*, 29/116 (Nov. 1995), 513–36, at 513.
[34] Kinealy, 'Beyond Revisionism', 31.   [35] Ó Gráda, *Black '47 and Beyond*, 11.

Irish historians have always acknowledged the importance of the 'Story of Ireland' and its symbiotic relationship with the country's history— hence the profusion of books and articles entitled 'The Story of Ireland' by eminent Irish writers such as Roy Foster, Alexander M. Sullivan, Emily Lawless, Justin McCarthy, and Standish O'Grady. Foster emphasizes the growing importance of this narrative mode, with its sense of progression and definable parameters, in the disordered context of nineteenth-century Ireland: 'A powerful oral culture, a half-lost language, the necessary stratagems of irony, collusion and misdirection which accompany a colonized culture, maybe even the long wet winter nights— all these give a distinctive twist to the way the Irish account for themselves.'[36] And yet early Famine historians were uneasy with this symbiosis of history and narrative, and were careful to separate them. This may be because the Famine was such a recent event, and the audience was expected to be sufficiently *au fait* with the facts: Mitchel refused to go into details in *The Last Conquest of Ireland (Perhaps)* because the facts were 'sufficiently known', and Davitt followed suit: 'The facts of this unparalleled famine are matters of history, and do not require reproduction in this story.'[37] History, story, or autobiography—Mitchel and Davitt seem to be cautiously weighing up categories, self-consciously unsure of their status. Mitchel's *History of Ireland* seems purposely written as a historical version of *The Last Conquest* (which is presumably the story version). The reader is informed that the facts of *The Last Conquest* have been recycled in the *History*, importantly 'excluding generally the inferences and opinions of the writer', as 'indignant declamation would but weaken the effect of the dreadful facts we shall have to tell'.[38] In *Jail Journal* and *The Last Conquest*, Mitchel is ostentatiously present in his capacity as hero of the story, but in the *History* he stiltedly insists on referring to himself as 'Mr. Mitchel' throughout. It is all, of course, a charade: the opinions and allegations are not toned down in the least. But it does make clear Mitchel's recognition that the appearance of impartiality, the mask of the historian, would strengthen the effect of his argument and become an important propaganda tool. For Mitchel, history is simply third-person narrative, displaced autobiography. And yet he does not feel comfortable using this medium for his story.

[36] Roy Foster, *The Story of Ireland: An Inaugural Lecture delivered before the University of Oxford on 1 December 1994* (Oxford: Clarendon Press, 1995), 5.

[37] Mitchel, *Last Conquest*, 117; Davitt, *Fall of Feudalism*, 52.

[38] John Mitchel, *The History of Ireland, From The Treaty of Limerick to the Present Time*, 2 vols. (1868; Dublin: James Duffy, 1869), i, p. v.

Modern historians are still concerned about status. What is the historian's role in narrating the Famine? Should they stick rigidly to the facts or make moral and evaluative judgements? Should self-censorship be an issue? Should they allow their language to be inflected with emotional and psychological imagery? Most Famine historians seem abnormally concerned about anachronisms. Oliver MacDonagh did his best to avoid 'impertinent moral judgments' by absolving landlords of responsibility for inherited views—the inference being that by questioning such views the historian was overstepping the mark.[39] Cecil Woodham-Smith, too often seen as the mouthpiece of nationalist Famine history, warned that 'The eighteen-forties . . . must not be judged by the standards of today', and pointed out that the British government, within a few years of the Famine, was to treat its own soldiers in the Crimea with as much parsimony and callousness as it had the starving Irish.[40] More recently, Daly has commented that 'it does not appear appropriate to pronounce in an unduly critical fashion on the limitations of previous generations', and Edward Garner has recommended that one should judge 'in the light of lives preserved'.[41] Famine historians seem obtrusively cautious, meek, reticent, and precise in methodology in a futile attempt to placate the critics—and, given the attacks, this is hardly surprising. Yet an avoidance of unseemly anachronism seems to involve a rejection of the importance of many contemporary sources, including ignoring the fact that Mitchel was not just a fanatic, but also provided necessary insights into contemporary public opinion, as is shown by the huge interest in the *United Irishman* in 1848, both in Ireland and in mainland Britain, and the enduring relevance of *Jail Journal*. Famine historians are called upon to prove their credentials as 'professional' historians by abandoning Mitchel and concentrating on what is perceived as 'real' history. When Gerard Mac Atasney began his study of the Famine in Lurgan and Portadown, he discovered that: 'social aversion, political expediency and historiographical avoidance have ensured that the study of the Famine in Ulster was not a subject for "real" historians'.[42] Similarly, Mitchelite musings on exports and genocide are not subjects for 'real' historians, and those who are seen to uphold Mitchel's conclusions are consigned to the amateur heap.

[39] Oliver MacDonagh, 'Irish Emigration to the USA and the British Colonies During the Famine', in Edwards and Williams (eds.), *The Great Famine*, 335, 340.

[40] Woodham-Smith, *The Great Hunger*, 407.

[41] Mary Daly, *The Famine in Ireland* (Dublin: Dublin Historical Association, 1986), 113; Edward Garner, *To Die By Inches: The Famine in North East Cork* (Cork: Eigse, 1988), 66.

[42] Gerard Mac Atasney, *'This Dreadful Visitation': The Famine in Lurgan/Portadown* (Belfast: Beyond the Pale, 1997), p. xvi.

The most notable casualty has been Woodham-Smith, whose *The Great Hunger* has suffered from its popularity with the general public and with President Éamon de Valera, who much preferred it to the 'professional' history he had commissioned from Edwards and Williams.[43] Ó Gráda sees Woodham-Smith's success as Edwards and Williams's lost opportunity:

> Woodham-Smith's book has many weaknesses but, to its lasting credit, it laid bare anew the horrors of the tragedy glossed over in *The Great Famine*. That Irish historians in the 1950s should have sought to rid Irish history of its undue emphasis on the tragic is understandable; but the appalling catastrophe of the 1840s was an unhappy choice for that campaign.[44]

As a result, *The Great Hunger* has been accused of cashing in on the melodrama, *The Great Famine* of detraumatization. The latter charge, we have seen, is not wholly true, and the former is certainly unjust. In many respects, Woodham-Smith can be seen as a trailblazer in Famine historiography. Her assertion that people died not because there was no food in the country, but because they had no money to purchase it, not only refutes Mitchel's emphasis on exportation, but looks forward to the work of economists such as Amartya Sen on entitlements during food scarcities.[45] Her recognition that emigration was 'historically the most important event of the famine' is a stance that seems justified by research in the 1990s, such as O'Sullivan's *The Irish World Wide*, Crawford's *The Hungry Stream*, and David Fitzpatrick's *Oceans of Consolation*. She was also one of the first to argue that people from the North of Ireland also suffered, many being forced to survive on subsistence foods like nettles and weeds—a claim that is only now being investigated.[46] Even her much criticized focusing of cruelty in the person of Trevelyan is being reprised in the work of one of the most influential Famine historians of this generation, Christine Kinealy. There is no doubt that Woodham-Smith's value is now largely accepted, in spite of attacks on her as an amateur. Both Kinealy and Ó Gráda cite, as an example of anti-Woodham-Smith prejudice, a University College Dublin history exam paper from the 1960s which posed the question: '*The Great*

---

[43] Ó Gráda suggests that it was de Valera, in his capacity as Chancellor of the National University of Ireland, who was responsible for awarding an honorary doctorate to Woodham-Smith.

[44] Ó Gráda, 'Making History in Ireland', 97, 99.

[45] Amartya Sen, *Poverty and Famines: An Essay on Entitlement and Deprivation* (Oxford: Clarendon Press, 1981).

[46] Woodham-Smith, *The Great Hunger*, 165, 206, 136–7.

Hunger is a great novel. Discuss.'[47] The question may indeed reflect the climate of debate surrounding the book, but in general examiners do not tend to provide the answer in their questions; they must certainly have expected that a valid case could be argued on the other side. Also, the notion that the greatest insult that can be offered to a historian is to label her work a novel indicates the profound distrust of fiction, the story of Ireland, which persists among modern historians.

Famine historians face difficult choices and consequences, walking the tightrope between indifference and melodrama, unable to avoid the inevitable criticism. Uncertain about their own role as historians, they seem to have no choice but to acquiesce to the reader's demands. The problem is they are expected to be all things to all men, historians and *seanchaís* combined. Daly has suggested that 'Ultimately only a blend of analysis and emotion, politics, folklore, and poetry will meet the needs of scholarship and popular memory alike. Whether historians can deliver this, it is impossible to say.'[48] Daly sounds resigned to the attempt, but perhaps the question needs to be: *should* historians deliver this? It would appear inhuman to expect it, superhuman to achieve, indicating as it does the failure of other forms individually to satisfy the needs of the community. Paradoxically, history is being accorded mythic status as a kind of metanarrative that draws all strands together to illuminate and explain.

Perhaps we should not be surprised that the boundaries between history and literature are not fixed: as Hayden White has pointed out, history is 'ineluctably poetic', and the principal philosophers of history, Hegel, Marx, Nietzsche, and Croce, were 'quintessentially philosophers of language'.[49] And, as Tom Dunne has argued, history is primarily a literary construct, wholly dependent on documents, and textually complicit:

The long search for a more scientific history has been frustrated, in part, by the lack of a specialised language, and the historian's dependence on 'ordinary edu cated speech' means that his reading and writing of texts is powerfully conditioned by the complex of social, cultural and psychological codes of which such language is composed.[50]

[47] Kinealy, 'Beyond Revisionism', p 33; Cormac Ó Gráda, *Ireland Before and After the Famine: Explorations in Economic History, 1800–1925* (Manchester: Manchester University Press, 1988), 80.

[48] Daly, 'Revisionism and Irish History', 86.

[49] Hayden White, *Metahistory: The Historical Imagination in Nineteenth-Century Europe* (Baltimore and London: Johns Hopkins University Press, 1993), p. xi.

[50] Tom Dunne, 'A Polemical Introduction: Literature, Literary Theory and the Historian', in Tom Dunne (ed.), *The Writer as Witness: Literature as Historical Evidence* (Cork: Cork University Press, 1987), 5.

As early as 1875, O'Rourke was stressing the urgency of collecting as
much information as possible before eyewitnesses passed away: now, as
Christopher Morash has commented, the Famine is 'primarily a retrospective, textual creation'.[51] The records may lack the immediacy of the
voice of the victim, but this is not to deny the power of the historical text
to shape the Famine, retrospectively or otherwise. Mitchel's writings have
been credited with the 'creation' of the Famine: 'An historian—or rather
a political activist writing as an historian—"invented" the Great Irish
Famine of 1845–49, that is, gave it initially the place it has come to occupy
in commonly perceived historical and imaginative understanding.'[52] What
the historian chooses to examine is what survives: therefore exports and
genocide have remained part of the discourse of the Famine long after they
have been proved to be historically irrelevant; thus earlier famines are
passed over despite huge, if not comparable, death-tolls; thus Skibbereen
and Schull have become notorious while areas that suffered equally but for
which there were few records have been consigned to oblivion. Kieran
Foley's work on the Killarney Poor Law Guardians challenges standard
histories in their bias towards the negative: 'Ironically, it would appear
that had they been incompetent and neglected the destitute in their area,
or had they refused to strike sufficient rates or not bothered to ensure their
collection, then they would have been more likely to have attracted the
attention of historians.'[53]

    Mitchel did not 'invent' the Great Famine; it would not have disap-
peared from memory if he had not written about it, as some earlier famines
had disappeared, simply because its impact was too profound. His central
dogma of genocide and exportation was already being voiced even by mod-
erates like Isaac Butt, disgusted by British duplicity, and by the novelist
William Carleton. But Mitchel's representation of the Famine does bor-
der on the fictional. Bearing in mind Tom Dunne's injunction against the
rejection of imaginative writing as primary evidence, Hayden White's
recognition of the part 'invention' plays in the historian's operations, and
Edwards's admission that Mitchel had as much right to be listened to as
'professional' historians, this is not to his discredit. But the form of *Jail
Journal* and *The Last Conquest* follows more closely the model we come to
expect in fiction, where the Famine becomes the background to a related

    [51] Christopher Morash, *Writing the Irish Famine* (Oxford: Clarendon Press, 1995), 3.
    [52] Patrick O'Farrell, 'Whose Reality?: The Irish Famine in History and Literature',
Historical Studies, 20/78–81 (Apr. 1982–Oct. 1983), 1–13, at 1.
    [53] Kieran Foley, 'The Killarney Poor Law Guardians and the Famine, 1845–52', MA
thesis (University College Dublin, 1987), 1.

concern: inheritance in *Castle Richmond*, violence and murder in *The Black Prophet*, religious conversion in many late nineteenth-century novels, and injustice, rebellion, and autobiography in *Jail Journal*. He even adopts the tone of a serial novelist in *Last Conquest*. Of O'Connell's abortive monster-meeting at Clontarf, which Mitchel reads as Ireland's last chance to save herself not only from conquest but also from the Famine, he announces dramatically: 'The curtain rises on the fifth act'; and he whets the reader's appetite to know what happened at O'Connell's trial by ending with a cliff-hanger: 'By what means they sought to secure this result [O'Connell's conviction] . . . I shall narrate in the next chapter.'[54] This, despite the fact that he is probably already preaching to the converted, to Irish and Americans sympathetic to his cause, and for whom this story was already well-known history. The Famine becomes a rhetorical effect in his works: punctuation in the *History of Ireland*: 'Throughout all these scenes the horrible famine was raging as it had never raged before . . .';[55] occupatio[56] in *Jail Journal*, where the reader is told 'There is no need to recount' the atrocities of famine, but is then treated to a long list, including the consumption of asses, cannibalism, mothers stealing from their children, husbands and wives fighting like wolves for food, and concluding with the final, worst iniquity: 'how, in every one of these years, '46, '47, and '48, Ireland was exporting to England, food to the value of fifteen million pounds sterling, and had on her own soil at each harvest, good and ample provision for double her own population, notwithstanding the potato blight'.[57] His final rhetorical flourish could be said to be aposiopesis,[58] registered by his failure to take Ireland up to the time of writing. His *History of Ireland*, which could have ended with the Fenians, chooses a much earlier cut-off point: 'At this point—the middle of the current century—the present history closes. It leaves in full operation the whole system of British rule in Ireland.'[59] *Jail Journal* and *Last Conquest* also break off after the Famine.

Morash suggests that Mitchel arrests Ireland during the Famine in order to spur the contemporary reader to rebellion:

[54] Mitchel, *Last Conquest*, 37, 45.   [55] Mitchel, *History of Ireland*, ii. 442.
[56] 'a rhetorical device . . . by which a speaker emphasizes something by pretending to pass over it', Chris Baldick, *The Concise Oxford Dictionary of Literary Terms* (Oxford: Clarendon Press, 1990), 154.
[57] Mitchel, *Jail Journal*, 16.
[58] 'a rhetorical device, in which the speaker suddenly breaks off in the middle of a sentence, leaving the sense unfinished. The device usually suggests strong emotion that makes the speaker unwilling or unable to continue', *Concise Oxford Dictionary of Literary Terms*, 15.
[59] Mitchel, *History of Ireland*, ii. 472.

A reader encountering the *Jail Journal* or the *Last Conquest of Ireland* would find that Irish history after 1848 enters a state of suspended animation in the midst of the Famine . . . the incomplete narrative acts in a Brechtian fashion as a powerful incitement for a reader to support action in the world outside of the text, action which will bring about the narrative closure the text refuses.[60]

It is an attractive and persuasive argument, and there is no doubt Mitchel intended to provoke anger at the proximity of the Famine. As he had learnt from Carlyle (particularly from *The French Revolution*), a mixture of inflammatory rhetoric, vivid narrative, and immediacy was extremely effective in holding the audience's sympathy and attention. Mitchel shared Carlyle's ability to immerse himself so completely in the material that he achieved total identification—easier for Mitchel as he actually did live through many of the event he narrated. But Mitchel's manipulation of his readers may be more prosaic than Morash suggests. Mitchel does in fact provide narrative closure for the Famine: 'At the end of six years,' he tells us, 'I can set down these things calmly; but to see them might have driven a wise man mad.'[61] In *The Last Conquest*, it is 'the six years' *Famine*', while the *History of Ireland* testifies to 'five seasons of artificial famine'.[62] The Famine is well and truly over as far as Mitchel is concerned, but there are other reasons why he might not want to take Ireland beyond 1850. The first is his own irrelevance: as he notes in *Last Conquest*, when he arrives at his own trial and transportation in 1848: 'the moment has arrived when I drop out of the history of Ireland, and disappear'.[63] His only subsequent contact with history-in-the-making was the rare newspapers he managed to get hold of while on his convict ship, months behind, already past history. Indeed, *Jail Journal* proclaims in 1854 his unfitness to write the book he produced in 1861: 'I know but by hearsay how the British government fulfilled the designs and administered the dispensations of Providence in Ireland,—how the famine was successfully *exploited* . . . In short, how the last *conquest* was consummated, let other pens than mine describe.'[64] The narrative breaks off not to continue the Famine, but to retain Mitchel's self-identification with Ireland and her history.

There was also a very good reason for pushing history back to mid-century in 1868, namely the failure of the Fenians in the previous year, which Mitchel coyly avoids: 'The compiler of this History of Ireland purposely stops short of the most recent events which have agitated that

[60] Morash, *Writing the Irish Famine*, 61.   [61] Mitchel, *Jail Journal*, 16.
[62] Mitchel, *Last Conquest*, 92; Mitchel, *History of Ireland*, ii. 458.
[63] Mitchel, *Last Conquest*, 182.   [64] Mitchel, *Jail Journal*, 19.

country, and disquieted and exasperated England. The time for relating the history of those events has not yet arrived.'[65] Even the title *The Last Conquest of Ireland (Perhaps)* gestures in its ambiguity towards an alternative progress that denies the stasis posited by Morash. The Famine is a 'dreary story' that Mitchel shapes to his purposes: it is six years, or five seasons, or 'three seasons of famine-slaughter' long; it is paradoxically both the culmination of a series, for 'as a matter of course she had her cruel famine every year', and unparalleled in history, for despite a level of misery Ireland had not suffered famine for twenty years.[66] His manipulation of the story enables him to trope himself as a martyr—even as a Christ-figure, as in his description of the trial:

Let any high-spirited Irishman try to conceive himself in my place on that day: confronting that coarse mimicry of law and justice; on the brink of a fate worse than a thousand deaths; stationed in a dock between two thieves, for having dared to aspire to the principles of freedom and manhood for myself and my children; with all the horrible sufferings and high aspirations of my country crowding on memory and imagination, and the moan of our perishing nation seeming to penetrate even there, and to load the air I breathed . . .[67]

Crucified between two thieves, Mitchel becomes his own Holy Spirit, but a demoralized people will not hear him: 'A whole Pentecost of fiery tongues, if they descended upon such a dull material, would fall extinguished in smoke and stench like a lamp blown out.'[68] After his own transmogrification into the Messiah, Mitchel has no qualms about metaphorically creating the Famine he wanted, neutralizing the shame of what he saw as cowardly starvation in the imagery of battle and blood sacrifice:

the story of an ancient nation stricken down by a war more ruthless and sanguinary than any seven years' war, that Europe ever saw. No sack of Madgeburg [*sic*], or ravage of the Palatinate, ever approached in horror and desolation to the slaughters done in Ireland by mere official red tape and stationery, and the principles of political economy.[69]

Mitchel's Famine is as evangelical as it is revolutionary, as personal as it is historical, and the reader is ruthlessly manipulated. Mitchel's Famine is 'artificial' in more ways than one.

Joseph Lee said that we all get the Famine we need—Mitchel and his readers got theirs, but Trevelyan and his readers were not deprived.[70]

---

[65] Mitchel, *History of Ireland*, ii. 479.
[66] Mitchel, *Jail Journal*, 95, 13; Mitchel, *Last Conquest*, 9.
[67] Mitchel, *Last Conquest*, 184–5.   [68] Ibid., 197.   [69] Ibid., 218.
[70] Lee, 'The Famine as History', 166.

Mitchel may have had to resort to metaphor in order to achieve his goal, but in some ways Trevelyan literally did get the Famine he wanted. His book, *The Irish Crisis*, first published as an article in the *Edinburgh Review*, abruptly curtailed the catastrophe: on the first page he refers to 'the great Irish famine of 1847', and after a description of government relief works, he provides narrative closure:

> The famine was stayed. The 'affecting and heart-rending crowds of destitutes' disappeared from the streets; the cadaverous, hunger-stricken countenances of the people gave place to looks of health; deaths from starvation ceased; and cattle-stealing, plundering provisions, and other crimes prompted by want of food, were diminished by half in the course of a single month.[71]

It is not difficult to imagine the effect this statement from the Assistant Secretary to the Treasury may have had on the public in 1848; it is certainly reasonable to suggest that it speeded up the 'donor fatigue' that began to be perceived even before the failed Rising. Trevelyan sent copies of his book not only to the Pope—who had been urging Catholics worldwide to donate to Irish charities—and to the King of Prussia, but to newly appointed relief officials in Ireland, who had to face at least another two years of conditions Trevelyan had described as long past. His own text was not the only one Trevelyan used to shape his Famine: all relief officials were provided with Edmund Burke's *Thoughts on Scarcities* and Adam Smith's *Wealth of Nations*, key texts on political economy, designed to steel sympathetic hearts against the importuning Irish. His final shaping text was the Bible. Trevelyan, with others in the government and in the public, was convinced that the Famine was providential in nature, and even if political economy had not forbidden a radical intervention in the markets, who could challenge the hand of God? The Famine was a 'great intervention of Providence to bring back the potato to its original use and intention' and, as far as Trevelyan was concerned, it had worked: 'on this, as on many other occasions, Supreme Wisdom has educed permanent good out of transient evil'.[72] The Providential theory of the Famine, explored recently by historians such as Peter Gray, was immensely pervasive. Sanctioned by Queen's Letters and fast days, it cast a particular light on the disaster which had definite repercussions: 'the power of providentialism was strong enough to hinder and qualify philanthropic reaction'.[73] Yet even those opposed to the government's handling of famine relief con-

---

[71] Trevelyan, *Irish Crisis*, 89.   [72] Ibid., 8, 1.
[73] Peter Gray, 'British Politics and the Irish Land Question 1843–1850', Ph.D. thesis (University of Cambridge, 1992), 283.

ceded providentialism: Isaac Butt spoke of 'the fearful blight with which
it has pleased an all-wise God to visit the food of her people', nationalists
argued that it was God's punishment on the Irish for cowardice in their
failure to free themselves from England, and Mitchel's famous dictum 'the
English created the famine' is preceded by the admission 'The Almighty,
indeed, sent the potato blight'.[74] Trevelyan was able to use widely
accepted ideologies like providentialism and political economy and the
texts that contained them to justify government policy during the Famine.

Trevelyan not only used various texts to shape the Famine, he also used
his experience of the Famine to shape various texts. Jenifer Hart has commented that 'whatever the subject, Trevelyan was often as much interested in compiling a history of its past and securing records for the future
as in solving the immediate problem'.[75] The vast collection of information
in Blue Books can be attributed to his influence, and it has been suggested
this accumulation was in some sense an alternative to proper relief: 'had
they contained some of the nutritive qualities which go to sustain human
life, they would have been an appreciable contribution towards feeding the
starving Irish people during the Famine'.[76] Furthermore, traditional
nationalists and anti-revisionists are not averse to using the demonized
Trevelyan when it suits them. As Revd John O'Rourke explained in his
early history of the Famine: 'Although far from agreeing with many of
Sir Charles' conclusions (he was Secretary to the Treasury during the
Famine), still the Author cheerfully acknowledges, that the statistical
information in the *Irish Crisis* is very valuable to a student of the history of
the Famine period.'[77] Trevelyan did his information-gathering so well
that O'Rourke and others were obliged to use his work to supplement their
own. W. P. O'Brien, although a former Poor Law and local government
inspector, admitted that he had kept no notes or records of his experiences
during the Famine, and many of his comments and conclusions are literally lifted from *The Irish Crisis*, the work of a man who had virtually no
personal experience of Ireland.[78] In a final ironic twist, although
Woodham-Smith suggests that Trevelyan went to face India softened and
tempered by his Irish experience, *The Irish Crisis* went to Indian famines

[74] Butt, 'The Famine in the Land', 501; Mitchel, *Last Conquest*, 219.
[75] Jenifer Hart, 'Sir Charles Trevelyan at the Treasury', *English Historical Review*, 75 (1960), 92–110, at 93.
[76] Revd John O'Rourke, *The History of the Great Irish Famine of 1847* (Dublin and London: M'Glashan & Gill; James Duffy, Sons, & Co., 1875), 337–8.
[77] Ibid., pp. viii–ix.
[78] W. P. O'Brien, *The Great Famine in Ireland and a Retrospect of the Fifty Years 1845–95* (London: Downey & Co., 1896); see 'Chapter IV: The Irish Crisis'.

to harden existing policies: during the Orissa Famine of 1865–6, in which 1,364,529 people—one quarter of the population—died, the government stood firm by 'classical famine policy', quoting *The Irish Crisis* to justify their actions.[79] The apologia became the textbook, making history for itself.

Other historical representations of the Famine have shaped lives and texts: Mitchel's texts made many nationalists—Douglas Hyde said, 'he would make a rebel out of me if I weren't one already'.[80] O'Rourke, along with James Connolly, may have influenced Liam O'Flaherty, whose novel *Famine* was published in 1937, while Woodham-Smith's title may have come from Patrick Kavanagh's poem 'The Great Hunger' (1942), which uses the Famine as a metaphor for the emptiness of modern rural life; in turn Woodham-Smith's work may have inspired Walter Macken's novel *The Silent People* (1962) and Tom Murphy's play *Famine* (1968), as well as such poets as Seamus Heaney and Eavan Boland. The word 'famine' is extremely resonant: 'Famine is one of the most powerful, pervasive, and arguably one of the most emotive, words in our historical vocabulary, and that in itself makes it all the more difficult to isolate its meaning and wider significance.'[81] It is no surprise, therefore, that government apologists tried to weed this emotive term out of their representations. O'Rourke listed several euphemisms used by relief committees and government offi-cials, including 'distress', 'destitution', 'dearth of provisions', 'severe suf-fering', and 'extreme misery'.[82] The word had even greater potency after 1850, serving as a political rallying cry for the Land League in the 1880s; the use of this term may have galvanized the government of the time to defuse the possibility of famine by issuing relief before it became political dynamite. Ironically, the word became so associated with oppression and misgovernment that when reports of famine conditions began to circulate during 1925, the new Irish government could not afford to allow it, and used euphemisms and rejected claims as vigorously as the British govern-ments of the 1840s, and with much greater success: 'a government attempting to restrict state expenditure was prepared to confront its critics on the question of western poverty in a way that no Westminster

[79] Patrick O'Sullivan and Richard Lucking, 'The Famine World Wide: The Irish Famine and the Development of Famine Policy and Famine Theory', in O'Sullivan (ed.), *The Irish World Wide*, 211.

[80] Quoted in Robert Welch (ed.), *The Oxford Companion to Irish Literature* (Oxford: Clarendon Press, 1996), 368.

[81] David Arnold, *Famine: Social Crisis and Historical Change* (Oxford: Basil Blackwell, 1988), 5.

[82] O'Rourke, *History of the Great Irish Famine*, 371.

administration could have after 1850. The era of famine in Ireland had finally drawn to a close.'[83] Although of course the 1925 shortages were nowhere near as severe as the Great Famine, the suggestion is that famine is only famine when it is allowed to be so, when the full range of associations attributed to the term are accepted. Given this, it seems odd that nationalists are as ready as anyone to renegotiate the language of famine. 'There was no famine' could serve as a rallying cry for both camps; indeed a mural on the nationalist Falls Road in West Belfast in 1995 proclaimed just that. Woodham-Smith's choice of the term *The Great Hunger* may be explained as a means of differentiating her work from its predecessor *The Great Famine*, but nationalist historian P. S. O'Hegarty was adamant in his discussion of 'the Starvation'; in his eyes there was no famine, because there was plenty of food available, though it was denied to the people.[84] There may also be a discomfort about using the term 'famine' rather than the Irish 'an gorta mór', in recognition both of those victims who spoke Irish, and that the Famine acted as an accelerator to the death of the language. Due to a semantic shift, both sides are united in indeterminacy. Of course, this does not mean that nationalist euphemisms seek to neutralize: on the contrary, even non-nationalist historians are today using terms that are, if possible, even more emotive than the word 'famine'. The connection was quickly made with modern famines like those in Ethiopia in the 1980s, and charitable organizations such as Trócaire play on the common heritage.

Other metaphors are less easy to assimilate. Patrick Hickey's description of Skibbereen in the Famine—'a Rwanda-like scene of bodies floating down the Ilen river'—effortlessly conjures up the words 'ethnic cleansing'.[85] The connection with the Holocaust was made early—even proleptically, one might say, as in 1904 Davitt described the Famine as 'the holocaust of humanity which landlordism and English rule exacted from Ireland in a pagan homage to an inhuman system'.[86] While he does not specifically mention the Jews, Hitler's Final Solution is obviously in Timothy O'Herlihy's mind two years after the end of World War II as an analogy for the role of landlords during the Famine: 'It is possibly accounted for by the fact that they belonged to an alien race and looked on

[83] Tim P. O'Neill, 'The Persistence of Famine in Ireland', in Póirtéir (ed.), *The Great Irish Famine*, 218.

[84] P. S. O'Hegarty, *John Mitchel, An Appreciation, With Some Account of Young Ireland* (Dublin and London: Maunsell & Co., 1917), 28.

[85] Patrick Hickey, 'The Famine in the Skibbereen Union (1845–51)', in Póirtéir (ed.), *The Great Irish Famine*, 194.

[86] Davitt, *Fall of Feudalism*, 50.

the Irish with the same contempt as the modern Herrenfolk regarded all non-Teutons.'[87] Recent comparisons are more specific: Kevin Whelan refers to 'the Famine holocaust', Anna Kinsella to 'this holocaust', while David Arnold has suggested that the importance of the Famine in Irish nationalist mythology is 'comparable, perhaps, in emotive terms to the Jewish Holocaust'.[88] Christopher Morash extends the analogy by comparing Famine and Holocaust literatures as affected by similar kinds of atrocities. This is not just a rarefied academic exercise: the state of New Jersey recently included study of the Famine in its Holocaust and Genocide curriculum for secondary level schools, and will no doubt be followed by other states. *Unit VI: Genocide* asks students to decide if the British were capable of deliberate extermination based on extracts from histories of Ireland, and the 'historical record': 'Briefly consider four issues: British treatment of American prisoners during the Revolution, British domination of the slave trade, British government-backed "Opium War", and British concentration camps used during the Boer War.'[89] As Colm Tóibín points out, this is 'as shocking in its carelessness and its racism as the *Times* editorials were about Ireland during and after the Famine. It is clear that the authors of the document want us all to be victims together. When they set foot in the Ireland of the Celtic Tiger, they will be in for a shock.'[90]

Most historians would agree that there is no real basis for comparison between the deliberate extermination of six million Jews, and maladministration that allowed one million Irish to die due to a disruption of the food supply, but the use of the analogy emphasizes the depth of feeling involved, and the extent to which historians are forced to bend the knee to the emotive issue. In the same way, although most historians agree that prevention of exports would not have meant prevention of starvation, and that the government was misguided but not genocidal, by continuing to evoke these concepts—which are largely literary constructs, rarely reflected in oral history—even in denial, repetition has worked to make them concrete and tangible. Ó Gráda may have proved that Ireland was a net importer of grain during the Famine, and that even if home produce

[87] O'Herlihy, *The Famine 1845–1847*, 36.

[88] Kevin Whelan, 'Pre and Post Famine Landscape Change', in Póirtéir (ed.), *The Great Irish Famine*, 32; Kinsella, *County Wexford in the Famine Years*, 40; Arnold, *Famine*, 115.

[89] 'The Great Famine', submitted to the New Jersey Commission on Holocaust Education on 11 January 1996, for inclusion in the Holocaust and Genocide Curriculum at the secondary level, prepared by the Irish Famine Curriculum Committee, 107.

[90] Colm Tóibín, 'Erasures: Colm Tóibín on the Great Irish Famine', *London Review of Books*, 20/15 (30 July 1998), 17–23, at 23.

had remained at home the shortfall still could not have been met, but his litany of government expenditure on other projects—£70 million in the Crimean War, £100 million fighting Napoleon, and Mitchel's favourite statistic, £20 million to compensate slave-owners—links him to Mitchel and genocide.[91] Crawford cannot consign exportation to the dustbin of history without leaving an opening: 'This is largely myth, although as with all myths it contains a kernel of truth.'[92] Even Peter Gray, who in his early work succeeds in steering attention away from the obsessive discussion of exports and genocide, which are largely retrospective concerns, and towards the more influential contemporary ideologies, cannot avoid using imagery that denies his assertion that British government policy was dogmatic but not genocidal: 'in the conditions of the later 1840s [government policy] amounted to a sentence of death on many thousands'.[93] Conversely, in the first edition of his *Modern Ireland 1600–1972*, Roy Foster described the Famine as a holocaust, but after a critical review by Nicholas Canny in the *London Review of Books*, he removed the term from subsequent editions; ironically, he has been criticized ever since for *not* describing it as a holocaust.[94]

Linguistic ambiguity is rife in Famine historiography, emphasizing interpretative uncertainty, circling around clichés about watersheds and oversimplifications: the treatment of the Famine as an accelerator is an oversimplification, condemnation of the government's relief programme is 'too simplistic', singling out the government is an 'oversimplification'.[95] Historians seem to be constantly seeking the moral high ground of complexity. Such complexity can be limiting, as can be seen in Daly's linguistic fumbling in describing evictions as 'One of the least attractive aspects of the famine years', instead of the verbally less complex but more satisfactory 'one of the worst aspects'.[96] Mitchel's choice of *The Last Conquest of Ireland (Perhaps)* for the title of his study of the Famine is remarkably ambiguous for a writer of such stridency: does 'Last Conquest' mean the final conquest, or the most recent one? Is the parenthetical 'Perhaps' revolutionary in its refusal to accept the final conquest, or resigned to a continuation in a series of conquests? In this highly controversial, emotionally

[91] Ó Gráda, *Before and After the Famine*, 117.
[92] E. Margaret Crawford, 'Food and Famine', in Póirtéir (ed.), *The Great Irish Famine*, 64.
[93] Peter Gray, 'Ideology and the Famine', in Póirtéir (ed.), *The Great Irish Famine*, 103.
[94] See Nicholas Canny, 'Upper Ireland: *Modern Ireland 1600–1972*', *London Review of Books*, 11/6 (16 Mar. 1989), 8–9.
[95] Cormac Ó Gráda, *Ireland: A New Economic History 1780–1939* (Oxford: Clarendon Press, 1994), 176; Daly, *The Famine in Ireland*, 84; Gray, 'Ideology and the Famine', 103.
[96] Daly, *The Famine in Ireland*, 109.

charged environment, tone becomes vitally important. In their obsession with complexity and self-generated polarity, and their delicate deployment of myth, narrative, and autobiography, Famine historians manifest an anxiety about their own role, their texts, and the status of the Great Famine in Irish history. But by embracing literary, sociological, and psychological language and forms, history may paradoxically have been inhibited rather than freed. As Foster has argued: 'Irish historical interpretation has too often been cramped into a strict literary mode . . . and there *is* a history beyond received narrative conditioning (though postmodernists may not admit it).'[97] In this realm, revisionism is a dirty word rather than a valuable historical tool. There is no doubt that a study of the literature of the Famine is uniquely valuable in creating new insights into the horror of that awful period, but historians appear to have gone too far in attempting to assimilate it. Their coalescence of fact and fiction has produced not truth but faction, in both senses of the word. It may be time for Famine historians to abandon the emotional high ground and regain their objectivity, deferring empathy to the reader as the ultimate arbiter of emotion.

[97] Foster, *The Story of Ireland*, 30.

2

War of Words: The Famine in
The Times *and* The Nation

It is rather disconcerting to look up the word 'Ireland' in the index to *The History of the Times* for 1841–84, and discover absolutely no reference to the Famine.[1] 'IRELAND: The *Times* "special commissioner" ', reads the main entry; elsewhere there are oblique references to the Irish Church Question and Land Question, but the Famine—not to mention the other Irish events which made headlines such as Repeal, the Fenians, the Land League, etc.—is absent. This is surprising, not only because the Famine was viewed from the outset as an important epoch in British and Irish history, but because it was also a major event in British and Irish journalism. Irish journalists were censored, prosecuted, and transported for what they wrote about the Famine, while 'English' journalists probed and commented on issues that had been agonized over for generations, alternately sympathetic and irate as circumstances altered.[2] Of course, English journalism's obsession with Ireland did not emerge with the Famine: reports of Irish misery and the progress of O'Connell's Repeal movement emanating from English—and more disturbingly, from foreign—travellers, fuelled media interest, and 'What is to be done with Ireland?' was the question that opened more than one leading article in the early 1840s. *The Times*'s 'Commissioner', Thomas Campbell Foster, was actually on the spot, touring Ireland, when news of the first failure of the potato crop broke in September 1845. From 1846 to 1849, virtually every day produced a leading article and an 'Ireland' column in *The Times* examining the distress and violence which followed in the wake of the blight. The interest was obsessive, partly because such a catastrophe was deemed out of sync with an age of advanced industry and civilization, partly from a feeling of responsibility for past injustices, partly from a fear that misery would spread. Such an omission from the *History of the Times* seems like retrospective amnesia; alternatively, one could read this omission as an

---

[1] *The History of The Times*, Vol. II: *The Tradition Established: 1841–1884* (London: *The Times*, 1939).

[2] Many of the journalists working on English newspapers that reported the Irish famine were in fact Irish or Scottish.

admission that the Famine was such a pervasive, well-known event that
the citing of 'Ireland' was, for an indexer, metonymic of its occurrence and
effects.

No one could have predicted in 1845 that the potato blight would have
such far-reaching consequences, and, ironically, journalists from both
sides of the Irish Sea seemed united from the outset in believing the
Famine would be the agent of good. *The Times* rejoiced in the breaking
down of barriers: 'The Orangeman and the Papist, Tory and Repealer,
Peer and tradesman, now meet together on one common ground, and for
one common purpose . . . It looks as if Irishmen required some great and
terrible calamity to remind them of their common duties and to restore
them to common sense . . .'.[3] Newspapers of all complexions condemned
the potato as an unnutritious food which took barely any effort to culti-
vate, making the Irish indolent and dependent; the change to a carnivorous
diet which all held to be inevitable—though few considered how it was to
be managed—would raise the Irish to a more civilized state. After all, as
The Nation noted, the potato was an English importation, another method
of keeping a conquered race under control, and the great men of Irish history had been fed on corn.[4] Despite an early concern for the fate of the
potato-eaters, *Punch* felt free to make jokes at the expense of the blighted
root: in September 1845, *Punch* was recommending Grimstone's Eye
Snuff to cure the black eyes of potatoes, and Rowland's Macassar Oil for
'the curl'.[5] In October it was advertising a new company for insuring the
lives of vegetables, and by November advocating an alternative use for bad
potatoes—pelting Repeal agitators: 'This is the use which a good Paddy
would make of a good-for-nothing Murphy.'[6] But in spite of the jokes, the
accusations of exaggeration, the suspicions, and the attacks on Irish politicians that the Famine afforded, 1845 saw most of the English newspapers
united in sympathy for the Irish. *Punch* commented on the 'dejected look'
of the New Year 1846: 'for he hears the voices of millions bewailing the
potato blight'.[7] *The Times*, never a noted Hibernophile, almost out-
stripped *The Nation* in its criticism of government delays in feeding the
starving; a series of leading articles in November 1845 berated the government for adding to Ireland's evils with its indecision, for doing nothing in
the two months since the blight had been discovered, ending with an
inspired metaphor for the experiment, in which Ireland was compared to
a woman on trial for witchcraft:

[3] *The Times* (4 Nov. 1845), 4.   [4] *Nation* (14 Mar 1846), 344.
[5] *Punch* 9 (July–Dec. 1845), 146; 'curl' was another kind of potato disease.
[6] Ibid., 157, 210.   [7] Ibid., p. iii.

Such are the alternatives in what we call the trial by letting alone. If the population are wrong in apprehending a scarcity, they have the comfort of knowing that the grievance will be indefinitely protracted. Should the event, on the contrary, prove them to be right, they will triumph in the argument, and die, or next door to it.[8]

This unanimity of sympathy must be read in the context of the perception of the crop failure of 1845 as a single event, not the forerunner of a famine of several years' duration. The blight of 1845 was a Europe-wide calamity, affecting many countries besides Ireland (including England), and compounded by the failure of other crops due to exceptionally bad weather. In November *The Times* was reporting 'a prospective dearth in England' due to fears of a wheat famine and the obligation to divert supplies to Ireland.[9] It quoted the French newspaper *La Presse* advocating the refusal of aid to starving neighbours—particularly England; *The Times* offered this as a lesson to those Irish whose sympathies lay with France, comparing England's admission of its duty to send aid to Ireland.[10] The Irish, for the moment, were fellow subjects, fellow sufferers, even if measures offered for relief, such as the Repeal of the Corn Laws, would benefit English rather than Irish poor. 'It will be no common dearth that will threaten Ireland,' noted *The Times*; 'so it will be no common exertion that will be required to meet it. Nor do we see how any human being can in his mind sever the Irish dearth from the English scarcity.'[11]

From the Irish point of view, of course, the situation was different. From *The Nation*'s perspective, 1845 was yet another manifestation of the English government's ignorance of Irish affairs and mismanagement of resources. In June 1845—four months before the announcement of the failure—a leading article in *The Nation* described England as 'a country which filled our soil with martyrs, and our statute-book with penal laws—which, finding the persecution of the sword insufficient, created famine by an elaborate process of desolation for the avowed purpose of exterminating us'.[12] Yet these iniquitous historical famines remained in the abstract, neutralized for the moment by favourable reports of this year's crop. *The Nation* was caught in a bind: crops had to be abundant to advertise the great natural resources of Ireland and the potential for national independence, but the undeniable poverty of the country and its dependence on English charity in previous famines had to be explained away in terms favourable to the Irish. On 28 June, *The Nation* quoted the *Ulster Conservative* with approval: 'From all parts of the country we have the

[8] *The Times* (22 Nov. 1845), 4.   [9] *The Times* (6 Nov. 1845), 4.
[10] *The Times* (7 Nov. 1845), 4.   [11] *The Times* (8 Nov. 1845), 4.
[12] *Nation* (7 June 1845), 568.

most gratifying accounts of the healthy state of the crops, which give every promise of an early and abundant harvest.'[13] The following week, a leading article on the Landlord and Tenant Bill obliquely raised the spectre of a controversy that was to rage throughout the Famine—exportation of food from a starving nation:

Food abundant, population willing, able and laborious, yet hunger more abundant still. Millions of food-producers, whose brawny arms make wealth untold, starving in the midst of their own abundance. They ask for food—is it wonderful? For it is they who create it, and food they must and shall have.[14]

Seven days later, the *Irish Farmer's Journal* was quoted: 'Our letters from all parts of the country contain cheering intelligence of the growing crops, which are, almost without exception, said to be most promising.'[15] Reports in farming journals became increasingly important to *The Nation* as the Famine progressed, not just for the impact failures would have on farmers and the starving, but on the potential for revolution also; in 1848, there would be no attempt to rescue Mitchel because the harvest was not ready to support a rebellion.

Strangely, *The Nation* was ready to concede in 1845 that England, the most prosperous country in the world, contained as much poverty as Ireland. This may have been designed partly as a pre-emptive strike on the findings of the *Times* Commissioner, who was beginning his much-publicized tour in Ireland, partly as a reaction to contemptuous articles on Ireland in the *Morning Post* and other English newspapers in July. A *Nation* leading article, 'First Principles', appeared in mid-August:

In England, where wealth is accumulated to an extent unthought of in any other country, the People suffer the most poignant ills of poverty. They are brutalised, ignorant, and sensual: in many parts they have not the least idea of GOD, or of man's moral responsibilities, and live in a state of indiscriminate indulgence of the lowest passions. At the same time that their labour is producing wealth, they lead a sordid life of barbarous poverty. Their wives and children labour beyond that degree which the robustest manhood ought to endure, and are ignorant beyond the ignorance of the worst of savages.[16]

Sensational reports of infanticide, wife-murders, and poisonings in English newspapers were seized on, and used to show the barbarity of the English as opposed to the newly sober, religious, pacific Irish. The issue of English poverty was indeed pressing, as the novels of Dickens and Gaskell, or contemporary newspaper reports on poorhouses in English

[13] *Nation* (28 June 1845), 629.   [14] *Nation* (5 July 1845), 633.
[15] *Nation* (12 July 1845), 646.   [16] *Nation* (16 Aug. 1845), 729.

towns, amply testify. And when it became clear that the crisis was no longer Europe-wide, but becoming centred in Ireland, *The Times* was quick to capitalize on English poverty as a reason not to have to contribute towards Irish relief. But at the outset, the prospect of a famine of major proportions afflicting any part of the empire was humiliating. It was a step backwards in civilization. At a public meeting in Leicester calling for ports to be opened, a local magistrate claimed that 'the people of this country were now in as much danger of famine as though they lived in the wilds of Siberia'.[17] By April 1846, when it had become part of the never-ending 'Irish Question', the famine in Ireland was being discussed as a frustrating brake on English progress and prosperity; as a leading article in *The Times* put it:

Ireland certainly is the fated instrument for humbling the pride of this empire. In the moment of our greatest successes, when the heart of the nation thrills with the sound of victory and the sense of achievement, when we seem to dare to do anything noble and generous, then Ireland recalls us to modesty, if not to despair.[18]

For all *The Times*'s posturing and *The Nation*'s insinuations, England's situation was entirely different from Ireland's. The potato had failed in England, but English labourers were not reliant on the potato in the way Scottish and Irish peasants were. England did not export food to the extent the Irish did, and had industries besides agriculture which were not available in Ireland; the collapse of the weaving industry in Ireland aggravated the extent of the Famine further still. The language and imagery surrounding early attempts to formulate a relationship between England and Ireland *vis-à-vis* the Famine make clear that they are benefactor and dependant, not fellow sufferers. Much of the imagery, predictably, is medical: Ireland is an 'ulcer' in the healthy body of England, the Irish are sick and the physician England must heal them. For *The Nation*, the English are quack doctors at best, at worst murderers: 'When will our physicians see that they are our "grievance"?'[19] Surprisingly, an even more damning indictment of government policy came from *The Times*, recalling the story of a celebrated anatomist who kept a wretch lingering in agony so that he could explain the nature of the disease to his students: 'The length of Parliamentary debates and the slowness of Parliamentary remedies over the convulsed and bleeding frame of Irish society appear a politico-clinical lecture hardly less inhuman.'[20] Another metaphor, making clear the polarity of the relationship, is the parable of Lazarus and

[17] *The Times* (29 Nov. 1845), 5.   [18] *The Times* (1 Apr. 1846), 4.
[19] *Nation* (27 Sept. 1845), 825.   [20] *The Times* (25 Mar. 1846), 4.

Dives.[21] As Sheila Smith has noted, this parable was commonly used in discussing the gulf between rich and poor in England;[22] but it gained extra potency in the Irish situation. The most enthusiastic employer of this metaphor was the *Illustrated London News*, one of the few English newspapers that seems to have accepted unequivocally that England was responsible for Irish misery. In the awful year 1847, when the *Illustrated London News* was reporting mass starvation in Skibbereen, Lazarus/Dives imagery proliferated in a frenzy of guilt. In the first issue of 1847, a leading article, 'The New Year', proclaimed English guilt and the failure of civilization:

Amid wealth, and skill, and energy, and knowledge, unexampled in extent and degree, our power is baffled, and our pride humbled, by the presence among us of Famine and Disease, spread over a third of the kingdom. Here is the reproach of our wealth, and the abatement of our satisfaction; we cannot fully enjoy our good things, knowing that there are hunger and want at our threshold; Dives has his Lazarus at the gate; there is a fly in the 'pot of ointment:' the lesson taught of old, and from on high, and intended for all time, is not wanting to us: shall we be able to do what it requires at our hands?[23]

In May of the same year, the flood of emigrants into England led the journal to use the metaphor again, to warn of the peril of leaving Ireland to starve: 'Dives sat careless at the feast with one Lazarus at his gate, and met no punishment on earth; but, with millions begging for the crumbs that might fall from the table, the richest of nations cannot securely eat on and refuse the alms.'[24] The proud *Nation* took umbrage at a metaphor that branded Ireland a nation of beggars craving crumbs from England's table:

Is Ireland, indeed, a loathsome LAZARUS, laid at England's gate full of sores— faintly craving such crumbs as may fall from her well-spread table—crying out to have his offensive wounds and endless 'grievances' probed, and salved, and experimented on, soliciting every cur to come and lick his sores? Do the English Press, and Legislature, and Public verily think of us after this manner?[25]

The Nation and Young Ireland politicians were anxious to counteract this image, and refused to accept that Ireland needed English alms; Thomas D'Arcy McGee was later to advise Americans to send money not to relief agencies but to the Repeal fund, a move which could only

---

[21] Luke 16: 19–31.
[22] Sheila M. Smith, *The Other Nation: The Poor in English Novels of the 1840s and 1850s* (Oxford and New York: Clarendon Press and Oxford University Press, 1980), 15–16.
[23] *Illustrated London News* (*ILN*), 10 (2 Jan. 1847), 2.
[24] *ILN* 10 (15 May 1847), 310.   [25] *Nation* (27 Sept. 1845), 824.

have been detrimental to Famine victims. But it is clear that the issue of representation was important from the outset; Irish journals needed to communicate the depth of the crisis without admitting the slander that the country was a nation of beggars; English journals wanted acknowledgement of their charitable acts, fearing misrepresentation. As early as October 1845, *The Times* was forecasting the nationalist reaction to the Famine:

Then there is really some reason to fear that the demagogue and the priest will deliberately stand between English charity and Celtic starvation. Every instinct of their fanaticism or their conspiracy will urge them to misrepresent and calumniate the good intentions of England, so as to paralyze both the hand that should give and that which should receive. When the report of dying myriads thrills through the unanimous and sympathetic hearts of England, the first impulses of an habitual benevolence will be instantly rewarded with the foulest of slanders, and, on the other hand, the perishing multitudes whom nature herself was teaching gratitude, will be instructed to see a worse death in the dole of English bounty.[26]

Of course, misrepresentation was not to remain so one-sided.

By early 1846, *The Times* appeared to be already suffering from compassion fatigue. A leading article of 21 January informed readers:

We have purposely abstained of late from directing the attention of the public to Ireland. The anomalous character of its grievances—the circular reaction of cause and effect in their diffusion and extension—the divisions among the people; divisions of blood, of caste, and religion—the outrages which they have produced the misery which has ensued from them—the quack remedies for them suggested by political empirics—all these have become as tedious and wearisome as a ten times told tale.[27]

Ireland was dominating parliamentary time, leaving very little for English issues, and as it was increasingly clear that the Famine was becoming confined to 'the weak extremities of the empire'[28] (that is Ireland and Scotland), *The Times* was getting peevish over the neglect of the English. Nevertheless, *The Times* felt obliged to confirm the reality of the tragedy and sympathize with Irish suffering due to attacks on the existence of the Famine by journals and individuals supporting Protection of the Corn Laws. A leading article on 5 January castigated the *Quarterly Review*'s denial of the crisis, and satirized its coolness in claiming that the Irish were used to famine, and had no use for corn: 'The natives, therefore, are pretty well accustomed to it by this time, and we need not put ourselves into a

---

[26] *The Times* (18 Oct. 1845), 5.   [27] *The Times* (21 Jan. 1846), 4.
[28] *The Times* (8 Sept. 1846), 4.

hurry about them.'[29] Ironically, once the scale of the expenditure on relief became clear, *The Times* was quickly to occupy this position itself; on 19 February a leading article objected to the government voting away money on an act of God, to a country that was used to famines.[30] Papers of all shades were ridiculing the Duke of Norfolk's suggestion that curry powder would make an excellent substitute for the potato. More unexpectedly, all argued against the exportation of food from Ireland. *The Nation* followed O'Connell's lead in calling for the ports to be closed, claiming an Irish government would have done so as a matter of course. Less predictably, the supposedly anti-Irish *Times*, while advocating Repeal of the Corn Laws and the opening of ports, admitted the anomaly of exporting food from a starving country. In language worthy of John Mitchel, it stated that 'The very poor are reduced to nothing; and yet in that state witness the exportation of grain which they have sown or reaped, with hardly an expectation that its price will redeem themselves from hunger.'[31] A few days later *The Times* expounded another future Mitchel doctrine, that there was enough food to feed all the people of Ireland several times over: 'This very year what she has sent out, in effect, to pay the rent of her landowners would cover again and again the deficiency in the potato crop.'[32] The peasant, the article continued, was merely the 'hungry sieve' through which English money passed to greedy landlords. An article listing the huge amounts of imports from Ireland for a week in March pointedly refused to comment on its own information:

we abstain from any remark on their number and importance at the present time, when the consideration of Ireland and the distress stated to exist in that country are occupying the most earnest attention of the Legislature and the British public, simply stating the facts and giving an authentic and correct list of the arrivals of such articles from the quarter alluded to, leaving the further consideration of the matter for those most interested and concerned.[33]

Cryptic as it is, the implication is clear: exportation from a poor to a wealthy country in a time of famine was unjustified. The *Illustrated London News*, remarking on the violence attending attempts to ship corn from Ireland, added: 'And we must admit, that, to a starving multitude, the spectacle of ship-loads of corn being taken away from where it is so grievously wanted is a painful and exciting one.'[34]

[29] *The Times* (5 Jan. 1846), 4.   [30] *The Times* (19 Feb. 1846), 4.
[31] *The Times* (28 Jan. 1846), 6.   [32] *The Times* (7 Feb. 1846), 4.
[33] *The Times* (27 Mar. 1846), 5.   [34] *ILN* 9 (10 Oct. 1846), 231.

Reports of food riots and attacks on carts became more frequent as 1846 progressed, interfering with the diffusion of sympathy by the media. *The Nation*, identified as the organ of 'physical' rather than 'moral' force in Ireland, was nevertheless anxious to distance itself from violence at this time, while simultaneously capitalizing on the threat to the Union. 'Between the people and food there is no obstacle that their breath would not brush away', a leading article tantalizingly stated, adding, however: 'And yet they hunger, but are patient. May GOD guard that holy virtue of theirs, which now stands in place of the safeguards that call vainly on the impotence of the Executive—may GOD guard it, and save His People!'[35] Reports of violence began to die down, however, to be replaced by panegyrics on the order of Irish demonstrations, frequently silent, and using only the traditional symbol of a loaf of bread on a pole. By June 1846, the *Illustrated London News* was protesting that as there was no violence, the projected Coercion Bill was wholly unnecessary. *Punch* had begun to ridicule the idea as early as April. 'How To Cure Ireland' rejected the usual remedies—steel, lead, and hemp—and recommended three meals a day and 'Friar's Balsam' (payment of Roman Catholic priests).[36] 'The Nation We Cannot Subdue' portrayed a mock battle using food, not weapons:

> Then hurrah! For the Sassenach, with *Punch* for their chief—
> Charge potatoes and buttermilk! Charge bread and beef!
> And charge absentee landlords—a thumping good tax,
> And we soon shall have 'Bellum' converted to 'Pax'.[37]

In spite of the provocation of Young Ireland, *Punch* returned to the fray in September, with 'We Must Invade Ireland':

> The van is to consist of grenadiers, to be called the 1st Life Potatoes, who are to shower the effective missile they take their name from on the quarters where it is most needed.
> The right wing is to be formed of the Household Bread and Meat Brigade; troops that may be depended upon for giving the enemy a bellyful . . .
> The whole army is to be flanked by a squadron of Schoolmasters . . .[38]

While these skits were patronizing and exactly what Young Ireland deplored, they were good-humoured and well-intentioned, which is more than could be said for many of the representations that were to follow.

---

[35] *Nation* (9 May 1846), 473.   [36] *Punch* 10 (Jan.–June 1846), 156.
[37] Ibid., 174.   [38] *Punch* 11 (July–Dec. 1846), 106.

The year 1846 also saw a major onslaught on Irish landlords in the English and Irish press. The eviction of 300 tenants from the estate of Mrs Gerrard at Ballinglass, County Galway on 13 March was universally condemned by the press and in the House of Commons. *The Times* reacted in fury that English legislature was acting in favour of the commission of such evil deeds: 'How often are we to be told that the common law of England sanctions injustice and furnishes the weapons of oppression? How long shall the rights of property in Ireland continue to be the wrongs of poverty, and the advancement of the rich be the destruction of the poor?'[39] *The Times*, no less than *The Nation*, was willing to admit that the increase in violent crime in Ireland was an index of desperation: 'murders are of daily occurrence. Grant it. But so also are the causes of murder. The population is daily starving. Evictions are daily enforced.'[40] Irish tenants were British subjects also, and deserved to be treated as such, *The Times* continued to affirm in the early days of the Famine. At this point, there appeared to be very little difference in the outlooks of *The Times* and *The Nation*. *The Times*'s zeal did not last long; by 22 April its Irish correspondent was tiring: 'Eviction and emigration furnish of late fruitful themes for Irish provincial editors. A little less repetition of the former would perhaps be more agreeable to the general readers of newspapers . . .'.[41] However, press opinion still seemed to merge in sympathy for the starving, outrage at indifferent landlords, and demands that the government should act. Indeed, the reader of *The Times* was imbibing many of the same opinions as the reader of the supposedly revolutionary *Nation*.

There was a similar consensus on the issue of emigration. Naturally *The Nation* was against it; in 1846 only comfortable farmers were leaving, taking their capital and energy with them, and there were fears that only the poor, weak, and aged would remain behind. Ireland was feeding England and Scotland, *The Nation* argued, and could easily afford to support all eight millions of her population; claims of over-population did not take into account unreclaimed land, etc. More significantly, *The Times* also recognized the anomaly and rejected emigration as a response to the Famine: 'The ejected or starved-out peasant who tries his fortune in a new world, obeys the same law that urges a man to leap from a burning vessel into a raging sea . . . we cannot look on emigration in any other light than as a great evil, less only than immediate starvation.'[42] The newspaper John Mitchel was later to accuse of hounding the Irish out of Ireland was thus in 1846 defending their right of existence and habitation.

---

[39] *The Times* (31 Mar. 1846), 5.   [40] *The Times* (18 Apr. 1846), 5.
[41] *The Times* (22 Apr. 1846), 7.   [42] *The Times* (15 Apr. 1846), 4.

The schism in opinion was largely political rather than social or economic. English newspapers were fiercely critical of O'Connell's Repeal Rent, especially when allegations were made that relief money was ending up in the Liberator's pocket. In December 1845, *Punch* delivered its damning indictment—'The Real Potato Blight of Ireland', a cartoon by John Leech portraying O'Connell as a gigantic potato with a begging plate.[43] Many papers reported the near-riot which took place at Conciliation Hall when Admiral Oliver suggested the Repeal fund should be turned over to a relief committee; O'Connell ordered Oliver out.[44] *The Nation*, in the halcyon days before its break with O'Connell, defended the Repeal Rent wholeheartedly. *The Times* was already warning in November 1845 that the English would begrudge giving charity to the Irish unless they were sure it would not go to Repeal, and a series of letters appeared on the thorny question of whether O'Connell would actually share his last potato with a starving peasant.[45] The Liberator's image had also been tarnished by the controversy over Thomas Campbell Foster's letters from O'Connell's property in County Kerry, where he was exposed as an 'absentee landlord' at a time when landlords were fair game. *The Times* followed up in March 1846 with a list of the huge salaries of the staff at Conciliation Hall, represented as battening on the starvation of the people they were supposed to be representing. The Irish correspondent suggested that the non-alarmist approach taken by Protectionists could only be aided by the call for O'Connell's Tribute at such a time.[46]

Other disincentives to charity quickly came to light. While Young Ireland was still adhering to 'moral force', leading articles in *The Nation*, principally by the firebrand Mitchel, argued otherwise. 'Threats of Coercion', which appeared in November 1845, while Mitchel was temporarily in charge of *The Nation*, offered practical methods to dismantle a railway and transform its materials into weapons; Duffy, who was working on a book on the Popish Rebellion, was quickly summoned back to Dublin to resume editorship.[47] The Young Ireland leader, William Smith O'Brien, was extremely vocal on Irish wrongs in the House of Commons, and was accused by *The Times* of giving a 'wild Irish howl' every time he raised the question of the Famine—this in spite of his English public school accent.[48] Certainly O'Brien's antics—such as his refusal to act on

[43] *Punch* 9 (July–Dec. 1845), 255.   [44] *ILN* 7 (8 Nov. 1845), 291.
[45] *The Times* (20 Nov. 1845), 4.
[46] *The Times* (14 Mar. 1846), 6; (7 Mar. 1846), 6.
[47] *Nation* (22 Nov. 1845), 88; Sir Charles Gavan Duffy, *My Life in Two Hemispheres*, 2 vols. (London: T. Fisher Unwin, 1898), i. 139.
[48] *The Times* (14 Mar. 1846), 4.

any committee that did not deal with Irish affairs, which led to his arrest
and incarceration in the cellars of the House of Commons for contempt
and earned him the soubriquet 'the martyr of the cellar'—did little to dispel English stereotypes of Irish 'enthusiasm'. *Punch* made clear its opinion
of the Young Irelanders with another Leech cartoon, 'Young Ireland In
Business For Himself', depicting a dwarfish, scowling Young Irelander
selling guns to a prognathous Paddy.[49] The tide of sympathy was turning
against Ireland.

Attitudes were further hardened by reports that supposedly starving
peasants were using English relief money to buy arms. English misgivings
were fuelled by reports in Irish newspapers confirming the increase in
sales of arms at markets. *The Times* affected a reluctance to believe such
ingratitude could be possible, but admitted: 'It is too natural to suspect—
nay, it is hardly possible to escape the conclusion, that a good deal of
"relief" money and rent money goes to the armourer.' It was too unnatural
to ask money from England to buy arms to destroy England, and the article ended by hoping 'that for lack of any other name, it will not have to be
called an Irishism'.[50] *Punch* was not so restrained. Leech's 'Height of
Impudence' portrayed a ragged Irishman asking John Bull: 'Spare a thrifle, yer Honour, for a poor Irish lad to buy a bit of—a Blunderbuss with.'[51]
In the same issue appeared 'Grateful Paddy', a poem which freely showed
the change in attitudes from early 1846:

> Och! Paddy, my honey, we've given you our money,
> And we freely came down with the dust, did we not?
> And now you enjoy it, the way you employ it,
> Is in laying it out upon powder and shot.[52]

The Nation protested that the 'popular armament' was in fact a run on
firearms by comfortable farmers who wished to defend their crops and
property against large bodies of the unemployed and starving, and admitted that the purchase of arms by the peasantry could bring only hatred,
punishment, and death; but the damage had been done.[53] The last straw
for English sympathy was the revelation of the huge sums which had been
deposited in Irish savings-banks in the year ending 10 October 1846; as
The Times acerbically commented: 'A few more famines, and Ireland will
become one of the wealthiest countries in the world.'[54]

[49] *Punch* 11 (July–Dec. 1846), 57.   [50] *The Times* (30 Nov. 1846), 4.
[51] *Punch* 11 (July–Dec. 1846), 245.   [52] Ibid., 252.
[53] *Nation* (12 Dec. 1846), 153.   [54] *The Times* (6 Nov. 1846), 4.

HEIGHT OF IMPUDENCE.

Irishman to John Bull.—"Spare a thrifle, yer Honour, for a poor Irish Lad to buy a bit of ——
A Blunderbuss with."

Figure 1. 'Height of Impudence', *Punch*, 11 (July–Dec. 1846)

The fact that it did not seem to occur to *The Times* that the really starving—and its own 'Ireland' column asserted there were undoubtedly many—could not buy arms or deposit savings indicates the chasm that existed between the *Times* writer or reader and the starving Irish peasant. The continuous exclamations of tedium by journalists testify to the complete lack of impact on their lives: 'We can easily imagine that our readers are beginning to be a little tired of Ireland. If it is any consolation to them, or any apology for ourselves, we beg to assure them of a most entire sympathy in their fatigue.'[55] Despite the newspaper's decision to print instructions on how best to treat diseased potatoes in the early days of the blight—as if assuming that its readers were one and the same with those most affected—the *Times* reader, as represented by its editors, was completely alien to suffering and deprivation: 'a column of small print headed "Another death by destitution," or a "leader" on its yesterday's predecessor, comes rather like a wet blanket on the warm curiosity of the gentleman in a dressing-gown, with a devilled drumstick on his plate, and a game pie in reserve'.[56] Thus, the *Times*'s readers were acknowledged to be wholly antipathetic to suffering, and it was the paper's moral obligation to expose 'sufferings which but for the activity of the press would be merged in the darkness of perpetual silence'.[57] But the alterity of Ireland, and the extent of the suffering there, led *The Times* to adopt a defensively Anglocentric tone. Its 'Ireland' column, composed chiefly of extracts from provincial newspapers such as the *Cork Examiner* and *Southern Reporter*, the *Tipperary Vindicator*, the *Clare Journal*, the *Mayo Constitution*, the *Erne Packet*, and the *Belfast Vindicator*, daily recorded death by starvation, horrendous murders, evictions, crimes of desperation. The leading articles, on the other hand, while condemning the violence and ingratitude of Ireland, consistently elevated English suffering over Irish. The English labourer—not a typical *Times* reader—became the symbol of an England oppressed and repressed by Ireland. The English labourer, the newspaper argued, had been hardest hit by the Famine, having to deal with the blight and cholera as the Scots and Irish had, but also having to foot the bill: 'How are the chief sufferers by this "great scarcity" to feed the Irish millions when they cannot get bread for themselves?'[58] The English are the 'chief sufferers' in this account, not the Irish, and to justify the claim, leading articles began to appear on the subject of English starvation. Articles on the horrors of the Poor Law system in Andover and Dorset appeared on the same page as panegyrics on the Poor Law as the potential saviour of

⁵⁵ *The Times* (11 Nov. 1846), 4.   ⁵⁶ *The Times* (1 Dec. 1846), 4.
⁵⁷ *The Times* (2 Dec. 1846), 4.   ⁵⁸ *The Times* (15 Sept. 1846), 4.

Ireland. Some of the names of those who starved to death in England, as reported in *The Times* and the *Illustrated London News*, sound suspiciously Irish: Mary Anne Ryan and Martin Finnigan in London and Liverpool, for example. *The Times* expressed its shock at Ryan's death: 'to think that human beings are dying of starvation in a land of plenty is a horror beyond the power of language to express'.[59] Had she died in Ireland, this observation would have been a potent comment on the system of exportation *The Times* had criticized early in the Famine; her death in England is disturbing in a different way. The starvation of Louisa Mordaunt, a poor London seamstress, through the neglect of local authorities raised an outcry in November 1846, as did the deaths of 2-year-old Joseph Woodward, a baby named Dovey in Worcester, and the Millers, a father and son from Preston-cum-Sutton in Dorset. These victims have names and stories, and leading articles lamenting their deaths; the Irish, even in sympathetic articles, are an entity, undignified by any individuality, tarred with the same brush, subject to ethnic prejudice and derogatory comments. In emphasizing the importance of the potato in the Irish diet, and consequently the impact of the blight in Ireland, *The Times* added:

But we entertain no doubt whatever that the hungriest and squalidest bogtrotter in Connaught, whatever his present condition—long-shanked, flat-footed, calfless, slouching, narrow-chested, high-cheeked, wide-mouthed, long-eared, short-nosed, as he may happen to be—if it should be considered an object, could with judicious treatment be brought to bear a dinner of turtle soup, roast beef, pheasant, and ice punch every day of his life, without being very much the worse for the change.[60]

Thus an entire nation is impoverished, and denied all possibility of respect, in uncompromising compound adjectives. Yet there was considerable ambivalence in the approach to racial difference. Part of the problem was that so many of the journalists writing on the degradation of the Irish for English newspapers—including the editor of *The Times*, John Thadeus Delane—were of Irish extraction. Indeed, the *Punch* cartoonist John Leech, who contributed such damning indictments on O'Connell, Young Ireland, and Irish ingratitude, was Irish on his father's side. William Makepeace Thackeray had travelled in Ireland several years before the Famine, was married to an Irishwoman, and was immersed in the world of London journalism. He described this milieu in *Pendennis*, published in 1848: 'Many of our journals are officered by Irish gentlemen, and their gallant brigade does the penning among us, as their ancestors

---

[59] *The Times* (20 Nov. 1846), 4.   [60] *The Times* (18 Sept. 1846), 4.

used to transact the fighting in Europe; and engage under many a flag, to be good friends when the battle is over.'[61] 'Jacob Omnium', the 'satirist of Belgravia', who wrote for *The Times* and the *Morning Chronicle*, visited Ireland in a serious capacity, as agent for the British Association for the Relief of the Destitute Irish, during the Famine, and sent letters to *The Times* detailing the misery he witnessed: 'I have found the naked bodies of women on the roadside . . . I have met mothers carrying about dead infants in their arms until they were putrid, refusing to bury them, in the hope that the offensive sight might wring charity from the callous townspeople sufficient to protract for a while the lives of the other children at home.'[62] A leading article in *The Times* the following day referred to 'Omnium''s letter, admitting the value of his report in putting the plight of the Irish into perspective, and praising 'the minuteness of detail which is in strong contrast with the generality of an account purely Irish'.[63] Ironically, 'Omnium' was 'purely Irish'; his real name was Matthew James Higgins, and he was born at Benown Castle, County Meath. His nationality, and his obvious sympathy for the sufferings of his fellow-Irishmen, did not however neutralize his fears about the dangers of English relief: 'English charity cannot do too much for Ireland, but what she does she must do systematically and cautiously', he warned, adding that the clergy were not reliable enough to have funds placed in their hands: 'we must beware of employing wolves to succour lambs'.[64] In the eyes of English journalism— and this seems to include Irish journalists working for English papers— the Celts were weak and dependent, and unable to deal with hardship as the Saxons could. Even within Celticism, there was a hierarchy of suffering: the Scots were seen as more hardy and stoical than the Irish, and less likely to complain.

Despite *The Times*'s attempts to distance the calamity to the 'weak extremities' of the empire, the familial metaphors commonly used at the time make it clear that the Famine was closer than English journalists might have liked. This is especially clear in *Punch* cartoons, where Britannia and John Bull were often portrayed as the elder, richer siblings of poor Hibernia. In 'Union is Strength', John Bull gives a basket of food to a starving family, saying: 'Here are a few things to go on with, Brother, and I'll soon put you in a way to earn your own living.'[65] More disturbingly, in 'Justice to Ireland', England is a wicked stepmother whipping

[61] William Makepeace Thackeray, *The History of Pendennis*, ed. John Sutherland (Oxford: Oxford University Press, 1994), 386.

[62] *The Times* (22 Apr. 1847), 6.   [63] *The Times* (23 Apr. 1847), 5.

[64] *The Times* (1 May 1847), 6.   [65] *Punch* 11 (July–Dec. 1846), 161.

her Irish children with a rolled-up Coercion Bill: 'She gave them some Broth without any Bread, | Then whipp'd them all Round, and sent them to Bed.'[66] 'The Irish Cinderella and her Haughty Sisters, Britannia and Caledonia' clearly exposes and condemns the exploitation of Ireland by Britain.[67] These last two *Punch* sketches indicate disquiet about the true nature of England's generosity. *The Times* is much less conscience-stricken about the relationship, and the familial metaphors are resolved much more in England's favour. England appears as a poor tradesman who helps his spendthrift son (Ireland), and is abused and betrayed in return.[68] Later, during the rate-in-aid crisis in 1849, Ulster reappears as the reluctant but more tractable son, being taught his duty to the less well-off: 'It [rate-in-aid] is the difference between giving alms in the presence of our children, and inducing them to contribute out of their own pocket-money.'[69] A survey of the year 1847 elicited admissions both of alterity and relationship from *The Times*: 'It will be difficult to most of our readers to feel near akin with a class which at the best wallows in pigsties, and hugs the most brutish degradation. But when we take the sum of the British people, the "ill-fed, ill-clothed, ill-housed" children of the Celt count with VICTORIA's own children . . .'.[70] For Irish journalists writing in England, the problem of identification must have been even more complex than that faced by the largely English middle-class readership of *The Times*.

Readership was also an issue for *The Nation* and Mitchel's *United Irishman*, as those who were starving were not those who read newspapers. *The Nation*, at 6*d.*, cost more than *The Times* (5*d.*), though as a weekly paper it was less expensive than the daily *Times*. Mitchel's journal and its successors, the *Irish Tribune* and the *Irish Felon*, were each 5*d.* per issue. *The Nation* was accessible to the masses in Repeal Reading Rooms until the break with O'Connell in July 1846, when many subscriptions were cancelled; but no doubt even after the break, whole communities would share a copy. However, *The Nation* openly appealed to landlords and Protestants to join Repeal, indicating its belief that its readership was wider than peasant Repealers. Indeed, some of the advertisements that appeared at the height of the Famine openly contradicted the bent of the leading articles. *The Nation* was fiercely anti-emigration, yet carried numerous advertisements for emigration ships in each issue. Readers were enticed to buy fine teas, turtle soup, London tailored clothing. *The Nation* even ran an advert for Trevelyan's *The Irish Crisis* in February 1848. In

---

[66] *Punch* 10 (Jan.–June 1846), 171.   [67] Ibid., 181.
[68] *The Times* (17 June 1847), 4.   [69] *The Times* (7 Mar. 1849), 5.
[70] *The Times* (3 Jan. 1848), 4.

THE IRISH CINDERELLA AND HER HAUGHTY
SISTERS, BRITANNIA AND CALEDONIA.

Figure 2. 'The Irish Cinderella and Her Haughty Sisters,
Britannia and Caledonia', *Punch* 10 (Jan–June 1846)

April 1847 it was attempting scare tactics obviously aimed at its middle-class readers, assuring them that the fever following in the wake of the Famine would inevitably kill more rich than poor: 'Who can be assured that *he* will not be the next victim of England?'[71] Deaths were strictly segregated by class: those of the poorer classes would usually appear in the 'State of the Country' column, those of the upper classes in 'Domestic News'. In March 1847, amid reports of evictions and leading articles calling on landlords to beware, this odd notice appeared:

IMPORTANT NOTICE

During the high price of Provisions and the non-payment of Rents, Ladies and Gentlemen have their Baths at Reduced Rates, at

THE MEDICATED BATHING ESTABLISHMENT

in Temple-street, from Six O'Clock in the Morning till Ten at Night.[72]

While it is tempting to read this as a satire on the heartlessness of the upper classes, there is nothing in the text to support such a conclusion.

One of the reasons Mitchel decided to separate from Duffy and *The Nation* at the end of 1847 was his complete loss of faith in the ability of the upper and middle classes to commit to Repeal. His choice of an epigraph from Wolfe Tone made clear Mitchel's feeling that *The Nation* had been dallying with the men of property too long, and to no avail: 'Our independence must be had at all hazards. If the men of property will not support us, they must fall: we can support ourselves by the aid of that numerous and respectable class of the community, *the Men of no property.*'[73] However, Mitchel's definition of 'men of no property', like that of Wolfe Tone himself, encompassed small farmers and tenants rather than the homeless, and his rhetoric was directed more often at them and those like them who had the means of arming themselves rather than at those who literally had nothing. Like his mentor, James Fintan Lalor (and the majority of his *Nation* colleagues), Mitchel was an elitist. In an article entitled 'The First Step—The Felon Club' published in the *Irish Felon* after Mitchel's transportation, Lalor called for clubs to be formed to arm and help others arm. Of course, one of the prerequisites was that members would agree with the club's principles: 'But this will not be enough, else a common labourer, unable to read or write, would be eligible . . . It is not the common labour, but the skilled labour of the country, we desire to engage and organise in this Club.'[74] The starving may have had vocal sympathy from the press, but no real representation.

[71] *Nation* (17 Apr. 1847), 440.
[73] *United Irishman* (12 Feb. 1848), 8.
[72] *Nation* (20 Mar. 1847), 384.
[74] *Irish Felon* (1 July 1848), 25.

The Famine was as provincial for Dublin-based newspapers as it was for those in London; both *The Times* and *The Nation* created a collage of extracts from provincial newspapers, often using the same ones—the *Cork Examiner* was a favourite. Sometimes reporting seemed skewed towards different areas: Skibbereen, which was receiving great coverage in the *Illustrated London News*, soon became a byword for famine; the distress in Mayo was highlighted because *The Times* and *The Nation* picked up a 'black list' of deaths which the *Mayo Constitution* began to publish weekly; but more surprisingly the Famine in Ulster was frequently referred to. This may have been a deliberate corrective to Protectionist protests that only remote areas were affected, and that the hardy Protestants of Ulster had withstood the blast. *The Times* quoted the *Belfast Vindicator* (previously edited by *The Nation*'s Charles Gavan Duffy):

If, through a false pride, with a view to show that no distress exists in Ulster, and such showy, aristocratic nonsense, the evil be permitted to make way, disease will follow destitution, and the fever will spread from the cabins of the poor to the houses of the rich; and he who now, for the *honour* of Ulster, forsooth, but to the disgrace of humanity, wants to have it said that there is no distress where poverty is, nevertheless, felt, in its most gloomy misery, may be the first to fall the victim of his own folly.[75]

It was understandable that Duffy and Mitchel, both Ulstermen, would be interested in the progress of the Famine in their native province, but there was an added incentive to follow stories about death on the streets of Belfast and on the public works: if these people, living in relatively wealthy areas, or supported by government relief, were dropping dead by the roadside, how much worse must it be for ejected tenants in Mayo or Cork? Journalists took care to manipulate the record for their own ends.

The return of the blight in 1846 made it clear that this was not to be a short-lived scarcity, and English attitudes hardened. *The Nation* also announced a change in policy, stating that previous articles had been toned down and self-censored:

Hitherto we have held ourselves under strong restraint in speaking of the awful abyss of misery that is swallowing up whole classes of our fellow countrymen. We have forborne to notice, and have tried not to see, the odious calumnies and rascal sneers of the English press, representing, we believe, too faithfully, the feeling of the English people, who, while they dole out to us a pittance of our own money plundered from us year by year, take ample security for it on the Irish soil, that they may hereafter plunder us *more*.[76]

[75] Quoted in *The Times* (14 Apr. 1846), 7.   [76] *Nation* (2 Jan. 1847), 200.

Nation readers may be forgiven for not having noticed the shift, as 'self-censored' articles seemed to be as critical and strident as later ones; as in Mitchel's *History of Ireland*, the appearance of objectivity was acknowledged as an important propaganda tool. But certainly such censorship can be seen in a newspaper that was sympathetic to Ireland, the *Illustrated London News*. In early 1847 a leading article in this journal rejoiced that it could act to remedy some of the evils its countrymen had committed:

> The advocacy of so holy a cause as that of 'feeding the hungry, and clothing the naked,' is a delightful task, and one of the very few sacred pleasures that fall to the lot of the journalist in his toilsome routine of professional occupation . . . The call should be responded to with the more alacrity on our part, as, we fear, much of the misery and suffering which now decimates the population of that ill-starred land is to be traced in its more remote, but not less certain, origin, to the long neglect and apathy with which we, the people of the governing island, have regarded that population and its affairs . . .[77]

The journal took its responsibility seriously, sending the Irish artist James Mahony to report from badly hit areas such as Skibbereen. Yet Mahony's sketches were not always as authentic as the journal promised; his sketch of Schull, accompanied by an article describing a crowd of up to 500 women trying to buy food, includes only four figures, and seems preoccupied by the details of the town rather than by the state of its inhabitants. In May the *Illustrated London News* ran a sketch of a food riot in Stettin, Germany, yet there were few images of the many food riots that were occurring in Ireland.[78] In late 1846 the journal had sent an artist to Dungarvan and Youghal, scenes of food riots, admitting the images he sent back would not be strictly true: 'The Artist has refrained from heightening the picturesqueness of these scenes; but they are stern and striking realities of the sufferings of the people, and must bespeak the sympathy of every well-regulated mind.'[79] For 'picturesqueness' read violence and horror. The artist encountered the difficulty faced by every journalist or enquirer in Ireland at the time: the locals assumed that he had been sent by the Board of Works to find out if public works were necessary: 'Our Artist was received somewhat roughly whilst he was sketching in the street, because he would not promise the mothers that their children, then working on the part of Government, should have an increase of wages over five or sixpence, which was insufficient to support them with Indian meal at 1s. 8d. per stone.'[80] In a sense, the artist *had* been sent as a relief agent;

---

[77] *ILN* 10 (16 Jan. 1847), 38.   [78] *ILN* 10 (15 May 1847), 320.
[79] *ILN* 9 (7 Nov. 1846), 293.   [80] Ibid., 293.

as the case of Skibbereen makes evident, newspaper reports had a definite impact on the provision of relief for various areas, and a visit from a journalist to a remote locality could mean the difference between survival and extinction; conversely, it could harden hearts and close purses.

Despite the huge death toll of 1847, attitudes had changed, and sympathy was much less readily available. A relief committee from Skibbereen visited England in January 1847 to try to raise funds, and found that the English were turning against them due to rumours of abuse of previous charity, the fact that the state of Ireland had not been improved by past generosity, the reports of popular armament by recipients of relief money, and the widespread apathy of the people—all staple topics of *Times* leaders on Ireland.[81] It was becoming clear that Ireland faced a terrifying prospect, and *The Times* was determined to make the point that England could not and would not pay. The scarcity that was once the concern of the empire was now 'a remote provincial famine' which had to be relieved by Irish landlords.[82] Yet again the newspaper came up with a powerful metaphor: 'Every working man in this island has an Irish peasant on his back, and may deem himself only too fortunate if both are not floundering in the mud before next August.'[83] By July 1848 matters had worsened so that 'every hard-working man in this country carries a whole Irish family on his shoulders', and in February 1849 *Punch* picked up the image with its cartoon 'The English Labourer's Burden; Or, The Irish Old Man Of The Mountain', in which an apish Irishman with £50,000 in a sack rides on the back of an honest Englishman.[84] Yet leading articles in *The Times* denying England's wealth and maintaining its inability to pay for Irish distress were frequently followed by boasts of the country's wealth and progress: 'The national income has been so steadily increasing during the last four or five years, that we now look for a surplus as a matter of course.'[85]

This new harsher tone from *The Times* included a note of nationalistic triumph. 'Ireland is now at the mercy of England,' one leading article brayed. 'For the first time in the course of centuries England may rule Ireland, and may treat her as a thoroughly conquered country.'[86] *The Nation*, for its part, was reviving the spectre of hated Cromwell: where once the choice offered to the Irish was 'to Hell or Connaught', now it was 'to Canada or the grave'.[87] Leading articles advocated 'England for the

[81] Report of Skibbereen Relief Committee, quoted in *The Times* (7 Jan. 1847), 5.
[82] *The Times* (24 Mar. 1847), 4.   [83] *The Times* (5 Feb. 1847), 5.
[84] *The Times* (26 July 1848), 5; *Punch* 16 (Jan.–June 1849), 79.
[85] *The Times* (6 Jan. 1847), 4.   [86] *The Times* (15 Mar. 1847), 4.
[87] *Nation* (17 July 1847), 648.

THE ENGLISH LABOURER'S BURDEN;

OR, THE IRISH OLD MAN OF THE MOUNTAIN.

[See *Sinbad the Sailor.*

Figure 3. 'The English Labourer's Burden; or, the Old Man of the
Mountain', *Punch* 16 (Jan.–June 1849)

English' and 'Irish for Ireland', and applauded the new note of nationalism in the Irish Conservative Press, and the formation of a Protestant
Repeal Association, including among its members such luminaries as
Samuel Ferguson. The journal begun by Thomas Davis to inspire national
feeling in all Irishmen was, however, a little reluctant to accept this off-
shoot, and Mitchel's acerbic pen can be traced in 'How We May Hold The
Island—Tenant-Right':

> Ireland for the Irish! THE IRISH NATION! Have we lived to hear words like these in
> an Assembly of Irish gentlemen, and so long after '82? . . . And do the landlords,
> the 'gentry,' 'the better classes,' the *English garrison*, as they were once, at least
> acknowledge a common nationhood *with* the tillers of the Irish soil, and *against* the
> English?[88]

It is easy to see that Mitchel was already contemplating the break with
Duffy.

By mid-1847 *The Nation* was convinced that two million people were
going to die in the Famine. Although Young Ireland had never agreed
with the hated public works, when the government announced they were
to be wound down, *The Nation* recognized this as a virtual death sentence
on those who relied on the meagre wages. It was becoming clear that the
accusation of genocide was going to be widely propagated. By October
1847, *The Times* was fulminating over 'the generation of an historical lie':

> 'In the dreadful winter of 1846,' it will be written and taught, 'when the only food
> of the Irish Roman Catholics had perished, the Protestant Government of England
> refused to take any measures to convey food to that miserable population, and sat
> with folded arms while two millions died. That any survived is owing to the bounty
> of America and other foreign nations . . .'[89]

Other 'Mitchelisms' were rearing their heads. The famous comparison of
the £20 million given to free West Indian slaves actually makes more
appearances in *The Times* than *The Nation* or *United Irishman*, in letters by
Archbishop MacHale and others, or retorts in leading articles that £20
million was nothing compared to what England would have to pay for
Ireland.[90] In October 1845, before the Famine had properly begun, 'T. S.
of Liverpool' wrote to *The Times* with an impassioned plea to save Ireland:
'Some three or four millions might do it. We were charged 20,000,000l. to
free the negroes,—shall we not be charged three or four to save from perishing a much greater number of our near neighbours and brethren?'[91]

[88] *Nation* (17 July 1847), 648.   [89] *The Times* (11 Oct. 1847), 4.
[90] *The Times* (1 Feb. 1847), 4.   [91] *The Times* (29 Oct. 1845), 8.

Mitchel's favourite dictum made an appearance in *The Nation* in January 1847: 'The potato blight is the dispensation of Providence—the famine is the work of a foreign Government.'[92] Yet as early as September 1846, *The Times* was already using this formula (in a more unwieldy form) to describe popular discontent in Ireland: 'The potatoes were blighted by a decree from on high, but labour is defrauded by the machinations of earthly power.'[93] Once more, tone is all, and a statement that became synonymous with Mitchel may have originated in a *Times* editorial.

It is instructive to compare *The Times* and *The Nation* of this time in their attitudes to the perceived Providential nature of the Famine. It might be expected that *The Times*, convinced as it was of the racial inferiority of the Irish and the unfitness of the potato for the food of civilized human beings, would have embraced the Providential theory wholeheartedly, while *The Nation*, blaming the English government, would angrily reject it as yet another excuse for exploitation. Indeed, Peter Gray has argued that the moral authority of those in government who believed implicitly in the Providential origin of the Famine, such as Trevelyan and Grey, was bolstered by the fervent support of *The Times*.[94] In fact, the only manifestation of a religious connotation to the calamity in *The Times* comes from extracts from Irish newspapers and memorials. Irish deputations to the Lord Lieutenant or Prime Minister were always prefaced with the admission that the Famine was undoubtedly a judgement from God—though of course, this may be more an indication of what was expected rather than what people actually believed. But *The Nation* quickly accepted it as such, interpreting the reasons why God was moved to strike Ireland to its own advantage. Biblical metaphors abounded: England was Pharaoh, keeping Ireland in chains: 'Israel in Egypt were weak in chariots and horsemen to the host of PHARAOH, but it is not recorded that their slavery was without an end.'[95] Treating both as equally historical, Joseph's actions during the seven years of famine in Egypt were compared to Russell's in Ireland: Joseph had destroyed free trade to save people, it was argued, and so should Russell.[96] Two months after the reports of the first blight, *The Nation* hailed the coming Famine as 'the greatest affliction which GOD sends as a trial or a punishment'.[97] By April 1846, it had decided that the Famine had been sent to rid the country of the conqueror's food, the

---

[92] *Nation* (30 Jan. 1847), 265.   [93] *The Times* (22 Sept. 1846), 4.

[94] Peter Gray, ' "Potatoes and Providence": British Government Responses to the Great Famine', *Bullán: An Irish Studies Journal*, 1/1 (Spring 1994), 84.

[95] *Nation* (17 Apr. 1847), 441.   [96] *Nation* (1 May 1847), 472.

[97] *Nation* (8 Nov. 1845), 57.

potato. By October the blight had come upon Ireland to destroy a defunct social system. In February 1847 it was a punishment for the abdication of nationality, and in June a judgement on Irishmen's sins against each other and dependence on England. So, while *The Nation* condemned the mere mention of Providence by English divines, it was not averse to using such theories for its own ends. Many English journals were noticeably more sceptical about Providentialism. *Punch* announced in September 1846 its 'Tremendous Potato Discovery'—that the blight had in fact been caused by the Maynooth Grant: 'But this is not the worst. The money voted to Maynooth—money is so wicked!—not content with spoiling the Irish potatoes, rotted the potatoes of Belgium, the potatoes of America, the potatoes of France . . .'.[98] The journal reacted indignantly to the assertions of English divines such as Revd Hugh McNeile, the evangelical canon of Chester, that the Famine was a divine retribution:

What—we ask it—have been the transgressions of the wronged and wretched peasantry? They have been ground to the dust by oppression, and they have never murmured. But—we think we discover the meaning of the preacher—they have been smitten for the patience with which they have endured long-suffering. Doubtless, thinks MR. M'NEILE, there is a point at which resignation becomes pusillanimity. If he do not mean this, we can see nothing in the words of the petition-monger—nothing save religion turned inside out.[99]

The *Illustrated London News* condemned the Archbishop of Dublin, Richard Whately, for making the same assertions: 'His arguments are singularly cold and hard, and, if it be not presumption to say it of a Prelate of the Church, completely at variance with the doctrines and precepts of the Gospel.'[100] *The Times*, although progressively more sure that the Irish had brought misery on themselves by their lack of forethought and their apathy and indolence, was dismissive of a Providential motive. When the Protectionist leader Lord George Bentinck tried to argue that the Famine was an act of God and therefore could not be relieved by Legislature, *The Times* retorted: 'Lord GEORGE will excuse us, but on the subject of miraculous interference we will not be content with even the word of a gentleman. When he produces a well-authenticated account of the angel, or other celestial informant, who told him why the potato has so universally failed this year, we will believe him.'[101]

    Christopher Morash has ably demonstrated that politicians like Trevelyan and Grey were convinced that the Famine was an act of God, and acted accordingly.[102] But, as observed in the curious unanimity of Famine historiography, things are never so clear cut: in a recent article in the *Spectator*, Paul Bew quoted a letter from Trevelyan to Father Mathew denying that the Famine was God's punishment on the Irish: 'Like you, I regard the prospect of Ireland with profound melancholy, but I fear less from the judgment of God than from the aggravation of man, owing to the ignorance, the selfish and evil passions of man.'[103] Hugh McNeile, who had indeed suggested that the blight was an act of Providence for the sins of the nation—tolerance of Roman Catholicism foremost among them— also argued that he was obliged to save his fellow men from starvation. In a letter to the Merchants, Bankers, Gentry, and Trading Class of Liverpool in January 1847, appealing for money for the starving Irish, McNeile pleads: 'Say not, you are feeding the poor Irish in your own streets, and must pay the enormously increased poor-rates incurred thereby. I know it; but *men, women, and children are starving to death.*'[104] English journalists came out against the paraphernalia of Providentialism, with its fast days and thanksgiving. This may have been just as detrimental to Ireland as denial of the Famine; *The Times* strongly opposed a Day of Thanksgiving and a Queen's Letter for the Irish in 1847, predicting:

The congregation will look black, the preacher look pale. Where a sovereign was given last year, it will be half-a-crown this; where half-a-crown then, a shilling now; where a shilling, nothing at all. The result will be that public benevolence, which at all times is rather hard to keep alive, will go out altogether; and neither Her Majesty nor her right trusty and entirely beloved counsellors, the Archbishops, will be able to extract more than a few paltry thousands for any purpose whatever.[105]

The prediction certainly came true, but whether it was a self-fulfilling prophecy remains unclear; the opinion of *The Times* was not to be ignored. Similarly, in March 1847 the newspaper ridiculed the idea of a day of solemn humiliation and prayer: 'A general fast in the British metropolis in the middle of the 19th century on account of a remote provincial famine will supply abundant materials both to the witty and the dull.'[106] Contrary to recent critical belief, *The Times* actually denied Providentialism in the Famine, but this did not make it any more sympathetic to the plight of the Irish.

---

[102] Christopher Morash, *Writing the Irish Famine* (Oxford: Clarendon Press, 1995).

[103] Quoted in Paul Bew, 'A Case of Compassion Fatigue', *Spectator* (13 Mar. 1999), 37–8, at 38.

[104] Revd Hugh McNeile, *The Famine A Rod of God: Its Provoking Cause—Its Merciful Design* (London and Liverpool: Seeley, Burnside & Seeley; Arthur Newling, 1847), 40.

[105] *The Times* (9 Oct. 1847), 4.   [106] *The Times* (24 Mar. 1847), 4.

Anti-Irish feeling was running high in 1847, with the flood of immigrants arriving daily. In January *The Times* announced that there were 15,000–20,000 Irish paupers in Liverpool, and forecast darkly 'a Mayo on the banks of the Ribble, and even of the Thames'.[107] By April the Irish in Liverpool were being described as 'pestiferous', and in October *The Times* announced that of all the fever patients in Edinburgh, nine-tenths were Irish. Both *Punch* and the *Illustrated London News* ran counter to this anti-Irish current: *Punch* criticized the '*Pseudo*-Saints of Liverpool' for their cruelty to Irish immigrants, and the *Illustrated London News* said of the treatment of the Irish at the hands of Liverpool parish officers: 'far more care would be taken of Irish cattle'.[108]

Several events in 1847 served to harden attitudes. The death of O'Connell in May, leaving his mediocre son John at the helm of Old Ireland, saw the focus of attention shift more and more towards Young Ireland. The Destitute Poor (Ireland) Act, popularly known as the 'soup kitchen act', which became law in February, permitted the administering of outdoor relief by poorhouse officials for the first time, and the French chef Alexis Soyer was recruited; he opened his model soup kitchen on Royal Barracks Esplanade in Dublin in April 1847. Although the Society of Friends had administered private soup kitchens throughout the Famine, and were praised by Young Ireland for doing so, this government-led initiative seemed the final humiliation for many nationalists. Only Shakespeare answered to the anger of *The Nation*: in 'Scene From The "Soup Kitchen" ', the witches from *Macbeth* make soup for the Irish, while 'Easter in Ireland' identifies the Irish with the hated Jew of *The Merchant of Venice*: 'Oh! Ireland, Ireland! has the very soul withered out of us? Have the heart, the brain, the blood, the very gall, clean gone from us? Have we yet senses, affections, passions, as a Christian hath? If you prick us do we yet bleed? If you poison us do we indeed die? If you wrong us have we forgotten the way to revenge?'[109] After his break from *The Nation*, Mitchel was to remember the soup kitchen act as the turning point; in a letter to the Prime Minister published in the *United Irishman* after Mitchel, O'Brien, and Thomas Meagher were charged with sedition, he recalled the opening of Soyer's kitchen:

We three criminals, my Lord, who are to appear to-day in the Court of Queen's Bench, were spectators of that soup-kitchen scene; and I believe we all left it with one thought—that this day we had surely touched the lowest point—that Ireland

---

[107] *The Times* (6 Jan. 1847), 4.
[108] *Punch* 12 (Jan.–June 1847), 56; *ILN* 11 (11 Sept. 1847), 166.
[109] *Nation* (3 Apr. 1847), 408; (10 Apr. 1847), 425.

and the Irish *could* sink no further; and that she must not see such another Easter Monday, though she should die for it.[110]

Thirty years later, Alexander M. Sullivan remembered the same scene with similar distaste:

Around these boilers on the roadside there daily moaned and shrieked and fought and scuffled crowds of gaunt, cadaverous creatures that once had been men and women made in the image of God. The feeding of dogs in a kennel was far more decent and orderly. I once thought—ay, and often bitterly said, in public and in private—that never, never would our people recover the shameful humiliation of that brutal public soup-boiler scheme. I frequently stood and watched the scene till tears blinded me and I almost choked with grief and passion. It was heart-breaking, almost maddening to see; but help for it there was none.[111]

Soyer's kitchens were also mocked in English newspapers, as in *Punch*: 'It is declared that SOYER must have prepared the new Prussian Diet, for it is so like his soup—there's nothing in it.'[112] But more often than not, grave London journalists lined up to taste the soup before the paupers could lift their chained spoons. *The Times*'s correspondent said: 'having been permitted to taste the soup, I found it to be very good, so much so, that if it but prove to be as nutritious as it is palatable, I think the Irish poor will have every reason to rejoice at the arrival of M. Soyer in this country.'[113] Unfortunately, it did not prove to be so, and *The Nation*'s nomination, 'dysentery-juice', would be recognized by modern historians as closer to the truth.[114]

The most powerful story of 1847, besides the huge and ever-increasing death-toll, was the murder of Major Denis Mahon, a landlord from Strokestown, County Roscommon, on 2 November. Mahon had been assisting emigration from his estate (recently inherited from a lunatic relative), and reports of 'coffin ships' and the rates of mortality from disease among emigrants at landing stations like Grosse Isle in Canada, had turned tenants against him. Despite many assassinations of landlords and bailiffs in the previous year, this one became notorious, and changed English opinion irremediably—especially as it coincided with the realization that the crop had failed once more, and the Famine was not coming to a close. For *The Times*, it was the end of optimism: 'this fearful catastrophe will be felt as a great blow and discouragement to the cause of Irish

[110] *United Irishman* (15 Apr. 1848), 152.
[111] A. M. Sullivan, *New Ireland: Political Sketches and Personal Reminiscences of Thirty Years of Irish Public Life* (Glasgow and London, 1877), 62.
[112] *Punch* 12 (Jan.–June 1847), 141.   [113] *The Times* (7 Apr. 1847), 3.
[114] *Nation* (10 Apr. 1847), 424.

regeneration'.[115] *The Times* had hoped that English capitalists would buy land in Ireland, and show a greater responsibility towards their tenants than Irish landlords had, but the collapse of the trade in land in Roscommon after the murder of Mahon disabused it of that idea. Even worse, the balance of sympathy shifted away from the evicted, starving Irish tenant, to the landlord in fear of his life. The perceived ingratitude of Young Ireland was already changing *Punch*'s mind; by October it felt it had answered the age-old question of what was to be done for Ireland: 'The "something," which "must be done for Ireland" is most unquestionably the English people.'[116] After Mahon's murder, its stance moved even closer to that of *The Times*. In 'What shall we do with our Criminals?' it suggested the worst should be converted into Irish landlords—as a form of capital punishment.[117] 'Punch and Paddy' portrayed Paddy as a puppet with a gun, Punch rebuking him: 'Put Away That Nasty Thing, And Let's Have A Merry Christmas.'[118] Things became even more heated when allegations were made that the parish priest of Strokestown, Father McDermott, had denounced Mahon from the altar days before the murder; leading articles in *The Times* raged about the power of the Roman Catholic Church in Ireland for life or death. In early 1848 *Punch* published 'Irish Game Laws': '1st *January*. LANDLORD shooting begins. 31st *December*. Landlord shooting ends. Certificates may be had from JOHN ARCHBISHOP OF TUAM, and FATHER MCDERMOTT.'[119] *The Nation* did little to neutralize the situation, declaring Mahon's assassination an 'Ejectment Murder', and stating that although it was appalled by the violence, it could not condemn an instinctive rebellion against conventional morality in a time of Famine, and, significantly, that it was possible the murders were a manifestation of God's justice—another kind of providence.[120] With this awful murder the tide of opinion turned, and English newspapers became far more interested in Irish crime than Irish starvation.

    The blight had not returned with its expected virulence in 1847, but the crop was unusually small, due to lack of money to buy seed, and the disincentive to plant provided both by the public works and by the fear of failure. Three years of scarcity and disease had weakened the people, and the death-toll continued to rise. 'Verily, this third famine year is the worst of the three,' intoned *The Nation*, 'as whoever will read that doleful miscel-

---

[115] *The Times* (6 Nov. 1847), 4.   [116] *Punch* 13 (July–Dec. 1847), 154.
[117] Ibid., 239. [118] Ibid., 245.
[119] *Punch* 14 (Jan.–June 1848), 29.
[120] *Nation* (6 Nov. 1847), 903; (27 Nov. 1847), 953.

lany of crimes, inquests and police intelligence, called "The State of the Country," may learn for himself.'[121] *The Times* expended most of its energy on a Special Commission into Irish crime; the majority of crimes appeared to be for stealing food and sheep.

Mitchel had broken with Duffy and *The Nation* at the end of 1847, and published the first issue of the *United Irishman* on 12 February 1848, to huge popular interest. From the outset, he proclaimed his public conspiracy to oust the government, daring the Lord Lieutenant the Earl of Clarendon to indict him and pack a jury to transport him. *The Times*, while mocking Mitchel and his cohorts, and their inability to stir up a rebellion, was eager to see them prosecuted for sedition, and urged the government on. The government seemed loath to take action, despite seeing its Viceroy labelled 'Executioner-General and General Butcher of Ireland'.

The turning point came with the French Revolution at the end of February. From this point it was accepted by all parties that an Irish Rising was inevitable. Mitchel was overjoyed: as Charles Gavan Duffy later recalled: 'Never was a man so metamorphosed; he used to be a modest and courteous gentleman, now he demeaned himself as if the French Revolution and the new opportunities it furnished were his personal achievements.'[122] Mitchel immediately called for the formation of Voluntary Defence Associations, and popular armament, using biblical rhetoric: 'Above all, let the man amongst you who has no gun, *sell his garment, and buy one.*'[123] *The Nation*, which had previously recognized the folly of taking up arms during a famine, also took up this cry, arguing disingenuously that a French Republic was likely to attack England, and Ireland was a convenient back door:

A million of the Irish people lie buried beneath the Irish soil, because we trusted their defence to England. They died of famine and fever. Another million may die defenceless as sheep, under the swords of a foreign soldiery, if we do not take precautions in time. The natural and only adequate precaution is a NATIVE MILITIA, or NATIONAL GUARD.[124]

In the same issue, *The Nation* ran a fictional report on the 'Second Week of the Irish Revolution'.

In England, the French Revolution was also seen as a trigger for Ireland, and attention focused more and more on the Young Ireland politicians, less and less on the sufferings of the ordinary people. The *Illustrated London*

[121] *Nation* (19 Feb. 1848), 121.   [122] Duffy, *My Life In Two Hemispheres*, i. 261.
[123] *United Irishman* (4 Mar. 1848), 56.   [124] *Nation* (11 Mar. 1848), 169.

News began to eschew its previous acceptance of English responsibility for Irish misery, and withdrew sympathy:

> If the Irish are led astray by such ravings as those of Mr. Mitchell [*sic*] and Mr. Meagher, it is their own fault, and on them the suffering will fall. If they will not learn, before rebellion, the notorious fact that Irishmen have every privilege which Englishmen have, except the unhappy privilege of being taxed, and that all classes of people in this country desire to see Ireland peaceful, industrious, free, and happy, they must necessarily pay the penalty of their ignorance.[125]

The £8 million sent by England to Ireland, the article continued, had been repaid by eight million curses, and the journal began publishing sketches of Irish pikes, evidently forecasting a massacre. *Punch* decided that the real disorder of Ireland was not the blight but madness, and published 'The Irish Ranters', featuring O'Brien, Mitchel, and Meagher.[126] In a pre-Darwin simian representation, Mitchel featured as a monkey in a joker's costume in 'The British Lion and The Irish Monkey', demanding: 'One of us Must be "Put Down" '; as Michael De Nie has noted, representations of Irish leaders in *Punch* differed greatly from cartoons involving English Chartists, who are portrayed as harmless, misguided, and most importantly, human, figures.[127] 'Charity and Pikes' objected that '*The United Irishman* would have the poor Irish pike the English people for relieving them, pierce them with steel for having been penetrated towards themselves with compassion.'[128] Now that O'Connell was dead and the landlords had been redeemed by assassination, Mitchel had become the great Irish bugbear, and his arrest and transportation were not long in coming.

The Times, for its part, was baying for Mitchel's blood: 'In our judgment, it is too hazardous to leave one-third of the empire open to the attempts of men clamouring for a republic, and of mobs shouting for "Pikes." '[129] Indeed, *The Times* was in favour of censorship of newspapers such as *The Nation* and the *United Irishman*; however, when they were censored, *The Times* complained they had become dull, perhaps indicating how much it relied on the Irish newspapers for self-definition in its pronouncements on Ireland. By April *The Times* appeared to have come out for Repeal itself, threatening to cast Ireland off forever if it did not stop hostilities. It had also changed its mind about emigration, accepting it as the 'door of safety' not only for Irish agitators, but also for English

---

[125] *ILN* 12 (15 Apr. 1848), 244.   [126] *Punch* 14 (Jan.–June 1848), 57, 139.
[127] *Punch* 14 (Jan.–June 1848), 147; Michael De Nie, 'The Famine, Irish Identity, and the British Press', *Irish Studies Review*, 6/1 (1998), 27–35, 31–2.
[128] *Punch* 14 (Jan.–June 1848), 156.   [129] *The Times* (29 Mar. 1848), 4.

Chartists.[130] By the end of the year, triumphing in yet another victory over the savage Irish, *The Times* was comparing English and Irish emigration; such unsurpassed movement of populations would have been fearful if it had been Saxon blood which was being drawn from the country, but as it was mainly the Celts who were leaving, there was little cause for alarm. However, the situation was not wholly good for the English: 'It is from Ireland that we draw our rough labour. The Celt—and we are bound to give him credit for it—is the hewer of wood and drawer of water to the Saxon. Can we spare that growing mine of untaught but teachable toil?'[131] In this return to a Spenserian language and tone, we see the rejection of British citizenship for the starving peasants of Ireland.

Even before the Rising, English newspapers were beginning to back the government in its Irish policy. *Punch* felt obliged to defend the Lord Lieutenant against slanders by the *United Irishman* and the *Irish Felon*; ' "My Lord Assassin" Clarendon Murdering The Irish' shows a beneficent Clarendon up against a wall while apish Irishmen fire blunderbusses.[132] The Irish Rising of July 1848, rather than freeing the country from foreign domination, seemed to have led to another conquest. It also signalled the virtual end of opposition. Mitchel had been transported, O'Brien and Meagher arrested for treason after a fiasco of a rising, Duffy had been arrested and the machinery and type of *The Nation* seized, including an issue edited by Mrs Callan (Duffy's sister-in-law) and Speranza (Jane Francesca Elgee, the future Lady Wilde) while Duffy was in prison. The successor journals to the *United Irishman*, the *Irish Felon* and the *Irish Tribune*, were suppressed, and their editors and proprietors—James Fintan Lalor, John Martin, Richard D'Alton Williams, and Kevin Izod O'Doherty—arrested. Even worse, the Rising was a mockery, parodied in *The Times* as a new *Iliad*, forever to be known as the 'Battle of Widow McCormack's cabbage patch'. It had had no popular support, yet English newspapers held the Irish people as a whole responsible, and those among the English people and press who had blamed the government and pitied the Irish people were changing sides. Due to the Rebellion, 'even those who most vehemently condemn the sins of omission and commission of the Russell Administration, cease their condemnation, and unite with its friends in support of the policy it has been so reluctantly compelled to follow in Ireland'.[133] The Rebellion had finally separated the countries, not by repealing the Union, but by convincing liberal Englishmen that the Irish were not to be trusted. As the *Illustrated London*

[130] *The Times* (27 Apr. 1848), 4.
[131] *The Times* (26 Dec. 1848), 4.
[132] *Punch* 15 (July–Dec. 1848), 17.
[133] *ILN* 13 (29 July 1848), 49.

News stated, it had been an insult not only to 'the unoffending English Government', but also to 'that generous and maligned people that paid so many millions of money which they could not well spare, to relieve their Irish brethren from the miseries of starvation'.[134] The only purpose the Rising appeared to have served was the alienation of previously pro-Irish newspapers like the *Illustrated London News*, which began to sound increasingly like *The Times*.

Conversely, the rate-in-aid crisis led Ulster newspapers to mimic the *United Irishman*. The *Northern Whig* even began to proclaim that 'unless any one is prepared to strike at the principle of the union, Yorkshire should be held as responsible as Downshire'.[135] *The Times*'s Irish correspondent was even more forthright:

> There is no use in mincing the matter. Ulster has become infected with downright Mitchelism, and the tone of the press and the platform insensibly brings one back to the palmy days when, without let or hindrance, people calmly talked of 'smashing the Castle gates,' and forwarding Lord Clarendon, per early mail, to England, as having no right of settlement in this 'our kingdom of Ireland.'[136]

A temporary truce was called with the visit of the Queen in August 1849; *The Times* announced that 'The QUEEN's visit to Ireland is the concluding chapter of the history of the Irish rebellion.'[137] The militant newspapers had been quashed, and the provincial press greeted the Queen's visit with such enthusiasm that all doubts about Irish loyalty seemed to have disappeared. *Punch*'s 'Landing Of Queen Victoria In Ireland' shows 'Sir Patrick Raleigh' laying his coat down for her.[138] But 1849 was yet another year of famine, even if Victoria was scrupulously protected from the sight of it. Distress was even more regional this year, and the emphasis shifted from Skibbereen and Schull to the west of Ireland, particularly Connaught. According to *The Times*, the whole nation was a lazar-house and an encumbrance on the generosity of England: 'The Celt counts with the lame, the blind, the sick, the aged, and the insane, as an impotent and destitute class. We have hospitals, poor-houses, prisons, asylums, and Connaught.'[139] As had happened time and again in this period of transition and change of tone, *The Nation* had come to agree with *The Times*. Revived in September 1849 by a disillusioned and much-prosecuted Duffy, the new *Nation* was a very different journal. Most of its writers were dead, transported, or fled, and the stalwart Speranza, who continued

---

[134] *ILN* 13 (29 July 1848), 49.   [135] Quoted in *The Times* (1 Mar. 1849), 6.
[136] *The Times* (5 Mar. 1849), 8.   [137] *The Times* (9 Aug. 1849), 4.
[138] *Punch* 17 (July–Dec. 1849), 47.   [139] *The Times* (8 Feb. 1849), 4.

to write reviews under a different pseudonym, had lost her enthusiasm for the *Nation* project following the failure of the Rising, for which she blamed the people, not the leaders. In the first issue, Duffy admitted that he had despaired of the Irish in Ireland, and contemplated giving up writing and leaving Ireland, though he had rejected these thoughts as cowardly (he was later to relent and leave for Australia). In a diatribe later reprinted in his *Conversations with Carlyle*, he argued that the Famine and landlords had created a new race in Ireland: 'I have seen on the streets of Galway crowds of creatures more debased than the Yahoos of Swift—creatures having only a distant and hideous resemblance to human beings.'[140] A week later, while in effect praising the Famine for achieving a revolution at relatively small waste of life and property—a point that the Duffy of 1848 would surely not have conceded—his regret and sense of loss and outrage emerged in a passage redolent of *Paradise Lost*:[141]

Connaught has reached that lowest depth in which there is no lower deep. I declare before Heaven that looking upon the peasantry of the West I have over and again been tempted to pray that GOD by some sudden merciful plague would cut them off the earth and save the land from another generation lower than men, and more unmercifully tasked and driven than the beasts of burden . . . The entire peasant children of Mayo seem to be reared up to whine with their first speech, 'give us a hep-ney.'[142]

As well as full-frontal assaults on Connaught peasants and 'jontlemen', Duffy also scarified the tenants he had the previous year been encouraging to hold the harvest: 'There are lazy besotted worthless tenants, wallowing in sloth and filth—vegetating on the land like its weeds from whom no good will come. And there are fraudulent tenants who would plunder for the sake of plunder, and from the justest landlord—but the system has made them, and it must bear the blame, and atone for the sin.'[143] Except for the final rushed attempt to place the blame elsewhere, this could have come straight from a *Times* leading article. As Thackeray wrote the year before Duffy's article appeared: 'though they cry out against the English for abusing their country, by Jove they abuse it themselves more in a single article than we should take the pains to do in a dozen volumes'.[144]

---

[140] *Nation* (1 Sept. 1849), 8.

[141] John Milton, *Paradise Lost* (1667), ed. Alastair Fowler (London: Longman, 1971); see Satan's speech in Book IV: 'And in the lowest deep a lower deep | Still threatening to devour me opens wide' (p. 194).

[142] *Nation* (8 Sept. 1849), 24.   [143] *Nation* (15 Sept. 1849), 40.

[144] Thackeray, *Pendennis*, 388.

A change in tone was also discernible in the Irish press at large. If Ulster newspapers were becoming Mitchelite, Repeal papers seemed to be becoming more conservative. *The Times* approvingly quoted articles from the *Cork Reporter* deploring the collection of money for the Pope while the Famine continued, and criticizing exaggerated stories about Irish distress. Duffy's conversion was even more of a coup:

> Indeed, when we read Mr. DUFFY's description of the recent movement, his account of its instigators, their characters, motives and hopes—the conditions under which they acted, the people whom they enlisted—we might almost believe that we were reading an article from an old file of *The Times*. Nothing that we have ever penned was more harsh than the castigations inflicted by Mr. DUFFY on his own party and his own countrymen.[145]

The Times attributed the change of tone to the Queen's visit, but in Duffy's case it was surely a reaction to the Famine and the Rising, both of which seemed to have destroyed any possibility of national renewal. The Rising's failure also stimulated calls by *The Times* and others for a new colonization of Ireland. What was needed was a substitution of 'the muscles and brains of Cumberland, Yorkshire, and Lancashire for the indolence, hopelessness, and servile content of the Connaught peasant'.[146] By the end of the year, *The Times* was deploring the fact that most of the purchasers in the Encumbered Estates Court were Irish, and claiming that there was a conspiracy to discourage English and Scottish farmers from buying. To counteract this, despite the continuation of the Famine into the 1850s, *The Times* adopted a new tone of optimism: 'We are happy to say that, notwithstanding their general helplessness, there is, at the present moment, no sign of scarcity in Mayo. Every cabin has a stack or two of corn behind it; potatoes are abundant and good; all parties admit that the distress is over and that the country is in process of amendment.'[147] It was no longer even a 'remote provincial famine', affecting only remote provinces of this remote province, and at a time when attention was being engrossed by the forthcoming Great Exhibition, interest was allowed to die away.

Famine journalists did not merely record the news; they made it. By raising consciousness about places like Skibbereen, Schull, and Erris, they were able to direct much needed attention and relief to these areas, undoubtedly saving lives. Conversely, by objecting, as *The Times* did, that money was needed at home, or as *The Nation* did, that Repeal was more important than relief, charity may have been hindered, and deaths caused

---

[145] *The Times* (11 Sept. 1849), 4.   [146] *The Times* (9 Mar. 1849), 5.
[147] *The Times* (18 Dec. 1849), 4.

by their insistence. Yet both *The Nation* and *The Times* were keenly aware
of the Famine as a historical event, and their own role in recording it. By
October 1846, *The Times* was already calculating how future historians and
economists would view the catastrophe:

> They will insist much on the fact that the food of millions did annually pass to the
> richer and happier shore. They will not reconcile this with the alleged improvid-
> ence of the Irishman quite so easily as we are wont to do. They will inquire very
> diligently what England gave in return. When their researches bring them to that
> crisis which we are now actually suffering, they certainly will be struck, perhaps
> even unduly, by the fact that while England was avowedly feeding Ireland . . .
> whole fleets of provisions were continually arriving from the land of starvation to
> the ports of wealth and the cities of abundance.[148]

By Black '47, *The Times* was wishing that Ireland possessed a writer of the
calibre of Thucydides, Virgil, or Defoe to record a calamity that had a
place amongst the most harrowing in history, and again quailed at the
thought of the future condemnation of England:

> Historians and politicians will some day sift and weigh the conflicting narrations
> and pronounce, with or without affection, how much is due to the inclemency of
> heaven, and how much to the cruelty, heartlessness, or improvidence of man. The
> boasted institutions and spirit of this empire are on trial. They are weighed in the
> balance. Famine and pestilence are at the gates, and a conscience-stricken nation
> might almost fear to see the 'writing on the wall.'[149]

The need for a history of Ireland had been a major part of the cultural project at *The Nation* since its inception, but the Famine superseded this
claim. When a reader complained that an advertised *Ballad History of
Ireland* had not appeared, the newspaper's editors retorted:

> What man with a heart would sit down to write Ballad History while his country
> perishes? There are great lessons in our history and great triumphs, and we
> delighted once, and may again, to dwell upon them . . . We are . . . 'making history'
> this year, not writing it; and very miserable and disgraceful history it will be, if it
> record only slavish patience and submission under our unparalleled wrongs.[150]

'Some unborn LINGARD or THIERRY' would record the history *Nation* journalists made. A later article on 'The Individuality of a Native Literature'
argued that men of action were needed in a year of famine and pestilence,
but: 'Of aught that tends to elevate the nation, and fuse together more tena-
ciously the various races and sects that compose it, literature is practical in

---

[148] *The Times* (30 Oct. 1846), 4.   [149] *The Times* (17 Sept. 1847), 4.
[150] *Nation* (1 May 1847), 472.

the highest sense, and the writer is a man of action.'[151] The *Nation* journalists were as good as their word; the Irish 'Revolution' was headed by
journalists rather than soldiers and politicians, more ink was spilled than
blood, and of those who were arrested and transported, most had little to
do with the Tipperary affray and everything to do with the War of Words.
The Nation and *The Times* self-consciously created the history of the
Famine, periodically propagating a potted history of a famine of genocide
and eviction, or of ingratitude and betrayal. The Almighty may have sent
the blight, the government may have exacerbated the famine, but the
Famine, the textual creation that remains to us, was created, related, and
exploited by journalists.

[151] *Nation* (21 Aug. 1847), 729.

3
Victims and Voyeurs:
Travelling in Famine Ireland

In spite of—or because of—its reputation for poverty, violence, and frequent famines, Ireland proved an attractive destination in the decades between the Act of Union and the Great Famine. English and foreign aristocrats, political and social commentators, philanthropists, economists, poets, journalists, and bona-fide travel writers thronged to this unlikely holiday resort. During the war with France, when the Continent was closed to English tourists, many made a virtue of necessity by declaring their *duty* to visit the sister-country, a part of Britain, yet less well known to English tourists than the Alps or the Norwegian fjords. Edward Wakefield complained in 1812: 'We have description and histories of the most distant parts of the globe . . . but of Ireland, a country under our own government, we have little that is authentic.'[1] Two years later, Lady Morgan could claim that Ireland's status as a tourist destination lay in her advance towards political freedom:

Not many years back, the few English persons of rank or consideration, who visited Ireland, came only on the imperious call of business; and probably considered their journeys as a mere pilgrimage of necessity to the shrine of interest . . . Silence and oblivion hung upon her destiny, and in the memory of other nations she seemed to hold no place; but the first bolt which was knocked off her chain roused her from paralysis, and as link fell after link, her faculties strengthened, her powers revived: she gradually rose upon the political horizon of Europe, like her own star brightening in the west . . . The traveller now 'beheld her from afar,' and her shores, once so devoutly pressed by the learned, the pious, and the brave, again exhibited the welcome track of the stranger's feet.[2]

Steamships, and later the expansion of railways in Ireland, made the journey cheap, comfortable, and quick. Moreover, at a time when travel literature was second in popularity only to fiction, there was a substantial profit to be made from an account of the journey. As Charles Dickens was setting off for America in 1842, William Makepeace Thackeray was heading

---

[1] Quoted in Constantia Maxwell, *The Stranger in Ireland from the Reign of Elizabeth to the Great Famine* (London: Cape, 1954), 218.

[2] Lady Morgan, *O'Donnel: A National Tale*, 3 vols. (London: Henry Colburn, 1814), i. 56–8.

for Ireland, frankly admitting his mercenary motive: 'for our trade is to write books and sell the same—a chapter for a guinea, a line for a penny'.[3] Chapman and Hall had rejected Thackeray's first proposal for an Italian tour, indicating their belief that the interest of the English reading public lay in Irish affairs. The same was true of the non-English audience. Gustave de Beaumont found great success with his *Ireland: Social, Political and Religious* in France, while the German Prince Hermann von Pückler-Muskau, travelling in England and Ireland in the late 1820s in search of a rich heiress to revive the family fortunes, struck gold instead in descriptions of peasant girls, faction fights, and wretched poverty.[4]

In an article on 'Twaddling Tourists in Ireland' in the *Dublin University Magazine* in November 1844, Charles Lever claimed that 'There probably never was a country so completely overrun by the book-making generation as this land of ours.'[5] In return, travel literature had an impact on Irish fiction. The traveller—such as Lady Morgan's ignorant or naïve English travellers in *The Wild Irish Girl* and *O'Donnel* or the incognito Irishmen of Edgeworth's *The Absentee* or Carleton's *Valentine M'Clutchy*—becomes an important plot device to expose English prejudice or Irish misdeeds. Joep Leerssen suggests that travel literature transformed the possibilites of Irish fiction by challenging English perceptions:

whereas the Gaelic Irish had universally been seen, until c.1750, as benighted barbarians, and the Anglo-Irish settlers as the upholders of European civilization, the travel descriptions of men like [John] Bush and [Arthur] Young did much to invert that view and to represent the Anglo-Irish upper class as duelling, profligate, loutish colonialists oppressing the honest, long-suffering Celtic peasantry. *Castle Rackrent* would have been impossible without the precursorship of Young's *Tour in Ireland*.[6]

This symbiosis was not deliberate; the most frequently cited reason for travelling in Ireland was not literary, but the need to discover the truth about Irish poverty. In an age obsessed with statistics, nothing was analysed with such fervour as the Irish question. From the end of the

[3] William Makepeace Thackeray, *The Irish Sketch Book*, 2 vols. (London: Chapman & Hall, 1843), ii. 326.

[4] The prince was known as 'Prince Pickle' in England, and appeared in Dickens's *The Pickwick Papers* as 'Lord Smorltork'; having divorced his beloved wife Lucie, after spending her fortune, he planned to find a rich wife who would maintain not only him, but also Lucie, in the manner to which they were accustomed.

[5] Charles Lever, 'Twaddling Tourists in Ireland', *Dublin University Magazine*, 24 (Nov. 1844), 505–26, at 505.

[6] Joep Leerssen, *Remembrance and Imagination: Patterns in the Historical and Literary Representation of Ireland in the Nineteenth Century* (Cork: Cork University Press, 1996), 64.

Napoleonic Wars until the Famine, the government scrutinized Irish poverty, setting up select committees in 1819, 1823, 1829, and 1833, filling innumerable Blue Books with impenetrable statistics. British newspapers were full of Irish poverty and unrest, and journalists were sent to report from the scene, as if from a disaster zone. This contemporary obsession with the state of Ireland was undoubtedly a major factor in the sale of Irish travel books, and stemmed partly from the fear of a prosperous Protestant nation that the geographic and political proximity of a poor, populous Catholic country would prove a serious economic and social liability. As Thomas Carlyle remarked in his 1839 essay 'Chartism', the steamships that brought the middle-class pleasure-seekers to Ireland also encouraged more Irish migrant labourers to seek work in England, prompting fears that English workers would be undercut, and living standards would decline to the Irish level.[7] While most travel-books claimed to be cultivating a closer relationship between England and Ireland, they were not averse to fanning the flames of fear: Henry Inglis claimed that Ireland in the mid-1830s was 'ripe for the re-establishment of the inquisition', while Mr and Mrs S. C. Hall, whose professed aim was to promote and maintain the Union, could not refrain from observing that 'during the periods England was most actively at war with France and Spain, vessels of both these nations frequented the ports of the south and west of Ireland'.[8] Fear—especially of retrograding to the Irish level—was the impetus for a comprehensive examination of society and culture in Ireland, a search for the truth that had little to do with humanitarian concerns. Nineteenth-century tourists routinely visited prisons, workhouses, and asylums, viewing them as indices of the social health of a country; but it is alarming to find what a prominent part such visits played in the itinerary of every traveller in Ireland. The travel narrative in this period became a vehicle for the expression of British anxiety about Ireland.

In spite of the glut of statistics and reports on the country, travellers still insisted it was their duty to discover the truth about Ireland. They were keen to explode misconceptions about Irish violence, but universally acknowledged that the Irish were congenitally incapable of telling the truth. This was quite convenient, as it meant British and foreign travellers could write books to warn of 'that power of misleading so essentially Irish',

---

[7] Thomas Carlyle, 'Chartism', in *Thomas Carlyle: Selected Writings*, ed. Alan Shelston (Harmondsworth: Penguin, 1980), 171.

[8] Henry Inglis, *Ireland in 1834*, 2 vols. (London: Whittaker & Co., 1835), ii. 342; Samuel Carter and Anna Maria Hall, *Ireland: Its Scenery, Character, &c.*, 3 vols. (London: Jeremiah How, 1846), ii. 117–19.

while Irish reviewers of these books could refute their conclusions by assuring the writer they were misled.[9] Undoubtedly, many tourists were 'humbugged': Elizabeth Smith, the Scottish-born landlady of Baltiboys, County Wicklow, wrote in her journal for June 1842 of the distress of her guest, Dr Eckford:

> He is forever asking them the most searching questions, accumulating facts upon the condition of Ireland, and they tell him the greatest parcel of falsehoods that their fertile imaginations can invent, keeping as grave all the while as Venetian Senators in a stage play—the bystanders hardly able to keep their countenances; he is quite distressed at our extravagant way of living—so much meat—so much variety—a round of beef is making him quite unhappy . . .[10]

Thackeray declared himself shocked to find that his predecessors, Inglis, de Beaumont, and de Tocqueville, had all been fooled by one man, who gleefully confessed to misleading them. As Robert Scally asserts, it was in a tenant's interest to keep his landlord in the dark about his financial affairs, and an element of caution was understandable and in a sense admirable: 'Their means of resistance—conspiracy, pretense, foot-dragging, and obfuscation—were the only ones ordinarily available to them, "weapons of the weak" like those employed by defeated and colonized peoples everywhere.'[11] Caution also extended to the stranger; journalists and travellers were often mistaken for Poor Law officials, and as such treated with suspicion, anxiety, and even anger. Inevitably, one class (or nation) commenting upon another was bound to cause distrust and offence, and the reader often senses the friction between traveller and native. On a visit to Erris in Connaught, the Anglo-Irish clergyman Caesar Otway asked a relatively innocent question about the wages of a needlewoman. The woman was rude to him, and when rebuked by a local coastguard for claiming she was

[9] William Smith, *A Twelve Months' Residence in Ireland, during the Famine and the Public Works, 1846 and 1847* (London and Dublin: Longman, Brown, Green & Longman, 1848), p. vi; see for example the objections of the *Cork Southern Reporter* to Foster's letters, quoted in Thomas Campbell Foster's *Letters on the Condition of the People of Ireland* (London: Chapman & Hall, 1846), 629–30, or the glee of *The Nation* at the revelation that a Ballinasloe Repealer had convinced Foster that Galwaymen pawned money, not knowing its value (*Nation* (1 Nov. 1845), 41).

[10] Elizabeth Smith, *The Irish Journals of Elizabeth Smith 1840–1850*, ed. David Thomson and Moyra McGusty (Oxford: Clarendon Press, 1980), 52. This scene was almost replayed in Trollope's *Castle Richmond*, written a decade later: the Irish clergyman Mr Townsend and his wife have to convince their English guest that a turbot is not a great extravagance in a time of scarcity (Anthony Trollope, *Castle Richmond*, 3 vols. (London: Chapman & Hall, 1860), iii. 164.

[11] Robert Scally, *The End of Hidden Ireland: Rebellion, Famine, and Emigration* (New York and Oxford: Oxford University Press, 1995), 14.

paid when in fact she taught poor women for free, she rounded on Otway's curiosity: 'What for does the like of him be coming and asking about such matters? what is it to him what I get?'[12] Suspicion was also manifested by the upper classes. Asenath Nicholson, an American who spent most of her time in Ireland in the cabins of the poor, was treated rudely by the Protestant missionary Edward Nangle; in language reflecting both commonplace English reactions to America at the time, and perhaps also a fear of exposure, Nangle accused Nicholson in his newspaper the *Achill Herald* of being 'the emissary of some democratic and revolutionary society'.[13]

Of course, the disadvantage of this obstructive defence was English reluctance to believe in the extent of Irish poverty, especially when the potato blight struck in 1845. The true value of the traveller in Ireland emerges in the effect on public opinion of the many books that appeared in the 1840s emphasizing the misery of Irish peasant life. As the German Johann Kohl discovered: 'Travellers in Ireland cannot speak too often of the extreme misery of the Irish poor, if it be only to confute those among the English who will not believe in the existence of this misery, and who even ridicule those who speak of it on the evidence of their own eyes.'[14] *The Times*, not known for its implicit belief in things Irish, conceded the value of the travel narrative in bringing home the extent of the disaster:

It is difficult for us, reposing in the tranquil contemplation of metropolitan wealth and general comfort, to realize the horrors which are told us of that which is truly a great famine. It is only when some one habituated to the luxury and opulence of England undertakes a pilgrimage of mercy to those shores of sickness and suffering, that we are made sensible of the fearful visitation from which we are separated by so slight an interval. Then it is that the enormity of what we escape and they endure is brought more forcibly to our minds . . .[15]

It is impossible to gauge the influence for good these books had on subscriptions for famine relief, but it is surely not unreasonable to suggest that things might have been worse in their absence.

The reluctance to rely on first-hand Irish testimony placed a great responsibility on the authors, who were often accorded extraordinary authority. The lawyer and journalist Thomas Campbell Foster was sent to

---

[12] Caesar Otway, *Sketches in Erris and Tyrawly* (Dublin and London: William Curry, Jr. & Co.; Longman, Orme, & Co., 1841), 329.

[13] Asenath Nicholson, *Ireland's Welcome to the Stranger: Or, Excursions Through Ireland in 1844 and 1845 for the Purpose of Personally Investigating the Condition of the Poor* (London and Dublin: Charles Gilpin; Webb & Chapman, 1847), 438.

[14] J. G. Kohl, *Ireland, Scotland, and England* (London: Chapman & Hall, 1844), 115–16.

[15] *The Times* (23 Apr. 1847), 5.

Ireland as *The Times*'s 'Irish Commissioner' in 1845—an unofficial title
which suggested a power that Foster did not possess; indeed, it is possible
that some of the people he questioned exaggerated the extent of misery in
the months prior to and after the first reports of the blight, because they
believed he was a Poor Law commissioner. Peter Gray notes that Foster's
articles were more widely read than the Devon report, and aroused greater
controversy.[16] In 1834, in the midst of contemporary debate about
whether the Poor Law should be extended to Ireland, the travel-writer
Henry Inglis set himself up as an alternative Poor Law commissioner. He
managed to procure a copy of the queries issued by the government to aid
the commissioners, and Chapter 16 of his book was given over to answer-
ing them. And he was taken seriously: his *Ireland in 1834* was quoted as an
authority in parliament in 1835, when the government was debating Poor
Laws for Ireland. In effect, Inglis set himself up as a legislator, and may in
fact have damaged the work of the real commissioners in the process.
Inglis's claims were well-intentioned but rather extreme: for example, he
asserted that 75 per cent of the Irish poor died of starvation.[17] The disparity between this figure and the more conservative 30 per cent destitution offered by Archbishop Whately's 1833–6 commission perhaps
prompted the government's third opinion: George Nicholls was sent on a
nine-week tour and returned with the more acceptable figure of 1 per cent
destitution—one example of the way in which travellers' tales would be
manipulated, and admitted into evidence as representative of Ireland as a
whole.

The position of unofficial authority adopted by travellers makes Irish
travel narratives fascinating but also potentially dangerous. Christopher
Woods makes an interesting analogy: 'As anecdotal evidence the traveller's account can perhaps be compared with the taxi-driver's remarks to
the journalist: the traveller, like the taxi-driver, is the ubiquitous, biddable
companion and guide, always ready to provide local information or an
opinion on the issue of the day. Is he any more reliable?'[18] It is perhaps
more accurate to see the traveller as the journalist in the back seat, filter-
ing the opinions of the taxi-driver through his own knowledge—or ignorance—of the political scene and his own eyewitness evidence, unsure of
what to believe and what to report. The question of reliability is one the

[16] Peter Gray, *Famine, Land and Politics: British Government and Irish Society 1843–1850*
(Dublin and Portland, Oreg.: Irish Academic Press, 1999), 77.
[17] Inglis, *Ireland in 1834*, ii. 324.
[18] Christopher Woods, 'Irish Travel Writing as Source Material', *Irish Historical Studies*,
28/110 (Nov. 1992), 171–83, at 171.

travellers returned to obsessively. Unable to rely on the testimony of the Irish, they felt obliged to witness at first hand. Lord Dufferin and the Honourable G. F. Boyle travelled from Oxford to the notorious Famine hot-spot Skibbereen in 1847 'in order to ascertain with our own eyes the truth of the reports daily publishing of the misery existing there', and they concluded: 'We have found everything but too true; the accounts are not exaggerated—they cannot be exaggerated—nothing more frightful can be conceived.'[19] In his letters from Ireland to *The Times*, Lord Sidney Godolphin Osborne said that he could 'hardly hope to be believed' in his statements on the condition of Ireland in 1849, and on his return to England, he could hardly even believe himself: 'I never read of, never dreamed of such romantic oppression as that which I have lately learned really exists; even now, when I look at the papers before me, attested as they seem to be, by scenes which, unless I dream, I surely saw, I can scarcely accept the reality, of what appears to be a page from some ill-conceived romance.'[20] Indeed, it had taken this trip to Ireland to make Osborne believe: his letters to *The Times* before his journey indignantly declaimed on Irish ingratitude and English generosity.[21]

Many travellers felt pressurized into offering an opinion of Ireland they did not feel competent to give. Thackeray wrote to his mother that 'a man ought to be forty years in the country instead of 3 months and *then* he wouldn't be able to write about it'.[22] Even offering that opinion could be dangerous: Foster was execrated as the 'gutter Commissioner' in the nationalist press for daring to criticize O'Connell as a landlord in Cahirciveen. Foster's letters were at times highly offensive, and he later defended himself on the grounds that he was being constantly abused: 'it is not to be wondered at that a tart expression should sometimes, almost unconsciously, escape from a writer who often saw himself coarsely designated as a "liar" and "slanderer" for stating the simple and undoubted truth'.[23] On one occasion John O'Connell read aloud in Conciliation Hall a forged letter purporting to be from Foster (the forger hadn't bothered to get his name right, and the O'Connells hadn't bothered to check), calling

---

[19] Lord Dufferin and the Hon. G. F. Boyle, *Narrative of a Journey from Oxford to Skibbereen During the Year of the Irish Famine* (Oxford: John Henry Parker, 1847), 5.

[20] Lord Sidney Godolphin Osborne, *Gleanings in the West of Ireland* (London: T. & W. Boone, 1850), 142, 208.

[21] See for example Osborne's letter 'Justice to Ireland', which is very much in the *The Times* mode of mid–1847, complaining that the good Englishman was being stinted to save the improvident bloodthirsty Irishman (*The Times* (19 June 1847), 8).

[22] William Makepeace Thackeray, *The Letters and Private Papers of W. M. Thackeray*, ed. Gordon N. Ray, 4 vols. (London: Oxford University Press, 1945), ii. 78.

[23] Foster, *Letters*, p. xii.

Daniel O'Connell a liar and blackguard; given the reverence for O'Connell among the majority of the people, no doubt Foster was at times in physical danger.[24] Thackeray's dedication of the *Irish Sketch Book* to Charles Lever precipitated a break between Lever and Samuel Ferguson, who stopped writing for the *Dublin University Magazine* in consequence; according to Duffy, Carlyle's posthumously published *Reminiscences of My Irish Journey* should have been suppressed, as its manifest lack of sympathy added to the backlash against Carlyle's reputation;[25] and the editor of Alexander Somerville's *Letters from Ireland during the Famine of 1847* suggests that Somerville's open condemnation of the government threatened his future career in England.

The danger inherent in proclaiming one's opinions on Ireland may have led to the development of a different kind of travel narrative. Inglis, who had written books on Spain, the Channel Islands, and the Tyrol, stressed that he was approaching Ireland in an entirely different way: 'allowing the interest which I felt in a fine and romantic country, to be lost in the higher interest, which attaches to the social condition of the people'.[26] Foster, a pragmatic lawyer who was well known for journalistic accounts of the Rebecca riots, rather wistfully conjured up an alternative account of the descriptions of Irish scenery he might have given, before crushing it with the iron 'I have a higher object'.[27] This 'higher object' and the onerous responsibility it placed upon them may have led writers of Irish travels to be more subjective than readers may have expected or wished, as a form of self-defence. Mary Louise Pratt, writing on travel narratives on Southern Africa in the late eighteenth century, speaks of what she calls 'the invisible eye/I' of travel literature, the effacement of the speaking and experiencing self from the text.[28] This is frequently not the case in Irish narratives. For a start, many began as letters to a newspaper, such as Foster's and Osborne's to *The Times*, Somerville's to the *Manchester Guardian*, and Martineau's to the *Daily News*. Others adopted the form of

    [24] Foster, *Letters*, 229.
    [25] William Ewart Gladstone noted in the flyleaf of his copy of Carlyle's *Reminiscences*: 'This book, in the first half of it especially is more egotistical and comes nearer to being trashy than any other of Carlyle's works. It has every where the art of succinct portraiture in few & telling words. He did not think the Irish worth a study, yet in other things he could not fail to see: as where he speaks of "the thing called law in Ireland".' (Gladstone's copy, held at St Deiniol's Library, Hawarden.)
    [26] Inglis, *Ireland in 1834*, i. 28–9.   [27] Foster, *Letters*, 270.
    [28] Mary Louise Pratt, 'Scratches on the Face of the Country; or, What Mr. Barrow Saw in the Land of the Bushmen', in Henry Louis Gates, Jr. (ed.), *'Race', Writing, and Difference* (Chicago and London: University of Chicago Press, 1986), 144.

the letter or journal entry for effect: Thackeray maintained the illusion of writing each day in a different location, when in fact he wrote most of the book in Charles Lever's house in Dublin. Publishing letters instead of reports was a way for gentlefolk to avoid the taint of plebeian journalism, but Thackeray and others were also using the epistolary form to emphasize their essential ignorance of Irish matters, and to reflect the change in their opinions as the journey progressed. This form may have been especially powerful during the Famine because of its immediacy, and the reinforcement of the sense of being an eyewitness.

There are certainly ellipses in our knowledge of these travellers: Inglis only mentions that he has been travelling with his wife to explain that the Irish trust women and are more likely to tell the truth to them than to male commissioners; the reader is unaware from their texts that de Beaumont and de Tocqueville were travelling together; several of the travel-guides were published anonymously, and that of Prince Pückler-Muskau was deliberately misleading, as it suggested the author was dead when it appeared; we have no idea if Catherine O'Connell was related to the Liberator, although she visited him in prison and at Derrynane, and incorporated a lengthy memorial to him in her text. But it is perhaps inevitable that the texts should seem more personality-based, partly because so many remarkable people visited Ireland in these years, and partly due to the anxiety travellers felt about the impact of their remarks, and their own status as either colonizers or fellow subjects—or both. As Martin Ryle has suggested:

whatever value travel writing may have as empirical evidence about the terrain it describes, it is itself primary evidence about the cultural relations which it necessarily represents, because it instantiates and embodies them. Travel writing, in other words, is to be relied on not as an account of the places described but as a record of how those places have been seen.[29]

Thackeray deliberately foregrounded his narrative persona, Michael Angelo Titmarsh: 'This is not a description of the Giant's Causeway (as some clever critic will remark),' says Titmarsh, 'but of a Londoner there . . .', and Thackeray's preferred title for the book was 'A Cockney in Ireland', emphasizing this dual interest.[30] A cursory glance at the list of travellers reads like an elite roll-call: Queen Victoria, two royal surgeons,

[29] Martin Ryle, *Journeys in Ireland: Literary Travellers, Rural Landscapes, Cultural Relations* (Aldershot: Ashgate, 1999), 6.

[30] Thackeray, *Irish Sketch Book*, ii. 260; Thackeray also used Titmarsh in his *Paris Sketch Book* (1840) and *Notes of a Journey From Cornhill to Grand Cairo* (1845), but the *Irish Sketch Book* was the first of his works to come out under his own name.

the future poet laureate, an ex–governor of Canada, a future governor of India, a future Chief Secretary of Ireland, the essayist Harriet Martineau (whom O'Connell had invited to visit and comment on Ireland in the 1830s, and who finally made it in 1852), and one of the most influential social commentators of his age, Thomas Carlyle. There were many subtle interconnections between the travellers and Ireland, and with other travellers. The political economist Nassau Senior, who visited in 1852, was the brother of the Poor Law commissioner Edward Senior, who was stationed in Ireland, and his opinions were obviously modulated by his brother's experience of workhouses during the Famine. Martineau was following the example of the English journalist and industrialist Spencer T. Hall, who had published his account of the Famine two years previously, and who was the person who cured Martineau of a lifelong nervous illness through mesmerism; Martineau's brother James, an eminent Unitarian divine, had served as a pastor in Dublin, and was chief promotor and first secretary of the Irish Unitarian Christian Society. Asenath Nicholson was irritated to find herself constantly compared to other women travellers such as Anna Maria Hall and Lady Chatterton. The future Chief Secretary W. E. Forster, then a young Quaker, travelled sometimes with his father and fellow Quakers William Bennet and James Tuke, sometimes alone, writing on the Famine for the Central Relief Committee of the Society of Friends; they met up often to exchange ideas. Bennet also travelled for a time with Asenath Nicholson, and Forster with Thomas Carlyle and the Young Irelander Charles Gavan Duffy. Their books are intensely intertextual, incorporating newspaper reports, extracts from Blue Books, references to novels such as Griffin's *The Collegians*, but especially quotations from other travel-writers. Green bindings sprayed with shamrocks were *de rigueur*, as Lever noticed when he warned readers: 'Let no fascinations of little green–bound volumes, all decked in shamrocks though they be, seduce you.'[31] Indeed, it is almost as if every publishing house were contributing to a matching library of Irish travel-books. When Sir Francis Head reached Westport in 1852, he found that 'the house was overflowing with English tourists, each carrying in his or her right hand a pea-green "Handbook", that had been given gratis at Euston Station, and which, very unfortunately for me, had gratuitously told almost everyone to come to Westport'.[32]

---

[31] Charles Lever, 'Twaddling Tourists in Ireland—No. II', *Dublin University Magazine*, 24 (Dec. 1844), 740–8, at 748.
[32] Sir Francis B. Head, *A Fortnight in Ireland* (London: John Murray, 1852), 151.

Not surprisingly, there is an obvious 'anxiety of influence' at work in these books, with authors struggling to repress and succeed their forebears by proving the excellence of their text and the redundancy of all others. Thackeray was appalled by the proliferation of Irish travel-books, which left less room for his own work: 'A plague take them! what remains for me to discover after the gallant adventurers in the service of Paternoster Row have examined every rock, lake, and ruin of the district, exhausted it of all its legends, and "invented new", most likely, as their daring genius prompted?'[33] Anxiety spilled over into personal rancour: both Hamilton and Fraser attacked Inglis—with more bitterness than justification—as 'a superficial writer who has monopolised too much of public attention'.[34] Otway denied Inglis's comparison of Killery Bay to a Norwegian fjord— even though Otway admitted he had never seen a fjord—and poured scorn on female tourists such as Mrs Hall and Lady Chatterton—whose books had been enormously successful—for being unable to scale cliffs:

> I wish Mrs. H——, or Lady C——, or any other petticoat tourist, were here to try it, I think the eagles would clap their wings, laugh out lustily, and cry, 'Well done, blue-stockings!' if, while cased in stays and bustle, and all the feminine armour trusted in to catch and captivate mankind, they should also conquer this diffi- culty.[35]

Such trivial squabbles are expected and rather healthy; more disconcert- ing is the remarkable homogeneity of these works. Travellers followed each other geographically through Dublin, Powerscourt, Killarney, Joyce Country, and the Giant's Causeway; socially to prisons, poorhouses, lunatic asylums, cabins, O'Connell's dinner-table, and Father Mathew's temperance meetings; and intellectually revolved on the same arguments about Irish poverty, education, religious strife, land tenure, the relation of landlord to tenant. Authors appeared to see themselves as successive edi- tors of the text *Ireland*, a text which was assumed to be stable, but which produced diachronic generalizations more often than synchronic truths. The travel-book became a palimpsest, overwritten by succeeding trav- ellers, preserving anachronistic interpretations, and indeed adding to them. It is disturbing to find George Saintsbury recommending in 1908 that anyone wishing to understand the Irish question need only read Spenser's *State of Ireland*, Wolfe Tone's *Autobiography*, and Thackeray's

---

[33] Thackeray, *Irish Sketch Book*, ii. 126.
[34] Charles Hamilton, *Leigh's New Pocket Road-Book of Ireland* (London: Leigh, 1835), 25.
[35] Caesar Otway, *A Tour in Connaught* (Dublin: William Curry, Jr. & Co., 1839), 272; *Sketches in Erris and Tyrawly*, 304.

Irish Sketch Book, which surely could not be relied upon for the state of early twentieth-century Ireland.[36] The Halls' three-volume *Ireland: Its Scenery, Character, &c.*, published 1841–3, recorded a vast improvement in all classes in Ireland since the 1830s: 'The peasantry are better clad than they formerly were, their cottages much more decent, their habits far less uncivilised.'[37] More remarkably, they suggested that the eating habits of Irish peasants had significantly altered for the better: 'we refer, in a great degree, to our recollections, when we describe the lower classes of the Irish as existing, almost universally, on the potato'.[38] Although this is not an Ireland that even their contemporary travellers would have recognized, the Halls were generally quoted with reverence. This beguilingly optimistic view was reissued—ostensibly as a new edition, and therefore supposedly updated—in 1846. The title-page incarnated all the stereotypes of 'Ould Oireland'—a harp flanked by two Irish wolfhounds, a trellis from which are suspended leprechauns and elves, weeping Erin, the ubiquitous Irish drunk, and a dashing Red Branch knight. Yet 1846 was the year of the second failure of the potato crop, and the Halls' assertion that the Irish no longer live on potatoes takes on a horrific new meaning in this context. Such a work, with such a title-page, published in such a year, may have seriously misled its purchasers about the state of famine in Ireland, yet the anachronism went unchallenged.

The fact is that the Irish travel-book in this period is less a dialogue than a monologue, a cumulative work that is self-referential and self-verifying. There is only a limited interaction with the subject. During the Famine, a chance traveller to a remote district could save lives, either by donating money or reporting his findings in the English press. Less positively, the ubiquitous guides and beggars were the products of tourism, and Catherine O'Connell traced the degeneration of the Irish peasantry to this source:

I will instance Killarney, where in late years the vast influx of rich and carelessly-generous Englishmen, has taught the poor mountaineer how easy it is to earn a shilling, and how much more agreeable to get it for a song, a jig, 'a plate of wild fruits,' 'a taste of potheen,' or even for attending your honour, than to toil for the half of it during a long summer's day.[39]

[36] George Saintsbury, 'Introduction' to *The Irish Sketch Book and Contributions to the Foreign Quarterly Review 1842–4, by William Makepeace Thackeray* (London, New York, and Toronto: Oxford University Press, 1908), p. viii.
   [37] Hall and Hall, *Ireland*, i. 3.   [38] Ibid., 83.
   [39] Catherine O'Connell, *Excursions in Ireland During 1844 and 1850* (London: Bentley, 1852), 9.

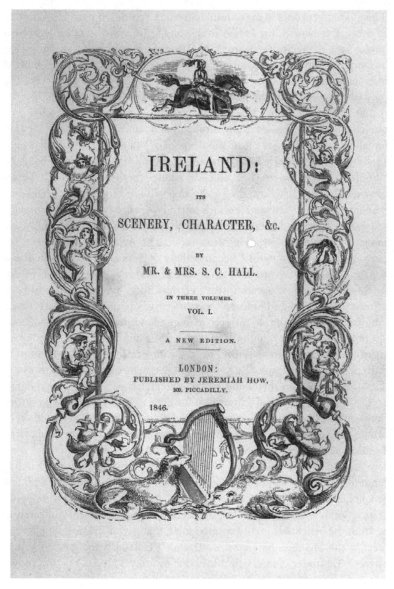

Figure 4. Title page, Samuel Carter and Anna Maria Hall's *Ireland: Its Scenery, Character, &c.*, 3 vols. (London: Jeremiah How, 1846)

The guides were able to make money from the names of past tourists such as Scott, Edgeworth, the Halls, Inglis, and Queen Victoria, while in turn guides such as the Spillanes and 'Sir' Richard Courtenay of Killarney were immortalized in books and sought out by later tourists. Even this limited interaction bred friction. In many cases the guides and beggars were the only lower-class Irish the tourists spoke to, yet they were hated by the people who used them. The Halls, harassed at Glendalough, said: 'For ourselves, we confess a strong desire to sink the whole tribe, male and female, into the deepest pit of the deep lake.'[40] Thomas Carlyle weighed his dyspepsia against Irish despair at Lough Gill, and screamed at beggars: 'Wouldn't it be worth your consideration, whether you hadn't better drown or hang yourselves, than live a dog's life in this way?'[41] Thackeray made a sly dig at his predecessors on the beggar's behalf: 'The unconscionable rogues! how dare they, for the sake of a little starvation or so, interrupt gentlefolks in their pleasure?'[42] The irritation at the need for personal contact is tangible, because these writers are engaging in a discourse of difference, quarantining Ireland from the rest of the civilized world. The sense of a community of travellers, hypersensitive to each other's movements and opinions, constructing a party-line in their books, emphasizes their essential difference from the Other, Ireland.

On his first day in Dublin, Thackeray was astonished at the announcement in the *Morning Register* of the consecration of the Bishop of Aureliopolis by the Pope: 'Such an announcement sounds quite strange *in English*, and in your own country, as it were; or isn't it your own country?'[43] This is a provocative question for the English traveller, who is torn between a strong sense of possession and an even stronger sense of alienation. The facts that these exotic places were only twenty-four hours from London, and that Ireland was the same country existing under the same laws were nervously reiterated, yet in the not so distant past, the English landlord Lane Fox had brought beads and mirrors to subdue his Wicklow tenants, and Inglis approached crossing the Shannon as if he were penetrating some remote jungle: 'an additional interest was communicated to it, from the belief that, to my countrymen, that part of Ireland lying to the west of the Shannon, is a *terra incognita*'.[44] Ireland was a land of superlatives: Alexander Somerville observed in 1847: 'Never, in the known

---

[40] Hall and Hall, *Ireland*, ii. 231.

[41] Thomas Carlyle, *Reminiscences of My Irish Journey in 1849* (London: Sampson Low & Co., 1882), 223.

[42] Thackeray, *Irish Sketch Book*, ii. 155.   [43] Ibid., i. 15.

[44] Inglis, *Ireland in 1834*, i. 265.

history of mankind, was there a country and its people in such imminent hazard of perishing utterly.'⁴⁵ Stereotypes were ruthlessly reinforced: the Irish peasant was presented as a one-dimensional creature, resolutely honest and hospitable if mindlessly violent, irretrievably superstitious though admirably pious, the inhabitant of a mud hut with a dung-heap at the door and a pig playing with the numerous children in a cesspool. Few registered any complexity: de Tocqueville realized that the people with the dung-heaps and pigs were actually the aristocrats of the peasant class, and joked that he would never sleep in a cabin without them.⁴⁶ But for most travellers, Irish meant poor and dirty, English industrious and clean. These essential polarities held true even for those writers who were Scottish, such as Inglis, Foster, Somerville, and Carlyle. 'Every Englishman,' said Foster, 'fresh from his own country, where almost every yard of it, through the length and breadth of the land, bears evidence of capital invested and of the application of intelligent industry, can scarcely avoid being filled with regret at seeing, as he traverses Ireland, so fine a country, so full of opportunities of improvement, so lamentably neglected.'⁴⁷ According to the guilty Mrs West, who crept round Limerick in 1846 grief-stricken for the broken Treaty of 1691, Ireland was 'the opprobrium of England in European eyes', and not surprisingly England tried to distance herself from it.⁴⁸ Comparisons were made with any other country to avoid making the connection with England: the scenery resembled Spain, Switzerland, Norway, or Germany; Irish cabins were like Indian wigwams, Eskimo igloos, or Hottentot kraals—only worse; the people were similar to the Spanish, native Americans, Canadians, negro slaves, Lettes, Estonians, Finlanders, Russians, Hungarians—to any nation, in fact, except the English. William Bennet impressed the proximity of the disaster on English minds in 1847, reminding his readers that this was happening to

a people, not in the centre of Africa; the steppes of Asia, the backwoods of America,—not some newly-discovered tribes of South Australia, or among the Polynesian Indians,—not Hottentots, bushmen, or Esquimeaux,—neither Mahomedans nor Pagans,—but some millions of our own Christian nation at

---

⁴⁵ Alexander Somerville, *Letters From Ireland During the Famine of 1847*, ed. K. D. M. Snell (Dublin: Irish Academic Press, 1994), 31.
⁴⁶ Alexis de Tocqueville, *Journey in Ireland July–August, 1835*, ed. Emmet Larkin (Washington, DC: The Catholic University of America Press, 1990), 7–8).
⁴⁷ Foster, *Letters*, 63.
⁴⁸ T. C. I. West, *A Summer's Visit to Ireland in 1846* (London: Richard Bentley, 1847), 152, 141.

home, living in a state and condition low and degraded to a degree unheard of before in any civilized community . . .[49]

Ulster was lauded as the country's saving grace: the reflection of England on Irish soil, an example of what the lazy Irish could do if injected with Scottish industry and the Protestant religion. Harriet Martineau deliberately began her tour in Derry, manipulating her readers into first seeing prosperous parts of Ireland, those that thrived under her country's rule, before descending to the underworld. There were hardly any suggestions in these books that the Famine had any impact on Ulster, as this would come too close to admitting that it could happen in England. William Bennet shied away from discussing the number of deaths from fever in Armagh: 'We heard of so many deaths occurring the very day of our being there that I am afraid to mention, lest it might not be credited.'[50] Although newspapers like the *Banner of Ulster* and the *Belfast Vindicator* were reporting on the impact of the catastrophe in the province, the American William Balch was the only traveller to openly describe the effects of famine in Ulster in 1848. In Derry he saw a woman sitting in a wheelbarrow eating dry meal; and his description of a County Monaghan fair-day could have been sent from Clifden or Skibbereen:

Here a mother thrust her skeleton child into our faces; an other exposed her cancer breast; a little girl led her blind father to us; a fourth exhibited a fractured leg. The most hideous looking being I ever saw in mortal shape was an old man, a complete skeleton, doubled together, his chin resting on his knees, with his fleshless legs and arms exposed to view. As we passed him, he turned upon us a deathly stare, and stretched out his long thin arm, muttering a prayer in the name of the Almighty and the Holy Virgin, that we would give him *something* to keep him from starving. His hollow cheeks, projecting jaws, eyeballs sunken deep in their sockets—oh, horror, I can not describe him—the image of Death, doubled together![51]

Everything, even the old man's obvious Catholicism, suggests a southern scene, and it could be suggested that Balch, who made no secret of his Anglophobia, was deliberately undermining perceptions of Ulster's superiority in order to shame the English.[52] Yet recent work on the

[49] William Bennet, *Narrative of a Recent Journey of Six Weeks in Ireland* (London and Dublin: Charles Gilpin; William Curry, Jr. & Co., 1847), 138.

[50] Ibid., 89.

[51] William Balch, *Ireland, As I Saw It: The Character, Condition, and Prospects of the People* (New York and London: Hallock & Lyon; H. K. Lewis, 1850), 411.

[52] Balch's untrustworthiness is perhaps best exemplified by his favourite experiment for measuring despair: he would ask Irish children if they wanted to come to America with him, and promise to send for them when he returned. As he claimed to be too soft-hearted to disabuse them, one imagines children all over the country waiting for Balch to send the money for them and their families to emigrate.

Famine in Ulster tends to corroborate Balch's testimony. In his book on the Famine in Lurgan and Portadown, Gerard Mac Atasney quotes a letter from John Dilworth, who was distributing funds from Christian friends in the area during the Famine. The letter, which appeared in the *Belfast Newsletter* in April 1847, describes a cabin visit that rehearses all the stock motifs such a visit in Connaught would inspire:

> oh! what a spectacle—a young man about fourteen or fifteen, on the cold damp floor, off the rubbish, dead!; without a single vestige of clothing, the eyes sunk, the mouth wide open, the flesh shrivelled up, the bones all visible, so small around the waist that I could span him with my hand. The corpse had been left in that situation for five successive days.[53]

Even closer to home than Ulster for the English tourists were scenes of starvation on the mainland. Despite several reports in *The Times* of starvation in London and Dorset, misery had become in English eyes a purely Irish characteristic: Robert Somers, describing the destitution of Scottish Highlanders during the Famine of 1847 remarked that it 'constitutes an Irish rather than a Highland picture. Yet there was nothing truly Irish there . . .'.[54] Lord John Manners, travelling in Ireland in 1846, asserted that 'in no part of England, however out of the way, have I seen so much squalor and dreary discomfort as is to be seen within ten minutes' drive of the viceroy's lodge'.[55] Yet Manners, an advocate of factory reform, had toured the industrial districts of Lancashire with Disraeli and George Smythe two years previously, and he must have witnessed conditions similar to those described in contemporary industrial novels, such as Elizabeth Gaskell's *Mary Barton*. Chapter 6 of this novel, set in Manchester and published in the year following 'Black '47', described the death by starvation and fever of an unemployed mill-worker in a fetid cellar—remarkably similar to reports of Famine victims dying in Irish cabins.[56] Thomas Campbell Foster, who defended England as the bastion of cultivation and civilization, contradicted himself when he tried to defend Irish exports during a Famine with an English analogy: 'surely the anomaly is fully as great to see, as is unhappily too often the case, in such a town

[53] Gerard Mac Atasney, *'This Dreadful Vistitation': The Famine in Lurgan/Portadown* (Belfast: Beyond the Pale, 1997), 61–2.
[54] Robert Somers, *Letters From The Highlands; or, The Famine of 1847* (London, Edinburgh and Glasgow: Simpkin, Marshall, & Co.; Sutherland & Knox; J. R. McNair, 1848), 96.
[55] Lord John Manners, *Notes of an Irish Tour* (London: J. Ollivier, 1849), 6.
[56] Elizabeth Gaskell, *Mary Barton, A Tale of Manchester Life*, 2 vols. (London: Chapman & Hall, 1848).

as Manchester, for instance, poor creatures half-clothed and perishing of cold in the middle of a town which clothes the whole world'.[57] There was certainly an element of culture shock in the reactions of English travellers to Ireland, but an element also of reluctance to admit that such misery could have anything remotely to do with England. Sidney Godolphin Osborne, depressed by the degradation and indolence of men in an Irish poorhouse, said: 'The yard in which what was called the able-bodied class of males was assembled, gave immediate, unmistakable evidence of the state of the Union.'[58] He was referring to the electoral union, but a dangerous double-meaning lurks behind: what is really at stake is the state of the legislative Union, an extremely sensitive issue for British and Anglo-Irish travellers.

So-called natives tread even more delicately. Caesar Otway declared that as a 'native' he was 'competent to afford information on subjects not exactly within the convenient reach of an American or Briton', but as a 'native', he was also reluctant to adopt theories, and was enraged by externs' persistence in doing so:

Why, if I were some English, American, or Continental tourist, who came to view our country through the coloured glasses of his own pre-conceived theory, I might have at once laid down the cause, and the cure for all this. But as I am a poor ignorant Irishman, who, of course, knows nothing of my own country, why I hesitate before I state the gnosis, the diagnosis, or remedy for this disease.[59]

Yet Otway certainly was not perceived as an Irishman by the people whose poverty he commented on. He remarked of the savage Irish-speaking boatmen of Killery Bay that they were 'very much out of humour at being obliged to leave their potato planting to go rowing a pair of idle Sassenach fools, as they evidently considered us to be'.[60] Samuel and Anna Maria Hall, both Irish-born, were scolded by an irate Irishman in the Devil's Glen in Wicklow:

You foreyners pass through Ireland, and instead of keeping your eyes and ears open, you want to bring everything—leaping torrents, mountains, hills, and all—down to the level of your own flat country. You believe nothing, and want to understand everything . . . You English want to *understand* all about Ireland, and yet you never understood an Irishman.[61]

The Halls were highly amused by this outburst, but the fact that one Irishman could not recognize another does indicate the gulf between the

<hr/>

[57] Foster, *Letters*, 613.   [58] Osborne, *Gleanings*, 53.
[59] Otway, *Tour in Connaught*, p. vi; *Sketches in Erris and Tyrawly*, 315.
[60] Otway, *Tour in Connaught*, 273.   [61] Hall and Hall, *Ireland*, ii. 248.

classes in Ireland, and the possibility that upper-class Irish suffered culture shock as often as their English counterparts.

James Johnson, surgeon to William IV, was brought up in Belfast, but
his overwhelming shame at the sight of Irish poverty prevented him from
identifying with the Irish in his travel narrative; he preferred to suffer the
guilt of the oppressor. In Clifden in 1844, he had a nightmare:

myriads of Troglodytes issued from their caves in endless forms of deformity—
some with 'heads beneath their shoulders,' some with broad Cyclopean visual orbs
in their foreheads, and others clad in the skins of various animals, from which they
could hardly be distinguished! They scowled fiercely on me, as they flitted past,
and I could frequently hear the words 'Saxon tyrant' applied to me in most fierce
accents![62]

This sense of estrangement grew even more pronounced during the
Famine. Charles Gavan Duffy, recently released from prison after the failure of his prosecution for treason-felony, depressed by the fiasco of the
failed Rising, and travelling in the company of the deeply prejudiced
Carlyle, must have been keenly aware of his own Irishness, yet took care
to evade its implications by suggesting that the Famine had created a 'new
race':

We saw on the streets of Galway crowds of creatures more debased than the
Yahoos of Swift—creatures having only a distant and hideous resemblance to
human beings. Grey-haired old men, whose idiotic faces had hardened into a settled leer of mendicancy, and women filthier and more frightful than the harpies,
who at the jingle of a coin on the pavement swarmed in myriads from unseen
places; struggling, screaming, *shrieking* for their prey, like some monstrous and
unclean animals.[63]

These beasts have nothing to do with the race Duffy and his colleagues
had hoped to regenerate through their cultural project at *The Nation*, and
in a sense this is Duffy's way of evading the trauma; his race is gone, and
he feels no obligation to, or sympathy for, this new debased breed. Lord
Dufferin, reporting from Skibbereen in 1847, was careful to identify himself as an Oxford student, not as the landlord of Clandeboye, in Ulster.
And William Wilde, who as a doctor attended the casualties of famine, and
compiled the 'Table of Deaths' for the 1851 census, deliberately excluded

[62] James Johnson, *A Tour in Ireland; with Meditations and Reflections* (London:
S. Highley, 1844), 201.
[63] Sir Charles Gavan Duffy, *Conversations With Carlyle* (London: Samson Low, Marston,
& Co., 1892), 121; Duffy had previously published this passage in *The Nation* (1 Sept. 1849),
8, without any mention of Carlyle.

the Famine from his 1849 travel-book *The Beauties of the Boyne.* 'As we
only engaged to present our readers with scenes of beauty or of interest,'
he lamely explained, 'we cannot be expected to devote much of our space
to a description of Navan!'[64] He asserted that the people of Trim were apathetic—a key term in the description (and criticism) of famine victims—
not because they were suffering from starvation and disease, but because
they were 'wanting the stimulus of the warder's bugle, and the exciting
scenes when De Lacy's lancers and mailed warriors careered through their
narrow streets, when the standard of royalty proudly waved from the tall
towers of their castle, and the mitred abbot and stole-girt priest, with all
the gorgeous paraphernalia of the Church, paraded their dull town'.[65]
Obviously romance was much harder to live without than food, and a
retreat into history was easier than facing hard facts.

It is hardly surprising that travellers, especially Irish ones, should want
to evade the horror of Irish poverty. 'The traveller is haunted by the face
of the popular starvation,' mused Thackeray in 1842: 'The epicurean, and
traveller for pleasure, had better travel anywhere than here; where there are
miseries that one does not dare to think of; where one is always feeling how
helpless pity is, and how hopeless relief, and is perpetually made ashamed
of being happy.'[66] If this was true in 1842, it was even more so in 1847 and
the following years. Asenath Nicholson, who had travelled from New York
to see for herself the state of affairs that was sending so many emigrants to
her country, had spent most of her time since 1844 living in cabins among
the people; but she found herself almost confined to a hotel room during
the Famine, for fear of what she might find in the cabins she had once frequented: 'I *did* not, and *could not* endure, as the famine progressed, such
sights, as well as at the first, they were too real, and these realities became
a dread . . . the horror of meeting living walking ghosts, or stumbling upon
the dead in my path at night, inclined me to keep within when necessity did
not call.'[67] Spencer Hall and Samuel Hole said that they were unable to eat
while in Ireland because of the starvation all around them, while others suffered from nightmares. The American philanthropist Elihu Burritt, a committed pacifist, abolitionist, and ex-blacksmith from Connecticut who
became famous as a self-taught mathematician and linguist, was lecturing
in England when he heard of the plight of the Irish, and he travelled there
in the hope that his account of his journey would raise money for famine

---

[64] William Wilde, *The Beauties of the Boyne, and its Tributary, the Blackwater* (Dublin,
London, and Liverpool: James M'Glashan; William S. Orr, 1849), 133.
[65] Ibid., 81.   [66] Thackeray, *Irish Sketch Book*, i. 146–7.
[67] Asenath Nicholson, *Lights and Shades of Ireland* (London: Charles Gilpin, 1850), 330.

victims. Burritt, who spent three days in Skibbereen in 1847, was deeply affected by the sight of a 12-year-old boy with dropsy, whose body had swollen to three times its normal size: 'It has haunted me during the past night, like Banquo's ghost. I have lain awake for hours, struggling for some graphic and truthful similes or new elements of description, by which I might convey to the distant reader some tangible image of this object.'[68] For Burritt and his fellow writers, no such images existed. 'I cannot describe . . .' is the constant refrain. For one thing, even before 1845, the Irish travel-book had developed into a genre that insisted on the use of superlatives to describe Irish poverty. Writers had to struggle against the redundancy of over-used and exhausted metaphors. Christopher Morash describes 'a haunting of language' during the Famine, suggesting that 'In the living skeletons and spectres who materialise again and again in the pages of Famine writing, we see a discourse of the Famine taking shape, with its own particular vocabulary.'[69] The 'living skeleton' is an image that proliferated wildly during the Famine; the monologue on Ireland had shifted to horror, and the texts remained largely homogeneous in content, language, and tone. Skeletons abounded: Elizabeth Smith recorded in her journal that the roads were 'beset with tattered skeletons'; Spencer Hall found 'a crowd of living skeletons' in his host's kitchen; Revd John East observed babies who were 'mere breathing skeletons'; and James Tuke recalled a 14-year-old boy in Clifden: 'The ghastly livid face and emaciated form, wasted with hunger and sores, of this breathing skeleton, told me that to him this world would soon pass away.'[70] Alexander Somerville recognized the power of the image by substituting it for the word 'person', dehumanizing a starving family, transforming them into a ghastly nightmare:

They were skeletons all of them, with skin on the bones and life within the skin. A mother skeleton and baby skeleton; a tall boy skeleton, who had no work to do; who could now do nothing but eat, and had nothing to eat. Four female children

---

[68] Elihu Burritt, *A Journal of a Visit of Three Days to Skibbereen, and its Neighbourhood* (London and Birmingham: Charles Gilpin; John Whitehouse Showell, 1847), 10. Burritt's public standing in England is indicated by an advertisement in the *ILN* for 'a Characteristic and carefully-finished PORTRAIT' of Burritt, costing 5s. for prints, 7s. 6d. for proofs (13 Mar. 1847, 175).

[69] Christopher Morash, 'Spectres of the Famine', *Irish Review* (Winter 1995), 74–9, at 75–6.

[70] Elizabeth Smith, *Irish Journals*, 246; Spencer T. Hall, *Life and Death in Ireland, as Witnessed in 1849* (Manchester and London: J. T. Parkes; Simpkin, Marshall, & Co., 1850), 12; Revd John East, *Glimpses of Ireland in 1847* (London, Bath, Bristol, and Dublin: Hamilton, Adams & Co.; C. Godwin, Binns & Godwin, T. Noyes; J. Chilcot; J. M'Glashan, 1847), 20; James Tuke, *A Visit to Connaught in the Autumn of 1847* (London and York: Charles Gilpin; John Linney, 1848), 14.

skeletons, and the tall father skeleton, not able to work to get food for them, and not able to get enough of food when he did work for them.[71]

But this image is not, as Morash suggests, part of a developing vocabulary of the Famine, but part of a literary convention of the description of Irish poverty, a database stretching back to Spenser and beyond. Henry Inglis, writing in 1834, encountered 'a living skeleton' in a Limerick cellar in a time of no great scarcity.[72] More revealingly, Kohl, travelling in 1843, recalled a 'Living Skeleton' freak show he had seen in England—the exhibit had been an Irishman.[73] The 'living skeleton' image is symptomatic of the inability of travel writers to extricate their descriptions of Ireland during the Famine from equally extreme accounts of poverty in previous years.

This is not to deny the power of the motif to shock the reader, or its concreteness for the observer. One of Burritt's more horrifying descriptions was of starving children: 'three breathing skeletons, ranging from two to three feet in height and *entirely naked*. And these human beings were alive! If they had been dead, they could not have been such frightful spectacles, they were alive, and *mirabile dictu*, they could stand upon their feet and even walk; but it was awful to see them do it.'[74] The constantly stressed ineffability of language would suggest that 'living skeleton' was as close as one could get to an adequate representation of the horror.

Another recurring motif is the 'spectre', as in Catherine O'Connell's representative 'gaunt spectre-like mother', Nicholson's abstract 'spectre of poverty', and Johnson's view of Ireland as 'a half-dead, half living spectre'.[75] Obviously the image has connotations of horror, apparitions, ghosts, and ghouls, perfectly appropriate for such a theme. Sir Francis Head described the experience of entering Galway in 1852: 'here almost immediately I first met with that afflicting spectacle, or rather spectre, that almost without intermission haunted me through the whole remainder of my tour, namely, stout stone-built cabins unroofed for the purpose of evicting therefrom their insolvent tenants'.[76] The spectres that haunted Head were the inanimate, sepulchral cabins of tenants who were probably dead. But by juxtaposing the words 'spectre' and 'spectacle', Head recognized their common etymology from the Latin *specere*, 'to see'. The 'spectre' motif is therefore very apt, as travellers were haunted by the spectacle

[71] Somerville, *Letters from Ireland*, 96.   [72] Inglis, *Ireland in 1834*, i. 304.
[73] Kohl, *Ireland, Scotland and England*, 50.   [74] Burritt, *A Journal of a Visit*, 14.
[75] Catherine O'Connell, *Excursions in Ireland*, 238; Nicholson, *Ireland's Welcome*, 35; Johnson, *A Tour in Ireland*, 274–5.
[76] Head, *A Fortnight in Ireland*, 116.

of Famine. Having erected a *cordon sanitaire* by insisting on the absolute alterity of Ireland, its essential Otherness, and instituting a monologue on Irish poverty, there could be no dialogue with the Famine victim. Famine for the traveller was a purely visual phenomenon, with little or no linguistic contamination: Famine victims were to be seen and not heard. The howling of the impostor was sharply contrasted with the silence of the true sufferer, which the observer found much more moving. The wife of an Irish landlord who charged a penny for soup at her private soup-kitchen threw a clamorous woman and her two children out for protesting: 'All was, however, lost on me; I could not hear more than "is this your charity!" but I did not think it proper that she should continue, so I told the door-keeper to send to the next police station, unless that woman was silent immediately.'[77] The starving were often charged with apathy or indifference, yet when they spoke up they were ungrateful beggars.

The silence of the starving inevitably engenders pity, but it can also be terrifying. Alexander Somerville encountered a 'phantom farmer', Thomas Killaheel, in Newcastle, County Limerick in 1847, and suffered great discomfort when this 'spectre', this thing to be seen, stared back:

The lean man looked as if his spirit, starved in his own thin flesh, would leave him and take up its abode with me. I even felt it going through me as if looking into the innermost pores of my body for food to eat and for seed oats. It moved through the veins with the blood, and finding no seed oats there, nor food, searched through every pocket to the bottom, and returned again and searched the flesh and blood to the very heart; the poor man all the while gazing on me as if to see what the lean spirit might find; and it searched the more keenly that he spoke not a word.[78]

This cannibalistic interchange is so disturbing because famine victims first should not have names, and secondly should not look back. They are exhibits, 'framed pictures of woe' on the canvas of the 'dark picture', Ireland.[79] Anadyton[80] is a rhetorical trope, designed to intrigue the reader, but it is also symptomatic: these travel writers constantly chafed against the boundaries of their own medium, wishing they could exchange 'cold words' for a paintbrush.[81] 'Had I the graphic pen of a Mulcahy . . .' said Spencer Hall, 'I might do the subject greater justice', and others wished

[77] 'A Lady', *Christmas 1846, and the New Year 1847, in Ireland, Letters From a Lady*, ed. W. S. Gilly (Durham: G. Andrews, 1847), 35.

[78] Somerville, *Letters from Ireland*, 153.

[79] Bennet, *Narrative of a Recent Journey*, 19.

[80] 'the impossibility of expressing oneself adequately to the topic', Brian Vickers, *In Defence of Rhetoric* (Oxford: Clarendon Press, 1990), 491.

[81] Catherine O'Connell, *Excursions in Ireland*, 77.

for the skill of a Maclise or an O'Neil, to draw what they found so difficult to say.[82] Yet few actually included drawings of the starving in their work. Sketches of Glengariff, the Giant's Causeway, round towers, the Lakes of Killarney, abounded, but few of the people who lived there. Thackeray included sketches of ragged children running after coaches, but they were a picturesque afterthought. Even James Mahony, the artist whose sketches for the *Illustrated London News* brought notoriety to Skibbereen, could be evasive, as can be seen from his article on Schull, describing 500 women waiting for meal, yet accompanied by a detailed sketch of the town with only four people in the background for perspective.[83] And even when sketches of the starving were included, they were not always as shocking as the text would claim: as Catherine Marshall has noted, sketches such as Mahony's famous 'Boy and Girl at Caheragh' suggest poverty through raggedness, but the people are actually remarkably well-muscled for famine victims.[84] Mahony may not have wanted to alienate readers by portraying an Irish mob, and perhaps as Marshall suggests, artists trained in drawing anatomy from Greek sculpture had difficulty representing the 'living skeletons' that abound in written representations. This was not an Irish phenomenon: as John Barrell has argued, there were constraints on how the poor were represented in contemporary English paintings 'so as to be an acceptable part of the decor of the drawing rooms of the polite, when in their own persons they would have been unlikely to gain admission even to the kitchens'.[85] Irish travel writers had to tread the line between sensationalism and something that would be received in the drawing rooms of their audience. Even if they could have faithfully described what they saw, it is unlikely that they would have.

Another difficulty in the visual depiction of Famine Ireland was the limitations of the observer. Lady Chatterton, perhaps the most artistic of the travellers, was always misreading the signs in her search for the picturesque. What she called 'picturesque semi-dress', others would recognize as rags.[86] She enthused: 'the green pounded nettles in a black pan, held by a half-naked yet smiling girl, must be a dull reality to the rest of the cottage inmates; but to me it was all wonderful, and strange, and interesting—a

[82] Spencer Hall, *Life and Death in Ireland*, 42.

[83] *Illustrated London News*, 10 (13 Feb. 1847), 101.

[84] Catherine Marshall, 'Painting Irish History: The Famine', *History Ireland*, 4/3 (Autumn 1996), 46–50, at 46.

[85] John Barrell, *The Dark Side of the Landscape: The Rural Poor in English Painting 1730–1840* (Cambridge: Cambridge University Press, 1980), 5.

[86] Lady Chatterton, *Rambles in the South of Ireland During the Year 1838*, 2 vols. (London: Saunders & Otley, 1839), i. 9.

scene to dwell upon and sketch, in the mind, and with the pencil!'[87] She was totally oblivious to the fact that nettles were a subsistence food when the potatoes failed, and indicated extreme want. A more alert viewer could still remark on the desire to treat it all as landscape and avoid the consequences. Alexander Somerville, no stranger to poverty himself, described a convoy of meal being removed for export from a mob of impotent, squalid wretches: 'To look on all this from some prominent place it was extremely picturesque and striking on the perceptive senses . . . But how miserable was the scene when looked upon otherwise than as a picture; when dwelt upon in thought.'[88] The people themselves were generally portrayed as the complete antithesis of the land they inhabited, 'a blotch upon the face of beauty', as Balch called them.[89] Foster described 'cottages so wretched that no description can convey an idea of them, in the very midst of scenery which you would think would exalt and refine the taste of a savage', and there is more than a hint that perhaps a more compatible and worthy people could be found to inhabit this landscape.[90] Musing on the legend of a fall from rocks on the west coast of Mayo, Somerville turned to a contrast between landscape and people redolent of the biblical Fall:

But there is a fall which is no legend that we must submit to; a plunge which we must make from the mountains of Mayo, with all their grandeur of ocean, of islands, deep bays, high headlands, lakes, rivers, waterfalls, fertile meadows, and greenness which knows no withering; we must plunge from the grand and the beautiful in the inanimate works of nature—to the most degraded and farthest lost of her works—the men made after God's own image.[91]

This Irish Garden of Eden is still fresh and beautiful, but its inhabitants are tainted, blasted by Providence for tasting the Forbidden *root*. Most writers relented and introduced *chiaroscuro* with a distinct visual contrast: either the women of one area, often Limerick, were all stunning, or one woman was picked out in a crowd of beggars as astonishingly beautiful, in some way redeeming the rest. Lord John Manners saw a boy in a cabin whose face might have been 'a study for Canova', and a baby in a poorhouse, 'one divine face such as Raffael might have painted'.[92] Somerville found in a Limerick hovel a young woman who was 'a fac-simile in features and shape of head' of the most beautiful woman of the English aristocracy.[93] These tributes to the noble savage were the commiseration prize, however, and no antidote to the systematic effacement of the people from

[87] Chatterton, *Rambles*, ii. 114–15.
[88] Somerville, *Letters from Ireland*, 41–2.
[89] Balch, *Ireland, As I Saw It*, 157.
[90] Foster, *Letters*, 400.
[91] Somerville, *Letters from Ireland*, 108.
[92] Manners, *Notes of an Irish Tour*, 20, 130.
[93] Somerville, *Letters from Ireland*, 153.

the landscape, literally and metaphorically. Far from sketching the details of the horror, some Irish travel-books are the literary equivalent of an estate clearance.

The tourist, in Ireland to satisfy his own curiosity, in effect the voyeur of Irish distress, was usually the self-portrayed victim of what he witnessed. Traumatized and haunted by starvation, he displaced and effaced the faceless sufferers. 'My hand trembles while I write,' observed William Bennet. 'The scene of human misery and degradation we witnessed still haunts my imagination, with all the vividness and power of some horrid and tyrannous delusion, rather than the features of a sober reality.' Later, he wrote that 'my mind was at times so struck down, that for days together the pen has refused its office; the appalling spectacles have seemed to float between, whenever I attempted it, and to paralyze every effort'.[94] Of course, travellers had more to fear than writer's block. The threat of cholera was all-pervasive, and the upper classes were statistically more at risk; and despite the apathy of the people, the rumours that a rebellion was brewing persisted. Feelings of guilt, horror, and fear led to paranoia: landlady Elizabeth Smith spoke of herself as being oppressed by the poor, in a reversal of traditionally accepted roles.[95] The starving were described as 'wolfish' predators, the tourists as their innocent prey. Osborne described the scene as he and his travelling companion in their coach were chased by a crowd of starving people: 'No two luckless human beings were ever so hunted; no ravening wolves ever gave more open expression of their object—food'; it is as if these skeletal creatures were planning to feast on Osborne rather than ask for some money or bread.[96] The only way to avoid the spectre of Famine, like the monsters and bogeymen of childhood, is not to look. Revd East, lecturing beggars in his host's garden, said: 'their aspect was so terrifically repulsive in its expression of hunger, that I tried not to fix my eyes upon any of them while I was speaking to them . . .'.[97] Describing a family near Erris, James Tuke admitted they 'presented a perfectly appalling picture, so worn and emaciated I could not bear to look at them'.[98] Harriet Martineau found that Osborne was universally respected in Ireland, and spoken of as having rescued many people from starvation. Yet Osborne was so upset at the sight of children in Clifden workhouse that he admitted he would have preferred them to be dead, so that he would not have to see them: 'they looked in the yard so cold, so comfortless, so naked, and such a libel on humanity, that I was glad to have

[94] Bennet, *Narrative of a Recent Journey*, 26, 132–3.
[95] Elizabeth Smith, *Irish Journals*, 81.   [96] Osborne, *Gleanings*, p 80.
[97] East, *Glimpses of Ireland*, 51.   [98] Tuke, *A Visit to Connaught*, 64.

them called in again to the close and infected atmosphere of the crowded day room'.[99] His only comfort, he frequently observed, was that they would all soon be dead. The voyeur is the victim, and anything that removes the terrifying spectacle is a mercy.

Perhaps it was Alfred Tennyson's short-sightedness which protected him from despair on his tour—or perhaps a more determined self-imposed myopia. The poet spent three months at Aubrey De Vere's Curragh Chase estate in County Limerick in early 1848; his conditions for accepting the invitation were that he should not be expected downstairs for breakfast, he should be able to smoke in the house, he must have half the day alone for writing—and there was to be no mention of Irish distress.[100] De Vere remembered that Tennyson was fond of reading poetry aloud to the family after dinner: 'on one occasion after finishing "A Sorrowful Tale" by Crabbe, [he] glanced round reproachfully and said, "I do not see that any of you are weeping!" '[101] Only Tennyson could have expected a family who were confronted daily with scenes of destitution and death to weep at a poem. Tennyson later visited the Knight of Kerry at Valencia to see the waves, of which he was passionately fond. A mysterious man, no doubt attracted by the poet's notoriously odd appearance, followed him up a mountain to ask conspiratorially: 'Be you from France?'[102] The only reference in his work to this visit, during which he must have witnessed—reluctantly—the most awful suffering and degradation, is the lyric 'The splendour falls on castle walls' in *The Princess*, inspired by hearing a bugler (probably Spillane, who is mentioned in most tourist guides) playing in Killarney.

For the post-Famine tourist, landscape and people were even more thoroughly divided. Travelling by railway distanced the observer: Spencer Hall described it as a photographic experience, a series of quick snapshots instead of the panorama previous travellers discussed.[103] The post-Famine tourist was haunted not by the ravening hordes, but by the symbol of their absence—the unroofed cabins. Sir Francis Head was so disturbed by the unroofed cabins of Ballinrobe that he had nightmares about the evicted tenants, and visited Lord Lucan to seek reassurance that eviction was necessary for progress. Although he and others were convinced that the ends

[99] Osborne, *Gleanings*, 74, 33, 39, 53.

[100] Robert Bernard Martin, *Tennyson: The Unquiet Heart* (Oxford: Oxford University Press and Faber & Faber, 1980), 318.

[101] Hallam Tennyson, *Alfred Lord Tennyson: A Memoir*, 2 vols. (London: Macmillan & Co. Ltd., 1897), i. 288.

[102] Ibid., 291–2.   [103] Spencer Hall, *Life and Death in Ireland*, 8.

justified the means, they remained uneasy. Even the pragmatic Harriet Martineau was chilled:

For miles together, in some places, there is scarcely a token of human presence but the useless gables and the empty doorways and window-spaces of pairs or rows of deserted cottages. There is something so painful—so even exasperating in this sight, that one wishes that a little more time and labour could be spared to level the walls, as well as take off the roof, when tenants are ejected, or go away of their own accord.[104]

Travellers attempted to assuage their discomfort at this sight by defining their distress as characteristically *English*: according to Tuke, 'it is impossible for an Englishman to contemplate one of these wholesale evictions without feelings of the deepest pity for the sufferers and indignation towards the inflictors', while Osborne asserted that 'the eye and heart of every Englishman' were 'painfully offended' by the sight of unroofed cabins.[105] The Englishman becomes a helpless bystander, witnessing the extermination of the Irish cottier by the Irish landlord. This discomfort is perhaps explained by the fact that the language of improvement had re-entered the Irish travel-book in the post-Famine period, with a colonial twist. The disaster could only be explained if there was some reason for the people to have been starved out—a hope for regeneration. Catherine O'Connell, revisiting Ireland in 1850, found 'a broken-spirited people' and a society in transition, 'crushed and altered' by the devastating experience.[106] The problem of over-population, cited as a major factor of Irish poverty in the pre-Famine period, no longer applied, and Ireland now appeared to be the perfect field for investment. William Bennet described the people as 'perfectly malleable' and ready to be 'socially remodelled' as part of England, for the first time since its conquest, and he subtitled his book 'The Character, Condition, and Prospects of the People'.[107] The dual meaning of the word 'prospect' emerged as the subtext of many post-Famine tours: when John Ashworth spoke of the 'glorious prospect I now enjoyed', he referred simultaneously to the view and the future riches he expected to extract from the land.[108] Ashworth, as an Englishman planning to emigrate to Ireland at a time when anyone who could get enough money was emigrating out of it, was highly sensitive to the paradoxical and

---

[104] Harriet Martineau, *Letters From Ireland* (London: John Chapman, 1852), 77.

[105] Tuke, *A Visit to Connaught*, 24; Osborne, *Gleanings*, 22.

[106] Catherine O'Connell, *Excursions in Ireland*, 223–4, 244.

[107] Bennet, *Narrative of a Recent Journey*, 120–3.

[108] John Ashworth, *The Saxon in Ireland: or, The Rambles of an Englishman in Search of a Settlement in the West of Ireland* (London: John Murray, 1851), 46.

morally suspect stance of those who sought to profit from Irish misery. He defended his own resettlement by arguing that emigration was entirely unnecessary: 'So long as such land remained in Ireland neglected and almost unappropriated, it was sheer wickedness to ship off luckless emigrants to the barren plains of Australia, or the ferny wastes of New Zealand.'[109] Indeed, in spite of the Malthusian paranoia about pre-Famine Ireland, no one seems to have been in favour of post-Famine emigration: Head described it as centrifugal ejection.[110] Yet advertisements for sales of Encumbered Estates recognized that unless it was clearly stated that the tenants were gone, no one would buy. If Irishmen would go, the conscience-salving argument went, it was the moral duty of Englishmen to inhabit and prosper.

Enthusiasm did not last long. Most of the purchasers in the Encumbered Estates Court were Irishmen, and Martineau's letters register her increasing despondence and loss of faith in a new Ireland. The idea that the Famine would be beneficial had taken the sting from the horrible deaths for her:

> It was this view which consoled us during many a day's journey through an almost unpeopled country, and through districts where the unroofed cottages outnumbered the occupied. It was this which kept up our spirits under the stories we have heard in workhouses, and the sight of crowds of orphans within and without the walls. And now, after all this, we find the landlords trying to bring back the old state of things—the potato diet—the competition for land, the sub letting, and all the consequent deterioration of land and people.[111]

Martineau and other travellers in 1852 (the year after the Great Exhibition, the symbol of the prosperity of the empire) were also appalled by the return of the potato blight, the ultimate sign that things had not changed for the better. Thomas Carlyle's apocalyptic tone would seem to have been justified: 'Society is at an *end* here, with the land uncultivated, and every second soul a pauper . . .'.[112]

The sense of a ghost-land, almost entirely deserted, is partly due to the expansion of railway travel, and the corresponding lack of contact with ordinary people. It is also partly due to the guilt of the survivor. Sir Lucius O'Brien, himself both an Irish landlord, implicated along with others in the clearances, and the brother of the transported rebel William Smith O'Brien, observed in 1848: 'When we remember how many have perished, both of high and low, rich and poor, in this calamity, while we remain

---

[109] Ibid., 146.　　　　　[110] Head, *A Fortnight in Ireland*, 235.
[111] Martineau, *Letters from Ireland*, 144–5.　　　　[112] Carlyle, *Reminiscences*, 206.

alive, we cannot but be deeply affected with the recollection.'[113] The survivors obviously suffered great psychological damage, and many simply
refused to speak of the Famine; when Sir Francis Head rather tactlessly
asked his driver if he had suffered much during the Famine, he received a
curt and indignant reply: 'And indade I did *not*, thank God!'[114] Cormac Ó
Gráda has noted that in all the accounts recorded by the Irish Folklore
Commission in the 1930s, 1940s, and 1950s, there was no mention of family members or relations as workhouse inmates:

This silence could mean that the descendants of inmates were not represented
among the narrators, or it may simply echo the shame of people forced to rely on
workhouse relief or the soup line. There are occasional mentions of family members who had been employed on the public works, but, significantly, they refer
mostly to people who served as foremen or clerks.[115]

The sense of shame, either for having suffered or for having survived, is
tangible. Even more striking than these evasions for the post-Famine traveller was the lack of contact with the people: Martineau described the few
people she met as 'chance survivors of some plague'.[116] The survivors
reacted with silence, allowing travel writers to mouth their empty optimism. The Famine had worked a great change for the better, they said; even
though people had died and fled their native land, still, better times were
coming, there was plenty to go round now, and the great generosity of
England to her Irish sister in her time of need had brought the Irish to a
true understanding of the benefits she received from the Union. Such
optimism was, of course, ill-founded. Many years later, Sidney Godolphin
Osborne, writing in the same newspaper that had printed his account of
Ireland in the late 1840s, traced the roots of Irish discontent to the Famine:

When I re-peruse the statements I published in your columns of what I saw in the
many miles I travelled in Ireland more than thirty years ago; when I had, from day
to day, to inspect the workhouses containing thousands under their roofs of this
race thus pauperised, hopeless, if disease spared them, ever again to find a home, I
felt satisfied that thus was sown the seed of a disaffection one day to bear bitter
fruit, and so I have lived to see it come to pass.[117]

[113] Sir Lucius O'Brien, *Ireland: The Late Famine, and the Poor Laws* (London: Hatchard
& Son, 1848), 5.
[114] Head, *A Fortnight in Ireland*, 197.
[115] Cormac Ó Gráda, *Black '47 and Beyond: The Great Irish Famine in History, Economy,
and Memory* (Princeton: Princeton University Press, 1999), 196.
[116] Martineau, *Letters from Ireland*, 114.
[117] Sidney Godolphin Osborne, *The Letters of S.G.O.: A Series of Letters on Public Affairs
Written by the Rev Lord Sidney Godolphin Osborne and Published in 'The Times' 1844–1888*, ed.
Arnold White, 2 vols. (London and Sydney: Griffith & Farren, 1890), i. 277–8.

The date was January 1886; the 'bitter fruit' was Home Rule agitation.

The silence of the spectre-victims descends on the survivors, and iron-ically, it has been left to the travel-books, limited, anachronistic, and one-sided as they are, to record the progress and effect of the catastrophe. Places once full of people were wiped from the map, and exist only in the recollections of English tourists: 'the place which once was Keem,' mused Martineau, 'still spoken of in the Irish guide-books as living, and moving, and having a being on earth'.[118] They read like elegies to the lost. In 'That The Science Of Cartography Is Limited', Eavan Boland explores the inability of the strictly visual, the lines and curves of the map of Ireland, to contain the horror of Famine: 'the line which says woodland and cries hunger | and gives out among sweet pine and cypress, | and finds no horizon | will not be there.'[119] The travellers, deprecating their ability to represent in words the terror 'this dark picture' inspired, often wished for the lines and curves they believed would be more faithful, not knowing that their faint reflections would be all that remained.[120] It is a monologue, because those other travellers, teeming the roads on the way to union-houses and ports and graves, did not have the time, or the energy, or the language, to let us see.

[118] Martineau, *Letters from Ireland*, 123–4.
[119] Eavan Boland, 'That The Science Of Cartography Is Limited', *In A Time Of Violence* (Manchester: Carcanet, 1994), 5.
[120] Bennet, *Narrative of a Recent Journey*, 19.

4
The Immigrant's Evasion: The Subtext of Trollope's 'Famine' Novels

In September 1841 the 26-year-old unknown Anthony Trollope arrived in Ireland to take up the position of clerk to the Post-Office Surveyor in Banagher, King's County. When he returned to England eighteen years later, he had established a reputation as a highly efficient trouble-shooter, and as the promising author of several novels and travel-books, including *The Warden* and *Barchester Towers*. He had been commissioned to write a leading serial for the *Cornhill Magazine*—*Framley Parsonage*—and was poised on the brink of his first major success. In England he had been neglected, indebted, maligned, and in absolute despair of ever improving his position. In Ireland he was respected and successful. There could be no higher accolade than this inclusion in the 'Domestic News' column of *The Nation*:

We see by the southern papers that, as the Kerry mail car was leaving Cork both springs broke and all the passengers, including Mr. Trollope, the post-office inspector, were pitched off, and a heap of luggage piled on and about them. This is the car of the substitution of which for a four-horse coach the Cork journals have been long complaining; but, as the post-office inspector shared in the present adventure, we may safely predict that redress is at hand.[1]

He was obviously accepted as a person of some standing in the community, even by those who would have been inclined to label Trollope as part of the English garrison. Trollope had no hesitation in attributing his metamorphosis to Ireland: 'But from the day on which I set my foot in Ireland all those evils went away from me. Since that time who has had a happier life than mine?'[2]

If the *Nation* extract signals Trollope's acceptance into Irish life as a professional, his inclusion in the *Oxford Companion to Irish Literature* recognizes how profoundly his Irish experience influenced his writing

---

[1] *Nation* (27 Nov. 1847), 957.
[2] Anthony Trollope, *An Autobiography*, 2 vols. (London: Oxford University Press, 1883), i. 80.

career.[3] He began and ended his literary life preoccupied with Irish themes, and he frequently returned to Irish settings and characters, attracted by an exoticism and perceived decadence that was not available to him in England.[4] To a certain extent, Trollope's outlook is Anglo-Irish: 'He is perhaps the only nineteenth-century Englishman—perhaps one of the few Englishmen in history—to have benefited from an involvement in what Conor Cruise O'Brien likes to call "the Irish predicament".'[5] He certainly came to identify himself strongly with the Irish and, even after he returned to England, the bond remained unbroken: 'when I meet an Irishman abroad, I always recognize in him more of a kinsman than I do in an Englishman'.[6]

In the context of mid-nineteenth-century Ireland, however, Trollope's happiness is deeply ironic. As Irish travel narratives of the time testify, pre-Famine Ireland was often as miserable and poverty-stricken as it was after the potato blight had struck. The agricultural depression that followed the end of the Napoleonic Wars was still having repercussions, and the 1830s and 1840s saw an increase in agrarian unrest. O'Connell's monster meetings and announcement of 'Repeal Year' in 1843 posed a serious threat to the Union, while his trial and conviction for conspiracy in 1844 caused uproar, and an ignominious reversal in the House of Lords following allegations of jury-packing. Thackeray's depression seems a much more natural response than Trollope's identification. Trollope appears to have been unaffected by the misery around him. Entering his magical 'Tír na nOg',[7] the years of oppression and depression were sloughed from him, and he began life anew. He was no longer in the ambiguous social position of son of a bankrupt lawyer and a woman who wrote for money. Instead, his position as an Englishman and a Protestant seemed to assure his place in the Ascendancy. Living in the very house in Clonmel said to have been occupied by Cromwell after his conquest of the town in 1650, Trollope appears as a symbol of colonial power, blissfully insulated from the ravages exacted on the peasant population around him.

Yet, as a writer, Trollope emerges as 'a uniquely valuable interpreter of mid-nineteenth century Ireland', perhaps because of, rather than in spite

---

[3] Robert Welch (ed.), *Oxford Companion to Irish Literature* (Oxford: Clarendon Press, 1996).

[4] Compare, for example, the graphic treatment of seduction and betrayal in *An Eye For An Eye* with the defensive preface to *The Vicar of Bullhampton*.

[5] Robert Tracy, ' "The Unnatural Ruin": Trollope and Nineteenth-Century Irish Fiction', *Nineteenth-Century Fiction*, 37 (Dec. 1982), 358–82, at 359.

[6] Quoted in N. John Hall, *Trollope: A Biography* (Oxford: Clarendon Press, 1991), 85.

[7] 'Land of Youth.'

of, his foreignness.[8] In his Irish writings, especially those that could be
termed his 'Famine' works—*The Macdermots of Ballycloran*, *The Kellys
and the O'Kellys*, and *Castle Richmond*, and the non-fictional *Six Letters to
the Examiner* and *An Autobiography* —Trollope is indeed a valuable interpreter—with the proviso that the reader is able to deconstruct the narrative. For Trollope's historiography is heavily skewed by his reluctance to
admit the extent of the catastrophe. The relief inspector who reported on
soup-kitchens in Clonmel in January 1847 was greatly distressed by the
experience, writing: '*I have witnessed such scenes . . .*'.[9] Trollope, who as a
resident in the same town must have been accosted daily by the same
scenes, echoed this sentiment in his attack on Sidney Godolphin Osborne
in *Six Letters*: 'Heaven knows that he can describe no worse than I have
witnessed.'[10] As to Trollope's personal trauma, however, we know nothing, as he denied that he witnessed anything at all. The fact is that the
Famine, and later the Land War, were to Trollope irrefutable proofs of his
alterity, placing an intolerable strain upon his cherished relationship with
Ireland by forcing him to choose between conflicting loyalties. To cata-
logue the extremity of the Famine would be to question the very Union
which enabled him to be stationed in Ireland, while to remain silent would
be a betrayal of the Irish people. As an English civil servant, it was
inevitable that Trollope would feel obliged to publicly support the policies
of the British government in Ireland; but as a private resident, a sensitive
and highly observant individual, it is hardly to be expected that he could
mechanically mouth government opinions without reservations. Trollope
therefore embarked on a process of historiographical pluralism. The public Trollope—the 'official' Trollope, as Overton calls him—stridently
supported the Encumbered Estates Bill, as the 'prolonged existence' of
improvident landlords was 'an injustice to those who are still able to keep
their tenants'; but the private 'unofficial' Trollope remembered friend-
ships with these same landlords, and implicitly questioned the integrity of
the bill: 'Poor Jack! I fear that the Encumbered Estates Court sent him
altogether adrift upon the world.'[11] Forced by his nationality to record the
Famine 'I will not say as an alien or foreigner but still as a stranger',

[8] Oliver MacDonagh, *The Nineteenth Century Novel and Irish Social History: Some
Aspects* (Dublin: National University of Ireland, 1970), 9.
[9] Quoted in Victoria Glendinning, *Trollope* (London: Pimlico, 1992), 164–5.
[10] Anthony Trollope, *Six Letters to the Examiner 1849–50*, ed. Lance O. Tingay (London:
Silverbridge Press, 1987), 6.
[11] Ibid., 24; Anthony Trollope, 'The O'Conors of Castle Conor', *Tales of All Countries*
(London: Chapman & Hall, 1867), 32.

Trollope's anxiety about British government policy is submerged in his writing, only to emerge clandestinely, in the subtext of his Irish novels.[12] The fact that Trollope's first novel, *The Macdermots of Ballycloran*, is a very powerful Irish tragedy reveals how much he had learnt since arriving in this 'land flowing with fun and whisky'.[13] Even the comic novelist Charles Lever, who made his living by exploiting the English misconception of the laughing Irishman, recognized its anomaly: 'Melancholy is indeed the badge of all our tribe . . . The poetry of the land, its music breathes but one voice, and that is one of sorrow . . .'.[14] Lever's work reflects his understanding of what English readers wanted, rather than his own conception of Irish character. Trollope had yet to learn the distinction, and was beginning his career with a distinctively Irish novel, employing the fall-of-the-house theme central to the genre.[15] He had been familiar with Maria Edgeworth's novels since boyhood; her *Castle Rackrent* is echoed in the title of his *Castle Richmond*, and both deal with the demise of the landlord class. He also read Lady Morgan, the Banims, Griffin, and Carleton at Coole Park, the home of his Harrow contemporary, William Gregory.[16] He was evidently influenced by these writers: for example, there are clear parallels between *An Eye For An Eye* and Griffin's *The Collegians*, and between *The Macdermots* and Morgan's *The Wild Irish Girl*. The prototype for Morgan's Prince of Inismore, and Trollope's senile drunken patriarch, share the name Macdermot; Trollope is perhaps gesturing towards his deliberate degeneration of the old Irish aristocracy and stock Irish themes. Feemy Macdermot, who walks 'as if all the blood of the old Irish Princes were in her veins', has exchanged the robes of Morgan's Glorvina for a dirty dress, the harp for a novel, the wealthy English lover for an illegitimate Protestant policeman, and the legendary Irish chastity for a death by miscarriage.[17] The age-old stereotypes are evoked only to be destroyed, and replaced with a stark social realism.

From the outset, Trollope displayed an unusual understanding of Irish society, where misconception was more often the badge of residence than

---

[12] Trollope, *Six Letters*, 5.   [13] Trollope, *Autobiography*, i. 82.
[14] Charles Lever, 'The Irish Sketch-Book', *Dublin University Magazine*, 21 (June 1843), 547–55, at 551.
[15] It is perhaps significant that Feemy Macdermot's seducer is named Ussher, recalling not only the famous seventeenth-century Archbishop of Armagh, whose chronology is still used in English Bibles, but also Poe's 'The Fall of the House of Usher', which first appeared in 1840.
[16] Hall, *Trollope*, 97–8.
[17] Anthony Trollope, *The Macdermots of Ballycloran*, 3 vols. (London: T. C. Newby, 1847), i. 17; the heroine of Trollope's *Castle Richmond*, Clara Desmond, may have come by her name through Morgan's *St Clair; or the Heiress of Desmond*.

perception. Most often cited both by contemporary reviewers and subsequent critics is his remarkable religious tolerance. The Ireland he portrays in the 1840s and 1850s is one of Protestant bigotry, and Trollope is
more than ready to expose O'Joscelyn in *The Kellys* and the Townsends
and Aunt Letty in *Castle Richmond* to the reader's supposedly superior
understanding. His patriarch priests—Father Giles of the autobiographical 'Father Giles of Ballymoy', Father John McGrath of *The Macdermots*,
Father Geoghegan of *The Kellys*, and Father Barney McCarthy of *Castle
Richmond*—are warm and liberal, and if not quite 'gentlemen', are perfectly adequate company for gentlemen. Trollope's novels of this period
have none of the evangelical fervour of those written by English men and
women after the re-establishment of the Catholic hierarchy in England in
1850.

Perhaps more remarkable is his mapping of social ambivalence in
Ireland. His examination of Ribbonism in *The Macdermots*, for example,
exposes the paranoia of his countrymen, and his Irish co-religionists,
which converted 'the scattered outrages of a suffering peasantry into a
political and religious insurrection, supported by French influence, and
having for its object the restoration of the Stuarts, and of the Catholic religion'.[18] Trollope revealed the falsity of this rationale by diversifying the
social structure of Ribbonism. The nominal peasant, Joe Reynolds, drifts
into Ribbonism because society has failed to provide for him: 'he was a
reckless man, originally rendered so by inability to pay high rent for miserably bad land, and afterwards becoming doubly so from having recourse
to illegal means to ease him of his difficulties'.[19] The middleman, Pat
Brady, who would have no hesitation in applying to the law to prosecute a
tenant, is a Ribbonman for cynical self-serving reasons. Trollope's master-
stroke, however, was to involve Thady Macdermot with this supposedly
anarchic force; he has recognized the fact that many of those involved in
agrarian crime were fairly well off, frequently the sons of strong farmers,
and has simultaneously exploded the stereotypical polarity of landlord and
tenant.

An Irish landlord, in the perception of a typical English reader of the
1840s, was irresponsible, profligate, and indifferent to the tenants he rack-
rented and evicted. A landlord in name, Thady is a vastly different creature from the idle rich of Brown Hall. His language, in both content and
form, marks him as a member of the oppressed majority: 'I'd strike a blow

---

[18] George Cornewall Lewis, *On Local Disturbances in Ireland; and on the Irish Church
Question* (London: B. Fellowes, 1836), 14.
[19] Trollope, *Macdermots*, i. 60.

for the counthry, and then, if I war hung or shot, or murthered any way, devil a care.'[20] One review of *The Macdermots* read such 'startling anomalies' as Thady's social position as evidence of Trollope's satiric intention: 'there is an air of tarnished chivalry in the demeanour of Thady, the last representative of the M'Dermots, which is infinitely amusing'.[21] Such a ludicrous interpretation sheds light on the distance between Trollope and the average contemporary English commentator on 'the Irish Question'. Thady's social isolation, far from providing amusement, is his ultimate downfall. An unlikely landlord, he cannot find fellowship among his 'feudal vassals': 'He had not slept, eat, and worked with them—he was not leagued to them by equal rank, equal wants, and equal sufferings.'[22] Scraping a living in the hinterland between landlord and poor cottier, Thady is less a symbol of the old Celtic order than of the new rising Catholic generation, legally emancipated in 1829, but still reeking of poteen and firearms, and still to be distrusted. Thady's social ambivalence enables his prosecutors to present his private act of defence as a public act of violence, an attack on the state rather than on his sister's seducer. He is judged as a landlord, by other landlords, and found unworthy of his social position. He is deviant, a landlord who has crossed the artificial boundary between landlord and tenant. So shocking a betrayal as this has profound social implications: the aptly named prosecutor Allewinde tells the jury that 'if you value the peace of your country—the comfort of your hearths—the safety of your houses—and the protection of your property', then Thady Macdermot must hang.[23] As in his treatment of the O'Connell trial in *The Kellys*, however, Trollope undermines the integrity of this ruling by questioning the justice of those who judge. The same landlords who are sitting in judgement on Thady are themselves judged and found wanting. Thady shows his mettle in refusing to sell the land to Keegan, who plans to eject the tenants. The wealthy Jonas Brown pays his labourers a starvation wage, while the supposedly beneficent Sir Michael Gibson is 'neither a bad nor a good landlord—that is to say, his land was seldom let for more than double its value'.[24] These are the men who judge Thady on his misconduct as a landlord, and these are the men who send him to the gallows, unperturbed by the fact that their prejudices and fears, and their ill-treatment of tenants, are more responsible for Thady's death than his own actions.

[20] Ibid., 101–2.
[21] *New Monthly Magazine* (June 1847); quoted in Donald Smalley (ed.), *Trollope: The Critical Heritage* (London and New York: Routledge & Kegan Paul, 1969), 552.
[22] Trollope, *Macdermots*, ii. 97.   [23] Ibid., iii. 278.   [24] Ibid., 21.

Trollope raised the topical question of the absenteeism of Irish land-lords in all his Irish novels; absenteeism was a key issue in the Irish debate, and fruitful ground for novels such as Maria Edgeworth's *The Absentee* (1812). In 1849 *The Times*, commenting on the death of Edmund Knox, Lord Bishop of Limerick, noted that the bishop drew £4,973 per year from his diocese, yet lived in Italy: 'But we cannot forget that while the Whig Bishop of LIMERICK was absent in the "sweet south," the peasantry of his diocese were perishing by famine, pestilence, and cold.'[25] Trollope's contempt for this class is nowhere so virulent as in *The Macdermots*. His vehemence may in part be traced to the rancour he felt for William Maberly, his previous civil-service superior, who was himself an Anglo-Irish absentee; this antipathy becomes focused in the novel in outrage at the conduct of Lord Birmingham. The squalid cabin on Birmingham's land at Mohill prefigures the Famine in the misery, disease, and malnutri-tion it fosters, and the injustice of the land system is condensed into one short sentence: 'And yet for this abode the man pays rent.'[26] The situation is ironized by Lord Birmingham's active intervention on behalf of every people but his own. The narrator's diatribe indicates great empathy for the people whose welfare rests in the hands of the absentee:

Yet shall no one be blamed for the misery which belonged to him; for the squalid sources of the wealth with which Poles were fed, and literary paupers clothed? was no one answerable for the grim despair of that half-starved wretch, whom but now we saw, looking down so sadly on the young sufferers to whom he had given life and poverty? That can hardly be.[27]

That can hardly be. And yet it was the case, and not only for absentee Irish landlords. In 1848, the year after the publication of *The Macdermots*, in spite of the revulsion of feeling caused by the Young Ireland rebellion, *The Times* was still outraged that balls were being held to raise money for the Poles:

We protest against that morbid sectarianism of sentiment which expands itself to all that is distant and remote, but which locks itself up against the appeal of domes-tic supplication and the eloquence of contiguous suffering—which has wine and oil for the denizen of Liberia and the slave of Cuba, or the exile of Poland; but which has neither scrip, nor coat, nor kindly words for the misery which pines in an English alley or an Irish hovel.[28]

The controlled anger of Trollope's passage demands retribution from the ultimate source of this misery, but this is where his argument founders, as

---

25 *The Times* (10 May 1849), 5.   26 Trollope, *Macdermots*, i. 204.
27 Ibid., 208–9.   28 *The Times* (11 Nov. 1848), 4.

he has deliberately elided this ultimate source. A self-conscious awareness of his own exteriority seems to have led Trollope to systematically avoid an English–Irish confrontation, and to concentrate instead on internal divisions such as rent and religion. Like the Banims and Griffin, he employed the unpalatable figures of the bigoted Ulster Protestant Ussher and turncoat Irishman Brady as objects of violence, suppressing the more explosive Anglo-Hibernian antibiosis. Trollope's fictional Englishmen do not have his good fortune in Ireland: the Molletts of *Castle Richmond* prosper in their blackmail until they confront Sir Thomas on his own ground, and Fred Neville ends up at the bottom of a cliff in County Clare in *An Eye For An Eye*. By highlighting the in-fighting of Irishmen, Trollope can avoid a confrontation that would alienate him.

Trollope was obviously aware of the potential for violence in Ireland. In *An Autobiography* he joked: 'The Irish people did not murder me, nor did they even break my head.'[29] While he is mocking both English prejudice and Irish patois—the use of the word 'murder' for any injury—the brutality of his depictions of Irish violence betray a certain anxiety. Archibald Green, the narrator of the autobiographical anecdote 'Father Giles of Ballymoy'—said to have occurred on Trollope's first night in Drumsna, the setting of *The Macdermots*—is apprehensive on arrival in this last bastion of Old Ireland, fearing 'that Ballymoy was probably one of those places so far removed from civilisation and law, as to be an unsafe residence for an English Protestant'.[30] After throwing—of all people—the parish priest, the epitome of Irish Catholicism, down the stairs, this English Protestant is almost proved right; an angry mob gathers, and he has to be put in gaol overnight for his own protection. Violence is all-pervasive in Trollope's Irish fiction, from his own near-lynching to the murder and mutilation of *The Macdermots*, the revenge of Mrs O'Hara in *An Eye For An Eye*, and the shooting of young Florian Jones in *The Landleaguers*. There is no romance about the two blows that shatter Ussher's skull, and we are spared nothing of the mutilation of Hyacinth Keegan:

a third, and a fourth, and a fifth [blow] descended, crushing the bone, dividing the marrow, and ultimately severing the foot from the leg . . . he got up and hobbled to the nearest cabin, dragging after him the mutilated foot, which still attached itself to his body by some cartilages, which had not been severed, and by the fragments of his boots and trowsers . . .[31]

[29] Trollope, *Autobiography*, i. 86.
[30] Anthony Trollope, 'Father Giles of Ballymoy', *Lotta Schmidt and Other Stories* (London: Alexander Strahan, 1867), 143–4.
[31] Trollope, *Macdermots*, iii. 13.

By focusing on the tenuous relationships between landlords, tenants, and middlemen, Trollope attempted to isolate this violence within Ireland. Indeed, this is the only 'Irish' novel Trollope wrote that is set wholly in Ireland: the threat is confined, the Irish alone suffer, and the English–Irish confrontation is reduced to the culture shock encountered by the English audience reading it. But by attempting to avoid the colonial question and focus on absenteeism, the subtextual inference is exposed: if it were not for the Union, there would be no absentees.

The horror of the cabin at Mohill is a single unrepeated incident, a moment of anger evoked to chastise Lord Birmingham. While violence is all-pervasive, pre-famine poverty, 'the face of the popular starvation', is rarely glimpsed, and for the most part the starving are kept discreetly out of sight.[32] To portray them would be to raise the question of the partnership of this regressive agricultural society with the most progressive industrial nation in the world. This underclass, which may be said to include the majority of Irishmen, emerges only in subtext: all of the misery, apathy, and hunger of the stereotypical Irishman are incarnated in one figure—Andy McEvoy.

Thady, hiding from the law in McEvoy's cabin, would rather give himself up to be hanged than remain in this soul-destroying lethargy: 'it was as sitting with a dead body, or a ghost, as that sitting there with that lifeless, but yet breathing creature'.[33] The old man is activated only by food; he watches Thady intently while he eats, then gobbles up what the young man has left. Apathy and hunger, the two characteristics most remarked upon by travellers such as Thackeray and Carlyle, are here taken to extremes: 'though he might have no demon thoughts to rack his brain, the vulture in his stomach tortured him as much'.[34] Thady's overwhelming desire is to escape this man: his horror can be read as Trollope's reaction to the starving Irish, and his need to escape them. The onset of Famine, the engendering of thousands of Andy McEvoys, meant that he had to adopt strategies of avoidance, and drive the issues deeper into subtext.

While he acknowledged that *The Macdermots* failed miserably with the reading public—only *La Vendée* was to fail more completely—Trollope recommended it as 'worth reading by any one who wishes to understand what Irish life was before the potato disease, the famine, and the Encumbered Estates Bill'.[35] This is the key to the tenor of *The Macdermots*:

---

[32] William Makepeace Thackeray, *The Irish Sketch Book* (London: Chapman & Hall, 1843), i. 146.

[33] Trollope, *Macdermots*, ii. 345.   [34] Ibid., 352.

[35] Trollope, *Autobiography*, i. 94.

it is the only one of Trollope's novels born free from the original sin of Famine. As Trollope was signing the agreement for *The Macdermots* with Newby in September 1845, the news was breaking that a mysterious disease was destroying the potato crop, and nothing would ever be the same. Free for the moment from this primordial guilt, Trollope had unleashed in *The Macdermots* an extremely powerful critique of the state of Ireland, highlighting absenteeism, rackrenting, intolerance of Catholics, and the injustice of the law. He would not be so critical after the disaster: 'Never again was Trollope so strong a tribune of the people.'[36]

The Famine is also the key to the early reception of *The Macdermots*, which R. C. Terry terms 'the most neglected first novel of any English author of recognised achievement'.[37] In view of the novel's criticisms of the landed gentry, its scenes of blatant violence, and its unfortunate timing—finally appearing in 1847, the so-called 'Famine Year', when the media were in Ireland-overload—it is hardly surprising that many of the reviews were bad. Trollope claimed that there were no reviews of the novel in England and no one in Ireland had read it; in fact, there were at least seven reviews, and the novel was well enough known in Ireland for Isaac Butt to quote it at the trial of post-office worker Mary O'Reilly in 1849, at which Trollope was a key witness. Whatever Trollope's reasons for suppressing this information, he had clearly decided that the frankness of *The Macdermots* had been a mistake. While his next novel continued with the Irish theme, Trollope compromised with his English audience by transforming the tragic Irish experience into a comedy of manners.

While *The Kellys and the O'Kellys* was no more of a financial success than *The Macdermots*, the reviewers heaved a sigh of relief: 'though not more powerful, it is less painful'.[38] After the unmitigated gloom of the first novel, and contemporary reports of the Famine in British newspapers, the return to a Leveresque Ireland was more than welcome. But by the time the novel appeared in 1848, English readers had entered a phase of compassion fatigue, and had been disgusted by the Rising, and this is reflected in the early critical reception: 'we cannot sympathize at the present moment with the whimsicalities of that strange, wild imaginative people, herein so characteristically described, when these whims are exhausting themselves in disloyalty and rebellion, and threatening rapine and bloodshed'.[39] Timing is also central to the novel itself, which is atypical of

---

[36] R. C. Terry, *The Artist in Hiding* (London and Basingstoke: Macmillan, 1977), 187.
[37] Ibid., 181.
[38] *Athenaeum* (15 July 1848), 701; quoted in Smalley (ed.), *Critical Heritage*, 547.
[39] *New Monthly Magazine* (Aug. 1848), quoted in Smalley (ed.), *Critical Heritage*, 555.

Trollope in its precise dating. The novel opens with the O'Connell trial in the first months of 1844, and the main action is concluded with the wedding of Frank and Fanny on 21 May 1844. Anty's letter to Barry is dated February 1844, and Kilcullen arrives at Grey Abbey on 3 April 1844.[40] The reason for such precise references is clear: Trollope was trying to establish and reiterate the fact that the Famine has not yet happened. In this retrospective treatment of Ireland on the very precipice of disaster, Trollope could not avoid historical inevitability; the Famine was imminent in the future of his protagonists, and in the minds of his contemporary audience. There is a singular lack of suspense maintained on the surface level of the story, as we are constantly reminded that Frank will succeed in the end: 'They might all have stayed at home; for Fanny Wyndham will never become Lady Kilcullen.'[41] Complicity has been established between author and reader by siting the narrative immediately prior to the inevitable Famine, so there remains no need for secrecy. Trollope has appropriated the role of the Irish *seanchaí*, relating a story his audience has heard many times, maintaining an artificial suspense with stock phrases such as 'Wait till I tell you'—the refrain of the unlovely O'Joscelyn as he expounds his particular brand of Irish history.

Yet all is not revealed. William Trevor asserted that *The Kellys* 'is best described by its secondary title, *Landlords and Tenants*, since that is what it is about'.[42] Yet, on the surface, this is manifestly what the novel is *not* about. Trollope used the subtitle as a paradoxical exegesis, revealing precisely because it conceals, suggesting that we look beneath the comic love story to the deeper issues submerged in the text. The trial of O'Connell, which Trollope mistakenly perceived as the end of political agitation in Ireland, is reduced to the level of a slanging match in Mrs Kelly's shop: 'Conspiracy, is it? . . . maybe, Ma'am, he'll get you put in along with Dan and Father Tierney, God bless them! It's conspiracy they're afore the judges for.'[43] The trial becomes the frame and background to the love story, a debased metaphor lurking suspiciously behind the comedy. Similarly, the patriotism of Young Ireland is parodied in the superficial nationalism of the names of Frank's horses—Finn McCoul, Granuell, and Brien Boru—and Martin's annual subscription to *The Nation*, while narrow sectarianism is mocked in

[40] Anthony Trollope, *The Kellys and the O'Kellys, or Landlords and Tenants, A Tale of Irish Life*, 3 vols. (London: Henry Colburn, 1848), i. 270; ii. 85; iii. 25.

[41] Ibid., 49.

[42] William Trevor, 'Introduction' to *The Kellys and the O'Kellys* (Oxford: Oxford University Press, 1982), p. ix.

[43] Trollope, *Kellys*, i. 153.

the O'Joscelyns. These aspects of the 'Irish Question' are translated to the comic sphere; but the landlord–tenant relationship referred to in the subtitle is ominously absent from Trollope's microcosm. The only such relationship we observe is that of The O'Kelly—Viscount Ballindine—and his distant relation, Martin Kelly, and this is not a representative relationship. Martin is obviously a rather well-off farmer from a solid mercantile family, and by the end of the novel he has become a landlord himself. He approaches Frank not to pay the rent, but to ask advice about eloping with an heiress. In a distinct reversal of roles, Frank borrows money from Martin. The title of the novel echoes Lady Morgan's *The O'Briens and the O'Flahertys* (1827), in which we find a corresponding relationship. The patriotic young aristocrat Murrogh O'Brien is deified by his faithful wood-kerne foster-brother and distant kinsman Shane na Brien, who act as his personal bodyguard. This powerful bond, the worship of 'the ould blood', has in *The Kellys* degenerated to purely financial terms. Money is the measure of success in *The Kellys*, and in the context of Famine Ireland, this is imperative: our 'heroes' have been sent out to accumulate as much cash as possible, and they must do so before a year has passed.

This financial anxiety, which provides the impulse behind the scenarios—the protagonists' marital bargains, Frank's gambling, and Barry's plot to kill his sister for her money—is the only ripple on the surface of the story, the only premonitory indication of imminent catastrophe. As MacDonagh says of *The Kellys*, 'In terms of conventional Irish historiography, it is all rather like an account of France between 1789 and 1799 with scarcely a mention of the revolution or the Directory.'[44] Instead of an account of the Famine, Trollope provides a fictional re-creation of the last months of pre-Famine Ireland, a revision that enables him to avert the disaster, at least for the chosen few. He appears to be preparing his microcosm for the Famine, by providing his 'heroes' with enough cash to make them immune, and by replacing irresponsible Anglo-Irish landlords and turncoat Irish middlemen with more conscientious individuals. Fanny Wyndham's £20,000 is not enough to shore up Kelly's Court, so Trollope throws in an extra £100,000 by killing off her brother Harry, just to make sure. Barry Lynch is exiled for treating his tenants as a by-product of the land. These invisible tenants are pawns in his plot to kill Anty: Barry offers to eject them from fifty acres and give the land to Dr Colligan at a nominal rent in return for the murder of his sister. Ejected tenants had become a *cause célèbre* by the time Trollope was writing *The Kellys*; cases such as the

44 MacDonagh, *Nineteenth Century Novel*, 9.

Gerrard evictions had been condemned by *The Times* and in the House of Commons. By the time the novel was published, however, the murder of Major Mahon had turned the tide of popular opinion. Nevertheless, Trollope was resolutely anti-eviction, as can be seen in the thwarting not only of Barry Lynch, but of Keegan in *The Macdermots*. In view of the clearances that were taking place all over Ireland as this scene was written, Barry's deal would have been as fatal to the tenants as to Anty. The rakish Kilcullen, already £80,000 in debt and with no interest in his estate, is similarly exiled. Kilcullen shares his name with the town Thackeray wrote of in 1842 as the first place where he encountered distress on his visit to Ireland, perhaps indicating the kind of landlord Kilcullen would have been during the Famine; Kilcullen's failure to extract Fanny's money can be seen as a moral judgement on his neglect of duty.[45] Frank, in contrast, often proclaims his disgust for absentees: 'Well, I hope I'll never live out of Ireland . . . a poor absentee landlord is a great curse to his country; and that's what I hope I'll never be.'[46] Kilcullen proves to be an unsuitable landlord, and becomes a part of his father's clearance programme, demanding money to emigrate: 'An eldest son would be a very difficult tenant to eject summarily.'[47] Frank, having proved his willingness to remain in Ireland, carries his bride and her fortune back to Kelly's Court, and will presumably survive the onslaught. The whole novel is 'a comic blue-print for social and economic recovery, which is to be effected by injecting fresh capital and renewing the partnership between landlord and tenant'.[48] Trollope orchestrates this regeneration from the other bank of the abyss, building an economic bridge to lead those he can to safety.

By giving *The Kellys* the subtitle *Landlords and Tenants*, and then failing to portray this relationship, Trollope perhaps also implies the disintegration of that other unrepresented partnership, the Union. Frank's counterpart in *The O'Briens and the O'Flahertys* is exiled because of his support for the Society of United Irishmen, whose abortive uprising in 1798 contributed to the Union of 1800. By this Union, Frank O'Kelly has lost both his name and his connection to his people. By echoing Morgan's novel in his title, Trollope emphasizes the disjunction of feudal values post-Union: Frank and Martin can no longer share the relationship of Murrogh O'Brien and Shane na Brien because Frank has lost his name. The Union reduced his grandfather to a court lackey, ruined his estate through the absenteeism

---

[45] Thackeray, *Irish Sketch Book*, i. 45.   [46] Trollope, *Kellys*, i. 74.
[47] Ibid., iii. 146.
[48] Bill Overton, *The Unofficial Trollope* (Brighton and Totowa, NJ: Harvester and Barnes & Noble, 1982), 20–1.

of both his father and grandfather, and bestowed upon him the un-Irish title Viscount Ballindine—'a more substantial though not a more respected title'—which translates him, denying the atavism of his Irishness.[49] Frank's dislocation and economic penury are paradigmatic of Ireland under the Union, in desperate need of a Trollopian rescue operation. Beneath the humorous courtship-and-marriage plot lies a serious subtextual appraisal of the forced 'marriage' of Ireland to England: 'It wasn't just the plight of the O'Kelly estate that grew from the Union.'[50]

Speaking of the conception and gestation of the ideas that he expressed in his *Six Letters to the Examiner* during the Famine, Trollope explained: 'My mind at the time was busy with the matter . . .'.[51] *The Kellys*, written as the relief operation was in progress, reveals how a mind 'busy with the matter' of Famine concealed its anxieties in subtext. *The Six Letters* were written between 1849 and 1850 in a spirit of hot-headed defence against the implications of Lord Sidney Godolphin Osborne's letters to *The Times*. They address the issue more directly than *The Kellys*, by actually admitting the Famine had occurred, yet obliquely, by describing the catastrophe in negatives: we approach it through a process of elimination, through what Trollope did *not* see, rather than what he did. His castigation of Osborne's anecdotal evidence—'what do such tales, true as they are, prove to us, but that there has been a famine and a plague in the land?'—gestures towards his own avoidance of fictional representation at this time.[52] His retort reveals the agenda of the *Six Letters*, which was to describe not the Famine, but Famine *relief*. Thirteen years would pass before Trollope wrote his own tale of the 'Famine Year', intertexing the polemic of the *Six Letters* with his narrative in order to make it self-destruct.

Trollope was well aware from past experience that Irish stories did not sell. Newby warned him in 1846 that Irish novels were 'very unpopular', and after the failure of *The Kellys*, Colburn acerbically commented: 'it is evident that readers do not like novels on Irish subjects as well as on others'.[53] Later, George Smith rejected *Castle Richmond* for the *Cornhill*. Fictional Barsetshire was proving far more popular than factual Ireland, and Trollope's reputation was established because he abandoned *Castle Richmond* to write *Framley Parsonage*. Trollope acknowledges the possibility of defeat in the opening lines of *Castle Richmond*: 'I wonder whether

[49] Trollope, *Kellys*, i. 30.   [50] Overton, *Unofficial Trollope*, 21.
[51] Trollope, *Autobiography*, i. 109.   [52] Trollope, *Six Letters*, 6.
[53] *The Letters of Anthony Trollope*, Vol One: *1835–1870*, ed. N. John Hall (Stanford: Stanford University Press, 1983), 13; Trollope, *Autobiography*, i. 105.

the novel-reading world—that part of it, at least, which may honour my pages—will be offended if I lay the plot of this story in Ireland!'[54] Yet he obstinately persisted with his Irish story, in spite of the overwhelming risk of rejection. In 1859, Trollope was transferred back to England, and *Castle Richmond* was conceived as a farewell to Ireland, a final statement: 'I am now leaving the Green Isle and my old friends, and would fain say a word of them as I do so. If I do not say that word now it will never be said.'[55] It is an auspicious opening, proleptic of revelation; and as Trollope was also revising *The Macdermots* in 1860, removing three chapters in order to intensify the tragedy, one might expect this 'word' to be of great significance. But the novel emerges as a didactic near-allegory of the merciful destruction of the nation, a moral tale forged from the material of the *Six Letters*. Furthermore, despite the blustering loyalty to 'the Green Isle', *Castle Richmond* is a farewell to Ireland that resists its Irish setting. The story is set precisely, in a part of Ireland Trollope had lived in and knew well, but it is then transferred wholesale out of Ireland: 'as regards its appearance Castle Richmond might have been in Hampshire or Essex; and as regards his property, Sir Thomas Fitzgerald might have been a Leicestershire baronet'.[56] Trollope is establishing that Sir Thomas will be a landlord along English lines and, unlike Irish landlords, will not neglect his tenants. But he is also in effect denying the testimony of contemporary travel-books—which insist on the absolute otherness of Ireland, and resist any comparison to England—in order to make the Union a tangible, physical fact. Post-Famine Ireland, it seems, is no longer a comfortable residence for Trollope's protagonists, and in *Castle Richmond*, as in *Phineas Finn*, *An Eye For An Eye*, and *The Landleaguers*, it proves impossible to keep people in the beleaguered country. The Fitzgeralds are ostensibly English in manners and tastes: both Sir Thomas and Herbert were educated in England, while Lady Fitzgerald and Lady Desmond were born there, the latter being 'English to the backbone'.[57] Their troubles originate in England, with the odious Molletts, but so does their salvation, in the form of the lawyer Prendergast. Indeed, Herbert revolves on the opposite axis of Trollope's wheel of fortune: Trollope's life was transformed in Ireland, while Herbert is restored to prosperity in England.

The interplay of Anglo and Hibernian 'plots' seems to gesture towards the simultaneous participation and abstraction of their English author in this Irish catastrophe. Trollope is fiercely defensive of his right to pronounce on Ireland. His tone is above all possessive. The ultimate rebuke

---

[54] Anthony Trollope, *Castle Richmond*, 3 vols. (London: Chapman & Hall, 1860), i. 1.
[55] Ibid., 3.   [56] Ibid., 5.   [57] Ibid., 16.

to Osborne is: 'I understood the country much better than he did'; it is reminiscent of Charles Lever's reaction to Thackeray as a tourist, as opposed to a better-informed resident.[58] In *Castle Richmond*, he defies anyone to dispute his claims: 'if I ought to know anything about any place, I ought to know something about Ireland'.[59] He seeks to dispel all doubt about the tendentious issues raised in the novel by inserting himself into the narrative as a primary eyewitness: 'I was in the country, travelling always through it, during the whole period . . .'.[60] Yet this proof of participation also indicates abstraction: the geographic spread of his knowledge is devalued by the transitory nature of travel. He does not engage, he merely spectates. By asserting his supremacy as the voyeur of misery, Trollope acknowledges that he was outside the experience, that for him at least there was always the possibility of escape.

Mary Hamer asserts that the significance of the Famine setting of *Castle Richmond* is that 'the main plot is constantly diminished by comparison with poverty and starvation'.[61] This *should* be the case but, on the contrary, the Famine victims are consistently effaced from the main plot. The decline and death of Sir Thomas overshadow the starvation of his tenants, and the mind of the reader, like those of the Fitzgeralds, is kept 'intent on other things'.[62] Matt Mollett is so preoccupied with his own misery that even in the presence of the starving he cannot transcend his own personal despair: 'But what were their rags and starvation to him? He was worse off than they were. They were merely dying, as all men must do. But he was inhabiting a hell on earth, which no man need do.'[63] The Famine struggles to intrude upon the narrative and displace the loves and tragedies of the Fitzgerald family, but is kept firmly in check by the narrative perspective. Critics have always commented on the discordance between the main plot and the Famine theme. One of the first reviews was perhaps the most perceptive: 'It is impossible not to feel that [the Famine] was the part of it about which Mr. Trollope really cared, but that, as he had to get a novel out of it, he was in duty bound to mix up a hash of Desmonds and Fitzgeralds with the Indian meal on which his mind was fixed as he wrote.'[64] The Famine was undoubtedly the impetus of the novel, the 'word' Trollope wished to say before leaving, but the domestic tragedy of

[58] Trollope, *Six Letters*, 3; Lever, 'The Irish Sketch-Book', 647–56.
[59] Trollope, *Castle Richmond*, i. 1.   [60] Ibid., 127.
[61] Mary Hamer, 'Introduction' to *Castle Richmond* (Oxford: Oxford University Press, 1989), p. xv.
[62] Trollope, *Castle Richmond*, iii. 28; ii. 117.   [63] Ibid., ii. 119.
[64] *Saturday Review* (19 May 1860), p. ix; quoted in Smalley (ed.), *Critical Heritage*, 113–14.

Fitzgeralds and Desmonds is not so disconnected from the background as a first reading might lead one to believe. A useful analogy is Terry Eagleton's textual rendering of the Union: 'What happened was that a metropolitan narrative was overlaid on a colonial one, to produce a radically undecidable text.'[65] In *Castle Richmond* the domestic narrative is laid over the national one, to produce an equally discordant text.

Trollope deliberately gives the family unit precedence. Individually, as he admitted, the characters are of little consequence: Owen is a 'scamp' and Herbert a 'prig'; Clara has 'no character' and her mother is 'almost revolting'.[66] Together, however, they are a lens through which Trollope refracts the devastation. Trollope used the family as a synecdoche for Ireland in *The Kellys*, where the Protestant 'half-sir' Barry and simple Catholic Anty represent religious and social divides. The Fitzgeralds and the Desmonds are historically two branches of the same family, the once mighty Geraldine dynasty, and can therefore be read as Ascendancy Ireland. By keeping the narrative perspective firmly on the problems of the Ascendancy during the Famine, Trollope can avoid writing about starvation for as long as possible. He magnifies the catastrophe for the middle class to a ludicrous extent: 'Is it possible to conceive a condition more pitiable than that of the landlord so situated? The last stage of misery, the empty tea-caddy, is not quickly reached; but it comes at last, and what can be more wretched than the period of its approach?'[67] It is not difficult to answer this question, but Trollope is 'deliberately myopic' when it comes to starvation.[68] Like Mr Green, the witness in the case of the disappearing oats, he shuts his eyes to avoid being implicated in the distress; it is no coincidence that the name he chose for the narrator of his autobiographical tales 'Father Giles' and 'The O'Conors' was also Mr Green, indicating both Irish sympathies and naivety.[69]

There are many reasons why Trollope would wish to deny the catastrophic effects of the Famine, not least of which is the guilt of being untouched. Clonmel and Mallow, the towns in which he lived during the crisis, had not escaped distress, and it is unlikely that Trollope could have avoided witnessing scenes of starvation and destitution. Politically, his hopes of entering parliament, or his career in the civil service, could have

    [65] Terry Eagleton, *Heathcliff and the Great Hunger: Studies in Irish Culture* (London and New York: Verso, 1995), 132.

    [66] Trollope, *Autobiography*, i. 208–9.   [67] Trollope, *Six Letters*, 23–4.

    [68] R. F. Foster, *Paddy and Mr Punch: Connections in Irish and English History* (London: Penguin, 1993), 145.

    [69] Trollope, *Macdermots*, iii. 237–9.

been seriously damaged by an examination of the Famine that raised disturbing questions; as Isaac Butt had discovered, to admit the crisis was
taking place was 'as sure a method of being branded as a radical, as to propose to destroy the church'.[70] Trollope's second cousin, Sir John
Trollope, had voted against his own party over the Corn Law Bill, and
Trollope was later to break with the Liberals over Gladstone's Irish land
policy; no doubt he was aware of the political ramifications of the Famine,
as of most manifestations of the 'Irish Question'. Trollope's friend
William Gregory had introduced the infamous 'Gregory Clause', restrict-
ing poorhouse relief to those who held less than a quarter-acre of land, in
effect colluding with landlords who wished to rid themselves of tenants;
another friend, the transport king Charles Bianconi, had acquired exten-
sive properties in the Encumbered Estates Court. Trollope, through personal and political allegiances, emerged as the mouthpiece of government
policy. This is particularly true of the *Six Letters*, which ruthlessly
manipulate the starving in order to eulogize the government victory. If the
government had not intervened 'the poor, instead of dying by hundreds,
would truly have died by thousands, till the deaths might have been
counted in millions'.[71] Given that conservative estimates now put the
death toll at over a million, and that between 1846 and 1850 excess mortality in County Cork was over one-eighth of the total population, is it possible Trollope could really have believed that only hundreds died?[72] We
have his own evidence against him. When it comes to praising 'our David
in Downing Street', the mortality takes on apocalyptic proportions:
'Famines there have been before, though I remember to have heard of
none since the days of Joseph in which the food of the stricken country
seems to have been so absolutely removed.'[73]

This biblical association is particularly apt in view of Trollope's adoption of Providentialism in *Six Letters* and *Castle Richmond*. It is significant
that he cast Russell—who was so small in stature that he appeared as a
baby in *Punch* cartoons—in the role of David to Famine, the Irish
Goliath—yet another manifestation of the representation of England as
the underdog or victim in the writings of English commentators on the
Famine. His pronouncements seem unnecessarily cruel, as in his
Malthusian lauding of the benefits of Famine *vis-à-vis* population control:

[70] Isaac Butt, 'The Famine in the Land', *Dublin University Magazine*, 29/172 (Apr.
1847), 501–40, at 502.
[71] Trollope, *Six Letters*, 7–8.
[72] James S. Donnelly. Jr., *The Land and the People of Nineteenth-Century Cork: The Rural
Economy and the Land Question* (London and Boston: Routledge & Kegan Paul, 1975), 121.
[73] Trollope, *Six Letters*, 5, 13.

'If the beneficent agency did not from time to time disencumber our crowded places, we should ever be living in narrow alleys with stinking gutters, and supply of water at the minimum.'[74] Eagleton justifiably dismisses this as 'moral crassness', and it is indeed puzzling that a man who was not rigidly conventional in his religious views—as his sympathetic delineations of Irish Catholic priests abundantly witness—should embrace this theory to explain the Famine. But in the *Six Letters*, Trollope was in fact reflecting the mind-set of those who were making decisions about relief. The Home Secretary, Sir James Graham, told Sir Robert Peel: 'It is awful to observe how the Almighty humbles the pride of nations. The sword, the pestilence and famine are the instruments of displeasure . . . These are solemn warnings, and they fill me with reverence; they proclaim with a voice not to be mistaken, that "doubtless there is a God, who judgeth the Earth".'[75] Providential pessimism, manifest not only among cabinet members but in the public at large, and reflected in fast days and Queen's Letters, was not a purely British phenomenon; it should be remembered that the blight appeared in other European countries. The Swiss author Jeremias Gotthelf describes the contemporary potato blight in his country in *Käthi die Großmutter*, transmitting the same didactic message through his heroine, an old woman whose livelihood is destroyed when her flax is washed away in a storm, and who is robbed of her food by the blight. Katie's explanation of her misfortune links it to Providence: 'God only meant to purify His poor people thoroughly, that they might not fail of reaching His heaven.'[76] The novel is an allegory of self-help, and eventually Katie is rewarded for her endurance with a wealthy daughter-in-law to save her from starvation.

This argument obviously possessed great currency and ideological power at the time Trollope was writing the *Six Letters*, but, as Boyd Hilton has argued, by the 1850s this particular brand of teleology was out of vogue— partly as a reaction to its use during the Famine.[77] Trollope certainly resists the idea of the Famine as a punishment in *Castle Richmond*, but, like Trevelyan, he maintains that 'Supreme wisdom had educed permanent

[74] Trollope, *Castle Richmond*, i. 126.
[75] Quoted in Peter Gray, 'British Politics and the Irish Land Question 1843–1850', Ph.D. thesis (University of Cambridge, 1992), 105.
[76] Jeremias Gotthelf, *The Story of an Alpine Valley or, Katie the Grandmother*, trans. L. G. Smith (London: Gibbings & Co. Ltd., 1896), 92.
[77] Boyd Hilton, *The Age of Atonement: The Influence of Evangelicalism on Social and Economic Thought 1785–1865* (Oxford: Clarendon Press, 1991), 250.

good out of transient evil'.[78] There are several interesting parallels between the expressed views of Trollope and Trevelyan. Both reduce the crisis to a single year, making it 'the great Irish famine of 1847'.[79] Five of Trollope's *Six Letters* are entitled 'The Real State of Ireland', echoing Trevelyan's opinion that the Famine 'exposed to view the real state of the country'.[80] Both embraced the Providential explanation rather than the more damaging socio-economic one and, finally, neither was entirely in harmony with his official line. Austin Bourke suggests that Trevelyan's apparent heartlessness in trying to save money instead of lives has been misconstrued: he was merely a civil servant following the orders of the government of the day. Bourke cites Trevelyan's subsequent service during the Indian famine: 'freed from the dead weight of Russell, Trevelyan resumed in India the more humane and flexible stance which he had shown in Ireland under Peel'.[81] His fellow civil servant Trollope, freed from the dead weight of his own official stance, resurrects the polemic of the factual *Six Letters* in the fictional *Castle Richmond* in order to subvert it. Eagleton, writing of the failure of the Union to operate in Ireland's favour during the Famine, asserts that 'the ultimate cause of this, whatever Trollope might have considered, was a matter of politics and property relations rather than of an all-merciful providence'.[82] In fact, in *Castle Richmond*, this proves to be precisely Trollope's point. The banal conclusions of the narrator are juxtaposed and denied by the narrative experience, leaving him discredited and ignored by the very tale he tells.

Incontrovertibly, *Castle Richmond* contains the seeds of its own destruction. Heralded as a companion-piece to the pro-government *Six Letters*, the novel contains 'scenes of desolation and starvation . . . grim enough to satisfy any patriot'.[83] The official policy of denial is stealthily undercut by a hidden agenda; as in *The Kellys*, where the subtitle draws attention to implicit criticisms submerged in the text, the opacity of the narrative in *Castle Richmond*, the lack of dialogue between narrator and text, arouses the reader's suspicion. In *The Kellys*, Trollope set Kelly's Court in the poverty-stricken west in order to intensify his point about the need for economic investment; but he seeks to soften the blow of Famine by making Castle Richmond the most prosperous estate in the neighbourhood.

---

[78] Charles Trevelyan, *The Irish Crisis* (London: Longman, Brown, Green & Longmans, 1848), 1.

[79] Ibid., 1.   [80] Ibid., 187–8.

[81] Austin Bourke, *'The Visitation of God'? The Potato and the Great Irish Famine* (Dublin: Lilliput Press, 1993), 177.

[82] Eagleton, *Heathcliff and the Great Hunger*, 26.

[83] Tracy, 'The Unnatural Ruin', 369.

Aby Mollett remarks that 'Even in these times the tenants are paying the rent, when no one else, far and near, is getting a penny out of them', and the only tenants we see are the prosperous O'Dwyer brothers of South Main Street and Kanturk.[84] Trollope's strategy of avoidance detonates a subtextual implosion that reveals the massive implications of the surface remark. The narrator says of the Fitzgerald estate: 'The tenants there had more means at their disposal, and did not depend so absolutely on the potato crop; but even round Castle Richmond the distress was very severe.'[85] If distress is severe around the prosperous estate Trollope has chosen for his case-study in Famine distress, what must it be like around the more typical estates? Like *The Nation* harping on the distress in Ulster, Trollope subtly manipulates the reader into a disturbing re-evaluation of the facts.

As in *The Kellys*, scenes of feasting are prevalent in *Castle Richmond*, as if to belie reports of starvation. Father Bernard, the parish priest of Drumbarrow, who has lost the source of his income through the reluctance of his parishioners to marry during a famine, is plied with food and drink by his niece and Mrs O'Dwyer.[86] His Protestant counterpart, Mr Townsend, and his wife treat their disapproving English clergyman guest to a huge turbot, explaining after a host of misunderstandings that it cost only one and sixpence—a higher than usual price in Ireland—due to 'an uncommon take of fish yesterday at Skibbereen'.[87] Trollope and his readers would have been well aware from the *Illustrated London News* and such travel narratives as those of Elihu Burritt or Lord Dufferin and the Honourable George Boyle that Skibbereen was notorious as the site of huge mortality from starvation. By placing his fish market in Skibbereen, Trollope makes two converse points at once: that there was abundant food available in Ireland during the Famine, and that the starving had no access to it. Writing of the poor quality of the meal sold to the people at Berryhill, the narrator remarks: 'The millers and dealers . . . of course made their profits in these times.'[88] The fact that it was so is registered, but not the obvious implication—the government policy of free trade had manifestly failed.

The inadequacy of government is similarly exposed. While the government is credited with funding the relief effort single-handedly—'They were responsible for the preservation of the people, and they acknowledged their responsibility'—in practice the burden of relief falls heavily on local relief committees and the landed gentry.[89] Lady Desmond sinks

---

[84] Trollope, *Castle Richmond*, i. 111.   [85] Ibid., 128.   [86] Ibid., ii. 51.
[87] Ibid., iii. 164.   [88] Ibid., i. 156.   [89] Ibid., ii. 62.

deeper into poverty through the crippling poor rates, while in Clady, a huge plot of land that had previously fed many families is left fallow: 'the whole proceeds of such land would hardly have paid the poor rates, and therefore the land was left uncultivated'.[90] The relative prosperity of the Castle Richmond tenants is wholly connected to the fortunes of the Fitzgerald family, who subsidize the meal shops and soup-kitchens of the area. The Fitzgerald ladies half-recognize this fact: 'it almost seemed as though the misfortune of their house had brought down its immediate consequences on all who had lived within their circle; but this was the work of the famine'.[91] Their impression is, however, proved correct, and the Fitzgeralds emerge as the only source of revenue in the area: 'They were now like enough to be in want of funds at that Berryhill soup-kitchen, seeing that the great fount of supplies, the house, namely, of Castle Richmond, would soon have stopped running altogether.'[92]

The failure of political economy, and the manipulative evasions of the narrative, are best illustrated in Herbert Fitzgerald's encounter with Bridget Sheehy. Faced with the stark reality of a starving individual, the narrator's first desperate instinct is to trope her as a type of the Irish race: 'It is strange how various are the kinds of physical development among the Celtic peasantry in Ireland. . . . The peasants of Clare, Limerick, and Tipperary are, in this way, much more comely than those of Cork and Kerry.'[93] The narrator tries to neutralize and naturalize the scene, reading rags and starvation as localized phenomena, a macabre tourist attraction, interesting in an anthropological sense. But the neutral image is shattered, and the object becomes an eloquent subject, when the type identifies herself, and we discover that Bridget Sheehy, married to Murty O'Brien, who earns four shillings a week at Kinsale, stands before us with her five starving children.[94] One by one, all the supposed defences against such misery are proposed only to be exposed as inadequate. For a member of the relief committee for Kanturk, Herbert seems woefully ignorant of the regulations surrounding relief. He tells Bridget to go into Kanturk poorhouse with her children; yet, as the narrator acknowledges much later, married women were not admitted if their husbands were working, for fear of fraud.[95] The choice of Kanturk is particularly apt, as mortality there was extremely high, and its workhouse horrendously overcrowded.[96] Due to government restrictions on outdoor relief, Bridget and her children would probably have been turned away empty-handed. Finally, Herbert suggests that she should

---

[90] Ibid., iii. 69.   [91] Ibid., 57–8.   [92] Ibid., 159.   [93] Ibid., ii. 42–3.
[94] Ibid., 44.   [95] Ibid., iii. 76–7.
[96] Donnelly, *Land and the People of Nineteenth-Century Cork*, 73, 94.

get a ticket for meal twice a week at the Clady shop his family subsidizes. Apart from the obvious fact that meal twice a week would not feed a family of seven, the meal, known as 'Peel's Brimstone', had a very bad reputation. Enterprising merchants ground the husk with the meal in order to make a greater profit, and Bridget shows the effect of such meal on her child:

its little legs seemed to have withered away; its cheeks were wan, and yellow and sunken, and the two teeth which it had already cut were seen with terrible plainness through its emaciated lips. Its head and forehead were covered with sores; and then the mother, moving aside the rags, showed that its back and legs were in the same state.[97]

It is a terrible and intolerable exposure, both of physical suffering and of misguided policy, and in the end there is nothing Herbert can do but give the woman some money. It is only when the scene is over that we discover that this is no isolated incident: 'In spite of all his political economy, there were but few days in which he did not empty his pockets of his loose silver, with these culpable deviations from his theoretical philosophy.'[98] The narrator appears to disapprove of Herbert's actions, but the whole scene has moved towards the conclusion that charity was unavoidable and political economy unworkable; human compassion wins out over cold theory. The final blow is administered at the end: 'But the worst of the famine had not come upon them as yet.'[99] If this is not the worst, how much more could be endured? Abstract concepts of Providence and political economy are displaced by the reality of starvation, and the horror of worse to come.

   In an even more terrible scene occurring just before Herbert's 'emigration' to England, he is once more confronted by the most vulnerable, a woman and her children. This chapter is paradigmatic of the pluralism of the narrative: titled 'The Last Stage', it initially refers to Herbert's last day in Ireland, the crisis-point of the domestic narrative, but it is transferred to the 'last stage' of starvation by Herbert's chance meeting with a dying woman. Like Bridget, this woman's husband would rather work than put his family in the poorhouse and surrender his land—giving the lie to allegations that the lazy Irish wanted to eat for free. The results are clear: despite his exertions, Mike cannot earn enough to keep his family alive. Significantly, this woman, whose child is called Kitty and whose husband is called Mike, can be identified with the Kitty who confronts Clara at Berryhill over the poor state of the meal she had received. That scene works against Kitty, who appears aggressive and is dismissed by the narrator as ungrateful—as so many recipients of so-called charity were. Yet it

   [97] Trollope, *Castle Richmond*, ii. 46.   [98] Ibid., 47.   [99] Ibid., 48.

emerges that Kitty has little to be grateful for: 'Who says it war guv' me?
. . . Didn't I buy it, here at this counter, with Mike's own hard-'arned
money? and it's chaiting us they are. Give me back my money.'[100] Once
again, the narrator is upstaged by his own text.

The Famine background intrudes on the main plot in full force in 'The
Last Stage', ousting Herbert from centre-stage by laying claim to the
chapter-title for the starving, outdoing his emotional misery by rendering
him powerless in the face of death: 'But what was he to do?'[101] He mimics
his author: he covers the corpse of the dead child with his silk handkerchief, as Trollope in the *Six Letters* shrouded the starving with words.[102]
Both fail. Herbert promises to send help, but it comes too late; Trollope,
who has maintained that God is merciful, and who has moreover assured
the reader that such things could not have happened because he did not
see them, owes us a happy ending he cannot provide: 'the mother and the
two children never left the cabin till they left it together, wrapped in their
workhouse shrouds'.[103]

Other metaphors of famine and disease, like 'last stage', litter the *Six
Letters* and *Castle Richmond*. Most interesting of all are the metaphors of
food and famine surrounding Owen and Clara. Owen, baulked of his prize
by Herbert, transforms Clara into food: 'Shall I see the prey taken out of
my jaws, and not struggle for it?'[104] Clara's love for Owen is described in
similar terms: 'That passion doubtless would die from want of food. Let it
be starved and die; and then this other new passion might spring up '[105]
These metaphors are easily read as nationalist and unionist allegories, with
Owen as the nationalist—perhaps as Daniel O'Connell—Clara as an
Anglicized Cathleen ní Houlihan, and Herbert as England, who steals her
away. Owen's cry for his lost prey resembles the complaint of the Irish that
England was stealing their food in exports while they were starving. The
'new passion' that will follow starvation and death reflects the hope that
the Famine would quell the Repeal movement—which it did—and signal
a new union between England and Ireland born of gratitude—which it did
not. Eventually, Owen becomes a Famine exile, driven out by the starvation of the old passion, and the marriage—union—of Clara and Herbert.

Owen is a highly glamorous and attractive character, with all the graces
of his namesake, Burgo Fitzgerald of Palliser fame, and none of his failings:

[100] Ibid., i. 156–7.   [101] Ibid., iii. 79.
[102] This echoes a scene in Charles Dickens's *Bleak House* (1853): in Chapter 8, 'Covering
a Multitude of Sins', Esther covers the dead child of the brickmaker with her handkerchief.
[103] Trollope, *Six Letters*, 14; Trollope, *Castle Richmond*, iii. 80.
[104] Trollope, *Castle Richmond*, iii. 16.   [105] Ibid., i. 140.

'a fine, high-spirited, handsome fellow, with a loving heart within his breast, and bright thoughts within his brain'.[106] Like Burgo, he has a bad reputation, but in Owen's case, much of this is slander—just as the Irish had acquired a bad reputation in Britain, usually due to stereotypes rather than actions. It is striking that Owen is described in much the same terms as Daniel O'Connell, the bogeyman of British politics, in the *Six Letters*:

the strong mind anxious for right but more anxious for success, the capacious intellect bright enough for any effort but that of discerning good from evil . . .[107]

To yield to him was ignoble, even though he might know that he was yielding to the right. To strive for mastery was to him noble, even though he strove against those who had a right to rule, and strove on behalf of the wrong.[108]

In both cases, an opening clause acknowledging the essential goodness of the man is modified by a second clause emphasizing his inherent flaws. O'Connell, like Owen, had been much maligned, as Trollope implicitly admitted in *The Kellys* by reiterating the fact that O'Connell's trial had been cast into doubt by the exclusion of Catholics from the jury. Owen behaves exceptionally well over the issue of ownership of Castle Richmond but, like O'Connell, he is a rebel, striving for a Repeal of the Union—that of Herbert and Clara. And like O'Connell, he fails.

Owen's failure, however, is not the logical conclusion of a novel professing to uphold the Union: the various 'unions' enacted by *Castle Richmond* are too problematic to achieve an affirmation of the political Union in the end. The scions of the Geraldine dynasty, the old Earl of Desmond and Sir Thomas Fitzgerald, have allied themselves with English women, in a reworking of the sexual metaphor of the Union as a marriage between John Bull and Cathleen ní Houlihan. Both marriages are questionable. The old Earl and Countess of Desmond married for mercenary motives, only to discover that each had been tricked.[109] Their marriage is paralleled by the declining fortunes of their family: the Desmonds, who 'had been kings once over those wild mountains', are reduced to penury by the actions of the old Earl's father, the aptly named self-centred Desmond Desmond, Earl of Desmond, 'who had repaired his fortunes by selling himself at the time of the Union'.[110] Like the O'Kellys, the Desmonds come to rue the acceptance of the bribe. The central disputable union of the novel is, of course, that of Sir Thomas and Lady Fitzgerald. The possibility that their marriage was bigamous has terrible consequences, bastardizing their children, leaving

[106] Trollope, *Castle Richmond*, iii. 14.
[108] Trollope, *Castle Richmond*, ii. 139.
[107] Trollope, *Six Letters*, 28.
[109] Ibid., i. 7–8.   [110] Ibid., 9.

them prey to the foul Molletts, questioning their right to the land they possess, threatening to disinherit Herbert, the child of the Union, and bestow
the estate on his vibrantly Hibernian cousin. Even when Herbert is rein-
stated as the rightful heir, the prevalent tone is one of sorrow. Sir Thomas
dies from excessive contemplation of the dubiety of his Union, 'the absolute
naked horror of the surmised facts' having been 'kept delicately out of sight'
for so long.[111] The Famine exposes the invalidity of the Union with
the ruthlessness of the Molletts, rending the domestic and national fabric
of society with stark and unpalatable truths. In a sense, Trollope, like
Sir Thomas—and the British government—bribes the reader to accept the
Unions—that of Ireland and Britain, Clara and Herbert—in return for a
happy ending. But that ending is so discordant and so sombre that the colonial narrative displaces the metropolitan, the continuing national crisis
gapes through the artificially resolved domestic one, warning us to reject the
bribe. The novel that had announced itself as the vindication of government
policy in Ireland has become retrograde, and a powerful critique of the basis
of government rule in Ireland.

As in *The Kellys*, Trollope offers a subtitle for *Castle Richmond* that does
not really fit the bill: 'A Tale of the Famine Year in Ireland'. Aside from its
obvious chronological inaccuracy, Trollope himself refers to its artistic inadequacy: 'But if one did in truth write a tale of the famine, after that it would
behove the author to write a tale of the pestilence; and then another of the
exodus. . . . And then the same author going on with his series would give in
his last set,—Ireland in her prosperity.'[112] This series has to a certain extent
been enacted in the main plot—in the Famine, the Molletts, Herbert's
migration to London and return in triumph, title intact. But Trollope's
attempt at an organic historical pageant is marred by the last novel in his
Irish 'set', *The Landleaguers*, which portrays an Ireland that is anything but
prosperous and peaceful. *The Landleaguers* addresses many of the same
issues as *The Macdermots*, but from an antithetical standpoint. One can sense
Trollope's identification with Sir Nicholas Bodkin, the old Catholic landlord
who had once been in tune with his tenants, but now 'he was at one with
them no longer'.[113] While Trollope had shown some sympathy and understanding towards Ribbonmen, the Landleaguers were anathema to him. He
was particularly shocked by the murder of Lord Frederick Cavendish in
Phoenix Park on 6 May 1882, as his friend, W. E. Forster, Cavendish's predecessor as Chief Secretary of Ireland (and, as we have seen, someone who
had laboured valiantly to ameliorate the condition of the starving during the

---

[111] Ibid., ii. 14.   [112] Ibid., iii. 284.

[113] Anthony Trollope, *The Landleaguers*, 3 vols. (London: Chatto & Windus, 1883), i. 150.

Famine), had resigned the post only two days before. Trollope was now in complete sympathy with the landlords, and conformed so closely to the Establishment that his tolerance of Catholicism vaporized. Florian Jones, described by John Cronin as 'one of the most improbable converts in the whole history of either religion or the novel', becomes a 'pervert' to Catholicism, partly as an adolescent prank to gain attention, and partly as a way to express his identification with the Irish.[114] But the substance of his religion seems to be the ability to shield criminals; Catholicism here takes on the guise of a secret society. Most of the other Catholics in the novel repel both narrator and reader just as the people of Ballymoy terrified Archibald Green, but now it is in earnest, not in jest. Perhaps the clearest sign of all that Trollope is thoroughly alienated from those with whom he once identified with is the interruption of the hunt by the Landleague: hunting was Trollope's passion and, in his eyes, those who could deprive gentlemen of their beloved sport must have been unmitigatedly evil.

Significantly, many of the root causes of the disturbances in this last novel are traced to the very Famine Trollope had hailed as the harbinger of prosperity. Philip Jones bought Ballintubber and Morony under the Estates Court in 1850, implicitly from a landlord bankrupted by the Famine. The ideas of the Landleague, according to Trollope, had filtered back from America, the land to which many bitter Irishmen emigrated. The 'villain' of the novel, Pat Carroll, shares his name with the typical Irishman of the *Six Letters*: 'Pat Carroll and the little Patlings must now be fed. That the law has enacted, and there is no avoiding it; his right to livelihood off the land comes before my own, even mine, the landlord's. He must eat, though I starve.'[115] Finally, Lax shoots Florian from a van-tage-point afforded by a cutting in the road commenced during the Famine, and never completed.[116] Forty-five years after the so-called 'Famine Year', Trollope is still enacting the Famine in subtext. Trevelyan saw the Famine as an exposure: 'The abyss has been fathomed.'[117] For Trollope, its result was obfuscation; the Famine muddied the clear waters of his land of rebirth, confirming his alterity, rendering him unable to translate the 'unintelligible rags' of the starving Irish without betraying his English heritage. Forced into artistic pluralism by the dichotomy of nationality, the English civil servant is systematically undermined by the subtextual strategies of his Anglo-Irish self.

---

[114] John Cronin, 'Trollope and the Matter of Ireland', in Tony Bareham (ed.), *Anthony Trollope* (Plymouth and London: Vision, 1980), 33.
[115] Trollope, *Six Letters*, 20.   [116] Trollope, *Landleaguers*, ii. 256–7.
[117] Trevelyan, *Irish Crisis*, 187–8.

5
William Carleton in Retrospect:
The Irish Prophecy Man

Ben Okri wrote (in the very different context of the execution of Ken Saro Wiwa): 'If you want to know what is happening in an age or in a nation, find out what is happening to the writers, the town criers; for they are the seismographs that calibrate impending earthquakes in the spirits of the times.'[1] William Carleton is one such seismograph, charting the political, historical, and literary earthquakes of his Ireland. In his lifetime, Carleton never had to defend his right to describe Famine Ireland, as Anthony Trollope had. A 'peasant's son', he was able to use his privileged access to the dying Gaelic Ireland to help originate a new Irish literature, based in and on Ireland.[2] A convert to Protestantism, he was initiated into the enclaves of the Dublin intelligentsia, contributed to all the leading Irish periodicals of the day, and used his literary contacts to become the self-appointed spokesman of his people. An acknowledged and loudly self-proclaimed authority on the Irish peasantry, he became indispensable to diverse groups, including Evangelicals, Conservatives, and Young Irelanders. He was a central figure of the Irish literary revival of the 1830s, and a powerful posthumous influence on the Gaelic Revival of the 1890s, notably on W. B. Yeats. In his own time he was lauded as the novelist of Ireland; yet only twenty years after his death he was vilified by nationalists, and Yeats had to scour the second-hand bookstalls for his best work. During his lifetime, he complained constantly of the cruelty of the reading public in neglecting his works and his pecuniary needs, and reluctantly resigned himself to the prospect of sharing the fate of his literary forebears, in achieving lasting success only after his death. However, he reached the apogee of his popularity long before his death in 1869, and rapidly drifted towards obscurity. In the late twentieth century, we find 'an author of acknowledged historical and literary importance . . . unhonoured, unsung, unavailable and uncatalogued'.[3] The complex intersections of allegiances that Carleton had

---

[1] Ben Okri, *Guardian* (1 Nov. 1995), 19.
[2] William Carleton, 'Introduction' to *Traits and Stories of the Irish Peasantry*, 3 vols. (Dublin and London: William Curry, Jr. & Co.; Orr, 1843–4), i, p. vi.
[3] Barbara Hayley, *A Bibliography of the Writings of William Carleton* (Gerrards Cross: Colin Smythe, 1985), 7.

132 William Carleton in Retrospect

exploited so successfully, and which had been accepted by his readers in mid-nineteenth-century Ireland, were in a post-Famine, post-Landleague world an abomination. Carleton's biographer, D. J. O'Donoghue, acknowledged the author's 'great genius', but was so distressed by what he perceived as anti-nationalist bias in works such as *The Tithe Proctor* that he accused the author of 'mental aberration', and approached his biography like a reluctant defence attorney:

An examination of the material placed at my disposal showed that it would be impossible to make a hero of Carleton, and proved the necessity of placing before the world the determining facts and circumstances (as it were) which make perfectly clear the extent of Carleton's great services to literature and to Ireland, no less than the disservice he had done himself.[4]

O'Donoghue and most of Carleton's critics have concluded that he was a pen-for-hire, a convert for convenience, who could switch from bitter invective against the Roman Catholic clergy for the *Christian Examiner*, to nationalist polemic and satire on the Established Church in *Valentine M'Clutchy*, according to who was prepared to pay. Caesar Otway has even been identified as the 'souper' who made Carleton a literary prostitute in his time of hardship.

Taken in context, however, the shifts in Carleton's literary stance can be attributed to changes in 'the Protestant mind' in the 1830s and 1840s, after Catholic Emancipation.[5] *The Nation* and the *Dublin University Magazine* shared a surprising number of contributors due to a pervasive Conservatism, and Denis Florence MacCarthy, Speranza, and James Clarence Mangan joined Carleton and others in writing for *The Nation* without breaking all ties with the *Dublin University Magazine*.[6] Three years before his breakthrough nationalist novel *Valentine M'Clutchy*, *The Nation* was forced to deny that Carleton was its sole writer. In 1848, when Carleton was writing the supposedly anti-nationalist *The Tithe Proctor*, he was also writing for the nationalist and revolutionary *Irish Tribune*, which

[4] D. J. O'Donoghue, *The Life of William Carleton: Being His Autobiography And Letters: And An Account Of His Life And Writings, From The Point At Which The Autobiography Breaks Off*, 2 vols. (London: Downey & Co., 1896), i, pp. x, xi; ii. 121.
[5] Edward Kelly, 'William Carleton: Ascendancy Novelist', MA thesis (University College, Cork, 1988).
[6] Tom Dunne, 'Haunted by History: Irish Romantic Writing 1800–50', in Roy Porter and Mikulas Teich (eds.), *Romanticism in National Context* (Cambridge: Cambridge University Press, 1988), 68–91, at 73; Joseph Spence, 'The Philosophy of Irish Toryism, 1833–52: A Study of Reactions to Liberal Reformism in Ireland in the Generation between the First Reform Act and the Famine, with Especial Reference to Expressions of National Feeling among the Protestant Ascendancy', Ph.D. thesis (Birkbeck College, University of London, 1991).

Figure 5. William Carleton (Age 46), by Charles Grey, R. H. A.

was also forced to deny Carleton's proprietorship of this journal—indicating the continuing conviction of readers (or perhaps enemies) of his national feeling.[7] A convergence of national-mindedness in 1845 saw the emergence of proto-nationalist novels by Anna Maria Hall (who also published travel-books with her husband), Charles Lever, and Joseph Sheridan Le Fanu, as well as Carleton's much-disputed *Valentine M'Clutchy*.[8] Moreover, although O'Donoghue stressed that Carleton had offended all Irishmen at one time or another,[9] the memorial attached to his application for a state pension in 1847 bears eloquent witness to the admiration he inspired in all sections of the community:

Carleton in a sense united his country: the list of eminent persons who petitioned the government to grant him a pension in 1847 represents all the different ways of being Irish. Nothing else could have brought together the President of the Catholic College at Maynooth and Colonel Blacker, the Orange leader, in the presence of Maria Edgeworth, Dan O'Connell's son, Oscar Wilde's father and Rev. Dr. Henry Cooke from Belfast.[10]

Or, as Thomas Flanagan placed it more sensationally in the context of the forthcoming Young Ireland insurrection: 'men who were soon to be accused of treason, some of the witnesses against them, the lawyers who prosecuted, and the judges who sentenced them to death'.[11]

Yet despite this evidence of ecumenical enthusiasm, Carleton remains a figure of controversy, not so much for the strong anti-Catholic bias of his work at the beginning of his career—which was very much in the mainstream of Irish Evangelical writing at the time—but because he has been perceived as a spoiled priest who had sold his religion and his people to achieve success as a writer in the Protestant camp. Carleton suffered the fate of the convert: rejected by his own people, but never allowed to become fully integrated into his chosen sphere. Too often, his work is criticized in terms of betrayal and blasphemy, rather than bad writing. The problem of register in Carleton's work, for example, becomes an issue of loyalty. In several of his stories, the local idiom of the protagonists is framed by the standard English of the narrator, or authorial 'we', who comments on and sometimes translates their dialogue. Most notorious is

[7] O'Donoghue, *Life*, ii. 56; *Irish Tribune* (8 July 1848), 72.

[8] Hall's *The Whiteboy*, Lever's *St Patrick's Eve*, and Le Fanu's *The Cock and Anchor*.

[9] O'Donoghue, *Life*, i, p. x.

[10] Norman Vance, *Irish Literature: A Social History: Tradition, Identity and Difference* (Oxford: Basil Blackwell, 1990), 137.

[11] Thomas Flanagan, *The Irish Novelists 1800–1850* (New York: Columbia University Press, 1959), 323.

the dazzling and accomplished 'Wildgoose Lodge', where the narrator-as-protagonist, a Ribbonman, speaks in dialect, while the narrator-proper marks the shift in his social and moral allegiances by speaking as an educated man. Barbara Hayley links this to Carleton's constant revisions of his work: 'It is very likely that his own way of speech changed as he developed from half-educated peasant to famous literary figure, so that he would cease to accept as normal usage some of his own natural pronunciations and habits of speech; and his ear would detect as wrong, comic, or Irish, sounds which he had previously taken as standard.'[12] This framing of the narrative in a distinctive idiom has, of course, a didactic element: where Carleton was serious about teaching his fellow Irishmen or about correcting English prejudice, standard English was much more likely to be effective. For Terry Eagleton, however, this interplay of registers symbolizes a clash of national cultures, with Carleton colluding with the system by using its language. Carleton's use of 'bureaucratese', Eagleton suggests, warps his judgement to such an extent that he can no longer write in an idiom commensurate to his protagonists. He cites the words of Condy Dalton on the beauty of Sarah M'Gowan in *The Black Prophet* as an example: 'Upon my honour, Donnel, that girl surpasses anything I have seen yet. Why she's perfection—her figure is—is—I havn't words for it—and her face—good heavens! what brilliancy and animation!' Eagleton objects that Dalton, as 'one of the labouring poor', 'has all too many words for it; but he is conforming to the Victorian convention that the gentility of a character's speech is in direct proportion to his or her moral stature'.[13] The implication is that Carleton has renounced a Gaelic tradition he fully comprehended for a Victorian convention that is alien to his subjects. The problem with Eagleton's argument is that the words are, in fact, spoken not by the virtuous Condy, but by the profligate squireen, Young Dick-o'-the-Grange Henderson, a practised seducer of young girls.[14] The gentility of Henderson's speech is therefore no index to moral stature, and merely differentiates him from those he and his agent father prey upon. Eagleton's misprision is symptomatic of the suspicion with which Carleton's works are scrutinized, and reveals far more about what the critic expects of the religious and cultural apostate than about Carleton's use of language.

[12] Barbara Hayley, *Carleton's Traits and Stories and the 19th Century Anglo-Irish Tradition* (Gerrards Cross and Totowa, NJ: Colin Smythe, 1983), 27.

[13] Terry Eagleton, *Heathcliff and the Great Hunger: Studies in Irish Culture* (London and New York: Verso, 1995), 209.

[14] William Carleton, *The Black Prophet: A Tale of Irish Famine* (London and Belfast: Simms & M'Intyre, 1847), 118.

Given this suspicion, it is hardly surprising that Carleton was obsessively anxious to establish the authenticity and truth of his writing. The authenticity of Carleton's narratives is the rock on which his work is based. He goes so far in the 'General Introduction' of the 1843–4 definitive edition of his masterwork, *Traits and Stories of the Irish Peasantry*, as to assert that his familiarity with the Irish peasant is '*the only merit which I claim*'.[15] His first literary production, 'The Lough Derg Pilgrim', is 'a perfect transcript'—'There is not even an exaggeration of any kind in my account of it.'[16] In the 'Preface' to *Valentine M'Clutchy*, he boasts that 'the man has never lived who could lay his finger upon any passage of my writings, and say "*that is false*" ', while *The Black Prophet* is based on Carleton's memories of the famines of 1817 and 1822.[17] His stories are punctuated with footnotes, appendices, letters from antiquarians, extracts from contemporary journals to verify his facts, and by the time of *Castle Squander*, his own previous works had become so 'authentic' that extracts were introduced as corroborating testimony. Carleton was so successful at passing himself off as 'a peasant's son', a man of the people, that his authenticity was never seriously questioned in the way that his intentions or sincerity were. Maria Edgeworth acknowledged that her position as an Anglo-Irish landowner left her at a severe disadvantage compared to Carleton when it came to representing the majority of the Irish people: 'I have read all the works that Carleton has yet written, and I must confess that I never knew Irish life until I had read them.'[18] Even late twentieth-century critics continue to accept complacently Carleton's self-projected cultural status: 'Avant tout, il était et resta toute sa vie un paysan.'[19] Even Patrick Kavanagh, protesting 'he was no more a peasant than is your obedient servant', is simply imposing an anachronistic reading on the term 'peasant'.[20]

Carleton's insistence on his peasant origins does, however, leave him open to misunderstanding and underestimation. More an anthropologist than a novelist, his critics say, he lacked the creative imagination to write convincing fiction, so settled instead for social documentation based on

[15] Carleton, 'General Introduction', *Traits and Stories*, i, p. xvii.

[16] Ibid., p. xvi; O'Donoghue, *Life*, i. 101.

[17] William Carleton, *Valentine M'Clutchy, The Irish Agent; Or, Chronicles of the Castle Cumber Property*, 3 vols. (Dublin: James Duffy, 1845), i, p. vi.

[18] Quoted in *Illustrated Dublin Journal* (2 Nov. 1861), 132.

[19] 'Above all, he was and remained all his life a peasant.' André Boué, *William Carleton, romancier irlandais (1794–1869)* (Paris: Publications de la Sorbonne, 1978), 145.

[20] Patrick Kavanagh, 'Preface' to *The Autobiography of William Carleton* (London: MacGibbon & Kee, 1968), 11.

memory. Carleton's very authenticity as a peasant, Frances Cashel Hoey argues, meant he did not possess the intellect or acumen to form the proper—presumably nationalist—conclusions his own writing should have suggested: 'while he glorified his origin by interpreting his people to the world, he retained its salient characteristics and its distinctive limitations'.[21] Horatio Sheafe Krans explains that as an Irishman, Carleton could not be expected to be rational: 'He was blood and bone of the peasants of whom he wrote, and like them untrained mentally, morally, and emotionally . . . Though endowed with the finest, deepest feeling, he seems incapable of thought and reason, and is only himself under the inspiration of strong impulse.'[22] Carleton is a much more complex writer than this reductive, blinkered criticism would allow, and certainly Carleton the didactic and utilitarian author is unrecognizable from Krans's description. It is a mistake to assume that Carleton's authenticity confines him to a rigid, easily definable category. To begin with, Carleton may describe himself as 'a peasant's son', but it is doubtful whether he ever thought of *himself* as a peasant. Like Thomas Carlyle, whom he met on the latter's first visit to Ireland in 1846, he had abandoned his peasant roots for an intellectual life. In his autobiography, he imperiously rebuked the artist Henry McManus, commissioned by Curry and Orr to produce an illustration of his birthplace for *Traits and Stories* in 1842, for drawing 'as vile-looking a hovel as ever sheltered a human being; and this he calls "Carleton's Birthplace" '.[23] He assured the reader that his birth was 'beyond doubt humble, but then it was unquestionably respectable', and dwells with satisfaction on the fact that his father's funeral had been the largest the parish had ever seen—a sure sign of Irish respectability.[24] Moreover, Carleton was highly conscious of being set apart from his neighbours, both Catholic and Protestant. He had been classically educated for the priesthood, and so was singled out from his siblings as above manual labour. Even after the passage of forty years, he could not quench his anger at the temerity of his brother Michael, who suggested William should work to help their impoverished family, even though 'he knew that I read the classics several hours a day'.[25] He agreed to be apprenticed to the stone-cutter Lanty Doain because Lanty knew some Latin, and was thus placed 'out of the category of common stone-cutters', and moreover he was 'not only my friend, but a warm admirer', and therefore unlikely to

---

[21] O'Donoghue, *Life*, i, pp. xix–xx.

[22] Horatio Sheafe Krans, *Irish Life in Irish Fiction* (New York and London: Columbia University Press; Macmillan, 1903), 320–1.

[23] O'Donoghue, *Life*, i. 4.   [24] Ibid.   [25] Ibid., 114.

tax the budding author's physical strength.[26] Carleton's sense of being set apart was not merely contemptuous snobbery—though no doubt there was an element of this; he was precociously aware of his own potential, and terrified that it would be wasted. On the day of what he claimed was his greatest triumph—not the publication of a novel, but the leap over the Clogher Karry river at a point he says was known for many years afterwards as 'Carleton's Leap'—the prospect of sinking into obscurity tormented Carleton: 'There I stood before them, a fine well-dressed young fellow, in my twenty-first year; an individual from whom great things were expected—yet what would I be in a week? A working-man, no better than one of themselves, with a paper cap on my head and a coarse apron before me.'[27] Carleton may have lived among the peasantry, may have understood them well enough to chronicle them, but he never considered himself to be one of them.

Even Carleton's 'Irishness' can be called into question. His contemporary, Patrick Murray, Professor of Theology at Maynooth, pronounced him 'not only Irish, but thoroughly Irish, intensely Irish, exclusively Irish', but in the same breath regionalized him by noting his familiarity with the *Ulster* peasantry, of Scots–Irish descent, and relative ignorance of those of the south and west of Ireland.[28] Carleton had to a certain extent obliterated the distinction between Ulster and the rest of Ireland in *Traits and Stories* by suppressing the Scottish–Hibernian accent of the North in favour of a more national, characteristic, recognizable Irish accent—a decision which involved, as Barbara Hayley asserts, 'a good deal of double-think, both in his lack of admiration for the real life speech of his allegedly true-to-life characters, and in its departure from the truth in representing it'.[29] It also brings into question Carleton's claim to be writing for an Irish audience. Potentially more problematic is the issue of the trilingual Carleton—fluent in Irish, Latin, and English—renouncing the Gaelic oral tradition in favour of English, the language of his people's traditional enemy, but also the language of his patrons and the market. Carleton's mother, a famous songstress, was once asked to sing the English version of 'The Red-Haired Man's Wife', a popular ballad. Carleton recalled: 'she replied, "I will sing it for you, but the English words and the air are like a man and his wife quarrelling—*the Irish melts into the tune but the English doesn't*" . . . She spoke the words in Irish.'[30] Presumably Carleton, while recording her words in *English*, and while writing in

---

[26] O'Donoghue, *Life*, i., 116.   [27] Ibid., 117–18.
[28] Patrick Murray, *Edinburgh Review*, 96 (Oct. 1852), 384–403, at 388.
[29] Hayley, *Carleton's Traits and Stories*, 25.   [30] O'Donoghue, *Life*, i. 8.

English a novel called *The Red-Haired Man's Wife*, remembered his mother's words, and pondered his own alienation from her Catholic, peasant, Irish-speaking world. Many of Carleton's villains adopt English as their badge of difference: Buck English's surname and ridiculous 'prononsensation' identify his ambitions and ruthless betrayal of his people;[31] Hycy Burke, who is prepared to convert to Protestantism to marry an heiress, is furious when his fellow villain Teddy Phats addresses him in Irish, and pretends ignorance although he is fluent in the language (significantly, Teddy is equally fluent in English, but as he runs an illicit still and the gauger only speaks English, it is convenient to be ignorant);[32] and the indifferent, heartless landlords the Squanders carry nothing back from England for their famine-stricken tenants but their English accents: 'they contrived to superinduce upon the brogue, such a travestie of the English accent as constituted a bastard language, which was disgraceful to either country'.[33] The ambivalence of Carleton's position, caught between the peasant world he rejected and the Ascendancy world that would not accept him, both empowers and compromises his representations of nineteenth-century Ireland.

Carleton's social insecurity, which led to an almost obsessive concern with the establishment of ethnic authenticity, also compelled him to insist on the truth of his narratives—hence the frequent footnotes testifying to the facts on which his text is built. Despite this constant self-verification, Carleton's relationship with his texts is far more complex than his protestations would suggest. Truth was a weapon for Carleton, and, like Joyce, he uses it as a threat, a form of revenge. As an Irish Catholic, powerless against the Ascendancy, truth was 'the only retribution which I can now exact for all the unknown distress and sorrow which their dishonesty has caused me and my family to suffer'.[34] *Valentine M'Clutchy*, he claimed, was written in revenge for a midnight raid on the Carleton home by Orangemen—known to be neighbours—in which Carleton's sister was wounded in the side with a bayonet. The story enacts a revenge-fantasy: 'Little they dreamt that there was a boy present, not more than ten years of age, who would live to punish them with a terrible but truthful retaliation.'[35] Fiction becomes a mask for truth, and, like Thomas Love Peacock, Carleton adopted allegorical names—M'Clutchy, M'Slime, O'Drive,

---

[31] William Carleton, *The Tithe Proctor* (London and Belfast: Simms & M'Intyre, 1849), 4.
[32] William Carleton, *The Emigrants of Ahadarra* (London and Belfast: Simms & M'Intyre, 1848), 26, 36.
[33] William Carleton, *The Squanders of Castle Squander*, 2 vols. (London: Illustrated London Library, 1852), i. 129.
[34] O'Donoghue, *Life*, i. 2.   [35] Ibid., 33.

Lucre—to satirize people he knew. Yet Carleton admitted that he had transformed one of the narrators of the opening fireside sequence of tales in *Traits and Stories*, Ned M'Keown, into a henpecked husband out of malice, as the real Ned had been a bully who had taken a dislike to young William, and persistently chased him from the crossroads.[36] This is not an isolated incident: Carleton is more than willing to undermine his own proclamation of truth and authenticity. His admiration of the Irish ability to lie in 'The Geography of an Irish Oath' is only partly tongue-in-cheek: 'Fiction is the basis of society, the bond of commercial prosperity, the channel of communication between nation and nation, and not unfrequently the interpreter between a man and his own conscience.'[37] 'Phil Purcel, the Pig-Driver' plays on the type of the stupid Paddy to show how a wily Irishman tricks more than twenty-four Englishmen into buying the same pig.[38] Surprisingly, even the most strident nationalists, those most concerned with raising the profile of the Irish in England and abroad, relished the representation of the cunning Irishman. *The Nation* gleefully reported that a Ballinasloe Repealer had fooled the *Times* 'Commissioner' Thomas Campbell Foster into believing and reporting that Galwaymen had pawned money: 'we are delighted that there is in every locality such men as Mr. MURRAY, able to mystify impertinent vanity . . .'.[39] Carleton's farcical 'The Resurrections of Barney Bradley', in which the verdict in an inquest on a supposedly dead man is 'Kilt by Andy Murtagh, and found beatin' the coroner afterwards', is sardonically offered as a corrective to English prejudice: 'we beg leave to recommend this *authentic* story to John Bull's perusal, and that it may serve to correct his views of Irish life and character, is the earnest and sincere wish of the writer. Amen.'[40] Carleton is assuming the position of the Irish peasant pulling the wool over the stranger's eyes. He is obviously poking fun at his own self-imposed role as translator of the nation, and his own—and other writers'— pretensions to a truthful exhibition of national characteristics, designed to obviate English prejudice. Truth was a malleable substance in Carleton's hands, and considering the influence he exerted on the many groups who took his representations on trust, it was a dangerous weapon.

In his more serious moments Carleton presented himself as a historian, and he was highly aware of the historical value of his work. He was conscious

[36] Carleton, 'The Three Tasks', *Traits and Stories*, i. 50.
[37] Carleton, 'The Geography of an Irish Oath', *Traits and Stories*, ii. 3.
[38] Carleton, 'Phil Purcel, the Pig-Driver', *Traits and Stories*, i. 407–27.
[39] *Nation* (1 Nov. 1845), 41.
[40] Carleton, 'The Resurrections of Barney Bradley', *Traits and Stories*, i. 328.

that he lived in a society in transition, and recognized the importance of his work in literary and historical terms, and the currency and market value of recording a dying race:

in connexion with this particular subject, there is, probably, something unparalleled in the annals of literature; for the author has reason to think that several of the originals, who sat for their portraits here presented, were the last of their class which the country will ever again produce—a fact calculated of itself to occasion an interest which a mere perusal of them could not give.[41]

Written on 16 June 1845, on the very eve of the Great Famine, this prediction was to prove true more quickly than Carleton could have known. Grounded as his work is in the major events of early nineteenth-century Ireland—the tithe campaign, agrarian unrest, the temperance crusade, Orangeism, Ribbonism, emigration, land, and famine—it is hardly surprising that many have taken his claims as a historian seriously, notably Yeats: 'William Carleton was a great Irish historian. The history of a nation is not in parliaments and battlefields, but in what the people say to each other on fair-days and high days, and in how they farm, and quarrel, and go on pilgrimage. These things has Carleton recorded.'[42] These things, and much more. Oliver MacDonagh suggests that the nineteenth-century novelist is as close as one gets to a historian in literature; the special insights of the novelist shed 'streaks of brilliant light' on the work of the historian.[43] Carleton is a prime example, yet his special circumstances—his apostasy, his unashamed campaign for and eventual award of a government pension, the subjective nature of his accounts—can dissuade bona-fide historians from looking again at Carleton's work. Tom Garvin, considering Carleton's writings on Ribbonism—and as Carleton had been initiated as a Ribbonman in 1814, his evidence is almost unique—concludes that he is an unsafe witness: 'Carleton was, admittedly, a story-teller, and he had changed sides by changing religion from Catholic to Protestant.'[44] 'Story-teller' here takes on strong pejorative connotations, and even what may have been a perfectly rational and sincere decision to change religion appears to undermine the ability to tell the

[41] William Carleton, *Tales and Sketches Illustrating the Character, Usages, Traditions, Sports and Pastimes of the Irish Peasantry* (Dublin: James Duffy, 1845), p. viii.

[42] W. B. Yeats, 'Introduction' to *Stories from Carleton* (London, New York, and Toronto: Walter Scott; W. J. Gage & Co., 1889), p. xvi.

[43] Oliver MacDonagh, *The Nineteenth Century Novel and Irish Social History: Some Aspects* (Dublin: National University of Ireland, 1970), 3, 19.

[44] Tom Garvin, 'Defenders, Ribbonmen and Others: Underground Political Networks in Pre-Famine Ireland', in C. H. E. Philpin (ed.), *Nationalism and Popular Protest in Ireland* (Cambridge: Cambridge University Press, 1987), 233.

truth. Carleton may have left Catholicism and Ribbonism behind, but he never became an Orangeman, and the trauma of the persecution of his family by Orangemen never left him; it is unlikely he would have falsely maligned Ribbonism, as this would have morally elevated its natural enemy, Orangeism.

Yet Carleton's view of history is suspect, not for the reasons Garvin suggests, but for the casual attitude Carleton adopted towards it. He is willing to subvert history for his own ends. Conscious as he was of his role as a cultural historian, he made frequent use of the works of antiquarians, and indeed claimed to be a unique storehouse of stories and songs passed down to him from his mother and father, the lineal descendants of old Gaelic artists: 'At this day I am in possession of Irish airs which none of our best antiquaries in Irish music have ever heard, except through me, and of which neither they nor I myself know the names.'[45] But having set himself up as the repository of Gaelic tradition, Carleton emphatically spurned the idea of any kind of Celtic civilization:

If there were the civilisation and learning they talk of, where are their monuments to be found, either in our ancient literature or our ancient architecture? Is there any great poem that the country can claim as particularly her own? . . . Away then with the cant of ancient civilisation. We Celts never were civilised, nor will be properly so for at least another half century, if even at that period.[46]

In *The Tithe Proctor*, Carleton openly rewrites history by introducing into his 'Preface' his source, *The Murder of the Bolands*, 'a narrative whose force and graphic power will serve only to bring shame upon the feeble super-structure which I have endeavoured to erect upon it'.[47] Carleton follows the source so closely that the reader cannot but expect that the Purcels will share the tragic fate of the Bolands—the men killed defending their home, the women carried off as prizes—and it comes as an anticlimax to find that only the obnoxious tithe-proctor and his horsewhip-wielding son are killed, while the others are saved by the *deus ex machina*, the mysterious Cannie Sugah. The exigencies of fiction are ostentatiously pandered to at the cost of historical accuracy.

In examining the historical outlook of the Irish Tories who wrote for the *Dublin University Magazine*, Joe Spence concludes that they 'retreated into biography when Irish history became too awful to contemplate', forg-ing in the 'Gallery of Illustrious Irishmen' a new, exclusively Protestant, Ascendancy history.[48] Carleton, divorced from this history, developed his

[45] O'Donoghue, *Life*, i. 10.
[46] Carleton, *Castle Squander*, ii. 207.
[47] Carleton, *Tithe Proctor*, p. viii.
[48] Spence, 'Philosophy of Irish Toryism', 173.

own escape mechanism, by retreating into autobiography. An early poem by Carleton, 'The Retrospect', exemplifies the fluidity of past, present, and future in his work. The poem looks back to the joys of nature and domestic happiness in boyhood, but the persistent use of the future tense, and the completion of each stanza with the words 'Will still, will still be sweet', drives the experience into the future. In the last stanza, we realize that the speaker is looking forward to a life after death, when he will relive his childhood; thus the poem is as much a prospect as a retrospect.[49] This sleight of hand recurs in Carleton's work, not always intentionally. His stories are so firmly rooted in the social problems of his age—poverty, famine, the troubled relationship of landlord and tenant—that in a sense his work becomes prophetic rather than historical. Carleton had a love–hate relationship with the figure of the Irish prophecy man, once a common sight in the countryside, selling broadsheets of the prophecies of 'Pastorini' and Colmcille. Their prophecies of the downfall of Protestantism in the year 1825 were of course repugnant to the moralist Carleton, and defunct once 1825 passed and the Protestants remained, but the atavistic Carleton's familiarity with the prophecies of 'Pastorini' affirmed his authenticity and his connections with peasant nationalism. A manuscript note (dated 1825 and probably by the scholar and divine Henry Cotton, who would have been archdeacon of Cashel at the time) bound with a copy of 'Pastorini''s *General History of the Christian Church* bears witness to Carleton's privileged access to such material·

Certain passages extracted from this work have been printed on a broad sheet and most extensively circulated (gratuitously) among the Roman Catholics of the South of Ireland.—But this has been done in the most secret manner; the extracts are not to be purchased or procured by Protestants; no answer is to be obtained to enquiries made respecting them: and the very existence of such a paper was solemnly denied to me personally in the shop of Rd. Coyne, (the accredited book-seller of the Roman Catholics, in Capel St Dublin,) by his wife.[50]

Carleton ostensibly deplores these peasant prophets, yet he had himself turned back from his journey to Munster to become a poor scholar due to a dream of a bull, and though he spoke with contempt of a gypsy who told him he would never be a priest, but would go to Dublin and become a great

[49] William Carleton, 'The Retrospect', *Dublin Family Magazine*, 1/5 (Aug. 1829), 293–4.
[50] Manuscript note bound with 1812 edition of Pastorini [Charles Walmesley], *The General History of the Christian Church, From Her Birth To Her Final Triumphant State In Heaven: Chiefly Deduced From The Apocalypse of St John, The Apostle and Evangelist* (Dublin: J. Mehain, 1790), in the Bodleian Library, Oxford, shelfmark 110.i.196(i).

man, he never forgot, and no doubt it influenced the course of his life.[51] His work abounds with prophets and prophecies, and his unique insights into Irish society make him seem remarkably prescient. Carleton becomes the prophet of the Black Stone, foretold in 'Barney M'Haigney, The Irish Prophecy Man', who 'always prophecies backwards, and foretells what has happened'.[52] For example, in *Valentine M'Clutchy*, published in 1845 but supposedly looking back to 1804, Carleton wrote of the 'extermination' by M'Clutchy of twenty-three families from the village of Drum Dhu on Christmas Eve, during which a young man, Torley O'Regan, dies of exposure.[53] Seven years later, Carleton inserted all fifteen pages of this scene into *Castle Squander* as representative of the suffering caused by evictions during the Great Famine, and in particular those of the Blake estate in Connaught during the winter of 1847–8:

> In the course, however, of about three years *after* the work [*Valentine M'Clutchy*] in which that scene had appeared had been published, there occurred in the west of Ireland an extermination so miraculously parallel to it in every circumstance, even—as far as we can recollect—to the very Festival on which both occurred, that it would almost seem as if the exterminators alluded to had gone with 'Valentine M'Clutchy' in their hands, in order to perform—act by act—the identical scenes recorded in it, precisely as if they had previously rehearsed them from it.[54]

It is less a case of life imitating art than a testament to the recurring crises of Irish agrarian life. Carleton combines the roles of historian and prophet with that of *seanchaí*, recording in his fiction the cycles of life and death that affect his people. This is most true of his examinations of famine.

In the late twentieth century, Harold Orel asserts, Carleton's true achievement is 'having recorded, more honestly and in greater detail than any of his contemporaries, the world of pre-Famine Ireland'.[55] This may be true, but it is important to remember that until 1846 there was no pre-Famine Ireland, and yet Carleton's reputation as a literary giant was well established by the time he published the second series of *Traits and Stories* in 1833. In January 1841, the *Dublin University Magazine* paid tribute to an established and unrivalled talent: 'William Carleton can vindicate his undisputed claim to the title of the novelist of Ireland. Whatever be his faults or his merits, he is alone.'[56] Although Carleton is now valued for

[51] O'Donoghue, *Life*, i. 71, 213.

[52] Carleton, 'Barney M'Haigney, The Irish Prophecy Man', *Tales and Sketches*, 214.

[53] Carleton, *Valentine M'Clutchy*, i. 187 ff.   [54] Carleton, *Castle Squander*, ii. 102.

[55] Harold Orel, 'Colored Photographs: William Carleton's Contribution to the Short Story Tradition', *Éire-Ireland*, 19/2 (Summer 1984), 75–97, at 77.

[56] *Dublin University Magazine*, 'Our Portrait Galley.—no xv. William Carleton', 17 (Jan. 1841), 66–72, at 66.

his depictions of a lost pre-Famine world, his work is more representative of *famine* Ireland—the Ireland of those who were vulnerable to almost annual crop failures. As Carleton stressed in *The Black Prophet*, famine was a common concept in so-called pre-famine Ireland: 'Much for instance is said, and has been said, concerning what are termed "Years of Famine," but it is not generally known, that since the introduction of the potato into this country, no year has ever passed which, in some remote locality or other, has not been such to the unfortunate inhabitants.'[57] Indeed, there had been fourteen partial or complete potato famines in Ireland between 1816 and 1842,[58] and it is reasonable to believe that Carleton, when recording past famines in his work, did not speak with the detachment of an outsider, as Trollope or Sidney Godolphin Osborne spoke, but as a sufferer. If history was autobiography for Carleton, the prevalence of famine in his writing suggests the immediacy of experience. Carleton's earliest memory was of being carried by his mother to a wedding or feast, where there were tables groaning with food; he adds, poignantly, 'I suppose the depth of the impression was occasioned by the novelty of what I saw.'[59] The lavish spreads in stories such as 'Shane Fadh's Wedding', 'The Station', and 'Going to Maynooth' have a fetishistic feel to them, and, as Boué comments, are completely unrealistic: 'même en Ulster une telle abondance de nourriture ne pouvait se trouver que sur la table des paysans les plus fortunés'.[60]

The year 1817 was an important turning-point in Carleton's life and career. It was the year of Carleton's pilgrimage to Lough Derg, which would later form the basis of his literary début, and in his own analysis changed the course of his life: 'It was the pilgrimage and the reflections occasioned by it, added to a riper knowledge and a maturer judgment, that detached me from the Roman Catholic Church.'[61] But 1817 was also the year of a major famine in Ireland. The narrator of 'The Lough Derg Pilgrim' is particularly horrified by the priests' demands for money for confession: 'It is right to mention here, that this pilgrimage was performed in a season when sickness and famine prevailed fearfully in this kingdom.'[62] An old man and a young boy are forced to make the forty-mile journey home penniless in a time of famine and disease because they have

[57] Carleton, *Black Prophet*, 175.
[58] R. F. Foster, *Modern Ireland 1600–1972* (London: Penguin, 1988), 320.
[59] O'Donoghue, *Life*, i. 4.
[60] 'even in Ulster such an abundance of food could only have been found on the tables of the most fortunate peasants' (Boué, *William Carleton*, 179).
[61] O'Donoghue, *Life*, i. 101.
[62] Carleton, 'The Lough Derg Pilgrim', *Traits and Stories*, i. 265–6.

paid the priests for confession. The narrator objects to this treatment, and injures his prospects of entering the priesthood as a result; thus the link between famine and one of the defining moments of Carleton's life is forged. In another early story, 'Dick Magrath', a farmer ruined in 1817, 'a time of peculiar sickness and famine', takes to selling scapulars in the guise of a blessed friar, makes his fortune on the back of papist superstition, and ends up 'in much more comfortable and independent circumstances than he was ever in before'.[63] These early stories are primarily anti-clerical, and concerned with the damaging effects of Papism on the character of the Irish peasantry, so famine becomes an ideal time to exploit religious super-stition. Other stories, such as 'Tubber Derg' and 'The Poor Scholar', employ the famine of 1817 to criticize landlords rather than priests. 'Tubber Derg' tells of the ruin of the honest farmer Owen M'Carthy, who is precariously balanced on the edge of financial ruin; the 1817 famine and subsequent disease spell disaster, and, unaided by an unfeeling landlord, Owen's family are evicted and his daughter dies. This emotive tale is an unconcealed attack on Irish landlords, whom Carleton blames for the severity of these years of famine: 'Common policy, common sense, and common justice should induce the Irish landlords to lower their agricul-tural produce, otherwise poverty, famine, crime, and vague political spec-ulations, founded upon idle hopes of a general transfer of property, will spread over and convulse the kingdom.'[64] In view of the fate of the land-lords in the Encumbered Estates Court, and the rise of the Tenant League after the Famine, this warning was also prophetic. Famine in 'Tubber Derg' is an exacerbation of an already fraught situation, and this is true of many of Carleton's portrayals of famine. Famine for Carleton was 'the Irish situation *in extremis*', the Irish character raw and exposed.[65] In his justly renowned 'The Poor Scholar', the Bishop, rector, and landlord become interested in Jemmy because of his emaciation and suffering due to famine fever, and the ethereal aspect these give him; his sufferings indi-rectly lead to the regaining of his family's unjustly repossessed farm.[66] Famine is a redemptive force in *The Black Prophet*, reconciling the feud-ing Daltons and Sullivans, softening the tempestuous Sarah.

Famine is the outward manifestation of society's ills, and so integral to Irish malaise that it becomes a metaphor for Carleton. For example, in the

---

[63] Carleton, 'Dick Magrath, A Sketch of Living Character', *Dublin Family Magazine*, 1/5 (Aug. 1829), 336–43.

[64] Carleton, 'Tubber Derg, or, The Red Well', *Traits and Stories*, ii. 372–3, 382.

[65] Flanagan, *The Irish Novelists*, 318.

[66] Carleton, 'The Poor Scholar', *Traits and Stories*, ii. 257–348.

'General Introduction' to *Traits and Stories*, Carleton compares the state of Irish literary production and publishing before his decision to publish exclusively in Ireland, to a state of famine:

> During some of the years of Irish famine, such were the unhappy circumstances of the country, that she was exporting provisions of every description in the most prodigal abundance, which the generosity of England was sending back again for our support. So was it with literature. Our men and women of genius uniformly carried their talents to the English market, whilst we laboured at home under all the dark privations of a literary famine.[67]

Metaphors of literary famine and absenteeism constitute a powerful vindication of Carleton's much-vaunted resolve to revive his country's industry. But it is also fascinating to realize that here, in 1842, three years before the onset of the Great Famine, Carleton is employing one of the key arguments of the nationalist mythos surrounding the Famine: that England drained Ireland of provisions while Ireland starved. Moreover, this criticism, which was to become the mainstay of Mitchel's argument about England's genocidal agenda, occurs even earlier in Carleton's work. 'Phil Purcel, the Pig-Driver', which first appeared in the second series of *Traits and Stories* in 1833, sardonically laments the changes that have taken place since the advent of political economy:

> It was then, simply pig-driving, unaccompanied by the improvements of poverty, sickness and famine. Political economy had not then taught the people how to be poor upon the most scientific principles, free trade had not shown the nation the most approved plan of reducing itself to the lowest possible state of distress; nor liberalism enabled the working classes to scoff at religion, and wisely to stop short at the very line that lies between outrage and rebellion.[68]

Once upon a time, the narrator continues, an Irishman could have eaten his own bacon, but now he must make do with cold theories and potatoes. He refers to the practice of exporting to Britain while the Irish starve in a barely veiled threat:

> But it is very condescending in John to eat our beef and mutton; and as he happens to want both, it is particularly disinterested in him to encourage us in the practice of self-denial. It is possible, however, that we may ultimately refuse to banquet by proxy on our own provisions; and that John may not be much longer troubled to eat for us in that capacity.[69]

[67] Carleton, 'General Introduction', *Traits and Stories*, i, p. v.
[68] Carleton, 'Phil Purcel, the Pig Driver', *Traits and Stories*, i. 408.   [69] Ibid., 410.

Even Mitchel would be hard-pressed to equal such concentrated venom. 'The Poor Scholar', also published in 1833, is a mine of information on how the people survived during famines by eating blood mixed with oatmeal, or chickweed and nettles; this extremity is contrasted with the immense amount of food leaving Ireland: 'the very country thus groaning under such a terrible sweep of famine is actually pouring from all her ports a profusion of food, day after day; flinging it from her fertile bosom, with the wanton excess of a prodigal oppressed by abundance'.[70] Published four years after the granting of Catholic Emancipation, Carleton's revolutionary language pre-dates not only the militant language of Mitchel in a post-Famine and supposedly alien world, but also the foundation of O'Connell's Repeal Movement.

Similarly, Carleton's interest in famine as psychological trauma seems to look forward to twentieth-century studies. Fardorougha Donovan,[71] the anti-hero of Carleton's first novel, is one in a long line of rustic misers in Carleton's work, who keep back their crops until the markets are high, and pray for a year of famine, when meal will be at a premium. Carleton created in Darby Skinadre of *The Black Prophet* so repulsive a figure of this type that the *Athenaeum* balked at it, spending the entire review defending provision-dealers, asserting against common reason that 'There is no class of men that suffers more severely, and in general more undeservedly, than provision-dealers in a season of scarcity.'[72] In his temperance tract *Art Maguire*, Carleton depicts a conversation between two such misers, Cooney Finigan and Jemmy Murray, who are downcast at the prospect of a good harvest, until Cooney has a happy thought: 'sure it's only the beginning o' May now, and who knows but we might have the happiness to see a right good general failure of the praties still? Eh? ha, ha, ha!'[73] Fardorougha is differentiated from Carleton's other misers, and becomes an object of sympathy, because, although he preys on the poverty of others, he is genuinely terrified by the prospect of famine. When his wife bears their only child after a prudent thirteen years of marriage, Fardorougha is thrown into a Malthusian hysteria: 'Think of what a bad saison, or a failure of the crops, might bring us all to! God grant that we mayn't come to the bag and staff before he's settled in the world at all, poor

[70] Carleton, 'The Poor Scholar', *Traits and Stories*, ii. 307.
[71] Carleton frequently forgets his characters' names, and Donovan often becomes O'Donovan.
[72] *Athenaeum*, 1011 (13 Mar. 1847), 278–9, at 279.
[73] William Carleton, *Art Maguire; or, The Broken Pledge. A Narrative* (Dublin and London: Simpkin, Marshall & Co., 1847), 56.

thing.'[74] Fardorougha spends his life torn between avarice and love for his son. Money is 'the famine-struck god of the miser', the only thing preventing an ignominious death.[75] The thought of parting with money, even to save Connor's life when he is charged with arson, torments the miser, and when his nightmare becomes reality and the county treasurer runs off with his hoard, leaving him penniless, Fardorougha's terror of starving as a pauper blots out everything else: 'I knew—I knew—I always felt it was before me—a dog's death behind a ditch—my tongue out wid starvation and hunger . . .'.[76] Asleep in the condemned Connor's prison cell, the old man cannot rid himself of the horror of dying of starvation, and screams out in a nightmare:

I'm dyin' wid hunger—will no one give me a morsel? I was robbed an' have no money—don't you see me starvin'? I'm cuttin' wid hunger—five days widout mate—bring me mate, for God's sake—mate, mate, mate!—I'm gaspin'—my tongue's out; look at me, like a dog, behind this ditch, an' my tongue out![77]

Fardorougha's pathetic monomania is particularly interesting in the context of Carleton's lifelong struggle with poverty. Like Fardorougha, Carleton had mixed feelings on the birth of his first child, Mary Anne: 'I felt divided between a feeling of happiness and care.'[78] The miser's insanity is no far cry from the anxiety of the writer on the edge of destitution.

Valentine M'Clutchy, written to help *The Nation* in its campaign for tenant right, is often seen as Carleton's volte-face, and a declaration of solidarity with Young Ireland. In fact, *Valentine M'Clutchy* reworks many of the issues he had been preoccupied with since the beginning of his career: absenteeism, the bad practices of middlemen and agents, the suffering of the people in times of scarcity, the inhumanity of eviction. Indeed, a comparison of 'The Poor Scholar' (1833), *Valentine M'Clutchy* (1845), and *The Squanders of Castle Squander* (1852) testifies to the consistency of Carleton's opinions, even though only one was written for a specifically nationalist audience.

As we have seen, *Valentine M'Clutchy* is peculiarly prophetic in some of the scenes it presents. The arms of the Topertoe family, who, like the eponymous O'Kellys in Trollope's novel, sold their country at the time of the Union, depict a man standing on the neck of 'a famine struck woman, surrounded by naked and starving children', in order to reach a purse and lead coronet, and 'such is his eagerness to catch it and the coronet, that he

[74] William Carleton, *Fardorougha the Miser, or the Convicts of Lisnamona* (1838; Belfast: Appletree Press, 1992), 18.
[75] Ibid., 13.   [76] Ibid., 105.   [77] Ibid., 109.   [78] O'Donoghue, *Life*, i. 257.

does not seem to care much whether he strangles her or not'.[79] The consequence of the Union, the arms predict, is famine. The novel is set four years after the Union, and the representation of famine is played out against the background of a critique of souperism, the allegation that Evangelicals converted Catholics with bribes of food in times of famine.[80] Protestant colonies such as those at Dingle and Achill had already stirred up the accusation of souperism before 1845—as in the critiques of Nangle in the travel narratives of the Halls and Asenath Nicholson—but Carleton places his charges specifically in terms of famine. The religious attorney Solomon M'Slime hands out tracts such as 'Spiritual Food for Babes of Grace' to the hungry, and is warned even by the unscrupulous Darby O'Drive: 'a hungry man—or a hungry woman, or her hungry children, can't eat bibles; although it is well known, God knows, that when hunger, and famine, and starvation are widin them and upon them, that the same bible, but nothing else, is handed to them by pious people in the shape of consolation and relief'.[81] Darby's advice on how to convert his neighbours is to catch them during the present famine: 'Bait it wid a flitch of bacon on the one side, and a collop o' fresh meat on the other, now before the praties come in, and you're sure of him.'[82] Darby maliciously spreads the rumour that Revd Lucre, M'Slime's rival in the conversion stakes, is offering five guineas per convert—resulting in a flood of potential Protestants. Lucre's consternation is meant to be blackly comic, but the scene is also heart-rending: Paddy Cummins, 'a ragged, famine-wasted creature', offers himself, his wife, and eight children, all starving, for the money as a last resort, but they are turned out to starve.[83] The scene takes on apocalyptic dimensions when the idiot-savant Raymond–na–hattha bursts in, and proceeds to expound the Bible: 'Let us see, then—Murdher and bloodshed, hangin' and starvin', huntin', purshuin', whippin', could and nakedness, hunger and sickness, death and then madness, and then death agin, and then damnation! Did I explain it?'[84] Raymond leaves after asking 'to borrow the loan of your religion till the new praties come in'.[85] It is a damning indictment of souperism, and it is doubtful whether Carleton could have made a more damaging assault even had he waited for the accusations that would be made in the following years. Nevertheless, the novel is uncannily prescient.

[79] Carleton, *Valentine M'Clutchy*, ii. 294.
[80] It is significant that in spite of accusations that he had taken the bribe himself, Carleton openly criticizes souperism and conversion for gain here and elsewhere.
[81] Carleton, *Valentine M'Clutchy*, i. 66–7.   [82] Ibid., ii. 39.   [83] Ibid., 103.
[84] Ibid., 120.   [85] Ibid., 122.

The Black Prophet has achieved fame in our time as the first literary representation of the Great Famine, but Carleton has been criticized for not
creating a plot commensurate to the atrocity. Eagleton sees *The Black
Prophet* as one of 'a number of curious literary near-misses',[86] while
Malcolm Brown, like many others underestimating Carleton's intellect
and overestimating his peasant status, believes that he was simply incapable of understanding the enormity of the Famine: 'beyond communi-
cating the raw feel of human pain, Carleton's peasant brain had trouble
seizing the meaning of the catastrophe'.[87] In fact, *The Black Prophet* was
one of those curious prophetic quirks of Carleton's fiction, arising from
the depth of social knowledge submerged in his works. The novel first
appeared in the *Dublin University Magazine* between May and December
1846; so, when it began to appear, there had only been the partial blight of
1845, and no sign that the destruction would recur. Even when Carleton
wrote his polemical 'Preface' to *The Black Prophet* when it was published
by Simms and M'Intyre in February 1847, he could foresee that there
would be great hardship due to the unexpected second failure in 1846, and
he knew from his own experience that disease would follow, but he could
not have predicted the low yield of 1847, or the failure of 1848. It is for this
reason—the fact that the Great Famine did not exist as a concept when he
began to write *The Black Prophet*—and not for any inability to compre-
hend the tragedy, that Carleton chose to use the Famine as a background
to a murder mystery. After all, no one would criticize 'The Poor Scholar'
or 'Tubber Derg', which Carleton also wrote from his experience of the
1817 famine, for using famine as background to issues of land or education. Despite the well-intentioned but misguided defence of *The Black
Prophet* by critics such as Sophia Hillan King, that one 'need not go to this
novel for plot, but rather for its evocation of the realities of famine', this is
not at all what Carleton intended.[88] The principal interest of the novel, he
stresses in the same 'Introduction' in which he criticizes the government
for failing to protect Ireland from Famine, should not be 'so gloomy a
topic as famine', but 'the workings of those passions and feelings which
usually agitate human life, and constitute the character of those who act in
it'.[89] *Howitt's Journal* of April 1847, and Barbara Hayley in 1985, unite in
describing *The Black Prophet* as 'well-timed', but it was in fact nothing less

[86] Eagleton, *Heathcliff and the Great Hunger*, 13.
[87] Malcolm Brown, *The Politics of Irish Literature From Thomas Davis to W. B. Yeats*
(London: Allen & Unwin, 1972), 92.
[88] Sophia Hillan King, ' "Pictures Drawn From Memory": William Carleton's Experience
of Famine', *Irish Review* (Winter 1995), 80–9, at 82.
[89] Carleton, *Black Prophet*, p. iv.

than a pre-emptive strike on the market.[90] For Carleton, it was simply the latest in a long line of failures—a fact made clear by the non-specific subtitle, *A Tale of Irish Famine*—and he was using his knowledge of the 1817 failure, as he had often used it before, to show Irish character under duress. As far as Carleton was concerned, this famine would soon be forgotten, and it would be a shame to let it pass without making some literary, political, and financial capital from it: 'National inflictions of this kind pass away, and are soon forgotten by every one but those with whom they have left their melancholy memorials.'[91] Cormac Ó Gráda would agree with Carleton's analysis: 'Ironically, had the potato famine of 1845 lasted just one year, it would have merited no more than a few paragraphs in the history books.'[92]

Carleton seized the opportunity to use the blights of 1845 and 1846 as the ultimate witness to the authenticity of his previous work. *The Black Prophet* is based on personal experience of the famine of 1817, but it is written in the midst of corroborating evidence: 'The pictures and scenes represented are those he himself witnessed in 1817, 1822, and other subsequent years, and if they be false or exaggerated, there are thousands still living who can come forward and establish their falsehood. They have been depicted, however, in the midst of living testimony, and they not only *have* escaped contradiction, but defy it.'[93] This is *living testimony*, the ultimate proof. But while Carleton is verifying his personal observation of past famines, he is also distancing himself from the experience of famine by identifying with it as a writer, not as a peasant. In a rather unsubtle reference to his ongoing campaign for a literary pension, Carleton reminds the Prime Minister, Lord John Russell: 'there is no party in this country so well qualified to afford authentic information on this particular subject, as those who have done most in giving an impulse to sustaining the literature of their country'.[94] Writers, he implies, are starving due to the ingratitude of the people and the government, and his own poverty precludes him from offering anything to famine relief but this novel. In *Red Hall: or, The Baronet's Daughter*, written in 1850, when people were still dying of starvation and related disease, the unsavoury Lord Dunroe turns the horror of famine, including newspaper reports of prosecutions for cannibalism, into a theatrical melodrama:

[90] *Howitt's Journal*, 1/17 (24 Apr. 1847), 236–7, at 236; Hayley, *Bibliography*, 149.
[91] Carleton, *Black Prophet*, p. iv.
[92] Cormac Ó Gráda, *Ireland Before and After the Famine: Explorations in Economic History, 1800–1925* (Manchester: Manchester University Press, 1988), 5.
[93] Carleton, *Black Prophet*, p. iv.   [94] Ibid., 'Dedication'.

On Saturday, the 25th inst., a tender and affectionate father, stuffed by so many cubic feet of cold wind, foul air, all resulting from extermination and the benevolence of a humane landlord, will, in the very wantonness of repletion, feed upon the dead body of his own child—for which entertaining performance he will have the satisfaction, subsequently, of enacting with success the interesting character of a felon, and be comfortably lodged at his majesty's expense in the gaol of the county.[95]

Divorced from the threat of actual starvation, Carleton appears to be trivializing famine, and the question of middle-class writers using the suffering of others for artistic and financial gain becomes highly relevant. And yet perhaps Carleton suffered more than we know, certainly more than many of his fellow writers on famine. Notoriously unwise in his dealings with publishers, Carleton had to support his wife and ten children on the proceeds of his pen. In a letter to Sir Robert Peel, he complained: '*I have never received for all I ever wrote—eleven volumes—the sum of seven hundred pounds! The reason of this is—because I published at home.*'[96] Even after his pension was granted in 1848, Carleton was always in debt. Like Fardorougha, he may have been haunted by the possibility of death by starvation. He had almost certainly seen starving men on the road to Lough Derg, he had slept alongside beggars, cripples, and hucksters in a cellar in Dirty Lane in Dublin. Perhaps he suffered more than he was prepared to admit. In his autobiography, he hints that his memory is selective: 'I have gone through scenes which, if related, would strip my narrative or my suffering of all claims to the dignity of ordinary experience.'[97] The narrator of *Castle Squander* in a post-famine Ireland recalls that the Famine was

something so utterly unprecedented in the annals of human life, as the mingled mass of agony was borne past us upon the wild and pitiless blast, that we find ourselves absolutely incompetent even to describe it. We feel, however, as if that loud and multitudinous wail was still ringing in our ears, against which and the terrible recollections associated with it, we wish we could close them and the memory that brings them into fresh existence.[98]

The use of the words 'recollections' and 'memory' remind us that Carleton was much more than an eyewitness. But, although he is not ashamed to tell of wandering the streets of Dublin penniless, of sleeping

---

[95] William Carleton, *Red Hall: or, The Baronet's Daughter*, 3 vols. (London: Saunders & Otley, 1852), ii. 51.

[96] Quoted in Boué, *William Carleton*, 348.   [97] O'Donoghue, *Life*, i. 188.

[98] Carleton, *Castle Squander*, ii. 105.

in the horrid cellar in Dirty Lane, of leaving boarding-houses without paying, his experience of famine is too awful to relate or to remember.

While Carleton strives to make the public at large understand what happens in a time of famine in Ireland, he is continually stressing the distance between reader and experience, and our utter inability to empathize with a starving person. To begin with, this is 'an exclusively Irish subject', so English readers, who ironically made up most of his contemporary audience, were automatically excluded: 'Alas, little do our English neighbours know or dream of the horrors which attend a year of severe famine in this unhappy country.'[99] Even for his Irish readers, the sufferings of famine victims are 'such as no human pen could at all describe', and even if he could describe this horror, our contemplation of it in retrospect is not enough: 'If, however, the abstract consideration of it, even at a distance, be a matter of such painful retrospect to the mind, what must not the actual endurance of that and worse have been to the thousands upon thousands of families who were obliged, by God's mysterious dispensation, to encounter these calamities in all their almost incredible and hideous reality.'[100] Another obstacle to the reader's understanding is the metamorphosis of the starving individual into something inhuman, which leaves the reader able to pity, but not to empathize. This has already been seen in the representations of famine victims in travel narratives as wolfish and aggressive. The hordes of starving people who attack meal carts and merchants' houses in *The Black Prophet* are brutalized by suffering, and even Carleton betrays more fear and fascinated disgust than empathy: 'Their cadaverous and emaciated aspects had something in them so wild and wolfish, and the fire of famine blazed so savagely in their hollow eyes, that many of them looked like creatures changed from their very humanity by some judicial plague that had been sent down from heaven to punish and desolate the land.'[101]

It is intriguing that Carleton, like Trollope, plays with this idea of the Famine as Providential retribution. Carleton the didactic writer had scoffed at Irish superstitions, but *The Black Prophet* is loaded with signs and portents, dreams and prophecies. Donnel Dhu, the eponymous prophet, is presented as a cunning villain, who uses prophecies to manipulate people, but they appear to come true against his will. Donnel tells Mave that the first man she meets as she passes the Grey Stone will raise her to wealth and happiness (he has previously arranged that Young Dick,

---

[99] Carleton, *Black Prophet*, 'Dedication'; 180.   [100] Ibid., 260–1, 148.
[101] Ibid., 176–7.

to whom he hopes to prostitute Mave, would already be there); thanks to the intervention of Donnel's daughter Sarah, and Mave's own initiative, she meets (and later marries) Condy Dalton. Donnel's dream that Mave gives him Condy's hammer to make his own coffin can be seen to be ful-filled, as the Cannie Sugah discovers Donnel's plot through the young lovers. Donnel's most powerful prophecy, his tour-de-force, is that of famine:

> Isn't the Almighty, in his wrath, this moment proclaimin' it through the heavens and the airth? Look about you, and say what is it you see that doesn't foretell famine—famine—famine! Doesn't the dark wet day an' the rain, rain, rain, fore-tell it? Doesn't the rottin' crops, the unhealthy air, an' the green damp foretell it? Doesn't the sky without a sun, the heavy clouds, an' the angry fire of the West fore-tell it? Isn't the airth a page of prophecy, an' the sky a page of prophecy, where every man may read of famine, pestilence, an' death?[102]

The power of this Evangelical language, the menacing repetition and the use of rhetorical question create an oppressive sense of doom, but Donnel is prophesying in much the same way as Carleton: the state of the country is an open book, 'a page of prophecy' that is open to all. Carleton plays along with the idea of Providential retribution, allowing us to believe, along with the people of Glen Dhu, that the Daltons' decline and fall into poverty and then starvation and sickness is because of a murder commit-ted by Condy's father twenty years before: 'it became too certain to be doubted, that the slow but sure finger of God's justice was laid upon them as an additional proof that crime, however it may escape the laws of men, cannot veil itself from the all-seeing eye of the Almighty'.[103] In fact, old Condy is innocent, and his decline is due to the ruthless grasping of the middleman Dick-o'-the-Grange, who wants to evict the Daltons so that he can profit by the £500 improvements they have made on their farm; and to their landlord, an absentee English nobleman, who draws £32,000 a year from his estate, yet who contributed only £100 to the relief of his famine-stricken tenants—a point that Carleton footnotes 'A recent fact';[104] and by implication to the government, whom Carleton had criti-cized in the 'Dedication' for not legislating to prevent such disasters. Moreover, Providence is exposed as false currency by its use in the justi-fication of the cruelty of the miser Darby Skinadre. Darby, who is 'like the very Genius of Famine', exploits the poverty of his clients in order to secure their possessions in return for a pittance of meal.[105] Jemmy Duggan is forced to give Darby the heifer he had been keeping for the rent, in

---

[102] Ibid., 15.   [103] Ibid., 99.   [104] Ibid., 198.   [105] Ibid., 50.

exchange for meal to save his wife and six children; Darby's 'consolation' is cold comfort: 'the thruth is, we have brought all these scourges on us by our sins and our thransgressions; thim that sins, Jemmy, must suffer'.[106] Such a doctrine in such a mouth cannot but be discredited. As in Carleton's previous examinations of famine, fault lies not with a sinful people, but with a social chaos.

When he had finished *The Black Prophet*, Carleton, who like Jemmy Donnelly in 'The Poor Scholar' had promised not to return home until he had fulfilled his potential, finally returned to the Clogher Valley. He may have been spurred by anxiety, to see how his family and neighbours were coping in Black '47. Carleton promised Charles Gavan Duffy: 'As soon as I return I shall publish a narrative (in *The Nation*) of my visit, my impressions, &.c., in all senses and in all moods—on returning after twenty years to my native place.'[107] The narrative never appeared. Carleton found the town of Ballyscally desolate, and all the tenants evicted, except his first love, Anne Duffy, and her husband. His interest in the 'exterminated' villagers ends here, and we receive a long description of how the middle-aged lovers were platonically reunited. Perhaps, had Carleton lived to complete his autobiography, he might have dealt at greater length with the Famine; but the famine of 1817, which recurs frequently in his fiction, doesn't even get a mention. As evidenced in Famine historiography, fiction seems to be a much less emotive, less painful medium than factual representation.

In a letter to his daughter Jane during his visit to the Clogher Valley in 1847, Carleton spoke ecstatically of his fame in County Tyrone, but not of the state of the country. 'Certainly I am a prophet—not the Black one—honoured in his own country,' he wrote, punning on his latest novel; but in a sense, like the Irish prophecy man, Carleton had sealed his own doom.[108] The Irish Prophecy Man, once a fixture in Irish villages, had prophesied himself into a corner by basing his system on the predictions of 'Pastorini' that the Protestant Church would be destroyed in 1825. When 1825 came and went, and when the great hope of Irish prophecy, Bonaparte, was imprisoned, the Irish prophecy man was discredited, and dwindled away and died. In 1842, on the basis of his own exertions in periodicals and books, Carleton announced a new age of Irish literature. By 1847 that dream was dead. Carleton's first publisher, William Curry, Jr., and seventy-two other Irish publishers, were declared bankrupt between

---

[106] Carleton, *Black Prophet*, 53.

[107] Sir Charles Gavan Duffy, *My Life in Two Hemispheres*, 2 vols. (London: T. Fisher Unwin, 1898), i. 221.

[108] O'Donoghue, *Life*, ii. 90.

1844 and 1848, reflecting a widespread economic destruction.[109] The Belfast firm Simms and McIntyre continued to publish Carleton in their 'Parlour Library' series, which were popular due to the extremely low price of one shilling for three volumes, and on a visit to London in 1850, Carleton found that *The Black Prophet* had achieved a wide English audience. However, Carleton, like Trollope, was to discover that readers were suffering from compassion fatigue, and had tired of gloomy Irish subjects. Carleton even betrayed his principles by approaching English publishers: the London publisher Maxwell declined to publish a Carleton novel in 1850, telling him that 'the Irish are not able to buy it, and the English will not', and making the bizarre suggestion that the Irish national novelist should 'go to Lancashire, reside there, and devote his gifts to English subjects'.[110] James Duffy, the notable survivor among Irish publishers (who, by the way, held a grudge against Carleton for having persuaded him to publish *Paddy Go-Easy*, a tract against Irish indolence), warned Carleton in 1855: 'The people seldom think of buying books, because they are luxuries, which they can do without.'[111] Carleton's disillusionment with both Irish literature and Ireland itself can be traced in *The Squanders of Castle Squander*, published—in London—in 1852.

O'Donoghue was quick to point out that Carleton referred to *Castle Squander* not as a novel, but as 'my work upon Ireland'.[112] Based on 'a knowledge of more than fifty years of my people and the country', the 'work' also charts the destruction of fifty years of Irish literature, beginning with an Edgeworthian comic framework, and ending with a literary nervous breakdown.[113] The novel begins with the first-person narrative of Randy O'Rollick, and the promise of exposition à la Thady Quirk; O'Rollick, the bailiff's son, even mentions that bailiffs often make their sons attorneys in order to swindle their masters of their land, much as Jason Quirk had done in *Castle Rackrent*.[114] But as the narrative grows progressively darker, the authorial 'we' supplants O'Rollick with greater frequency, even to identifying himself as Carleton by acknowledging *Valentine M'Clutchy* as his own production, and inserting extracts from it into the text. O'Rollick's narrative is further usurped by extracts from the *Dublin University Magazine*, Trevelyan's *The Irish Crisis*, letters by Hancock and J. S. Mill, references to Dante's *Inferno*, Mary Shelley's *Frankenstein*, and Defoe's *The Great Plague*.

---

[109] Charles Benson, 'Printers and Booksellers in Dublin 1800–1850', in Robin Myers and Michael Harris (eds.), *Spreading the Word: The Distribution Networks of Print 1550–1850* (Winchester: St Paul's Bibliographies, 1990), 47–59, at 57.

[110] O'Donoghue, *Life*, ii. 176–7.   [111] Ibid., 215.   [112] Ibid., i. 182.

[113] Carleton, *Castle Squander*, i, pp. iii–iv.   [114] Ibid., 3–4.

The book begins and ends in famine. Carleton has shifted his viewpoint to the Big House, an unusual step for the delineator of the Irish peasant. Like Carleton, Randy has been assimilated into the Establishment, and feels regret at its passing: 'The truth, however, is, that I became attached to the family, and not the less so that I saw the house absolutely tottering to its fall.'[115] A constant critic of Irish landlordism, Carleton has placed a fifth column in its ranks in the shape of O'Rollick, yet finds the spy has become a convert, sympathizing in the dying throes of an enemy. Nevertheless, Randy's testimony is damning. The book opens in a year of famine, and Randy witnesses the excesses of the Squanders' entertainments while their tenants starve. Masses of food lie about in the dust of the kitchen floor, the dogs are treated to bins of oatmeal and potatoes, and we are reminded:

Now it so happened, that the year in question was one of severe famine, and I could not help reflecting, even then, that the sum of five pounds, subscribed to the relief fund by Mr. Squander, took a very inhuman shape, when associated with the profuse abundance thus lavished in his kennel, whilst so many of his fellow creatures, nay, of his own tenants, were literally perishing for want of food.[116]

A few years later, during another period of famine and disease, the Squanders become absentees, taking off to London for a spot of horse-racing—a move Randy castigates as inexcusable.[117]

However, whereas in his previous works these famines would have provided a catalyst exposing the Irish peasant character, here they simply highlight the immoral excesses of Irish landlords. There is an impassable gulf established between the Big House and the cabin, which not even Randy can breach. Once he is established at Castle Squander, his mother, 'sportheen' stepfather, pretty sister, and other siblings virtually disappear from view. In *The Black Prophet*, the reader had been admitted into the midst of death, had seen the starving woman and her children whom Sarah had saved, had witnessed the death of a woman and her baby from starvation in a cabin.[118] In *Castle Squander*, the process of dehumanization intensifies, and we receive not such sentimental set-pieces, but brutalized horror. Carleton was an experienced writer of the macabre: as Harold Orel asserts: 'It is difficult to name another British writer of the 19th century

---

[115] Carleton, *Castle Squander*, 219.

[116] Ibid., 44; Squander's £5 donation may be a sly reference to nationalist claims that Queen Victoria donated only £5 to famine relief.

[117] Ibid., 107.

[118] Both of which scenes are remarkably similar to parallel scenes in Trollope's *Castle Richmond*, published several years later.

who could, or would, describe putrefying flesh of hanged conspirators in details as fulsome as Carleton did in "Wildgoose Lodge".[119] Carleton's interest in violence and horror, appropriate as it is to the nineteenth-century Irish scene, permeates his work. In 'Wildgoose Lodge', we have not only the rotting bodies of Devaun and his co-conspirators, but the attack on the Lodge itself, where a woman's burning head is transfixed by a bayonet and a pike, and thrust back into the flames. Carleton several times refers to the Irish peasantry as 'Frankensteins',[120] and almost forty years before Le Fanu's 'Carmilla', and sixty-four years before Bram Stoker's *Dracula*, he was describing ruthless agents as 'vampyres'.[121] In an early scene in *The Black Prophet*, the enigmatic Sarah M'Gowan attacks her stepmother with a knife; her beauty is transformed into a terrible expression of cruelty, and she becomes a 'beautiful vampire that was ravening for the blood of its awakened victim'.[122] When she can't stab Nelly, Sarah bites her cheek instead, exclaiming in triumph: 'I've tasted your blood, and I like it—ha, ha, ha!'[123] Elsewhere, Carleton even deals with ghoulish body-snatching.[124] But nothing prepares us for the amount and intensity of horror in *Castle Squander*. Squire Squander is bluff, jovial, a Sir Condy Rackrent for the 1840s, generous to a fault, but with the abhorrence of the unwashed masses typical of his class and time. Yet Carleton turns the sentimental Victorian deathbed scene on its head in an extraordinarily minute description of the physical change as Squander dies:

his face became first crimson, then the hue deepened until it turned into purple, and immediately almost into black; his head fell down on his breast, he gave one long, deep-drawn gasp, his under jaw relaxed and dropped from its natural position, giving to the open mouth a wild and fearful character, whilst the eyes still remained fixed and staring as before, only that the inanimate glare of death now added to the horror of their expression.[125]

Added to this are the supernatural manifestations surrounding Squander's death—strange and appalling sounds, jingling tumblers, windows rattling 'as if a large bird, with huge pinions, had fiercely dashed against them', a voice calling Squander.[126] The horror does not end there. On a visit to

[119] Orel, 'Colored Photographs', 76.

[120] For example, *Castle Squander*, ii. 88; Carleton makes the common mistake of believing 'Frankenstein' was the monster, not the creator.

[121] Carleton, 'Poor Scholar', *Traits and Stories*, ii. 332; Carleton, *Valentine M'Clutchy*, ii. 175.

[122] Carleton, *Black Prophet*, 10.   [123] Ibid., 11.

[124] Carleton, 'The Misfortunes of Barney Branagan', *The Fawn of Springvale, The Clarionet, and Other Tales*, 3 vols. (Dublin: William Curry, Jr. and Co., 1841), iii. 119.

[125] Carleton, *Castle Squander*, i. 236–7.   [126] Ibid., 236.

Squander's tomb later in the book, Mrs Squander, Emily, and Tom seem to enter an Inferno, where rotting cholera victims are tossed into trenches, only to be dragged out by ravenous dogs. We are spared the sentimental scenes of human suffering and the death of individuals only to be appalled by general death and degradation:

Legs and arms stripped of the flesh and bearing about them the unnatural marks left by the bloody fangs of some hungry mastiff, were scattered about. Some had been dragged into the neighbouring fields, as might be learned by the eager and interrupted howl of the half-gratified animal, as he feasted upon the revolting meat. In a different field might be seen another wolfish hound, with a human head between his paws, on the features of which he was making his meal.

Now, all these frightful pictures were facts of that day, and were witnessed by thousands![127]

In *Red Hall*, published the same year, the animals who eat putrid flesh are human beings, and with the final taboo, cannibalism, falls the myth of family solidarity in the face of famine:

all the impulses of nature and affection were not merely banished from the heart, but superseded by the most frightful peals of insane mirth, cruelty, and the horrible appetite of the ghoul and vampire. Some were found tearing the flesh from the bodies of the carcasses that were stretched beside them . . . fathers have been known to make a wolfish meal upon the dead bodies of their own offspring. We might, therefore, have carried on our description up to the very highest point of imaginable horror, without going beyond the truth.[128]

While famine offers the ultimate in artistic licence, this is Carleton's nightmare, a vision he strove desperately to escape. The authorial 'we' admits that the sufferings of the Irish people at this time would have driven him to violence, and although he deplores the débâcle of the Young Ireland rising, he seriously questions the people's want of spirit: 'we have often, in the burning indignation of the moment, asked ourselves what had become of the Celtic spirit—and why the people, in self-defence, did not spurn that law which gave them no protection, and forget themselves into the execution of natural justice'.[129] Even Randy, in his capacity as under-agent to that embodiment of Famine, the gargantuan Greasy Pockets, is overcome by an atavistic fury: 'I felt a sense of injustice that almost turned my sympathy into madness, and prompted me to drag the aggressive villain out of the house and trample him under my feet.'[130] Carleton deals with this powerful tribal anger linking him to Famine victims by deliber-

---

[127] Carleton, *Castle Squander*, ii. 139.   [128] Carleton, *Red Hall*, ii. 34–5.
[129] Carleton, *Castle Squander*, ii. 232.   [130] Ibid., 95.

ately distancing them; first by dehumanizing them, making them carrion for dogs or worse, for each other; then, by isolating the Famine in the south and west of the country.

In a comic scene near the start of the book, Randy is interviewed for the post of tutor by kindly old Dr M'Claret, the Protestant rector. When M'Claret asks Randy to solve a mathematical problem he finds impossible, Randy evades by asking M'Claret in Irish what the last news from Purgatory had been, and if M'Claret's father had been redeemed yet. M'Claret, who, like Carleton, had begun life as a Northern Catholic, does not understand Irish, and asks Randy to explain:

'It is the vernacular, sir, of a certain country, with whose history you are evidently unacquainted. Of a country, sir, whose inhabitants live upon a meal a month; keep very little—for sound reasons—between themselves and the elements, and where abstinence from food is the national diversion.'

'God bless me!' exclaimed the parson, 'that's very odd, very odd indeed, I shall take a note of that; how very like Ireland!'[131]

Irish is thus established as the vernacular of a famine-stricken people, iso-lating it among the peasantry from whom Carleton had escaped. But the North of Ireland, Carleton's homeland, is spared in *Castle Squander*, despite contemporary reports in the *Banner of Ulster* and the *Belfast Vindicator*, and historical evidence that Ulster certainly partook of the Famine. Tom Squander's property luckily lies in an industrious Northern county, and even during the Famine his income is maintained. Henry Squander, the black sheep of the family, who demeaned himself by marry-ing into a merchant family and setting up business in the north, is in the end able to buy up his ancestral residence in the Encumbered Estates Court. On a visit to Henry's home in Ulster, Randy is amazed at the con-trast: 'The trim hedges, the neat and clean culture, the superior dress, the sober and thoughtful demeanour, and the calm air of self-respect and inde-pendence which marked the inhabitants of the north, were such as could not for a moment be mistaken.'[132] While Carleton is scoring a didactic point about the virtues of his adopted religion, he is also denying that his people, the people of Ulster, were affected by famine. He had suppressed their accent in *Traits and Stories* to achieve cohesive nationality, but now he resurrects it as a barrier against the vernacular of a famine-stricken people. He had revisited the Clogher Valley in 1847 and found it deserted, but in *Castle Squander* it is repeopled, newly prosperous, untouched. Carleton went even further, cursing Ireland with an astonishing vehemence, and

---

[131] Ibid., i. 31.   [132] Ibid., ii. 185.

declaring his resolution to emigrate from his ungrateful country: 'Only may the curse of God alight doubly on Ireland and may all she has suffered be only like the entrance to Paradise compared to what she may suffer.'[133] His language suggests not only fury but fear, and the desire to escape. Like Lord Dunroe of *Red Hall*, he has come to associate Irishness with starvation, brutality, and cannibalism: 'call me profligate—spendthrift—debauchée—anything you will but an Irishman.'[134]

A disillusioned, angry Carleton rejected the notion of a Celtic civilization in Ireland, retorting: 'We Celts were never civilised, and are not civilised, nor will be properly so for at least another half century, if even at that period.'[135] The Famine had proved that, and had destroyed not only his hopes for Irish literature, but the people who had formed the raw material of his work. Brandishing the 1851 census, he tells us to seek the missing people of 1841 in the grave.[136] Carleton entered what Yeats called his 'Iliad of decadence', ironically scoring his greatest success in 1855 with the fatuous *Willy Reilly and his Dear Colleen Bawn*, which quickly ran through forty editions, catering for an audience tired of tragedy and in need of romance.[137] The final prediction of this Irish Prophecy Man was the death of the brief literary revival he had helped initiate, and his own fall into disfavour:

Banim and Griffin are gone, and I will soon follow them—*ultimus Romanorum*, and after that will come a lull, an obscurity of perhaps half a century, when a new condition of civil society and a new phase of manners and habits among the people—for this is a *transition* state—may introduce new fields and new tastes for other writers, for in this manner the cycles of literature and taste appear, hold their day, displace each other, and make room for others.[138]

Twenty years later, W. B. Yeats would envy Carleton his Celtic eyes, and hope the prophecy was made for him, but his passion soon cooled; in a copy of *Stories from Carleton* which the poet gave to John Quinn in 1904, he wrote: 'I thought no end of Carleton in those days & would still I dare say if I had not forgotten him.'[139] But after the half a century predicted by Carleton, the most famous Irish novelist of the twentieth century would

---

[133] To Charles Gavan Duffy, quoted in Boué, *William Carleton*, 352–3; it is significant that these remarks were made to Duffy, who was at the time equally disillusioned, and expressing similar fury in the newly revived *Nation*.

[134] Carleton, *Red Hall*, ii. 50.   [135] *Castle Squander*, ii, 207.

[136] Carleton, Ibid., ii. 237.   [137] Yeats, *Stories from Carleton*, xvi.

[138] O'Donoghue, *Life*, ii. 293.

[139] W. B. Yeats, *Uncollected Prose by W. B. Yeats*, Vol. I, ed. John P. Frayne (London: Macmillan, 1970), 142.

leave his native place and, like Carleton, spend the rest of his life re-creating it. Another half century, and a fellow Ulsterman would confront his literary forebear on the road to Lough Derg, and seek to make his peace with a disillusioned, angry man who outlived his time.[140]

[140] Seamus Heaney, 'Station Island II', *New Selected Poems 1966–87* (London: Faber & Faber, 1990), 166–8.

6

'A Ghastly Spectral Army': History, Identity, and the Visionary Poet

A ghastly, spectral army, before the great God we'll stand,
And arraign ye as our murderers, the spoilers of our land.

('Speranza', 'The Famine Year', *Poems by Speranza*
(Dublin: James Duffy, 1864), 7.)

The Chinese author and intellectual dissident Hsien–Liang Chang spent the late 1950s and most of the 1960s in a gulag, accused of thought-crimes. Like most Chinese during the reign of Mao Tse-tung, political prisoners were in constant danger of starvation: the title of Chang's autobiography, *Grass Soup*, reflects the state of his diet for many years. Yet, despite his own sufferings, and the constant deaths from starvation of camp colleagues, he continued to write. Sometimes there was an ulterior motive: if he let it be known that he was writing a poem in praise of Chinese technology, or the camp commander, he would be given more food, or assigned lighter tasks. But even he was amazed at his own resilience:

Still, it was surprising that I was moved to write poetry. People were dying one after another in front of my eyes, dying right next to me, yet I still raised my voice in song. Famine not only took countless lives, it also murdered countless poems. If I had been able to eat to my fill, I could certainly have written thousands of eulogies.[1]

Irish poets must have been similarly surprised by their ability to continue writing poetry in the midst of Famine. The columns of *The Nation* and other periodicals burgeoned with their offerings; as *The Nation* noted: 'It is a ghastly inspiration that Famine kindles. Cypress, and yew, and nightly-shrieking mandrake, furnish the dismal coronals that our poets are gathering for us in these days.'[2] Certainly it would seem to be a topic chosen with reluctance: in 'The Old Story', William Pembroke Mulchinock charted the disappointment of a young poet who hoped to find fame by singing of his country, only to discover that 'The poor were ne'er in fashion':

---

[1] Hsien–Liang Chang, *Grass Soup*, trans. Martha Avery (London: Minerva, 1995), 75.
[2] *Nation* (14 Mar. 1846), 344.

> I've seen around me scatter'd wide
> Decay and desolation—
> I've seen it, and I sadly sighed,
> To draw thence Inspiration.[3]

But for Irish poets of the late 1840s, Famine was the theme no one could avoid. In practical terms, it disrupted literary careers, as publishers went out of business, *The Nation*'s 'Library of Ireland' programme, for which many of them were writing, was dropped, and Thomas Davis's longed-for 'Ballad History of Ireland' was discontinued on the grounds that the Famine made politics infinitely more important than poetry. Readers who wrote to *The Nation* enquiring about the 'Ballad History' were asked: 'What man with a heart would sit down to write Ballad History while his country perishes?'[4] Ballads had become important disseminators of historical and political knowledge in Ireland, and Davis and Duffy hoped to use them to raise political awareness among readers of *The Nation* and its anthology, the *Spirit of the Nation*. Ballad history was to be the ideal complement to dry, statistical facts, teaching its readers to love virtue and nobility and deplore shame and sorrow, and to remember the deeds of great men: 'these are the highest duties of history, and these are best taught by a ballad history'.[5] The abandonment of the project was significant because it acknowledged that the Famine marked a change in the course of history, which led to a subtle reinterpretation of the importance of history on the part of all Famine poets. Indeed, the poets of the Famine period could be said to be engaged, on an individual level, in the creation of a ballad history of the Famine. Almost twenty years after the event, the *Dublin Review* described the poems of Speranza as a running commentary on the Famine, a kind of memory bank:

[Her] gloomy series of images recalls to us the awful state of the country—the corpses that were buried without coffins, and the men and women that walked the roads more like corpses than living creatures, spectres and skeletons at once; the little children out of whose sunken eyes the very tears were dried, and over whose bare little bones the hideous fur of famine had begun to grow; the cholera cart, with its load of helpless, huddled humanity, on its way to the hospital; the emigrant ship sending back its woeful wail of farewell from swarming poop to stern

---

[3] William Pembroke Mulchinock, 'The Old Story', in Chris Morash (ed.), *The Hungry Voice: The Poetry of the Irish Famine* (Dublin: Irish Academic Press, 1989), 66–7.
[4] *Nation* (1 May 1847), 472.
[5] Thomas Davis, in Pádraig O Dálaigh (ed.), *A Ballad History of Ireland for Schools* (Dublin and Cork: The Educational Company of Ireland, 1929), 5.

in the offing; and, far as the eye could search the land, the blackened potato-fields, filling all the air with fetid odours of decay.[6]

Speranza's poems serve as the quiddity of Famine, the locus from which memory radiates, expanding her images into a history of the disaster. The frequent anthologizing of 'The Famine Year' ensures that her version of history, and her identification with the calamity, has survived; when Mulchinock lamented there were 'No wreathes for Inspiration' drawn from misery, he cannot have taken into account the spectacular rise of Speranza.

But, as Chris Morash asserts, there was a vast disparity between poets such as Speranza and the suffering poor she claimed to represent. Most of the contributors to *The Nation*, the *Irishman* and the *United Irishman*— journals that published most of the Famine poets—were middle-class professionals: Richard D'Alton Williams and Kevin Izod O'Doherty were doctors, Thomas Davis, John Mitchel, and John O'Hagan were lawyers, Speranza and other female contributors such as 'Eva' (Mary Kelly) and 'Thomasine' (Olivia Knight) were from genteel families, or married to professionals. Furthermore, Morash claims, the whole basis of their enterprise was a linguistic fallacy, as they were writing in English to preach rebellion to an Irish-speaking peasantry, and, even worse, using English as the medium of a concept that was inherently alien to it:

Famine, perhaps more than any other agent of change, forces the poet to make difficult choices; for while the sight of so many of his fellow creatures driven to the limits of existence cries out for some sort of response, famine does not sit comfortably in any of the established poetic idioms of the English tradition. Had the Great Famine taken place a half century earlier, it could have found expression in a native Gaelic tradition that embraced a long history of famine, exile and destitution.[7]

However, Morash is being uncharacteristically simplistic in order to overstate his case. Although many of the poets were professionals, it does not follow that they were wholly divorced from the suffering—the fact that many of them were doctors would suggest otherwise, as they would have been in daily contact with the casualties. When Richard D'Alton Williams, a practising doctor, was tried for treason-felony for his writings in the *Irish*

---

[6] *Dublin Review*, Apr. 1865, quoted in Joy Melville, *Mother of Oscar: The Life of Jane Francesca Wilde* (London: John Murray, 1994), 20. The 'hideous fur' of the children refers to the medical condition whereby malnourished children experience increased hair growth, especially on the face.

[7] Morash (ed.), *Hungry Voice*, 18.

Tribune in 1848, his lawyer and fellow poet Samuel Ferguson defended him on the grounds of his sufferings during the Famine:

Thus it came, that having been among the poor during the year of the famine, and during the year of supplemental famine, he is now here because for these two years he has been made practically familiar with the misery of his countrymen—has been convinced that the state of society in which such horrors have occurred can only be remedied by a rejection of that English legislation which has made this, our unhappy country, the abode of misery, distrust, and disaffection.[8]

The jury obviously accepted this argument, as Williams was the only Young Irelander tried in the summer and autumn of 1848 to be acquitted.[9] Moreover, many Famine poets were certainly not middle-class professionals: James Clarence Mangan worked only periodically as a clerk and transcriber, John Keegan was a hedge-school teacher, John De Jean Frazer was a carpenter. All three died in penury—Mangan and Keegan in 1849, Frazer in 1852. All three deaths could be related to the Famine they chronicled. There was not always a disparity between the poet and his subject.

Morash's theory that the poets were uncomfortable writing about a purely Irish phenomenon in the language of a culture that had no tradition of famine is also a non sequitur. First, there is no evidence of discomfort in the poetry; in fact, the inability topos, the constant 'I cannot describe . . .' that infiltrates so many of the novels and travel-books of the period, rarely occurs in Famine poetry. Secondly, Morash is denying the flexibility of the English language by suggesting it can never accommodate new forms and themes—which begs the question how English literature could have developed and dealt successfully with innovations such as the Industrial Revolution or world war, or could more recently have expanded the canon to include post-colonial literatures. In addition, the form of the ballad, chosen by Davis as the ideal medium for Irish history and employed by many Famine poets—notably Mangan—had been imported from England and Scotland in the seventeenth century, and became increasingly popular with the spread of the English language.[10] Joep Leerssen argues that 'songs and balladry constituted, in fact, one of the

[8] Samuel Ferguson, quoted in Lady Ferguson, *Sir Samuel Ferguson in the Ireland of his Day*, 2 vols. (Edinburgh and London: William Blackwood & Sons, 1896), i. 206–7.

[9] Duffy claimed Williams got off because his father's close friend, Mr Kemmis the Crown Solicitor, manipulated the evidence against him—but this may be due to Duffy's desire to be the only political survivor; see Sir Charles Gavan Duffy, *My Life in Two Hemispheres*, 2 vols. (London: T. Fisher Unwin, 1898), i. 292.

[10] Robert Welch (ed.), *Oxford Companion to Irish Literature* (Oxford: Clarendon Press, 1996), 28.

most important cultural expressions of the Irish peasantry, and testifies to their uncertain position between two languages, English and Irish, and between the registers of orality and literacy'.[11] Also, the concept of famine was not new to either the English language or the English experience. *The Times* reported on individual deaths by starvation in London and Dorset in the 1840s, making reference to English famines in previous centuries, before the implementation of the Poor Laws, and also denying that England was immune to famine in the mid-nineteenth century—admittedly in part to justify the reluctance to save Ireland at all cost, but also reflecting very real fears. Finally, even if these poets were faced with the dilemma of translating an Irish theme into English, this should not have posed a problem. Many Irish poets were famed for their skill in translation: Ferguson was an accomplished translator of Irish; the vast majority of Mangan's poems were translations from Irish, German, and Persian; Denis Florence MacCarthy was best known for his translations of the Spanish dramatist Calderón; Speranza translated from a wide variety of European languages, including Swedish; and many of the poems of Williams and McGee were based on early Irish verse forms and themes. Such linguistically eclectic poets were unlikely to be perturbed by the lack of English experience of famine.

In fact, instead of translating their experience of Famine Ireland, these poets seem to be translated and transformed by it: Mangan and Williams struck a more serious tone and became more committed to Young Ireland and physical force; McGee moved away from his fascination with anti-quarianism and became immersed in politics; Speranza turned away from her genteel Protestant arch-Unionist respectability to write seditious poetry and leaders for *The Nation*; Samuel Ferguson became a Protestant Repealer—a group perhaps even rarer than Protestant nationalists today; Aubrey De Vere, who was already contemplating his transfer from Protestantism to Catholicism, ceased dreaming and became a man of action. Famine poets became bifurcated, divorced from previous modes and stances, reluctantly dragged from their comfortable historical certainties to the terrible present and terrifying future, determined and desperate to make a difference yet impotently lapsing into visionary revenge. Their differences in education, class, religion, gender, and literary styles dropped away as they embraced the epic, exhortatory register of famine poetry. Their poems are remarkably similar in tone and style, and all,

[11] Joep Leerssen, *Remembrance and Imagination: Patterns in the Historical and Literary Representation of Ireland in the Nineteenth Century* (Cork: Cork University Press, 1996), 173.

regardless of the social and political beliefs they expressed in prose, accepted in their poetry that the Famine was a divine retribution. Their real feeling that the Irish nation was about to be translated—either into oblivion or the kingdom of heaven—transformed them.

For James Clarence Mangan, writing about the Famine was less a case of interpreting a new phenomenon, and more a recognition of his own psychic despair and sense of destiny. As Ellen Shannon-Mangan has pointed out, most of his Famine poetry is not about the agony of famine, but its role as pathetic fallacy, a metaphor for his own life: 'In the national disaster he found a representation of his personal dissolution; he did not call up images of personal dissolution to serve as metaphors for the national disaster. In the midst of Ireland's tragedy he is almost breathtakingly self-concerned.'[12] Like Carleton, Mangan was accepted as 'the Banshee of the famine'[13] and accorded prophet status: but unlike Carleton, Mangan saw the 'Coming Event' not as the last in a long line of disasters, but, as an apocalyptic moment, redolent of the Book of Revelation rather than 'Pastorini' and agrarian tension. Carleton in his rural Clogher valley may have had direct experience of famines such as those of 1817 and 1822, which the Dubliner Mangan, whose father was a well-to-do grocer before bad business sense bankrupted him, would have been shielded from. As David Lloyd has suggested, although Mangan's last years were spent in penury, his own autobiography and later biographies read this back into his earlier life: 'Chronic as his psychic pain may have been, it is constantly associated by Mangan's biographers with hypothetical economic and material deprivation.'[14] His prophetic Famine poems are therefore more remarkable for the fact that he may not have realized the devastation the potato-blight could inflict.

But this is only half the story; Mangan's psyche was already radically divided before he came to deal directly with the Famine. Mangan was not the melancholy seer he and his biographers would have us believe he was. Any reader of Mangan must first dismiss the tortured-poet myth that surrounds him—allegations of alcoholism and drug-addiction which have exercised the minds of his biographers, and which are not dispelled by

---

[12] Ellen Shannon-Mangan, *James Clarence Mangan: A Biography* (Dublin: Irish Academic Press, 1996), 207.

[13] D. J. O'Donoghue, *The Life and Writings of James Clarence Mangan* (Edinburgh, Dublin, Chicago, and Peabody: Patrick Geddes & Co.; M. H. Gill & Son; T. G. O'Donoghue; P. V. Fitzpatrick; Nugent Bros., 1897), 234.

[14] David Lloyd, *Nationalism and Minor Literature: James Clarence Mangan and the Emergence of Irish Cultural Nationalism* (Berkeley and London: University of California Press, 1987), 29.

poems such as the supposedly autobiographical 'The Nameless One', which suggests Mangan suffered the fate of Maginn and Burns (alcoholism), and 'pawned his soul for the Devil's dismal | Stock of returns'.[15] His editor and biographer D. J. O'Donoghue is more than willing to accept that suffering ennobles in Mangan's case: 'So far as Mangan himself was concerned, life could not possibly have been a more helpless failure, but literature, and especially Irish literature, is immeasurably the richer for his having lived and possibly for his having lived in such misery.'[16] The image of the melancholy poet, perpetuated not only by critics and biographers but by Mangan himself, has unfortunately stuck, and Mangan has been cast as a Shelleyan Alastor-figure, prematurely aged and debilitated, ridiculous in his wig and false teeth, cloak and warlock's hat, roaming from tavern to tavern reciting 'Dark Rosaleen'. This is the Mangan who inspired Louis D'Alton's play *The Man in the Cloak*, and Brian Moore's novel *The Mangan Inheritance*. It is the Mangan of whom Yeats wrote: 'born in torpid days in a torpid city, [he] could only write in diverse fashions, "I am Miserable". No hopes! No philosophy! No illusions! A brute cry from the gutters of the earth!'[17] This is the side of Mangan that informs the poetry of doom and fear. But it is not the only side to Mangan. The man who could begin a description of the author of *Melmoth the Wanderer* with 'Maturin, Maturin, what a strange hat you're in',[18] was not simply delicately self-conscious, but delightedly aware of his own strange appearance and its effect on his audience. 'My Bugle and How I Blow It' links his identity firmly to the fact he is 'The Man in the Cloak', and he was as addicted to postures and masks as Yeats would ever be.[19] 'I should far and away rather be a great necromancer to being a great writer,' he announced in 'A Sixty Drop Dose of Laudanum': 'My natural propensities lead me rather to seek out modes of astonishing mankind than of edifying them.'[20] But this Mangan is anathema to those who cling to the tortured-poet myth, and there is great resistance to his sense of humour. 'We cannot endure mediocre burlesque in the author of *Dark Rosaleen*,'

[15] Mangan, 'The Nameless One' (1849), *The Collected Works of James Clarence Mangan*, Vol. IV: *Poems: 1848–1912*, ed. Jacques Chuto, Tadhg Ó Dúshláine, Peter Van De Kamp (Dublin and Portland, Oreg.: Irish Academic Press, 1999), 223.

[16] O'Donoghue, *Life and Writings*, 235.

[17] W. B. Yeats, 'Clarence Mangan', *Uncollected Prose by W. B. Yeats*, Vol. I, ed. John P. Frayne (London: Macmillan, 1970), 117.

[18] O'Donoghue, *Life and Writings*, 24.

[19] Mangan, 'My Bugle and How I Blow It. By The Man in the Cloak', *The Prose Writings of James Clarence Mangan*, ed. D. J. O'Donoghue (Dublin and London: O'Donoghue & Co.; M. H. Gill & Son; A. H. Bullen, 1904), 287.

[20] Mangan, 'A Sixty Drop Dose of Laudanum', *Prose Writings*, 202.

groans Louise Imogen Guiney, while John Mitchel assures us that 'Mangan's pathos was all genuine, his laughter hollow and painful.'[21] This is wishful thinking: Mangan delighted in fooling his readers, and he certainly seems to have succeeded in convincing them of his all-encompassing misery.

The jester/seer divide is echoed in his use of alternative identities. Many of his supposed translations were in fact original poems attributed to non-existent poets. His pseudonyms are both masks and a form of self-dramatization: he adopted the name 'Clarence' both as a way of distinguishing himself from his tyrannical father, who was also called James, and because he liked to make an impact on arrival by proclaiming, 'Clarence is come, false, fleeting, perjured Clarence.'[22] Several of his German 'translations' are attributed to 'Selber' ('himself') or 'Drechsler' ('turner'), and other interesting alter-egos include 'Joe King', 'Bham-Booz-eel', and 'Baugtrauter'. He wrote for the *Dublin Penny Journal* as its Italian correspondent, giving an address in Liverpool, despite the fact he had never been outside Ireland, and rarely outside Dublin, in his life.[23] Unlike his critics, Mangan did not take himself too seriously, and was not averse to poking fun at himself in his work, for example in his 'Treatise on a Pair of Tongs':

Standers-by are instantaneously stricken lifeless with astonishment at the golden tide of poetry which, in myriads of sunny streams and glittering rivulets, issues from my lips, poetry as far beyond what you, Public, are accustomed to get from me, as ambrosia is beyond hog-wash. With modest effrontery I take a chair, and if my quick eye detect the presence of anything in the shape of wine or punch on the table, I cheerfully abolish its existence . . . I may add that I re-establish the spiritless bottle upon the table, instead of putting it into my pocket, as a robber would do, or shattering it into shivers upon the hearth-flag, as a ruffian would do. Why is this? Because, Public, I, Clarence, am neither a ruffian nor a robber.[24]

Mangan was not entirely aberrant in his dual persona. His *Nation* colleague Richard D'Alton Williams wrote both serious and humorous pieces: his 'Misadventures of a Medical Student' appeared in *The Nation*

[21] Louise Imogen Guiney, *James Clarence Mangan: His Selected Poems*, ed. Louise Imogen Guiney (London, Boston, and New York: John Lane; Larsson, Wolffe & Co., 1897), 60; John Mitchel, 'Introduction', *Poems of James Clarence Mangan*, ed. D. J. O'Donoghue (Dublin and London: O'Donoghue & Co.; A. H. Bullen, 1903), p. xliv.

[22] O'Donoghue, *Life and Writings*, 35; the quotation is from Shakespeare's *Richard III*, but Shannon-Mangan suggests he may have taken it from Clarence Hervey in Edgeworth's *Belinda*, who also quotes *Richard III* (Shannon-Mangan, *James Clarence Mangan*, 85).

[23] O'Donoghue, *Life and Writings*, 34.

[24] Mangan, 'A Treatise on a Pair of Tongs', *Prose Writings*, 268–9.

172   *History, Identity, and the Visionary Poet*

alongside his religious and martial poetry. Morash, however objects to this duality: 'While it may not seem remarkable that Williams should have exhibited this form of cultural schizophrenia, it does seem striking in retrospect that neither he nor his editors should have found it disturbing or even incongruous that a university prankster should have been praying for Armageddon.'[25] Yet in the context of the times, when even Unionists were calling for a Repeal of the Union, such 'cultural schizophrenia' does not seem so strange. Morash seems to be missing the point: Williams was an essentially humorous, optimistic young student who was so disturbed by the worsening conditions around him that he felt impelled to become involved in rebellion, and to reflect it in poetry. *The Nation*'s series *Penny Readings for the Irish People*, begun in 1870, describes Williams as 'one of the liveliest, gayest, and sweetest poets of the *Nation*', and a fellow Famine poet, Martin MacDermott, said of Williams and his friend Denis Florence MacCarthy, that they 'threw off their levity' during the Famine, 'and gave us songs of lamentation'.[26] More interesting than Williams's transfer from comic to tragic writer is the vacillation between his calls to take matters into Irish hands, and admissions that the Famine was divinely inspired, and could not be assuaged through human agency. This dichotomy is mirrored by Williams's success in the post-1848 mutually exclusive realms of religion and revolution: Williams's 'Kyrie Eleison' was reported to have reduced Dr Murray, Archbishop of Dublin, to tears, while after Williams's death in Louisiana in 1862, a passing regiment of Irish-American soldiers raised a monument over his grave to show respect to a patriot who had died in exile.

Like many of his *Nation* colleagues, including Williams, Mangan was not a natural revolutionary; as David Lloyd has noted: 'His life appears resistant to a nationalist typology, and it frames a body of work that is equally inassimilable to a nationalist aesthetic.'[27] It is true that Mangan did not confine his writings to nationalist subjects and journals—few contemporary Irish writers did—but it is also true that he had a strong belief in national self-determination, and would have liked to have been part of the struggle towards that goal. Even his early poetry, such as 'To My Native Land', published in the *Comet* in 1832, testifies to this desire:

[25] Morash (ed.), *Hungry Voice*, 28.
[26] *Nation, Penny Readings for the Irish People, Conducted by the Editors of the 'Nation'*, 4 vols. (Dublin: A. M. & T. D. Sullivan, 1870–86), i/2, 33; Martin MacDermott, 'Introduction', *Songs and Ballads of Young Ireland* (London: Downey & Co., 1896), p. xxii.
[27] Lloyd, *Nationalism and Minor Literature*, 47.

Awake! arise! shake off thy dreams!
Thou art not what thou wert of yore:
Of all those rich, those dazzling beams,
That once illum'd thine aspect o'er
Show me a solitary one
Whose glory is not quenched and gone.[28]

Just before Mitchel's arrest for sedition in March 1848, Mangan sent him a public letter of support:

Insignificant an individual as I am, and unimportant to society as my political opinions may be, I, nevertheless, owe it, not merely to the kindness you have shown me, but to the cause of my country, to assure you that I thoroughly sympathise with your sentiments, that I identify my views of public affairs with yours, and that I am prepared to go all lengths with you and your intrepid friend, Devin Reilly, for the achievement of our national independence.[29]

Mitchel rather patronizingly commented, 'it did not intimidate the British Government much', and Mangan did not act further on his pledge of support, but there is no doubt that he was sincere, and that identification with Mitchel at this time was dangerous.[30] Duffy had to dissuade him from joining the Irish Confederation, as it would have jeopardized his relationship with his Tory employers,[31] but this did not prevent him from offering support in verse written for nationalist journals. Mangan was well aware that any role he could play would be limited:

My countrymen! my words are weak,
My health is gone, my soul is dark,
My heart is chill—[32]

This did not mean he would remain silent and inactive in the face of horror, and Mangan had no hesitation in offering his own weak services:

[28] Mangan, 'To My Native Land' (1832), *The Collected Works of James Clarence Mangan*, Vol. I: *Poems: 1818–1837*, ed. Jacques Chuto, Rudolf Patrick Holzapfel, Peter Mac Mahon, Pádraig Ó Snodaigh, Ellen Shannon-Mangan, Peter Van De Kamp (Dublin and Portland, Oreg.: Irish Academic Press, 1996), 47.

[29] Mangan, *United Irishman* (25 Mar. 1848), 106.

[30] Mitchel, 'Introduction', *Poems of James Clarence Mangan*, p. xxxvii.

[31] Duffy's memories may be disingenuous on this point; Shannon-Mangan argues that Duffy must have been aware that Mangan had lost his job at Trinity College Dublin library, so there was little for him to lose by joining the Confederation; it was more likely Mangan and fellow poet Frazer were refused because of their odd appearance and unruly behaviour (Shannon-Mangan, *James Clarence Mangan*, 341–2).

[32] Mangan, 'For Soul and Country' (1849), *Collected Works*, Vol. IV: *Poems 1848–1912*, 123.

> You, young men, would a man unworthy to rank in your number,
> Yet with a heart that bleeds for his country's wrongs and affliction,
> Fain raise a Voice to, in Song, albeit his music and diction
> Rather be fitted, alas! to lull to, than startle from, slumber.[33]

He was not afraid to voice his beliefs overtly, but he also worked under cover: the allegorical 'Song of the Albanian' covertly advocates violence as a means to free Ireland from bondage and famine:

> Were there a land whose people could
>   Lie down beneath heaven's blue pavilions
>   And gasp, and perish, famished slaves!
> While the ripe golden food
>   That might and should have fed their millions
>   Rotted above their graves—
>
> That land were doomed![34]

Evidently, he believed that he had made some contribution to the debate; in the posthumously published 'The Nameless One', Mangan implied that he had somehow saved himself in his writings on the Famine: 'But yet redeemed it in days of darkness, | And shapes and signs of fatal wrath, | When death, in hideous and ghastly starkness, | Stood on his path.'[35] Both Dandy and Romantic, Mangan was a poet of extremes—extreme levity, extreme melancholy. He saw life as 'a drama that so strangely united the two extremes of broad farce and thrilling tragedy', and these were the poles of his life until the Famine shifted the centre of gravity.[36]

So, when Mangan was found dying in a cellar in Bride Street by William Wilde, one would have thought he would have been elevated as a nationalist icon and a martyr to the Famine. On the contrary, there is a great deal of discomfort among commentators in admitting that Mangan died in the Famine. In his *Romances and Ballads of Ireland*, Hercules Ellis described how he rushed to the Meath Hospital to see Mangan's body, finding it 'an attenuated corpse, wasted to a skeleton, by want, and sickness, and misery, and despair'; Ellis asserted that Mangan died not from cholera, but from

---

[33] Mangan, 'A Voice of Encouragement—A New Year's Lay' (1848), *Collected Works*, Vol. IV: *Poems: 1848–1912*, 17.
[34] Mangan, 'Song of the Albanian (1826)' (1847), *The Collected Works of James Clarence Mangan*, Vol. III: *Poems: 1845–1847*, ed. Jacques Chuto, Rudolf Patrick Holzapfel, Ellen Shannon-Mangan (Dublin and Portland, Oreg.: Irish Academic Press, 1997), 340.
[35] Mangan, 'The Nameless One', *Collected Works*, Vol. IV: *Poems: 1848–1912*, 224.
[36] James Clarence Mangan, *Autobiography*, ed. James Kilroy (Dublin: Dolmen Press, 1968), 28.

'absolute starvation'.[37] Certainly the deathbed sketch by Frederick Burton, the only image of Mangan to survive, does not represent the poet as a skeleton, but as we have seen in drawings of the starving in newspapers and travel-books, it is impossible to draw conclusions from this. Forty-seven years later, the American Louise Imogen Guiney informed her readers that: 'Mr. Ellis's account was thought to be sensational when it was published. But there is a grave fear that it was the truth.'[38] D. J. O'Donoghue entered the fray the same year to deny categorically that Mangan died of starvation, while Mitchel avoids the subject altogether.[39] Even more inexplicable, Mangan's poems 'The Famine' and 'The Funerals', which appeared in the *Irishman*, and were republished in Ellis's collection in 1850, were ignored by Mitchel in 1859 and by O'Donoghue in 1897; both had almost certainly come across these poems, as O'Donoghue mentions Ellis's collection, and Mitchel recalled in *Jail Journal* reading issues of the *Irishman* while his prison-ship was at anchor off South Africa. This elision of Mangan from the role of Famine poet and Famine victim, like his exclusion from the Irish Confederation, may be explained by his supposed habits and his relationship with Young Ireland. It may be that Mitchel did not want to promote Mangan as the archetypal poet/victim because of that other, more damaging perceived duality in Mangan's psyche. 'There were . . . two Mangans,' wrote Mitchel, 'one well known to the Muses, the other to the police; one soared through the empyrean and sought the stars—the other lay too often in gutters of Peter Street and Bride Street.'[40] Mitchel was happy to allow Mangan to be an 'Irish papist rebel', but not that sacred thing, an Irish martyr.[41] Death by disease had a certain literary respectability—after all, Davis had died of scarlatina—but the admission that Mangan had died from starvation would have reflected badly on those of his friends who had remained in Ireland after the rising. The resistance to the idea that Mangan died of starvation is palpable, and has perhaps led to a diminishment of respect for him as both prophet and victim. In the end, perhaps it matters little whether he died from lack of food or not; the fact remains that the Famine created conditions in which it was very difficult for him to survive.

A similar mystery surrounds the Famine experience and death of John Keegan. In his *Dictionary of National Biography* entry on Keegan, O'Donoghue stated that the poet suffered greatly during the Famine, but

---

[37] Hercules Ellis, *Romances and Ballads of Ireland* (Dublin: James Duffy, 1850), pp. xiii–xiv.
[38] Guiney (ed.), *Selected Poems*, 31. [39] O'Donoghue, *Life and Writings*, 219.
[40] Ibid., p. xxxv.
[41] Mitchel, 'Introduction' to *Poems of James Clarence Mangan*, p. xxviii.

he volunteered no further information. Like Mangan, Keegan's life seems a web of misery and disappointments: 'from the time he reached manhood he seems to have met with more troubles than the average human being'.[42] A hedge-school teacher from Queen's County (present-day County Laois), Keegan's short stories seem to be modelled on Carleton's: his *Legends and Tales of the Queen's County Peasantry*, published in the *Dublin University Magazine* in 1839, bears an external similarity to Carleton's *Traits and Stories of the Irish Peasantry*, without ever approaching the latter's genius. Like Carleton, he based his claim to fame on the authenticity of his stories, but, unlike Carleton, and perhaps consciously in opposition to him, Keegan was a staunch O'Connellite, and wrote only for Catholic magazines: 'Certainly were I to take my position on anti-national and anti-Catholic grounds, I would soon have a purse full of the "yellow dirt". But I will not be a blackguard for filthy lucre.'[43] This may have been high-minded or narrow-minded, or simply a case of making a virtue out of necessity, but either way it was fatal: Carleton and his large family scraped by during the Famine; Keegan, who was estranged from his wife and daughter, didn't survive.

Surprisingly, Keegan had moved to Dublin and privation in the midst of the Famine in May 1847, abandoning a relatively lucrative position as clerk to a Queen's County relief committee. The committee offered to raise his salary to a pound a week, yet Keegan refused.[44] One pound was approximately five times what a labourer on relief works could expect to earn for a six-day week. It was a strange move to make in the middle of a Famine, and perhaps we can surmise that Keegan's experience of relief work, his contact with the starving, so distressed him that he felt he had to leave. Five months before his departure, Keegan wrote a poem based on a report in the *Kilkenny Moderator* on an inquest in Corbetstown on the bodies of a woman and her three children, found dead and partially eaten on the road. 'The Dying Mother's Lament' sensitively evokes the mother's distress at night, in a storm, in the knowledge that her children are dead:

> To see my ghastly babies—my babes so meek and fair—
> To see them huddled in that ditch like wild beasts in their lair;
> Like wild beasts! No! the vixen cubs that sport on yonder hill
> Lie warm this hour, and, I'll engage, of food they've had their fill.[45]

---

[42] D. J. O'Donoghue, 'Memoir', in John Keegan, *Legends and Poems by John Keegan*, ed. Very Revd J. Canon O'Hanlon (Dublin: Sealy, Bryers & Walker, 1907), p. vii.

[43] Quoted ibid., p. xxiii.   [44] Ibid., p. xxv.

[45] Keegan, 'The Dying Mother's Lament', ibid., 510.

The fact that Keegan, unlike most other Famine poets, uses the persona of a Famine victim, perhaps emphasizes his closeness to the calamity. A later poem, 'To the Cholera', published in the *Cork Magazine* in November 1848, also employs the persona of a victim. The speaker begs the personified Cholera to pass by his house: 'But if you're strong, be merciful, and spare | The trembling poet to his country's cause.'[46] But the cholera was not merciful, and in 1849 it killed John Keegan. He was buried in a pauper's grave in Glasnevin Cemetery.

Nothing could seem more remote from this than the experience of Jane Francesca Elgee. The future Lady Wilde, who wrote for *The Nation* as Speranza, was a member of a genteel Protestant, staunch pro-Unionist family. Elgee was not overly aware of public affairs in her own country; she had never even heard of Thomas Davis until she was surprised by the crowds thronging Dublin streets at his funeral. Much of her most powerful Famine poetry registers the surprise of a naïve but interested onlooker: 'Weary men, what reap ye?' opens 'The Famine Year', while 'The Enigma', whose title emphasizes the interlocutor's failure to understand, also opens with a question: 'Pale victims, where is your Fatherland?'[47] Yet this proves a surprisingly powerful stance, and Speranza is using her background to her advantage: her incomprehension overtly gestures towards Ireland's inexplicable lack of progress in an age of capital and industry, and covertly hints at its lack of power as the answer to the enigma: the victims have no Fatherland because their country has been taken from them, and they are unacknowledged by their supposed partners in the Union. Speranza saw the poet's mission to be Ireland's reinsertion into the stream of progress, the provision of a future for a country imprisoned by its past. In 'A Remonstrance', Speranza rebuked her fellow poet Denis Florence MacCarthy for living too much in the past, for being more an archaeologist than a living poet, and enunciated her own mission:

> O Poet-Prophets! God hath sent ye forth
> With lips made consecrate by altar fire,
> To guide the Future, not to tread the Past;
> To chaunt, in glorious music, man's great hymn,
> The watchword of humanity—Advance![48]

---

[46] Keegan, 'To the Cholera', in Morash (ed.), *Hungry Voice*, 58.
[47] Jane Francesca Elgee ['Speranza'], 'The Famine Year', 'The Enigma', *Poems by Speranza* (Dublin: James Duffy, 1864), 5, 8.
[48] Speranza, 'A Remonstrance, Addressed to D. Florence McCarthy, M.R.I.A.', ibid., 74.

Speranza was much more concerned with Ireland's progress—or lack of it—than her past glories. 'To-Day' evokes the past, but only to ask why it has faded:

> Has the line of the Patriots ended,
>   The race of the heroes failed,
> That the bow of the mighty, unbended,
>   Falls slack from the hands of the quailed?
> Or do graves lie too thick in the grass
> For the chariot of Progress to pass?[49]

As Morash has noted, many Famine poets—including Speranza—were 'members of a class who, were it not for Ireland's colonial status, would have been in positions of political power'.[50] The Famine was another symptom of the dispossession of this class, and Speranza's disenfranchisement manifests itself in a rejection of history and obsession with progress, which reveals that 'we alone of the Christian nations | Fall to the rear in the march of man':

> Ireland rests mid the rush of progression
>   Like a frozen ship in a frozen sea;
> And the changeless stillness of life's stagnation,
>   Is worse than the wildest waves could be,
>   Rending the rocks eternally.[51]

Here the stagnation of Mangan's 'Siberia' is extrapolated to circumscribe the whole nation, but the sibilant angry hiss of Speranza's words denies the resignation and despair of Mangan's poem. Speranza dedicated her *Poems* to her sons Willie and Oscar, adding: 'I taught them, no doubt, | That a Country's a thing men should die for at need!' But the men Speranza hoped to raise by her rallying call were to die not for freedom but for Progress and the proper Ascendancy. Speranza was a firm believer in established social hierarchy—a unexpected attribute in an outspoken revolutionary, but one shared by most Young Irelanders, who were remarkable for nothing so much as their conservatism. Speranza explained to a friend: 'No Democracy. Why should a rude, uncultured mob dare to utter its voice? Let the best reign, Intellect and Ability—you and I if they choose and an

---

[49] Speranza, 'To-Day', ibid., 70.   [50] Morash (ed.), *Hungry Voice*, 27.
[51] 'Who Will Show Us Any Good?', *Poems by Speranza*, 67; there may be a conscious echo here of Coleridge's 'As idle as a painted ship | Upon a painted ocean', given the poems' allied themes of suffering, doom, and atonement (*The Rime of the Ancient Mariner*, ll. 117–18).

admirable world we would make of it—but not the machine masses.'[52] Yet she reacted towards the sufferings of these 'machine masses' with powerful empathy and sympathy. Significantly, the puzzled interlocutor of 'The Enigma' is unusually replaced by a potential Famine victim in 'The Voice of the Poor': 'we—in our rags, and want, and woe'; few Famine poets attempt such a close identification. But the tangible pain of the voyeur, pervasive in travel-narratives of the time, is also present here:

> Before us die our brothers of starvation:
> Around are cries of famine and despair!
> Where is hope for us, or comfort, or salvation—
> Where—oh! where?[53]

'The Exodus' rejects cold statistical truth in favour of sympathy for the individual sufferer:

> 'A million a decade!' Count ten by ten,
> Column and line of the record fair;
> Each unit stands for ten thousand men,
> Staring with blank, dead eye-balls there;
> Strewn like blasted trees on the sod,
> Men that were made in the image of God.[54]

Ironically, the census on which this poem was based was compiled by her future husband, William Wilde.

There remains, however, a sense of unease in reading the Famine poems of a relatively wealthy woman. John De Jean Frazer, who died in penury soon after the Famine, and who lost a son in the cholera epidemic of 1849, registered this unease in 'The Three Angels': the angels of War and Pestilence are rather democratic, choosing their victims arbitrarily, and so not antagonizing class hatred: 'Still—one cold gleam of comfort shone | The rich—the poor—had not fallen alone.' The angel of Famine, however, is wholly discriminatory: 'But a murmur went up with the dying moan | That the poor—the poor—had been victims alone!'[55] Similarly, Speranza's *Nation* colleague Mary Kelly, who wrote as 'Eva of the *Nation*', contrasted a wretched mother starving in a cabin with a rich lady, implying the latter was responsible for the former's state:

[52] Quoted in Melville, *Mother of Oscar*, 33–4.
[53] Speranza, 'The Voice of the Poor', *Poems by Speranza*, 11.
[54] Speranza, 'The Exodus', ibid., 55.
[55] John De Jean Frazer, 'The Three Angels', in Morash (ed.), *Hungry Voice*, 185, 187.

> Far, far away, with pearls and gold
> My lady's hair is gleaming;
> For every gem our eyes behold
> A crimson drop is streaming!—
> For all the grace of silks and lace
> Some wretches naked shiver;
> For every smile upon her face
> Some death-blue lips will quiver![56]

For all her sympathy, Speranza could never be fully aware of the consequences of the Famine, so she—like William Smith O'Brien and John Mitchel—continued to call for revolution, blind to the fact that the starvation she deplored made it impossible. 'Signs of the Times', 'The Year of Revolutions', and 'France in '93' call on the Irish to follow the examples of Poland, France, and Prussia by breaking free at the point of the sword. While Duffy was incarcerated for treason-felony, Speranza and Duffy's sister-in-law Mrs Callan resolved to bring out *The Nation*; Speranza's stirring leader 'Jacta Alea Est' (The Die is Cast) landed Duffy in more trouble, but is an adequate indication of how far she felt Ireland should be prepared to go in these desperate times:

One instant to take breath, and then a rising; a rush, a charge from north, south, east, and west upon the English garrison, *and the land is ours*. Do your eyes flash— do your hearts throb at the prospect of having *a country?* . . . Is it so hard a thing then to die? Alas! do we not all die daily of broken hearts and shattered hopes, and tortures of mind and body that make life a weariness, and of weariness worse even than the tortures; for life is one long, slow agony of death.[57]

Ironically, she did not seem to realize that for many of *The Nation*'s readers, she was part of the 'English garrison' she urged them to overthrow. In July 1847 *The Nation* had reacted to the speeches of the new Protestant Repeal Association by asking: 'And do the landlords, the "gentry," the "better classes," the *English* garrison, as they were once, at last acknowledge a common nationhood *with* the tillers of the Irish soil, and *against* the English?'[58] The impact of the Famine on individual sufferers and on the prospects of the nation had led Speranza far from the traditional expectations of her class—and perhaps gender—yet not far enough for her to be wholly identified with either nation or people.

---

[56] Mary Kelly ['Eva'], 'A Scene for Ireland', *Poems by 'Eva' of 'The Nation'* (Dublin: M. H. Gill & Son Ltd., 1909), 58.
[57] *Nation* (29 July 1848), 488; this issue was seized and was probably never circulated.
[58] *Nation* (17 July 1847), 648.

Thomas D'Arcy McGee vacillated between sympathy for the sufferers and fury at their resignation. In 'New-Year's Thoughts', he recalled how the Irish were primed for rebellion when the Famine destroyed them:

> There was candor in the land,
>   And loud voices in the air,
> And the poet waved his wand,
>   And the peasant's arm was bare,
> And Religion smiled on Valor as her child;
>   But alas! alas! a blight
>   Came o'er us in a night,
>   And now our stricken plight
>   Drives me wild![59]

Only 21 years old in 1846, McGee was one of the youngest of the Young Irelanders—although, as the 24-year-old Martin MacDermott noted in 'A Very Old, Old Man', age counted for little when there were such awful sights to be seen.[60] He had emigrated to America aged 17, quickly made a name for himself as an orator and editor of the *Boston Pilot*, and was recalled to act as London correspondent for the *Freeman's Journal*. His fascination with the British Museum, and his articles for *The Nation*, soon led to a parting of the ways with the *Freeman*, and Charles Gavan Duffy was glad to employ the talented young writer. But his return to Ireland and the Famine in 1846 sharply diverted the course of his career: 'He had come from London and the British Museum with lofty ambitions to serve Ireland as a poet and scholar. Circumstances had made him in turn a political journalist, a propagandist, a conspirator and now it seemed he was to become an armed rebel.'[61] The Famine had a major impact on McGee. Although his poetry rarely dwells on the physical reality of starvation, his prose confirms that the sufferings of his fellow Irishmen were more than he could bear. In his speech to the Irish Confederation on 15 March 1848, in which he made the motion that Smith O'Brien and Thomas Meagher should be sent to Paris as the Confederation's delegates to the new Republic, he testified to his dismay at the sights he witnessed:

My heart is sick at daily scenes of misery. I have seen human beings driven like foxes to earth themselves in holes and fastnesses; I have heard the voice of mendicancy hourly ringing in my ears, until my heart has turned to stone and my brain to

[59] McGee, 'New Year's Thoughts', *The Poems of Thomas D'Arcy McGee* (London, New York, and Montreal: D. & J. Sadlier & Co., 1869), 88.
[60] Martin MacDermott, 'A Very Old, Old Man', in Morash (ed.), *Hungry Voice*, 192–4.
[61] Josephine Phelan, *The Ardent Exile: The Life and Times of Thomas D'Arcy McGee* (Toronto: Macmillan, 1951), 62.

flint from inability to help them. I cannot endure this state of society longer. Nothing green, nothing noble will grow in it. The towns have become one universal poorhouse and fever shed, the country one great graveyard.[62]

When he was later called upon to defend his actions as an Irish rebel to the Canadian parliament of which he became a member, he replied: 'I rebelled because I saw my countrymen starving before my eyes, while my country had her trade and commerce stolen from her . . . there is not a Liberal man in this community who would not have done as I did, if he were placed in my position, and followed the dictates of humanity.'[63] And yet for McGee, as for all Young Irelanders, politics came before relief, and he personally advised American organizations to send money to the Repeal Fund instead of charitable groups. He was not a natural rebel: in later life, he was vehemently opposed to the Fenians, and was murdered in consequence. In a leading article in *The Nation* after the arrest of Duffy in July 1848, McGee revealed the change in his conservative, elitist outlook wrought by the prolonged Famine and demoralizing public works: 'I opposed Tenant-right in '46, because I wished for a patriot aristocracy, and I thought the famine and the public works would have given it to us. But I wake in '48, and I am undeceived. I awake, and am for more than Tenant-right, for perpetuity of Tenure and the abolition of the law of Primogeniture.'[64] The fact that McGee was driven to rebel during the Famine is another manifestation of the desperation of the times, and its power to transform conservatives to rebels, poets to men of action.

McGee's antiquarian interests are reflected in the fact that although none of his Famine poetry is included in the *Ballad History of Ireland for Schools*, his 'The Celts' and 'The River Boyne' are.[65] In fact, his immersion in the heroic literature of the past means that many of his Famine poems are suffused with shame; having decided that he would become a rebel, he suddenly discovered that the Irish were no longer worth it. In 'The Search for the Gael', the speaker eventually discovers his race; they are misshapen and downcast—rather like Duffy's post-Famine descriptions of the people of Connaught—but the speaker resolves to fight for them anyway.[66] 'When Fighting Was The Fashion' looks back to the

[62] Quoted ibid., 54.
[63] Quoted in 'Biographical Sketch' by Mary Anne Sadlier, *Poems of Thomas D'Arcy McGee*, 31.
[64] *Nation* (15 July 1848), 457.
[65] Pádraig O Dálaigh (ed.), *A Ballad History of Ireland for Schools* (Dublin and Cork: The Educational Company of Ireland, 1929).
[66] McGee, 'The Search for the Gael', *Poems of Thomas D'Arcy McGee*, 91–2.

golden time when Ireland's grain could not have been stolen from her by exportation, and men could not have died by the roadside, and 'The Living and the Dead' argues that Gaelic chiefs would have struck a blow against such tyranny. 'The Exile's Meditation', which refers to Young Ireland anger at remarks by John O'Connell that men should die rather than defraud their landlords, contrasts past and present:

> I have read in ancient annals of a race of gallant men
> Who fear'd neither Dane nor devil; but it is long since then—
> And 'cowardice is virtue,' so runs the modern creed—
> The starving suicide is praised and sainted for the deed![67]

'Home Sonnets' suggests that the Famine destroyed the Irish so easily because they had become so degenerate they could be swept away like chaff:

> The sword no more an Irish weapon is—
> The spirit of the land no longer lives;
> Mother! 'twas kill'd before the famine came—
> The stubble was prepared to meet the flame;
> All manly souls were from their bodies torn,
> And what avails it if the bodies burn?[68]

Ironically, McGee appears to be agreeing that the Irish are apathetic, and have brought their troubles on themselves. This tone of resignation alternates with a more optimistic urgency. 'A Harvest Hymn' calls on the sufferers to hold the harvest: 'God has been bountiful—Man must be brave!'[69] Morash has pointed out that this poem, like Frazer's 'The Harvest Pledge', probably refers to the decision to defer the rebellion until after the harvest, so a note of covert optimism lurks beneath the title.[70] McGee's poem may also have inspired Fanny Parnell's 'Hold the Harvest', an address to Irish farmers in 1880 calling on them to remember the Famine and be brave:

> The yellow corn starts blithely up; beneath it lies a grave—
> Your father died in 'Forty-Eight'—his life for yours he gave—
> He died, that you, his son, might learn there is no helper nigh
> Except for him who, save in fight, has sworn HE WILL NOT DIE.[71]

---

[67] McGee, 'The Exile's Meditation', ibid., 106.
[68] McGee, 'Home Sonnets—Address to Ireland', ibid., 126.
[69] McGee, 'A Harvest Hymn', ibid., 100.   [70] Morash (ed.), *Hungry Voice*, 286.
[71] Fanny Parnell, 'Hold the Harvest', *Penny Readings for the Irish People*, iv. 294.

McGee's attitude to emigration is notably ambivalent, considering he emigrated twice, and spent his life in America and Canada campaigning for the rights of Irish immigrants. 'The Dawning of the Day' laments empty homes and full ships; McGee was perhaps thinking particularly of the fates of his friends and comrades who were being transported. 'Wishes' deplores exile even if it means Freedom. 'The Woful Winter', which suggests the Irish are fleeing from Ireland out of cowardice, seems rather harsh given that it was written in America, to which McGee had escaped dressed as a priest after the failed rising: 'They are flying, flying from her, the holy and the old, | Oh, the land has alter'd little, but the men are cowed and cold.'[72] However, 'An Invitation Westward', written in 1852, when there was a less urgent need for emigration, calls on the Irish to abandon their land: 'Though it grieve your souls to part from the land you love the best, | Fair Freedom will console you in the forests of the West.'[73] 'The Irish Homes of Illinois' celebrates the fact 'No landlord there | Can cause despair | Nor blight our fields in Illinois', while 'The Shanty' declares America a famine-free zone:

> The Famine fear we saw of old,
> Is, like a nightmare, over;
> That wolf will never break our fold,
> Nor round the doorway hover.
> Our swine in droves tread down the brake,
> Our sheep-bells carol canty,
> Last night yon salmon swam the lake,
> That now adorns our Shanty.[74]

The nightmare of Irish history was over for McGee's emigrants. It is clear that the history of Ireland was dramatically transformed in McGee's eyes; it was no longer a source of pride but a badge of shame to be forgotten by the individual who has escaped. Before, Ireland was the land of saints and heroes; now it is the site of famine and despair.

Samuel Ferguson's vision of history was also modified by the Famine. He had great faith in the power of history, and believed it was a great shame that Irish gentlemen were not more conversant with their own past: 'Whether a man seek for change or for continuance of existing institutions, he must ground a great part of his reasonings on historical

---

[72] McGee, 'The Woful Winter', *Poems of Thomas D'Arcy McGee*, 145.
[73] McGee, 'An Invitation Westward', ibid., 147.
[74] McGee, 'The Irish Homes of Illinois', 'The Shanty', ibid., 348, 350.

example.'[75] Unlike Speranza, who believed implicitly in progress and the future, Ferguson felt the pull of the past, and emphasized the Liberal Protestant view of the role of history as a means of amelioration and reconciliation: 'The history of centuries must be gathered, published, studied, and digested, before the Irish people can be known to the world, and to each other, as they ought to be.'[76] The descendant of Scots settlers in Ulster in the early seventeenth century, Ferguson may have immersed himself in Irish history in order to lay claim to a distinct Irish heritage, much as Yeats, who admired Ferguson greatly, was later to do. Indeed, he offered himself as the historical complement to the literary efforts of the *Nation* poets, whom he admired, but whose political views he could not share:

Davis and Duffy, Mangan and MacCarthy, and later on Thomas D'Arcy McGee, the greatest poet of them all, burst into song, and while I followed up the endeavour to elevate the romance of Irish history into the realm of legitimate history in the 'Hibernian Nights' Entertainment' in the 'University', awoke the whole country to high and noble aspirations through their fine enthusiasm in the 'Spirit of the Nation'.[77]

Yeats rewarded his efforts by naming him 'the greatest poet Ireland has produced, because the most central and most Celtic', and as Yeats followed Ferguson in dealing with many of the same legendary characters and themes, this is high praise indeed.[78]

In the second of his essays on 'Hardiman's Irish Minstrelsy' in the *Dublin University Magazine* in 1834, Ferguson celebrated the resilience of the Irish throughout history:

Seven hundred years of disaster, as destructive as ever consumed the vitals of any country, have each in succession seen our people perishing by famine or the sword in almost every quarter of the land; yet at this day there is neither mountain, plain, or valley that is not rife with generations of the unextinguishable nation: long may they walk upon our hills with the steps of freemen! long may they make our valleys ring with the songs of that love which has thus made them indomitable in defeat and ineradicable in a struggle of extermination![79]

Just over a decade later, he was to witness destruction by famine, extermination by landlords, the extinguishing of the songs of love and the language

---

[75] Lady Ferguson, *Sir Samuel Ferguson*, i. 95; significantly, Ferguson's position as Deputy Keeper of the Records of Ireland is engraved on his tombstone, but not the fact that he was a poet.
[76] Ibid., 40.   [77] Ibid., 139.
[78] Yeats, 'The Poetry of Sir Samuel Ferguson—II', *Uncollected Prose*, i. 103.
[79] Lady Ferguson, *Sir Samuel Ferguson*, i. 40–1.

in which they were sung, the headlong flight of generations away from the valleys and mountains. The Famine represented a serious challenge to Ferguson's theory of history.

Ferguson had spent 1845–6 on the Continent, recuperating after an illness and researching Irish manuscripts, and, according to his wife, the state of Ireland on his return was a complete shock: 'When Ferguson left Ireland at the close of 1845, the population exceeded eight millions, and her natural leaders—gentlemen of honour and position—seemed to be aroused to a keener sense than formerly of their public duties. When he returned a year later, he found famine and pestilence rife, and the people decimated by starvation.'[80] Of course, pre-Famine Ireland always looked rosy in hindsight, but Ferguson obviously shared the sense of loss that infused the writings of this transition time. Ferguson was infuriated by the government's failure to control the Famine by implementing adequate relief. He became honorary secretary to the cross-party Irish Council in 1847, and he and others believed that if the government had listened to that body's recommendations, the misery of 1848–9 could have been averted. Rumours were circulating in 1848 that the Lord Lieutenancy was about to be abolished, and the Courts of Law transferred to Westminster; Ferguson, as a lawyer, was understandably hostile. He also suspected that the government was using the Famine to centralize wealth and power in London; in May 1848 Ferguson gave a speech to that effect to the Protestant Repeal Association. He also accused the government of ignorance of Irish affairs and a level of neglect which led to the deaths of British subjects, and which could have been avoided by an Irish parliament:

It was perfectly evident that if, on the 1st of January, 1847, we had had a local legislature in this country, not only would monies have been raised adequate for preserving the lives of all her Majesty's subjects, who since that time, owing to the mismanagement of the Imperial Legislature, have lost their lives; but in applotting the taxation for that purpose, under any act passed in the Irish Legislature, no one class in the community would have been made to suffer more than another.[81]

The fact that his speech was favourably reported in both *The Nation* and the *United Irishman* is a measure of how far Ferguson had moved out of the Protestant Unionist enclave. He was still very far from the position of the Young Irelanders, in that he advocated the return of Grattan's Parliament rather than secession, and was evidently as interested in the rights of landowners, threatened with swamping poor rates, as with the

---

[80] Lady Ferguson, *Sir Samuel Ferguson*, 242.
[81] Speech of Samuel Ferguson, reported in *United Irishman* (13 May 1848), 203.

starving. Nevertheless it was a big shift, as Padraic Colum has pointed out: 'to the Unionists of the Trinity College of his day he must have seemed a crypto-nationalist'.[82] When he defended Richard D'Alton Williams against the charge of treason felony later that year, his transformation must have seemed complete.

In the summer of 1849, Ferguson, his wife, and two English friends (the author and publisher Charles Knight, and Douglas Jerrold, who was closely associated with *Punch*) visited Killarney. Ferguson spent a day climbing Carrantoul while his guests relaxed on the lakes; his wife records that he returned exhausted and hungry: 'The food he had carried with him had been shared with the starving people he met, for famine was sore in the land.' She adds that the tour would have been perfect, had it not been for 'the evidences everywhere painfully visible of the terrible effects of famine'.[83] Their English guests were evidently also shocked. Charles Knight wrote of the tour in his journal *The Land We Live In*:

Two emaciated little girls, preternaturally pallid, have watched the arrival of the stranger, and are come to offer their gleanings of the woods—a hart's horn—a wild nosegay. Poor wretched children, all mirth of childhood is vanished from their faces. In the mountain-hovel where they crouch there has been grievous want. They have become acquainted with the bitterness of life very early. And we are pleasure-seeking! We are surrendering ourselves to all sweet thoughts and influences! 'The sunshine of the breast' is driving out all remembrances of fear and trouble. But *now*, when we think of that quiet place in the luxuriant woods, the faces of these poor children still haunt the spot and make us sad.[84]

The sight and memory must have been even more disturbing and guilt-provoking for the native Ferguson. Indeed two poems he published in the *Dublin University Magazine* that year—'Inheritor and Economist' and 'Dublin'—display his unease. In the former, Irish complaints are figured as a lawsuit:

> So when ECONOMIST, as crier, bawled
> 'Celt *versus* Hunger,' Celt had to be called:
> The silent grave no Celt's complaint returned,
> The suit abated, and the court adjourned.[85]

It is interesting that the obnoxious ECONOMIST is identified as an officer of the court, as Ferguson was. But the victim is identified not as specifically

[82] Padraic Colum, in Samuel Ferguson, *The Poems of Samuel Ferguson*, ed. Padraic Colum (Dublin: Allen Figgis, 1962), 5.

[83] Lady Ferguson, *Sir Samuel Ferguson*, i. 223, 225.   [84] Ibid., 225.

[85] Samuel Ferguson, 'Inheritor and Economist—A Poem', *Dublin University Magazine*, 33 (May 1849), 638–49, at 644.

Irish, but as a Celt; Ferguson may not have been accepted as ethnically Irish, but he was certainly a Celt. The Famine was divorcing Ferguson and his class from their country; by identifying himself as a Celt and as a Repealer, he became more closely involved in the disaster. Like many of the poems of his Young Ireland friends, 'Inheritor and Economist' ends with impotent fury at the fate of his 'Poor native land!' and resignation to the will of God:

> Thy day prefixed in God's eternal doom
> May long be longed for; but the day will come
> When heaven shall also give its sign to thee,
> Thy Diocletian fallen, thy people free.[86]

The speaker of 'Dublin' is contemplating emigration away from the hell-on-earth of Famine Ireland:

> Here men of feeling, ere they yet grow old,
> Die of the very horrors they behold.
> 'Tis hard to sleep when one has just stood by
> And seen the strong man of sheer hunger die;
> 'Tis hard to draw an easy, healthful breath,
> In fields that sicken with the air of death;
>
> .   .   .   .
>
> Who, without shortened days could daily pass
> The tottering, fluttering, palpating mass,
> Who gaze and gloat around the guarded dole,
> That owned a heart of flesh, or human soul?[87]

The fact that Ferguson like Carleton, could speak of emigrating from a land whose literature and history he had done so much to promote, and which was so integral to his identity, indicates how much this horrible vision of reality had affected him.

While for Ferguson, the Famine had been a severe blow to his theory of history, for Aubrey De Vere it was strangely a confirmation. In his *Recollections*, he recalled his sudden realization of the unity of Irish history: 'It was after the lapse of many years that the meaning of Irish history flashed upon me. It possessed unity, although not a political one. Religion

---

[86] Ferguson, 'Inheritor and Economist—A Poem', ibid., 649.

[87] Samuel Ferguson, 'Dublin: A Poem. In Imitation of the Third Satire of Juvenal', *Dublin University Magazine*, 34 (July 1849), 102–9, at 109; in spite of the overt reference to Juvenal, the poem is also very reminiscent of Oliver Goldsmith's 'The Deserted Village' (1770), perhaps gesturing towards the irony of emigrating from one of the capital cities of the richest nation in the world.

was Ireland's unity . . . to the different nations different vocations are assigned by Providence; to one, an imperial vocation, to another a commercial one; to Greece an artistic one, to Ireland, as to Israel, a spiritual one.'[88] For De Vere, the Famine was a manifestation of Ireland's spiritual destiny, its atonement for sin through suffering. The Irish for him were a 'sacrificial People', 'Smitten of God, yet not in hate, but love'.[89] At first sight De Vere's motives may appear suspicious: the son of a County Limerick landowner and the nephew of ex-Chancellor of the Exchequer Lord Monteagle, the brother of a landowner who advocated large-scale emigration, a Protestant brought up to be a clergyman, dismissing the deaths of Catholic tenants as the will of God? For De Vere, however, the Famine paradoxically lowered these barriers of race, class, and religion. He was on the point of converting to Catholicism, which he did in 1851, and although he was impelled to do so more through his contact with Newman and Manning, and the Gorham Controversy, than with his own Catholic tenantry, he was doubtless influenced by the patience under suffering he witnessed among Famine victims. Like William Allingham's Laurence Bloomfield, De Vere was 'Irish born and English bred'; Bloomfield, brought up to be a staunch unionist, finds himself reconciled to his own country by witnessing famine, evictions, and the Land War: 'We Paddies, Downing, you must understand, | Count England as a dangerous heathen land!'[90] The Famine increased De Vere's sense of Irishness where it diminished Ferguson's: in his *English Misrule and Irish Misdeeds*, he sarcastically thanks England for reminding him that despite his English education and English friends, he was not English: 'There never was a time when I did not feel Ireland to be my country; and the stormy scorn with which for a year and more you have assailed her, trampling upon her in the hour of her sorest adversity, and embittering the flavour of the bread you gave, has pressed that sentiment around me with a closeness for which I thank you.'[91] While Ferguson sought his identity in the heroism of the past, De Vere was able to reconcile his Norman heritage with that of the supplanted Celts in the Encumbered Estates Court. In his dramatic monologue 'The Irish Gael to the Irish Norman', De

---

[88] Aubrey De Vere, *Recollections* (New York and London: Edward Arnold, 1897), 353–4.

[89] Aubrey De Vere, 'The Sisters; or, Weal in Woe. An Irish Tale', 'Ireland. 1851', *Irish Odes and Other Poems* (New York: The Catholic Publications Society, 1869), 174.

[90] William Allingham, *Laurence Bloomfield in Ireland. A Modern Poem* (London and Cambridge: Macmillan & Co., 1864), 6, 267.

[91] Aubrey De Vere, *English Misrule and Irish Misdeeds: Four Letters From Ireland, Addressed to an English Member of Parliament* (London: John Murray, 1848), 259.

Vere—pre-empting Mitchel—figures the Famine as the last English colonization of Ireland, and a betrayal by England of the race they once
upheld: 'Once more the Desmonds fall: | To-night old Wrongs shake
hands in History's hall.'[92] Although a 'Norman' by blood, De Vere was at
last united in opposition with his 'Gaelic' fellow Irishmen.

The Famine wrought great changes in De Vere's life. His father, who
had devoted his fading energies to relief, died in 1846, and for Aubrey and
his elder brothers, the work of relief became a duty to their father's memory. The dreamy poet who had rejected the career of the Church, but
could not find anything to interest him, astonished family and friends with
his energy and enthusiasm. He wrote to a friend in October 1846:

My ears are sometimes dinned for a day together by the wrangling of people at Relief
Committees or Road Sessions, and I assure you I have learned how to make use of
my eyes also. I was out from after breakfast till nine o'clock at night, a few days ago,
making a census of the people in want of food, and many a strange spectacle I saw
while engaged on this occupation. In this part of the country there is little *except
want* to contend with; but some of the scenes which I have witnessed in wilder parts
of the country are desolate indeed. In one day I have sat within nearly eighty mud
hovels, without windows or chimneys—the roof so low that you could not (in some
cases) stand upright, and within and around a mass of squalidness and filth . . .[93]

He was threatened by mobs throwing stones, and on several occasions by
armed men, but he bore this with courage and patience: his attitude mirrored that of his cousin, Stephen Spring Rice, who told him: 'We should
not blame our poor people for being riotous when they see their families
in danger of starvation. If they give me a good beating on some occasion
you will see how little grudge I shall bear them on that account.'[94]

De Vere's connections and those of his family enabled them to call attention to the plight of the starving while at the same time defending Irish
landlords, whom they understandably felt were being unfairly and indis-
criminately blamed, especially by the English press. His brother Stephen
travelled on an emigrant ship to Canada to witness the conditions Irish
emigrants endured; his letter describing their sufferings was read in the
House of Lords by the Secretary of the Colonies, Earl Grey, and helped to
get the 'Passengers Act' amended. The De Veres later paid to enable (and
encourage) their tenants to emigrate.[95] Several of De Vere's influential

---

[92] De Vere, 'The Irish Gael to the Irish Norman; or, The Last Irish Confiscation. 1850',
Irish Odes, 153.
[93] Quoted in Wilfrid Ward, *Aubrey De Vere: A Memoir Based on his Unpublished Diaries and
Correspondence* (London, New York, and Bombay: Longmans, Green, & Co., 1904), 120–1.
[94] De Vere, *Recollections*, 228.   [95] Ibid., 253–4.

friends visited Curragh Chase during the Famine and witnessed events for themselves. Tennyson proved resolutely indifferent, but other guests were not so implacable. De Vere took William Monsell (later Lord Emly) and Lord Arundel (soon to become Duke of Norfolk) to visit Kilkee. While there they entered a deserted cabin, and were shocked by what they saw:

Its only inmate was a little infant, whose mother was most likely seeking milk for it. On slightly moving the tattered coverlet of the cradle, a shiver ran over the whole body of the infant, and the next moment the dark, emaciated little face relapsed again into stillness. Probably the mother returned to find her child dead. Mr. Monsell burst into a flood of tears. Nothing was said; but a few days later, on Lord Arundel's return to England, the inspector at Kilkee received a letter from him enclosing a cheque for two hundred pounds to be added to the local relief fund.[96]

Although all three seem to have accepted that there was nothing to be done to save the child, and appear to have taken no measures to rescue it, this was not idle voyeurism: besides Arundel's donation, De Vere notes that Monsell's letter to the Irish Secretary describing the visit probably helped to prompt 'Labouchere's Letter', which attempted to supplement the Public Work Act by allowing reproductive works. These were influential witnesses: both represented County Limerick in Parliament (Arundel in 1850–2, Monsell in 1847–74), and Monsell was particularly vocal on the sufferings of the Irish during the Famine. He went on to have a distinguished career, becoming Under-Secretary for the colonies in 1868 and Vice-Chancellor of the Royal University of Ireland in 1885.

But as much as De Vere identified with the Famine, he was well aware that he, like Monsell and Arundel, was merely there to observe, and to help if possible. The Irish Gael reminds the Irish Norman that he will never suffer as the Gael has:

> Give thanks! How many a sight is spared to thee,
> Which we, thy sires in suffering, saw and see!
> Thou hast beheld thy country, by the shocks
> Of three long winters, driven upon the rocks
> High and more high. Thou shalt not, day by day,
> See her dismembered planks, the wrecker's prey,
> Abused without remorse to uses base . . .[97]

De Vere, like Trollope, responds by making that suffering all the more intense for the watching landed classes: 'The eyes which had witnessed what theirs had witnessed never wholly lost that look which then came into them; and youth had gone by before their voices had recovered their

[96] Ibid., 250.   [97] De Vere, 'The Irish Gael to the Irish Norman', *Irish Odes*, 160.

earlier tone.'[98] But De Vere, like his fellow Famine poets, was divided: the man who had responded in person with stirring energy, and in prose with powerful remonstrance and practical schemes, reacted in poetry with vision and resignation. In prose he laid the blame at the government's door; in poetry it was the work of God.

It seems to be a reflex of Famine poetry that even the most ardent nationalist and vituperative critic of the British administration accepts that the Famine was divinely sent to chastise the Irish: Speranza asks: 'O Christ! how have we sinned, that on our native plains | We perish houseless, naked, starved, with branded brow, like Cain's?'[99] Mangan, typically, sees it as an extension of God's punishment of him; his autobiography testifies to the indescribable terror of the future that haunted him from his earliest years, in spite of his disbelief in predestination: 'It was in its nature, alas! a sort of dark anticipation, a species of my melancholy foreboding of the task which Providence and my own disastrous destiny would one day call upon myself to undertake.'[100] This conviction of doom, which suffuses much of Mangan's poetry, pre-dated the Famine, and left him in a sense better prepared to deal with it. In 'Siberia', the exile becomes one with the landscape which destroys him: 'They are part, and he is part, | For the sands are in his heart, | And the killing snows.' But the poet also can be seen to identify with the barren wasteland and the dull pain of the exile; the short lines and languid rhythm emphasize not fear but numbness, expectation:

> Blight and death alone.
> No Summer shines.
> Night is interblent with Day.
> In Siberia's wastes alway
> The blood blackens, the heart pines.[101]

Siberia is Famine Ireland, recognized by Mangan as what always waited for him in the future, a wasteland of dull pain and death.

Mangan was highly aware of his stature as prophet of the Famine: in 'Irish National Hymn', published in the *United Irishman* in May 1848, just before Mitchel's arrest, he identifies himself as '*one whom some have called a Seer*'.[102] He also said that he always wanted 'to be aroused, excited—shocked even', and he was attracted to the wonderful and terrible in art and society: 'Descriptions of battles and histories of revolutions; accounts

---

[98] De Vere, *Recollections*, 249.
[99] Speranza, 'The Famine Year', *Poems by Speranza*, 7.
[100] Mangan, *Autobiography*, 9.
[101] Mangan, 'Siberia' (1846), *Collected Works*, Vol. III: *Poems: 1845–1847*, 158.
[102] Mangan, 'Irish National Hymn' (1848), *Collected Works*, Vol. IV: *Poems: 1848–1912*, 49.

of earthquakes, inundations and tempests; and narratives of "moving accidents by flood and field" possessed a charm for me which I could neither resist nor explain."[103] This taste for the ultimate disaster created a tone in his poetry that made it instantly amenable to the theme of Famine, so much so that many of his poems seem prophetic of horror. 'The Groans of Despair', published in *The Nation* in October 1849, as 'An Unpublished Poem By Clarence Mangan', is typical of Mangan's Famine poetry—the dream in which he sees his 'future doom', the fear he is lost and it is too late to repent, the signs that forecast the Coming Apocalypse:

> I see black dragons mount the sky,
>   I see earth yawn beneath my feet,
>   I feel within the asp, the worm
> That will not sleep and cannot die,
>   Fair though may show the winding sheet!
>   I hear all night, as through a storm,
>   Hoarse voices calling, calling
>   My name upon the wind—
> All omens, monstrous and appalling,
>   Afright my guilty mind.[104]

Yet 'The Groans of Despair' was first published in the *Dublin Unversity Magazine* exactly two years earlier as 'Moreen: A Love Lament', and represented as a translation from the Irish of Charles Boy Mac Quillan.[105] Mangan's famous translation of 'Dark Rosaleen', which Hardiman and Ferguson had attempted before him and disagreed over (Hardiman thought it was political allegory, Ferguson the song of a love-lorn priest) shows a similar manipulation in the symbiosis of lovesong and allegory in one of the most haunting, elegiac, and rousing poems of Irish literature:

> O! the Erne shall run red
>   With redundance of blood
> The earth shall rock beneath our tread,
>   And flames wrap hill and wood,
> And gun-peal, and slogan cry,
>   Wake many a glen serene,
> Ere you shall fade, ere you shall die,
>   My Dark Rosaleen![106]

[103] Mangan, *Autobiography*, 27–8.
[104] Mangan, 'The Groans of Despair' (1849), *Collected Works*, Vol. IV: *Poems: 1848–1912*, 219.
[105] Mangan, 'Moreen: A Love Lament' (1847), *Collected Works*, Vol. III: *Poems: 1845–1847*, 369–72.
[106] Mangan, 'Dark Rosaleen' (1846), ibid., 169–70.

Many of Mangan's translations have this dualistic quality, referring simultaneously to the far past, and to present Famine Ireland. 'Prince Alfrid's Itinerary Through Ireland', which Mangan published in 1846, based on John O'Donovan's unrhymed version in the *Dublin Penny Journal* in September 1832, could be read as an implicit criticism of the deterioration of Ireland under British rule. Prince Alfrid, in Ireland as a student in the late seventh century, is amazed by the wealth of Ireland:

> I travelled its fruitful provinces round,
> And in every one of the five I found,
> Alike in church, and in palace hall,
> Abundant apparel and food for all.
>
> Gold and silver I found, and money,
> Plenty of wheat and plenty of honey;
> I found God's people rich in pity,
> Found many a feast and many a city.[107]

This is a stark contrast to the conditions Alfrid's nineteenth-century countrymen were describing in travel narratives and newspaper reports at the time Mangan published this translation. Similarly, 'Cean-Salla', representing the words of Red Hugh O'Donnell on his departure from Ireland, published in *The Nation* in July 1846, reads more like an anti-emigration poem by Thomas D'Arcy McGee, or the words of a disillusioned John Mitchel:

> Weep not the brave Dead!
> Weep rather the Living—
>   On them lies the curse
> Of a Doom unforgiving!
> Each dark hour that rolls,
>   Shall the memories they nurse,
> Like molten hot lead,
> Burn into their souls
>   A remorse long and sore!
>   They have helped to enthrall a
> Great land evermore,
>   They who fled from Cean-Salla![108]

'The Sorrows of Inisfail', a translation of a poem by Geoffrey Keating (*c*.1580–*c*.1644), published in *The Nation* of December 1846, seems ideally

---

[107] Mangan, 'Prince Alfrid's Itinerary Through Ireland' (1846), ibid., 105.
[108] Mangan, 'Cean-Salla' (1846), ibid., 196.

chosen to reinforce the point that the Young Ireland message and Irish sufferings were not new:

> How long, O, Mother of Light and Song, how long will they fail to see
> That men must be *bold*, no less than *strong*, if they truly will to be free?
> They sit but in silent sadness, while wrongs that should rouse them to madness,
>   Wrongs that might wake the very Dead,
>   Are piled on thy devoted head![109]

The choice of these poems for translation serves as an extension of Mangan's prophetic status, as he uses dead poets as masks for his examination of Famine Ireland.

Mangan's original poems pick up the feeling of doom and disaster remarkably early. Like Carleton's *The Black Prophet*, Mangan's 'The Warning Voice', published in *The Nation* in February 1846, long before the second failure made deaths almost inevitable, is terrifyingly prescient:

> A day is at hand
> Of trial and trouble,
>   And woe in the land!
> O'er a once greenest path,
>   Now blasted and sterile,
>   Its dusk shadows loom—
> It cometh with Wrath,
>   With Conflict and Peril,
>   With Judgment and Doom![110]

Two months later 'The Peal of Another Trumpet' warned the Youth of Ireland what to expect:

> For the Pestilence that striketh
> Where it listeth, whom it liketh,
> For the Blight whose deadly might
> Desolateth day and night—
> For a Sword that never spared
>   Stand prepared!
> Though that gory Sword be bared
>   Be not scared!
> Do not blench and dare not falter!
> For the axe and for the halter
>   Stand prepared![111]

---

[109] Mangan, 'The Sorrows of Inisfail' (1846), ibid., 252.
[110] Mangan, 'The Warning Voice' (1846), ibid., 134.
[111] Mangan, 'The Peal of Another Trumpet' (1846), ibid., 163.

This poem seems to look forward not only to the starvation and disease of the next years, but also to the attempted rising of 1848. 'The Coming Event', published posthumously in the newly revived *Nation* in September 1849, when the worst could be said to have already occurred, seems an anomaly, predicting, as 'The Warning Voice' had done three years previously, the transition time:

> And shadows of CHANGES are seen in advance,
>   Whose epochs are nearing;
> And days are at hand when the Best will require
>   All means of salvation,
> And the souls of men shall be tried in the fire
>   Of the Final Probation.[112]

Yet 'THE EVENT and its terrors', which the poem so powerfully predicts, had already happened before the poem was published—it appears to be predicting past events. In fact, however, 'The Coming Event' was first published in the *Dublin University Magazine* in February 1844 as a translation by 'Selber', making it very much pre-Famine; it is perhaps significant that 'Selber' not only means 'self', but is an anagram of 'rebels'. Mangan had a habit of selling poems that had already been published to other magazines—perhaps due to pressing financial need, perhaps quite innocently forgetting he had done so—and it is likely that Duffy believed he was getting an unpublished poem about the Famine. 'The Coming Event', published before the Famine was a possibility, proves Mangan's state of mind accorded so well with the disaster that was to kill him and a million others, that the progress of his poetry flows seamlessly into the Famine.

Mangan enhances his prophet-status by introducing visions or dreams into many of his Famine poems. In this way, he evades the *present* horror by diverting it to *past* visions of *future* events. Like 'Prince Alfrid's Itinerary', 'A Vision of Connaught in the Thirteenth Century', published in *The Nation* in July 1846, is an implicit criticism of the government of Famine Ireland, contrasting its dearth with the abundance Ireland enjoyed under Cáthal Mór; but the final stanza makes the criticism explicit, exploding in a vision of terror:

[112] Mangan, 'The Coming Event' (1844), *The Collected Works of James Clarence Mangan*, Vol. II: *Poems: 1838–1844*, ed. Jacques Chuto, Rudolf Patrick Holzapfel, Peter Mac Mahon, Ellen Shannon-Mangan (Dublin and Portland, Oreg.: Irish Academic Press, 1996), 336–7.

> I again walked forth;
>   But lo! the sky
> Showed fleckt with blood, and an alien sun
>   Glared from the north,
>   And there stood on high,
> Amid his shorn beams, A SKELETON!
>   It was by the stream
>   Of the castled Maine,
> One Autumn eve, in the Teuton's land,
>   That I dreamed this dream
>   Of the time and reign
> Of Cáthal Mór of the Wine-red Hand![113]

The intrusion of the skeleton, the premier motif of Famine Ireland, is suppressed not only by the return to the thirteenth century in the last line, but also by the removal of the dreamer to 'the Teuton's land', outside the influence of either Cáthal Mór or the skeleton.[114] Similarly, the nightmare of 'The Funerals' is temporally displaced—'It was a vision of the night, | Ten years ago'—but the dreamer recognizes in his vision the culmination of the dark anticipations of his soul, such anticipations as had haunted Mangan:

> Here were the FUNERALS of my thoughts as well!
>   The Dead and I at last were One!
> An ecstasy of chilling awe
>   Mastered my spirit as a spell![115]

The dreamer wakes, realizes he has been dreaming, and dismisses his fear, but the vision returns nightly to haunt him, and he admits: 'I know there lives | A deep, a marvellous, a prophetic power'. The Funerals, capitalized in each stanza, are replaced in the last by the 'JUDGEMENT HOUR' which they attest to. But it is very much a personal apocalypse.

'A Vision: A. D. 1848' employs temporal displacement to enact the end of the Famine and the freedom of Ireland by creating the illusion of history. The Voice that addresses the speaker explains past signs: 'The Anointing:

---

[113] Mangan, 'A Vision of Connaught in the Thirteenth Century' (1846), *Collected Works*, Vol. III: *Poems: 1845–1847*, 199.

[114] 'A Vision of Connaught in the Nineteenth Century', which appeared in *The Nation* a year later as a parody of Mangan's poem, may, as Morash suggests, have been written by Mangan himself. In this poem, Cáthal Mór has been replaced by 'Randal Routh of the wine-red nose' (the civil servant in charge of distribution of relief during the Famine); while the Famine is referred to directly, its implications are evaded through humour (see Morash (ed.), *Hungry Voice*, 13).

[115] Mangan, 'The Funerals' (1849), *Collected Works*, Vol. IV: *Poems 1848–1912*, 118.

1839–1842'—Father Mathew's Temperance crusade, which has prepared the Irish for sacrifice; 'The Muster: 1842–1845'—O'Connell's monster-meetings; 'The Famine: 1845–1848'—explained providentially as the necessary purging of one-seventh of the Irish to prepare the Anointed for war; and finally 'The End: 1848–185*'—perceived by the speaker as a series of symbols 'ye read of in John's | Revelations of Wonders'. The speaker wakes before the conclusion, but the result is clear:

> But there seemed in mine ears,
>   As I started up, woken,
> A noise like fierce cheers,
> Blent with clashings of swords,
> And the roar of the sea![116]

The poem was published in the *United Irishman* early in 1848, and the vision seeks to fulfil itself not only by setting a date to the end of the Famine—that very year—and provisionally dating the time of deliverance to the 1850s, but also by urging readers of Mitchel's paper to take matters into their own hands.

The prophetic tone of many of Mangan's poems predicates a sense of apocalyptic doom which yet avoids the millenarian aspects emphasized by Morash in his *Writing the Irish Famine*. Certainly, Mangan, in common with many nationalists, appears to agree with the Providential theory of the Famine. 'I see GOD in all things. GOD is *the* idea of my mind,' he stated, and the will of God, and his use of Mangan as his prophet, is an evident concept in his poetry.[117] Like Siberia, other afflicted cities such as Pompeii and Jerusalem become symbols for him of the fate of Ireland, punished by God for an unknown sin: 'Hadst thou less guilt? Who knows? The book of Time | Bears on each leaf alike the broad red stamp of Crime.'[118] 'The Famine' sees the blight as a biblical cloud, rising to blot out the beautiful time before disaster, but it is divinely inspired: 'This work is Thine—/ To Thy decrees, Thy law, Thy will, we bow—/ We are but worms, and Thou art THE DIVINE!'[119] Nevertheless, as in 'The Funerals', it is much more a personal apocalypse than the destruction of the race envisaged by other apocalyptic poets, such as Speranza and De Vere. 'The Warning Voice' contains the destruction within Mangan's generation:

---

[116] Mangan, 'A Vision: A. D. 1848' (1848), *United Irishman* (26 Feb. 1848), 43 (also *Collected Works*, Vol. IV: *Poems 1848–1912*, 40); in *Hungry Voice*, Morash has enacted his own resolution by editing 'The End' to read '1848–1850', 146–9.

[117] Mangan, *Autobiography*, 15.

[118] Mangan, 'Pompeii' (1847), *Collected Works*, Vol. III: *Poems: 1844–1847*, 277.

[119] Mangan, 'The Famine' (1849), *Collected Works*, Vol. IV: *Poems: 1848–1912*, 138.

To *this* generation
The sore tribulation,
The stormy commotion,
And foam of the Popular Ocean,
    The struggle of class against class;
The Dearth and the Sadness,
    The Sword and the War-vest;
To the *next*, the Repose and the Gladness,
    'The sea of clear glass,'
And the rich Golden Harvest![120]

He does not dwell on the concept of national sin, focusing instead on a sense of personal sin, as if the Famine were the culmination of a series of punishments inflicted on him. The penances which he undertook in his youth were 'merciful dispensations . . . compared with those which the Almighty afterwards adopted for my deliverance'.[121] He came to consider his miserable condition as 'the mode and instrument which an all-wise Providence made use of to curb the outbreakings of that rebellious and gloomy spirit that smouldered like a volcano within me'.[122] It is as if the Famine had come for Mangan alone. 'When Hearts Were Trumps!' promises that love will overcome the present pain, but not for Mangan:

And, friends, trust me! your—(not *my*)—
Offspring will have wondered
Much at myriad changes—by
Anno Nineteen-hundred![123]

The new century will bring change, not destruction, for the Irish, but Mangan, issueless, will be long gone.

For De Vere, the Famine was both punishment and beneficial intervention: 'If Providence had not, in its merciful severity, interposed with this calamitous potato blight, the eventual ruin to which we were tending must have been to us even more signal, and to [England] even more disastrous, than the trial which has overtaken us.'[124] He responds by attempting to contain and explain Irish suffering as part of the nation's spiritual history. The Irish not only do not want the penitential chalice to pass from them, they actually beg for more: 'Give me more suffering, Lord, or else I

[120] Mangan, 'The Warning Voice' (1846), *Collected Works*, Vol. III: *Poems: 1845–1847*, 136.
[121] Mangan, *Autobiography*, 22.
[122] O'Donoghue, *Life and Writings*, 21.
[123] Mangan, 'When Hearts Were Trumps!' (1850), *Collected Works*, Vol. IV: *Poems: 1848–1912*, 235.
[124] De Vere, *English Misrule and Irish Misdeeds*, 115.

die.'[125] 'Persecution' reminds the reader that the angels were prevented
from rescuing Christ from crucifixion, and Ireland must also fulfil her des-
tiny: 'Peace, brethren, peace! to us is given | Suffering: vengeance is for
Heaven!'[126] But as in the work of other Famine poets, the intrusion of
vision and prophecy in De Vere's poetry betrays a deep-seated anxiety.
'Ode VII: After One of the Famine Years' affirms that the Famine is God's
work, and the speaker is powerless to prevent it:

> I come, and bring not help, for God
>   Withdraws not yet the chalice:
> Still on your plains by martyrs trod
>   And o'er your hills and valleys,
> His name a suffering Saviour writes—
>   Letters black-drawn, and graven
> On lowly huts, and castled heights . . .[127]

The writing of the Famine thus takes place outside this text, not in De
Vere's words but in the 'black-drawn' letters of the Saviour, and the poem
manifests great tension in its author's reluctance to write it. Famine victims, it argues, should join the dead of other ages in silence; like many critics, De Vere was obviously concerned about the ethics of representing pain
and suffering in literature:

> I come, and bring not song; for why
>   Should grief from fancy borrow?
> Why should a lute prolong a sigh,
>   Sophisticating sorrow?[128]

Moreover, the speaker is not even present in his native land; like Mangan
in 'A Vision of Connaught in the Thirteenth Century', De Vere employs
spatial displacement, situating the speaker in Paris and designating his
experience as a vision that haunts him: 'A cry from famished vales I hear,
| That cry which others hear not.'[129] This poem, promoting silence and
disapproving of memorials of the dead, would deny its own existence.

In 'Ode VIII: The Desolation of the West', the speaker has returned,
and is roaming a desolate land: 'Nearer I drew: the tale was told! | Grim,
roofless walls, and hearts long cold;— | The villagers were dead.'[130] The
speaker avoids the issue of personal guilt by a double displacement: first,

[125] De Vere, 'Ireland. 1851', *Irish Odes*, 160.
[126] De Vere, 'Persecution', ibid., 125.
[127] De Vere, 'Ode VII: After One of the Famine Years', ibid., 43.   [128] Ibid., 43.
[129] Ibid., 41.   [130] De Vere, 'Ode VIII: The Desolation of the West', ibid., 47.

in real time, it is ten years since the Famine, so although he has to face the consequences, he has escaped the full horror; secondly, he is told in a vision that Ireland has atoned for her sins and has become 'God's Altar in the West!'[131] 'Irish Colonization. 1848', which rebukes England for not organizing state-assisted emigration, enacts resolution with a vision: 'I heard, in deep prophetic trance immersed, | The wave, keel-cut, kissing the ship's dark side . . .'.[132] The speaker envisages a fair city beyond the sea, a new Britain populated by the Irish; but his vision is fractured by the image of Ireland as a skeleton: 'Pointing with stark, lean finger, from the crest | Of western cliffs plague-stricken to the West'.[133] This symbol of Famine Ireland is too powerful to be contained. Similarly, in the striking 'The Year of Sorrow', De Vere's attempt to contain the distress by submerging it in nature and religion, making it seasonal and sacramental rather than an abomination, is subverted by his evocation of Famine victims:

> And ye, O children worn and weak!
> Who care no more with flowers to play,
> Lean on the grass your cold, thin cheek,
> And those slight hands, and whispering, say,
>
> 'Stern Mother of a race unblest,
> 'In promise kindly, cold in deed,—
> 'Take back, O Earth, into thy breast,
> 'The children whom thou wilt not feed.'[134]

The horror of the peasant at the sight of the returned blight in the 'Summer' section cannot be mitigated by the speaker's fatalism, while the beauty of 'Winter' and the assurance 'The Rite proceeds!' seem only an empty attempt to make up for death and the loss of ceremony in the awful, ineluctable reality.

Williams's visions and prophecies are much less vague than Mangan's and much more militant that De Vere's. 'The Vision: a National Ode' foresees the destruction of the oppressor nation and the rise of 'Ul-Erin', while 'A Prophecy' predicts that the tyrant shall be crushed and dragged down to hell.[135] 'Gratias Agamus: A Paean to England' scornfully satirizes English complaints of Irish ingratitude:

---

[131] Ibid., 49.   [132] De Vere, 'Irish Colonization. 1848', ibid., 137.
[133] Ibid., 138.   [134] De Vere, 'The Year of Sorrow—Ireland—1849', ibid., 141.
[135] Richard D'Alton Williams, 'The Vision: A National Ode', 'A Prophecy', *The Poems of Richard Dalton Williams* (Dublin: T. D. Sullivan, 1883), 18.

> By the ghastly myriads sleeping
> In a coffinless repose,
> And the dying-living weeping
> For God's justice on our foes—
> Let us die for England![136]

Many years later, when he was practising medicine in America, Williams read Fenianism back into the realm of Famine:

> Lo! the ghastly spectre throng!
> Shroudless all in awful pallor!
> Vengeance! *Who* should right their wrong!
> *We* have arms, and men, and valor.
> Strike! the idol long adored
> Waits the doom just gods award her;
> To arms! away! with fire and sword!
> Our march is o'er the British border![137]

The Famine dead can no longer be saved, but their ghosts can be avenged. Williams attempts to heal the dichotomy between his martial and religious views by suggesting it is God's will men should fight, as in 'Hand in Hand': 'Let us bravely stand for our lives and land, | And prove that men have souls!'[138] 'Lord of Hosts', published in the wake of the French Revolution, calls on God to 'Smile on freedom's sacred steel'.[139] But 'Kyrie Eleison', written for James Duffy's *Irish Catholic Magazine* instead of *The Nation*, has a very different tone. Here the Famine is not caused by the tyrant (England) but by Irish national sin: 'The blight came down at Thy command'. Redolent of the leading articles of Mitchel and Duffy, the poem laments starvation as a waste of a life that could have helped free Ireland: 'Oh! had we fallen on the plain | In rapid battle swiftly slain, | We had not perished thus in vain—', but the message is clear: 'Human aid is sought in vain'.[140] 'Kyrie Eleison' prays for the Famine to be lifted from Ireland so that the enemy would have no excuse to gloat over Irish suffering as a punishment. The author of the anonymous 'Thanatos, 1849' interprets the Famine as a punishment for lack of action:

---

[136] Williams, 'Gratias Agamus: A Paean to England', ibid., 27.
[137] Williams, 'Song of the Irish-American Regiments', ibid., 50.
[138] Williams, 'Hand in Hand', ibid., 33.   [139] Williams, 'Lord of Hosts', ibid., 42.
[140] Williams, 'Kyrie Eleison', ibid., 150–2.

God sent a curse upon the land, because her sons were slaves;
The rich earth brought forth rottenness, and gardens became graves;
The green crops withered in the fields, all blackened by the curse,
And wedding gay and dance gave way to coffin and to hearse.[141]

Similarly, in 'The Harvest Pledge', John De Jean Frazer suggests that the Famine was an opportunity sent by God for the Irish to free themselves, and they had failed: 'They crushed not the crusher, nor freed themselves then! | May he load them, and scourge them, and starve them again!'[142] This rhetoric informed the writings of Michael Davitt in *The Fall of Feudalism*, when he maintained that those who starved deserved to die for being cowards. But for a romantic nationalist like Williams, dedicated to revolution, this ambivalence over the causation of Famine indicated a deep-seated anxiety about nationalist ideology and the means of extrication from Famine and England.

When the Rising failed ignominiously, Speranza was bitterly disappointed, characteristically blaming the people for not supporting it. Her disappointment is evident from a comparison of the defiant 'The Famine Year', published in *The Nation* in January 1847, and 'Foreshadowings', published in the same journal of September 1849. As Sean Ryder has noted, 'The Famine Year', despite its message that God alone can avenge, does not work as religious quietism: 'to read this as merely a plea to "suffer and be still" in the hope of divine retribution is to fail to realise the power of the political rhetoric which also suffuses the poem'.[143] A poem that opens with the controversial theme of exportation, and proceeds through the sufferings of women and children and the coffinless burials of the dead to the vengeance of God, demands more than the rising of a spectral army. The last stanza is pure concentrated venom:

Now is your hour of pleasure—bask ye in the world's caress;
But our whitening bones against ye will rise as witnesses,
From the cabins and the ditches, in their charred, uncoffin'd masses,
For the Angel of the Trumpet will know them when he passes.
A ghastly, spectral army, before the great God we'll stand,
And arraign ye as our murderers, the spoilers of our land.[144]

---

[141] 'Thanatos, 1849', in Morash (ed.), *Hungry Voice*, 165.

[142] Frazer, 'The Harvest Pledge', ibid., 176.

[143] Sean Ryder, 'Reading Lessons: Famine and the *Nation*, 1845–1849', in Chris Morash and Richard Hayes (eds.), *'Fearful Realities': New Perspectives on the Famine* (Dublin: Irish Academic Press, 1996), 151–63, at 157.

[144] Speranza, 'The Famine Year', *Poems by Speranza*, 7.

As in much of Williams's poetry, Speranza's apocalyptic stance is the position of enraged impotence, taking comfort in a justice of the afterlife at
least. Yet 'Foreshadowings', a more overtly apocalyptic poem, elides the
overthrow of the tyrannical oppressor in favour of an objectless martyrdom:

> I see in a vision the shadowy portal,
> That leadeth to regions of glory immortal;
> I see the pale forms from the seven wounds bleeding,
> Which up to God's Throne the bright angels are leading;
> I see the crown placed on each saint bending lowly,
> While sounds the Trisagion—Holy, thrice Holy![145]

Speranza was jolted back into her natural political conservatism by the
failure of the rising, and the prosecutions of Duffy over a series of leaders,
including her own 'Jacta Alea Est', and it shows in her change of tone. The
function of Famine victim as witness for the Divine Prosecution has been
reduced in her later poetry to a banal, tame sanctification.

The intrusion of the visionary and apocalyptic modes in McGee's
poetry, as in Speranza's and Williams's, indicated a recognition of impotence. 'The Famine in the Land', published in *The Nation* in April 1847,
opens with the despair its contemporary readers must have felt: 'Death
reapeth in the fields of life, and we cannot count the corpses'. The title of
the poem echoes Isaac Butt's paper 'The Famine in the Land', published
in the *Dublin University Magazine* in the same month. Whereas Butt's article is eminently practical if furiously condemnatory, McGee attempts to
subvert reality in mid-poem by revealing he has been dreaming: "Twas a
vision—'tis a fable—I did but tell my dream— | Yet twice, yea thrice, I
saw it, and still the same did seem.'[146] This recalls the continuous dream
of Mangan's 'The Funerals'. The poem began mimetically, but shifts
focus dramatically by suggesting the Famine, which was ravaging Ireland
in the reader's present, might never happen if the men of Ireland took a
stand. The central vision of 'The Three Dreams', the 'warrior throng' the
speaker zealously welcomes, cannot be sustained, and he wakes before its
fulfilment to be confronted by the nightmare of a silent 'dread Death-land'
and the ominous Prophecy Book of St Patrick:

[145] Speranza, 'Foreshadowings', ibid., 18.
[146] McGee, 'The Famine in the Land', *Poems of Thomas D'Arcy McGee*, 341.

> The skene and the sparthe,
> The lament for the dearth,
> The voice of all mirth
> Shall be hush'd on thy hearth,
> O Erie!
> And your children want earth
> When they bury![147]

Antique terms like 'skene', 'sparthe', 'Tanist', and 'kerne', and the promise that if men turn back to God and free themselves the curse will be lifted, attempt to remove the disaster to a safe distance, but fail. 'Lord Gl—Gall's Dream' has given up the ghost of armed rebellion for the rebellion of ghosts, as a skeletal crew, like the 'ghastly, spectral army' of Speranza's 'The Famine Year', rise to denounce this lord on Judgement Day:

> His lordship scarce could tell for fear,
> Of every name that met his ear;
> But he saw that the archangel took
> Note of them all in his blackest book—
> From Farney some, and from Skibbereen,
> From West and East and the lands between,
> Such a skeleton tryst has never been seen.[148]

As Ryder has noted with reference to 'The Famine Year', this is a form of political rhetoric; but it is the rhetoric of frustrated impotence, deferring vengeance because the speaker does not have the power to exact it in the present.

De Vere's 'Widowhood. 1848' unites the impotent individual with his suffering country in the act of witnessing: 'I saw the black robe and the aspect pale, | And heard in dream the country's dying wail.'[149] In all of these Famine poems, the vision functions either as a means of successfully resolving unfinished situations by ending the Famine or freeing the country, or as a distancing device, a sanitized substitute for real vision, which would mean seeing and acknowledging the horror of starvation. Very often, Famine poets had a real opportunity to make a difference in the disaster, whether by becoming more stridently militant, like Williams, Speranza, and McGee, or changing allegiance, like Ferguson, by using contacts to spread information, like De Vere, or by falling prey to it, like Mangan. At the height of the Famine, *The Nation* declared that 'the writer

[147] McGee, 'The Three Dreams', ibid., 105.
[148] McGee, 'Lord Gl—Gall's Dream', ibid., 154.
[149] De Vere, 'Widowhood. 1848', *Irish Odes*, 152.

is a man of action';[150] certainly these men and women were to prove themselves in their different capacities to be the unacknowledged legislators of
their world. In their real lives, each of these poets was forced to come to
terms with the Famine and how it transformed them; but in their poetry,
they attempted escapism, and a resolution that evaded them in reality.

[150] *Nation* (21 Aug. 1847), 729.

7
The Black Stream: Politics and Proselytism in Second-Generation Famine Novels

> Between the Ireland of the past and the Ireland of the present the
> Famine lies like a black stream, all but entirely blotting out and effac-
> ing the past. Whole phases of life, whole types of character, whole
> modes of existence and ways of thought passed away then and have
> never been renewed. The entire fabric of the country was torn to
> pieces and has never reformed itself upon the same lines again.
>
> (Emily Lawless, *The Story of the Nations: Ireland* (London and
> New York: T. Fisher Unwin, 1887), 401–2.)

Literary critics tend to agree that the generation following the Famine was
'among the most barren culturally in modern Irish history', providing little of value except to the antiquarian or anthropologist.[1] Few literary
works were produced at all, say the critics, even less a cohesive literature
of the Famine: 'There is a handful of novels and a body of poems, but few
truly distinguished works. Where is the Famine in the literature of the
Revival? Where is it in Joyce?'[2] Eagleton is so disturbed by this lack that
he felt the need to borrow *Wuthering Heights* in order to fill out the canon
of Famine literature.

Both assertions are misleading: the years between the Famine and the
Revival may have been comparatively barren, partly due to the destruction
of the publishing industry and the loss of many promising authors to
famine and exile or, like Carleton and Speranza, to disillusionment; but
nevertheless they yielded outstanding novels by Irish writers such as
Lever, Le Fanu, and Kickham. As for Famine representation, Eagleton is
not only obliterating it from less well-known Victorian novels, but also
diminishing its impact on the works of Somerville and Ross, O'Flaherty,
Macken, and Trevor in this century. In Eagleton's estimation, Yeats's failure to date *The Countess Cathleen* to the mid-nineteenth century, and

---

[1] Oliver MacDonagh, 'Introduction', in W. E. Vaughan (ed.), *A New History of Ireland*,
Vol. V: *Ireland Under the Union I 1801–70* (Oxford: Clarendon Press, 1989), p. lix.
[2] Terry Eagleton, *Heathcliff and the Great Hunger: Studies in Irish Culture* (London and
New York: Verso, 1995), 13.

Joyce's curious omission of the Famine from Dublin on 16 June 1904, clearly renders its claim to attention null and void. On the contrary, Christopher Morash's anthology of Famine poetry *The Hungry Voice* could easily be matched by a series of Famine novels stretching from the 1840s to the present day. They may not constitute a genre, and their authors may not rival Yeats and Joyce in literary ability, but they certainly indicate the continuing interest of Irish, British, and American readers in the Great Famine, and deserve attention as reflections of how various groups perceived the Famine at various times.

It is true that the brief Irish literary renaissance of the 1830s and 1840s was crushed by the Famine, and many Dublin publishers, including William Curry, Jr., who published many of Carleton's novels, were bank-rupted. Even the notable survivors, such as James Duffy, encountered problems; Duffy told Carleton in 1855: 'The people seldom think of buy-ing books, because they are luxuries, which they can do without.'[3] Nevertheless, Duffy continued to publish novels about the Famine, bring-ing out Thomas O'Neill Russell's *The Struggles of Dick Massey* in 1860, David Power Conyngham's *Frank O'Donnell* in 1861, and Richard Baptist O'Brien's *The D'Altons of Crag* in 1882. In England, the initial over-exposure of the Famine in newspapers, travel-books, and parliamentary reports seemed to inhibit the publication of novels on any Irish subject, as Trollope discovered when he offered *Castle Richmond* to the *Cornhill*. Yet religious publishers such as the Protestant evangelical Religious Tract Society, or the firm of Charles Dolman and Thomas Richardson (with his New York partner Henry Richardson), which published Catholic interest books, had no qualms about publishing Famine novels with a religious slant in London soon after the Famine, and bigger names such as Macmillan and Chapman and Hall began to show an interest in the 1870s and 1880s. By 1875 Annie Keary was able to establish her reputation with her Famine novel, *Castle Daly*, in a way Trollope could never have done with *Castle Richmond*. Margaret Brew's *Castle Cloyne* was so highly praised by *The Times*, the *Standard*, and the *Morning Post* in 1885, that the *Irish Monthly Magazine*, to which she had contributed many stories, expressed concern that anything which so delighted the English must be biased; the review concluded, however, that the novel 'has received these perilous commendations, and, nevertheless, is an excellent Irish tale'.[4]

---

[3] Quoted in D. J. O'Donoghue, *The Life of William Carleton: Being His Autobiography And Letters: And An Account Of His Life And Writings From The Point At Which The Autobiography Breaks Off*, 2 vols. (London: Downey & Co., 1896), ii. 215.

[4] *Irish Monthly Magazine*, 14/158 (Aug. 1886), 455–6.

Thomas Flanagan has noted that the Famine destroyed 'at least for several decades, the notion of Ireland as a picturesque hinterland',[5] but this did not prevent the publication of representations of a broken, drained, stricken Ireland, or theories as to its downfall.

In fact, the Famine appears in so many novels for so many reasons, that it seems to have been hijacked by manifold pressure groups for personal and political gain. Famine novels were written by evangelical Protestants, Roman Catholic priests, revolutionaries and politicians, landlords of both religions and the middle classes who succeeded to their estates, Irish language enthusiasts, emigrants and the descendants of emigrants. The turbulent times they lived through—the times of the Encumbered Estates Court, emigration, Fenian agitation, Disestablishment, the Land League, Home Rule, the Easter Rising—all seem to trigger novels about this ultimate catastrophe, and the Utopia that existed on the other side, and was lost forever. W. J. McCormack reads this as an idiosyncratic Anglo-Irish complaint: 'the Golden Age always existed before some movable disaster, before the Union, before the Famine, before the Encumbered Estates Court, the Land War, Parnell, the Rising, the Troubles, an accelerating succession of unfortunate falls each one briefly inaugurating some (retrospectively acknowledged) idyll which is itself soon dissolved by the next disaster'.[6] Yet the Famine seems to have withstood this dissolution, looming large in the minds of 'Anglo-Irish' and 'native' without discrimination.

Indeed, the issue of famine is employed by Irish writers as a blank canvas on which to explore their own anxieties, and to imagine future relations with England. In this way, all famine texts are strikingly similar, even when not written about the same famine: Revd Knox's *Pastoral Annals*, published in 1840 and dealing with the 1817 famine, or Mrs Berens's *Steadfast Unto Death*, about the famine of 1879–80, are recognizable famine texts because they are informed by the same language and imagery as novels about the Great Famine—a language and imagery that can be traced back to Spenser and sixteenth-century famine victims. Indeed, apart from the archaic language, Spenser's description of famine in *A View of the Present State of Ireland* (1596) reads very much like a travel narrative or journalistic report from Ireland in 1847:

Out of every corner of the woods and glynnes they came creeping forth upon their hands, for their legges could not beare them; they looked like anatomies of death,

[5] Thomas Flanagan, 'Literature in English, 1801–91', *New History of Ireland*, v. 509–10.
[6] W. J. McCormack, *From Burke to Beckett: Ascendancy, Tradition and Betrayal in Literary History* (Cork: Cork University Press, 1994), 10.

they spake like ghosts crying out of their graves; they did eate the dead carrions, happy where they could finde them, yea, and one another soone after, insomuch as the very carcasses they spared not to scrape out of their graves; and, if they found a plot of water-cresses or shamrocks, there they flocked as to a feast for the time, yet not able long to continue therewithall; that in short space there were none almost left, and a most populous and plentifull countrey suddainely left voyde of man and beast : . .[7]

The careful use of a vocabulary of famine—'apathy', 'silence', 'docks and nettles', 'walking ghosts', 'living skeletons', 'spectres', and 'wolfish voracity'—by famine authors forms a powerful shorthand to conjure famine and allow them to mould the tragedy to their own agenda. Famine was a recurring catastrophe in Ireland, and the similarity of language and incident in famine novels before and after the Great Famine can cause confusion. Revd Stephen Brown's useful *Ireland in Fiction* lists Russell's *Dick Massey* as a novel about the 1814 famine, when it actually describes 1845–7, and sets Charles Kennett Burrow's *Patricia of the Hills* during 'the Famine years, and the Young Ireland movement', when it is in fact set in the mid-1880s.[8] The scenes of famine and fever in Emily Fox's *Rose O'Connor* (1881) would definitely seem to indicate, as Brown suggests, that it is a story of 'the famine years' of 1845–9.[9] The heroine's younger brother starves to death with a piece of turnip uneaten in his hand—a recurring motif in both Famine fiction and newspaper reports—and the extremity of distress suggests only the Great Famine: ' "The famine was sore in the land." People were dying by the roadside, in their efforts to procure food. Whole families were found dead in their homes when they were entered by some of the good Samaritans, who were roused to exertion by the constant reports of "death by starvation".'[10] However, towards the end of the novel, George Stanley, who has emigrated to New York, writes home of the arrival of Parnell and Dillon in America, so dating the novel to the 1879–80 crisis.[11] Fox is evidently attempting to strengthen American support for the attempt to win Home Rule by employing the imagery of earlier famine novels to bolster her representation of contemporary suffering. The blank canvas effect seems to impose a remarkable

---

[7] Edmund Spenser, *A View of the State of Ireland* (1633), ed. Andrew Hadfield and Willy Maley (Oxford: Blackwell, 1997), 101–2.

[8] Revd Stephen Brown, *Ireland in Fiction: A Guide to Irish Novels, Tales, Romances and Folklore* (1916; Shannon: Irish University Press, 1969), 269, 48.

[9] Ibid., 159.

[10] Emily Fox ['Toler King'], *Rose O'Connor: A Story of the Day* (Chicago: Henry A. Sumner & Co., 1881), 108.

[11] Parnell and Dillon toured America from 2 January to 11 March 1880.

homogeneity on each Famine author: all at least hint at misrule, condemn the exportation of food from a starving country, regret emigration as draining the country of its lifeblood while land lies uncultivated, and demand that tenants should have rights. There are no Protectionists in Famine fiction, and no one claims that representations of suffering and death are overdrawn—on the contrary, we are told, they have been toned down.

One of the most frequent motifs of the homogeneous Famine novel is the female victim, usually a mother, in various poses: a dead mother suckling a living baby, a living mother with a dead child, an abandoned or widowed mother rejected at the poorhouse and left to starve with her children, a woman forced to abandon her baby to suckle an older child to enable him to work, a mother who abandons her child or steals food from him, and, most disturbingly, a mother who eats her dead child. Margaret Kelleher argues that Famine novelists chose the female as the 'archetypal victim', despite historical evidence indicating the higher survival rate of women during the Famine.[12] Their motivation to describe female famine victims, she suggests, is to confine the effects of the Famine to the domestic sphere, and so avoid discussions of the political causes and consequences: 'the portrayal of women as apolitical allows authors to evade discussion of famine as a political phenomenon'.[13] What Kelleher fails to explain is why Famine authors should want to avoid the political sphere. On the contrary, they often court it, and allegations of genocide against the government and landlords coexist with pathetic scenes of the starvation and death of women. Certainly, the *United Irishman* didn't make a point of isolating cases of male starvation in order to raise the political temperature. In many cases the fictional female famine 'victim' is in fact a survivor, no matter what she has suffered, or to what depths she has descended. It may be that the countless descriptions of women and children in cabins simply reflect the experience of gentlemen and philanthropists, who had easiest access to the starving family at a time and place when men might be absent in search of work or food—this is certainly true of the many cabin scenes in contemporary travel narratives. Nevertheless, given the importance of the figure of the 'Angel in the House' in the construction and perception of gender in the Victorian period, the idea of starving mothers in cabins must have carried an extra emotional charge. As a motif, it is a powerful reminder of and link to other Famine novels, and an economical way of

---

[12] Margaret Kelleher, 'The Feminisation of Famine: Narrative Representations of Irish and Bengali Famines', Ph.D. thesis (Boston College, 1992), 5, 227.

[13] Ibid., 363–4.

triggering information from remembered scenes. However, men are by no means unrepresented in Famine death scenes: the death by starvation of poor Tim Murphy in *The Hunger,* or Oonagh's discovery of the putrid skeletal remains of her lover John Molloy in *Castle Cloyne* are quite as disturbing as any female death scene.[14] In any case, the groups most likely to be affected by Famine were the old and children, but Kelleher does not complain about the under-representation of geriatric death scenes. Even if one chooses to see a disproportionate preponderance of female victims, this can easily be explained as an intention to capitalize on the vulnerability, pathos, and relative attractiveness—in a macabre sense—of mother and baby deaths.[15] Or, far from being apolitical, the female victim may be interpreted as an icon for an Ireland which can no longer feed her 'children', or has been deserted by her faithless 'husband' John Bull in the hour of most need. What is certain is that recurring motifs, including the female victim, constitute not evasion but consolidation of the Famine mythos.

First-generation Famine writers were keenly aware of the importance of their role: to preserve and document a phenomenon which changed Ireland dramatically, but which was passing rapidly from memory. Mildred Darby observed in 1910 that few of her generation knew anything but the broad outlines of the Famine taken from textbooks, and no more real or recent to them than the campaigns of Cromwell and King Billy.[16] Famine novelists attached great importance to the fact that they or their sources were witnesses to the tragedy, but perhaps a more vital clue to their interest is that they outlived it. The literature of the Famine, like the ideology of the Tenant League, was written by and for those who survived the Famine, not its victims, and any attempt to create a solidarity of suffering between those who starved and those who watched implies the guilt and shame of those who lived to tell the tale. One of the guests at Tom and Norah's wedding in *Dick Massey,* surrounded by the wedding feast in the midst of Famine, remarks: 'I'm greatly afeerd whoever lives until this time twelvemonths 'ill have quare stories to tell.'[17] In effect, Famine novelists

[14] Mildred Darby ['Andrew Merry'], *The Hunger, Being Realities of the Famine Years in Ireland 1845 to 1849* (London: Andrew Melrose, 1910), 222–4; Margaret Brew, *The Chronicles of Castle Cloyne; or, Pictures of the Munster People,* 3 vols. (London: Chapman & Hall, 1885), ii. 286. It could of course be argued that these female writers may have a different perspective to their male fellow Famine writers.

[15] See, for example, John Keegan's 'The Dying Mother's Lament', discussed in the previous chapter.

[16] Darby, *The Hunger,* 1–2.

[17] Thomas O'Neill Russell ['Reginald Tierney'], *The Struggles of Dick Massey; or, The Battles of a Boy* (Dublin: James Duffy, 1860), 281.

tell their 'quare stories' in order to drown the silence of the dead, and afford some share in history to those who survived.

The struggle to represent history as narrative can prove problematic or opportune: perhaps for Louis J. Walsh, the evocation of the dead heroes of Young Ireland in his novel *The Next Time* added resonance to his own political campaign. By 1919 most of the people who had lived through the Famine were dead, and it was history indeed; but novels about the Famine began to appear before it was acknowledged as a major historical event. William Carleton began writing *The Black Prophet* in 1846, before the Famine even existed; for him it was merely the last in a long line of scarcities. Mrs Hoare must claim the prize for the earliest fictional representations of the Great Famine: her *Shamrock Leaves*, written in 1846–7 and published in 1851, shows remarkable prescience. Her story 'The Living and the Dead: An Irish Sketch', celebrating Irish customs connected with 'waking' the dead, was written in the midst of an ongoing Famine, when such ceremonies were defunct: 'Buoyancy of spirit is gone with vigour of body; all the energies of mind are concentrated in the one fierce craving of animal life. "Food! Food!" is the cry that echoes through the land:—the short bleak wintry day, and the long dark frosty night, alike resound with the shrieks of those who perish from hunger and nakedness.'[18] Before turning to happier times and customs, she remarks that now those who die of starvation are tossed in mass graves without coffins—if the rats don't get to them first: 'Such scenes are horrifying to contemplate, yet they are true; nor can any human being foresee their termination.'[19] With no end in sight, it is safer to turn to the past. Similarly, Mrs Berens's *Steadfast Unto Death*, written during the 1879–80 crisis, seeks closure by evading the present. The novel opens in the winter of 1879 with Mora a little girl, but by the end of the novel she has been left a fortune of £500, grown up, married a Dublin porter, and become a mother. The novel ends abruptly: 'In vaticination we lay down our pen, for we have yet to complete the year of 1880.'[20] Brought down to earth with a crash, we realize that we have been deceived, and Mora is still a little girl, recovering from the deaths of her mother and her protector Black Hugh, with a very uncertain future. Like the Famine poets, Berens attempted evasion by displacing temporally, but her vision is unsustainable.

[18] Mrs Hoare, 'The Living and the Dead: An Irish Sketch', *Shamrock Leaves; or, Tales and Sketches of Ireland* (Dublin and London: J. M'Glashan; Partridge & Oakey, 1851), 95–6.
[19] Ibid., 96.
[20] Mrs Berens, *Steadfast Unto Death: A Tale of the Irish Famine of To-Day* (London: Remington & Co., 1880), 275.

There is a sense of urgency about first-generation Famine novels, a need to get everything down on paper before the witnesses disappear. John O'Rourke, who published the first history of the Great Famine in 1875, knew that his testimony should be written without delay:

Several reasons occurred to him why such a work should be done: the magnitude of the Famine itself; the peculiarity of its immediate cause; its influence on the destiny of the Irish Race. That there should be no unnecessary delay in performing the task was sufficiently proved, he thought, by the fact, that testimony of the most valuable kind, namely cotemporary testimony, was, silently but rapidly passing away with the generation that had witnessed the scourge.[21]

This seems to hold true even for those born immediately after the Famine. The Christian evangelist and socialist orator Alexander Irvine, who became a missionary among down-and-outs in New York, and served as a minister to the forces during World War I, was born in Antrim in 1862, the son of a Protestant shoemaker and his Catholic wife, who had suffered greatly during the Famine. The Irvines lost their second child, always afterwards called 'the famine child', because it was malnourished in the womb, and Alexander's father Jamie was caught stealing milk to save his wife and child from starvation. Yet, for the younger Irvines, the Famine was useful fiction, not history. Often hungry themselves, as their father was frequently unemployed, they used the Famine as a way to forget their own troubles: 'We had many devices for diverting hunger. The one always used as a last resort was the stories of the "great famine." We were particularly helped by one about a family half of whom died around a pot of stir-about that had come too late.'[22] This innocent ghoulishness indicates the blurring of the distinction between fact and fiction for the generation succeeding the Famine, and the need for the first generation to record their experiences before it was too late.

Of course, many of the authors who wrote Famine novels in the late nineteenth century were second-generation themselves—and some were not even Irish. But all were anxious to point out that, if they were not witnesses themselves, all of their information was obtained from reliable eyewitnesses. Even Louis J. Walsh, who was born in 1880, and published his novel in 1919, announced that *The Next Time* is 'very much "historical" and very little "novel" ', and 'founded on the actual experiences of

---

[21] Revd John O'Rourke, *The History of the Great Irish Famine of 1847* (Dublin and London: M'Glashan and Gill; James Duffy, Sons, & Co., 1875), p. vii.
[22] Alexander Irvine, *My Lady of the Chimney-Corner* (London: Eveleigh Nash, 1913), 150–1.

eye-witnesses'.[23] *The Hunger* reads more like a folklore archive than a novel, and O'Brien went overboard in *Ailey Moore* and *The D'Altons*, claiming to have been present at all events, even the supernatural, and to have overseen the cures he relates.[24] The authenticity of these authors' depictions of Famine Ireland is vital, not only to counter allegations of exaggeration, but also to fix themselves as partakers in this national calamity. But there is an admission of unease at the proximity of suffering: of all Famine narrators, only Mrs Hoare employs first-person narrative, in her short story 'Little Mary: A Tale of the Black Year'; to identify oneself as one of the brutalized starving comes too close for comfort. Many of these authors have only a precarious claim to victimhood, to their expressions of nationalist outrage—or even to Irishness. Annie Keary was born and brought up in England; Margaret Brew was the daughter of a County Clare landowner, and she dedicated *Castle Cloyne* to the anti-Home Rule activist Lady Florence Dixie; Louise Field, daughter of a County Cavan magistrate, dedicated *Denis* 'To my kinsfolk and friends, among the landowners of Ireland', while, as Christopher Morash has noted, Canon Sheehan was not even born when the events which 'spring up to memory' in *Glenanaar* occurred.[25] Everyone, it seems, is clamouring for recognition, proclaiming their own authentic Irishness by proving that they, and their kind, suffered too. Many of those writing, and many of those they were writing for, had connections among Irish landowners, who had been beleaguered on all sides during the Famine, and their novels seek to redress the balance by emphasizing the universality of the ruin. In Brew's *Castle Cloyne*, the poor are only the first to suffer, and many old aristocratic families are swept into oblivion by the 'terrible impartiality' of the Famine (which was obviously too democratic for Brew's tastes).[26] Landlords, she argued, were unjustly blamed for evicting their tenants to face starvation and death: 'It was the imperative instinct of self-preservation; the instinct of one swimming for his life, who must perforce

---

[23] Louis J. Walsh, *The Next Time: A Story of 'Forty-Eight* (Dublin: M. H. Gill & Son, Ltd., 1919), 5–6.

[24] In *Ailey Moore*, when Gerald reveals that he himself was the blind boy healed at the sacred well, O'Brien footnotes: 'It is an event of the life of the writer of this sketch' (p. 4). Similarly, A. M. Sullivan testifies to the truth of his story about a Protestant clergyman who attempted to save a dying man during the Famine by adding: 'I know this to be true. *I* was the "young friend" who went for and brought the wine.' (A. M. Sullivan, *New Ireland: Political Sketches and Personal Reminiscences of Thirty Years of Irish Public Life* (Glasgow and London: Cameron & Ferguson; Fleet Street, 1877), 65).

[25] Canon Patrick Sheehan, *Glenanaar: A Story of Irish Life* (London, New York, and Bombay: Longmans, Green & Co., 1905), 198.

[26] Brew, *Castle Cloyne*, ii. 161.

cast off with a determined hand the drowning comrade who clutches him with so convulsive a clasp that both are in danger of being drowned.'[27] But by this stage, in the 1880s, even Charles Gavan Duffy agreed with her.[28] The dual plot of *Castle Cloyne*, involving the separate attempts of the peasant Oonagh MacDermott and the aristocrat Hyacinth Dillon to survive the disaster, emphasizes the universality of suffering, but Brew made a point of foregrounding the better capabilities of the peasant class for reconstruction. Oonagh remains in Ireland, discovers a post-famine boom trade as a pedlar and makes a small fortune, whereas Hyacinth loses not only his estate, but his entire family, and is forced to go to America—the very last resort of the Famine novel. Brew perhaps unconsciously renounced universal suffering in her partiality for Hyacinth, redeeming his fortunes in classic *deus-ex-machina* fashion: first he strikes gold in California, then his wife's surprise inheritance enables them to buy back Castle Cloyne. Oonagh may die happy in her assurance of heaven, but Hyacinth's reward is much more immediate and substantial.

Brew attempted to authenticate her Irishness by transcending class barriers, but Annie Keary approached the problem of her authenticity with another kind of duality—that of nationality. The daughter of a County Galway gentleman who emigrated to England and took holy orders after the loss of his family's property long before the Famine, Keary spent only two weeks in her entire life in Ireland, while writing *Castle Daly* in the 1870s, and knew very few Irish people personally. But, as her sister has recorded, Keary had a very powerful imagination, stimulated by the tales her father told of his Irish childhood, which he would pretend had happened to Annie also. Eliza recalled how Annie,

letting her thoughts reach back to some dim, remoter period of existence, would see sweet, misty pictures of the west, hear the soft clatter of the Irish tongue, run barefooted across the bog with merry little foster-brothers and sisters, to fish in the blue mountain lough, or to feast upon sweet milk and potatoes at the foster-parents' board in the cabin where papa was nursed, and where he laughed and sported away so many careless hours—but, somehow, never without Annie, how could he ever have been anywhere without her?[29]

Annie and her father 'represented the Irish side of the family', so it is not surprising that when she came to write her Famine novel, this duality in

---

[27] Brew, *Castle Cloyne*, ii., 166.
[28] Sir Charles Gavan Duffy, *Four Years of Irish History 1845–1849* (London, Paris, and New York: Cassell, Petter, Galpin & Co, 1883), 46.
[29] Eliza Keary, *Memoir of Annie Keary* (London: Macmillan, 1882), 5.

her own family reappeared in the Dalys.[30] Squire Daly speaks of 'the Irish faction of us, Ellen and Connor and I', in opposition to the cold, formal, English faction of Mrs Daly and Pelham.[31] Ellen is in constant opposition to the English virtues of reason and rationalism: her English mother 'was her conscience',[32] while the English agent, John Thornley, tries to curb her impetuous sympathy for her people. Thornley's rationalism is acknowledged as repugnant:

He stood still and looked over the valley lying bright in the golden sunset, where the labourers stood in groups about the gates of their little garden enclosures, and the women came out and put the babies into their fathers' arms, and children filled the air with joyous evening clamour; and talked quite calmly of the inevitable evils attending on the subdivision of land, and the certainty that an over-stimulated population like the one he was surveying must come at last to the point of being decimated by want and sickness.[33]

But Anglo-Saxon rationalism is seen to save people, while Celtic emotion is impotent. In a letter to a relative, Keary revealed: 'I mean the Thornleys to be the strong-willed people: Ellen and Anne the sympathetic people, who alter those they live near not by subduing, but by permeating them with influence . . .'.[34] Her lack of knowledge of Ireland inevitably led to caricature, exemplified by the name of Anne O'Flaherty's house—Happy-go-Lucky Lodge, in Good People's Hollow. But the dualism of the novel indicates an internal struggle, where the 'Irish faction' of herself indignantly sympathized with Irish suffering, while the English side rationalized and sought to assuage it. In the end, she attempted to merge them by uniting the Irish Ellen to the English Thornley, the Hibernophile Lesbia to the Anglophile Pelham, symbolizing the general trend of the novel towards moderation and modernization, but at a heavy cost: the rebel Connor's long years of exile, and the desertion of a once-populous area.

Unlike Keary's attempt at reconciliation, many of these novels divide their demand for a share of history along sectarian lines. One of the most powerful and lasting accusations surrounding the Famine was that Protestant clergy or landlords on relief committees controlled the distribution of relief, and allowed access only to Protestants or those prepared to convert. This allegation—known as 'souperism' from the soup

---

[30] Ibid., 4.

[31] Keary, *Castle Daly*, i. 35; in *Writing the Irish Famine*, Morash states that Mrs Daly is dead, and Ellen has been fostered out in consequence (p. 33); in fact Ellen's mother is not dead, and she is fostered out in accordance with custom and not because of her mother's death. Ellen's opposition to her English mother is one of the central themes of the novel.

[32] Keary, *Castle Daly*, i. 29–30.   [33] Ibid., 151–2.   [34] Eliza Keary, *Memoir*, 152.

provided by private individuals and later by government-controlled agencies after the so-called Soup Kitchen Act (Temporary Relief Act) of
1847—caused lasting acrimony, and inflamed relations between
Protestant and Roman Catholic clergy during relief operations, contributing to a mutual paranoia, and perhaps accelerating the post-famine 'devotional revolution'. There is evidence for and against the existence of
souperism: O'Rourke was adamant that 'to deny that neither money nor
food were given, to induce persons to attend the Scripture classes and
proselytizing schools, is to deny the very best proven facts'.[35] A more
recent commentator has stressed that such allegations are difficult to either
prove or disprove, and that the charge of souperism was a 'handy shille-
lagh' to use on even the most disinterested of philanthropists.[36] Revd
Thomas Armstrong, a Presbyterian minister in County Mayo during the
Famine, provided contradictory evidence. On the surface, he presented a
picture of harmony between the classes and religions during the distress:
'As an evidence of the good impressions left on all, many years after, at a
time of severe distress and suffering, the Roman Catholic Bishop proposed
me as president of another Relief Committee, which honour I of course
declined in his favour; but I was unanimously appointed vice-chairman.'[37]
Yet Armstrong was an enthusiastic proselytizer and admirer of the missionary zeal of Edward Nangle and Alexander Dallas, and obviously tried
to emulate them in his own parish during the Famine, for which he was
physically attacked by a local priest. He was deeply disappointed when
British capitalists failed to take the opportunity offered by the Famine to
make another plantation in Ireland, finishing Papism forever.[38] It is certain that souperism did occur at least on a local level, even if it was not the
organized campaign some would suggest. In his unpublished autobiography, the Quaker Alfred Webb recalled the despair and misery that led
Catholics to feign conversion: 'Those who really became Protestants were
few and far between. The movement left seeds of bitterness that have not
yet died out, and Protestants, not altogether excluding Friends, sacrificed
much of the influence for good they would have had if they had been satisfied to leave the belief of the people alone.'[39] In general, the Friends did

---

[35] O'Rourke, *History of the Great Irish Famine*, 518–19.
[36] Desmond Bowen, *Souperism: Myth or Reality: A Study in Souperism* (Cork: Mercier
Press, 1970), 229.
[37] Revd Thomas Armstrong, *My Life in Connaught, With Sketches of Mission Work in the
West* (London: Eliot Stock, 1906), 15.
[38] Ibid., 95–6, 58.
[39] Quoted in R. F. Foster, *Modern Ireland* (London: Penguin, 1989), 329n.

not suffer the same opprobrium as Protestants; most were resolutely against discrimination, and this meant they were remembered as selfless, while Protestant rectors, who undoubtedly saved many lives, suffered accusations of genocide. This feeling manifests itself in the ruthless one-dimensional soupers of anti-proselytism novels, such as Revd Exeter Hall in Bowles's *Irish Diamonds*, and the portrayal of Quakers as self-sacrificing and impartial, like the Goodbodys in *The Hunger*.

Allegations of souperism did not begin with the Famine. The Irish Church Missions Society was founded in 1818, and it sent tracts and Scripture-readers throughout Ireland to convert the Irish through their own language. Controversial Protestant settlements were founded at Dingle and Achill, and were viewed—at least initially—with as much horror by liberal Protestants such as Archbishop Whately of Dublin, as by the Roman Catholic Archbishop MacHale of Tuam. Indeed, the opposition of liberal Established Church clergymen to Evangelical proselytism is often recognized in Famine novels as the contrast between the benevolent rector and the odious souper—a pairing matched in Protestant novels by the acceptable, liberal, Douai-educated gentleman priest and his fiery, uncouth, fanatic, Maynooth curate (Trollope's Irish novels spring to mind in this context). In Conyngham's *Frank O'Donnell*, Revd Smith not only condemns the evil souper Bob Sly, but actually financially supports the parish priest through the Famine, and takes in the Catholic O'Donnells when they are evicted.[40] The convert settlements were well aware of the disapproval they garnered from all sides, and seemed to view themselves as isolated outposts in the wilderness, adopting a paranoid siege mentality. As we have seen, Asenath Nicholson, who was not averse to handing out a bible or two herself, was verbally abused by the suspicious Nangle. Samuel and Anna Maria Hall, travelling a few years earlier, were equally unimpressed with the Achill settlement; they discovered that the autocratic Nangle had dismissed a boy from his school for no apparent reason, leaving him to beg or starve, and that poor Roman Catholics on the island would rather starve than join the colony.[41] The bribe of food for conversion was obviously being employed even before the Famine, during the frequent periods of scarcity, as can be inferred from Carleton's *Valentine M'Clutchy*; but Carleton's novel is high farce compared to post-Famine representations of souperism. Alexander Dallas, founder of the Dingle colony, recorded his visit to the

[40] David Power Conyngham ['Allen Clington'], *Frank O'Donnell: A Tale of Irish Life* (Dublin and London: James Duffy, 1861).

[41] Samuel Carter and Anna Maria Hall, *Ireland: Its Scenery, Character, &c.*, 3 vols. (London: Jeremiah How, 1846), iii. 398–400.

remote village of Derrygimla in Connemara. The inhabitants were waiting for the relief officer to arrive to distribute food, so Dallas seized his opportunity:

I found my way to the highest large stone in the place, on which I stood, asking in a loud voice what they came there for. 'For relief,' was the reply. 'I have got relief for you,' I said; and the words brought the scattered groups into a closer crowd around me. Speaking plainly and slowly, I said, 'Man shall not live by bread alone, but by every word of God'—that is God's own word.[42]

One can only assume the people of Derrygimla were too weak to retaliate to what must have seemed a cruel prank, but Dallas was obviously sincere in his belief that, thanks to the Famine, Irish souls would be saved even if bodies were sacrificed: 'At a very early period of this effort I was made sensible that the arrangements of Providence were wiser and better than my plans.'[43] Nangle shared his belief: 'It is said that Mr. Nangle frequently told his friends, that had it not been for the Famine of '47, his mission in Achill would have been a failure.'[44]

Evangelical—and even some liberal—Protestants viewed the Famine as a judicial punishment from God for a variety of sins: for the Maynooth grant, for Papism, for the murderous urges of the Irish. For the author Elizabeth Hely Walshe, famine was 'the sharp scourge . . . which should purify the land'.[45] But the Famine was also the perfect opportunity to convert the chastened Irish, and save their souls even if their bodies were beyond rescue. The fanatical Evangelist Lord Fitzwalter in *Denis* weeps tears of joy at the thought of converting Irish children through food.[46] The slightly more rational Margaret Percival devoted the profits of her novel *The Irish Dove* (1849) to the conversion of the Irish through their own language. Like Carleton, Percival set her novel during an earlier famine, but she referred frequently to the present as an opportunity for those who provided temporal help to turn it to spiritual gain: 'a still more holy—a still more glorious—a still more precious work: that of turning many to right-

[42] Revd Alexander Dallas, in *Incidents in the Life and Ministry of the Rev. Alex. R. C. Dallas, A. M., by his Widow* (London: James Nisbit & Co., 1873), 392.

[43] Ibid., 384.

[44] Revd John O'Rourke, *The Battle of the Faith in Ireland* (Dublin: James Duffy & Sons, 1887), 527; it could, of course, be argued that O'Rourke, as a Roman Catholic priest utterly opposed to Nangle's project, was a biased witness.

[45] Elizabeth Hely Walshe, *Kingston's Revenge: A Story of Bravery and Single-Hearted Endeavour* (London: The Religious Tract Society, 1917) (first published in 1865 as *Golden Hills: A Tale of the Irish Famine*), 134.

[46] Louise Field, *Denis: A Study in Black and White* (London and New York: Macmillan & Co., 1896), 222.

eousness, and saving the souls of those, whose crumbling frail bodies, you were made the happy instruments of rescuing from death'.[47] The institution of prayers and fast days for Ireland by the Established Church, sanctioned by the government, only served to intensify the zeal of those who believed Ireland's distress was Christianity's opportunity.

The idea of the Famine as chastisement did not leave the Catholic psyche untouched. As we have seen in the examination of newspapers during the Famine, many of the most strident proponents of the Providential theory were nationalists. Of course, many shared O'Rourke's view that this Providentialism was blasphemous, and that the elevation to Dean of Ripon of such a preacher as Hugh McNeile, whose sermon 'The Famine, a rod' advocated the theory, was an insult to Ireland.[48] But others were not so sure, and the signs and portents associated with the Famine in many texts—its sudden appearance (often overnight), the unnaturally heavy rain, the thick bank of fog settling on the fields, even pillars of fire—seemed to indicate supernatural forces at work.[49] Emmet Larkin sees the Famine as the culmination of a 'growing awareness of a sense of sin' which was exploited and channelled by the Catholic Church into a post-Famine devotional revolution.[50] This is certainly reflected in Famine literature. Emily Bowles's anti-souper novel *Irish Diamonds* contains a harangue by an Irish priest worthy of the most ardent anti-Papist, but turned outward, against the lapsed emigrants rather than the saintly Catholics at home:

It is our own sins, the sins of Irishmen in other lands, which perpetuate this evil. It is the drunkenness, the murders, the sacrileges, the impurity, which we hear of, like a hideous dream, but which, thanks for ever be to God! our eyes never behold in this country, which cling to us here, and oblige Him to lay upon us a heavy chastising hand. You tell me things of our people in London which haunt me even in my prayers.[51]

In Keary's *Castle Daly*, the people believe they are being punished for the murder of Squire Daly, while in Louis J. Walsh's *The Next Time*, the conservative Delaneys, loyal to O'Connell and Repeal, blame Young Ireland for calling down the Famine on them.[52] This sense of sin is cleverly sublimated,

[47] Margaret Percival, *The Irish Dove; or, Faults on Both Sides. A Tale* (Dublin and London: John Robertson; Simpkin, Marshall, & Co., 1849), 151–2.

[48] O'Rourke, *History of the Great Irish Famine*, 374, 516.

[49] For example, see Darby, *The Hunger*, 17.

[50] Emmet Larkin, 'The Devotional Revolution in Ireland, 1850–75', *American Historical Review*, 77/3 (June 1972), 625–52, at 639.

[51] Emily Bowles, *Irish Diamonds: or, A Chronicle of Peterstown* (London: Thomas Richardson & Son, 1864), 89.

[52] Keary, *Castle Daly*, ii. 84; Walsh, *The Next Time*, 144.

however, in the representation of the heroic martyrdom of Catholics in their refusal to convert for food.

The accusation that one had accepted food in return for conversion was 'a dreadful slander in the Catholic community' after the Famine, a slander that has not entirely abated.[53] The Irish-American James Carroll remembers hearing the word 'souper' for the first time:

Once, at the dinner table, I asked my Air Force father why his new Pentagon boss, an Irishman named Robert S. McNamara, was not a Catholic? Before my father could answer, my mother said, 'He's a souper.' 'A what?' 'Someone in his family took the soup,' she said, then explained that during the Famine the British government offered relief to the starving peasants at soup kitchens set up at the Protestant churches. In order to get the soup, a villager had to convert to Protestantism. Those who did so left a curse upon their village—a curse that made me shudder at my mother's mention of it.[54]

Such fear and resentment may explain the bitterness of Frank Hugh O'Donnell's attack on Yeats's *Countess Cathleen*; in this story of an Irish noblewoman who sells her soul to emissaries of the devil in order to save her people, the heroine is elevated to heaven and kissed by the Blessed Virgin for the motive, not the deed. This is certainly not acceptable behaviour in Catholic Famine novels; in essence, Countess Cathleen is a souper. According to Emily Bowles, those who gave in to souperism were merely weak: 'All had not the courage to hold their starving children on their knees, and see life ebbing from them drop by drop. All could not stand the sharp cry or moaning wail for bread which they could not supply.'[55] This may seem extreme, but as far as Bowles and other anti-souper novelists were concerned, a true Irishman should be prepared to watch his children die rather than take the bribe. It was vital that the victims be identified as exclusively Catholic, and that these 'martyrs of the nineteenth century'[56] should be contrasted with Protestants and converts, who are seen to have plenty of food in the midst of famine. The pages of these novels are littered with whole families who have starved to death rather than submit to souperism: the Porters in *Irish Diamonds*, the Sullivans in *Frank O'Donnell*, Paddy Hayes in *The D'Altons*—their deaths are pathetic and

[53] Desmond Bowen, *The Protestant Crusade in Ireland, 1800–70: A Study of Protestant–Catholic Relations Between the Act of Union and Disestablishment* (Dublin: Gill & Macmillan, 1978), 185.

[54] James Carroll, 'A Shawl of Grief', in Tom Hayden (ed.), *Irish Hunger: Personal Reflections on the Legacy of the Famine* (Boulder, Colo. and Dublin: Roberts Rinehart; Wolfhound Press, 1997), 211.

[55] Bowles, *Irish Diamonds*, 174.   [56] Ibid., 161.

moving, but, on this evidence, only converts would have been able to survive the Famine.

Soupers and converts are represented in these novels as universally bad,
a surmise that some commentators believe is close to the truth. Thomas
O'Neill notes that several Scripture-readers were convicted of theft, and
many converts were insincere: 'Even during the famine this lack of sincerity had been noticed by the missionaries when families, which nominally
had changed to Protestantism, insisted on Catholic burial for some of their
deceased members.'[57] Richard Baptist O'Brien, the ultramontane Dean of
Limerick, tolerated Protestants in the Ireland of his novels, but was unsur-
prisingly contemptuous of soupers and converts. In *The D'Altons of Crag*,
two starving men duck a souper who has been trying to convert them; a
Protestant gentleman saves the souper, but rails against the practice: 'This
purchasing of conversion is an abomination! It is transforming a number
of people into liars against God and against man; and preparing for a state
of things that will make life, property, and order unsafe. Kill the conscience, and what remains but mere force, and, in such a condition, society goes to pieces.'[58] This particular souper's character is rounded off
completely by the fact that his grandfather was an informer in the 1798
rebellion, providing him with a fine pedigree for a turncoat. O'Brien's
Ailey Moore, written only a few years after the Famine and in the midst of
the controversy, is even more condemnatory. O'Brien turned his attention
to the controversial Dingle settlement, claiming that only 200 of a population of 80,000 had converted, and revealing in a dialogue between the well-
named Evangelists Dr Creamer and Mr Salmer that those who had
converted were the dregs of Catholicism:

the converts are the off-scourings of the population: they have been completely
demoralized. Habits of labour have utterly disappeared from among them: they are
filthy in their appearance, and have an expression, every one, that marks them as
the countenance marks a Jew. No one trusts them. In a word, Mr. Salmer, they
have cost us nearly one thousand pounds a head, and only there is hope of their
progeny—the bible has been 'more penetrating than a two-edged sword' among
these wretched creatures, indeed—it has destroyed them, and the social harmony
of the districts where they live.[59]

---

[57] Thomas O'Neill, 'Sidelights on Souperism', *Irish Ecclesiastical Record*, 71 (Jan.–June
1949), 50–64, at 63.
[58] Richard Baptist O'Brien, *The D'Altons of Crag: A Story of '48 & '49* (Dublin: James
Duffy & Sons, 1882), 129.
[59] Richard Baptist O'Brien, *Ailey Moore, A Tale of the Times* (London and Baltimore:
Charles Dolman; J. Murphy & Co., 1856), 40.

By the end of the novel, inevitably, Salmer is exposed as a thief, and 'The Soupers are all gone or converted'.[60] The patience and faith of the Irish lead to conversions to Catholicism in *Ailey Moore, Irish Diamonds*, and *Kate Gearey*, and the emblem of Catholic martyrdom through the Famine is seen to purify and consolidate the Church against the Protestant threat.

The Protestant counter-attack to the myth of martyrdom began soon after the Famine. It is hardly surprising that Protestants would resent charges of souperism, as in many areas the Protestant minister was the last line of defence against starvation. In areas where priests were busy night and day administering the last rites to the dying, parsons, with their wives and daughters and useful contacts in English parishes, were indispensable for the administration and distribution of relief.[61] Indeed, Bowen goes so far as to suggest that in many cases, parsons were actually preferred as almoners, as some Catholics feared that priests, whose only source of income was their parishioners, would deduct their dues from any relief money before distribution.[62] The good Protestant rector rendered desperate by his attempts to save the poor appears in many novels, for example Revd Murray in *The Hunger*, and the Brookes in *Kingston's Revenge*, who live on turnips and meal to give food to the poor, but are still accused of souperism.[63]

Significantly, the language of martyrdom is appropriated in post-Famine Protestant novels, both from a genuine sense of grievance, and in a clever attempt to steal the thunder from Catholic claims of persecution. The Irish Society for converting through the Irish language is forced to meet in secret after dark in *The Irish Dove*; in a deliberate reversal of roles, penal laws have been transferred to inoffensive Protestants.[64] In the same novel, accusations of souperism are cunningly turned against Catholics: the industrious convert Reilly, ruined by the blight and forced to live on nettle-tops and half-decomposed potatoes, knows that he and his family could be saved from starvation if they return to the Catholic Church.[65] Accusations of counter-souperism did occur, no doubt fuelled by the suspicions and anti-papist sentiment inevitably roused by the re-establishment of the Roman Catholic hierarchy in England in 1850. Catholics were accused of proselytizing in poorhouses, a claim Bowen admits as probable,[66] and this idea was seized upon by the anonymous author of the Evangelical novels *Poor Paddy's Cabin*

---

[60] O'Brien, *Ailey Moore*, 308.
[62] Ibid., 183.
[64] Percival, *Irish Dove*, 284.
[66] Bowen, *Souperism*, 44.

[61] Bowen, *Protestant Crusade*, 182.
[63] Walshe, *Kingston's Revenge*, 280, 298.
[65] Ibid., 196.

and *The Irish Widow*. In the former, two orphan girls are taken in by a
benevolent Protestant woman, but the priest demands that they be taken to
the poorhouse to be brought up as Catholics; the girls are refused entry at
the poorhouse as there is no room, and they are left in a cart by the church-
yard to die horribly: 'and sure that was nothing if they died natural, but
'twould frighten one a'most to death to see 'em—with the dint of pain and
suffering they had scratched and torn each others little faces, like poor dying
cats, and their little hands and fingers were full of each others blood and hair
they tore off'.[67] In the sequel, *The Irish Widow*, the estate has been purchased in the Encumbered Estates Court by a Catholic who has been
ordered by his priest to remove the converts.[68] In both novels converts are
mercilessly persecuted—including being stoned, if proof was needed of
their martyr status—by their neighbours and the priests. The O'Connors
are forced to emigrate to America at the end of *Poor Paddy's Cabin*, but in
the sequel, Widow Desmond manages to convert the landlord to
Protestantism and to marry him, paving the way for more conversions and
the return of evicted converts from America. These novels rewrite the
Famine in terms of the sufferings of Protestants, not only as the derided
owners of large estates bankrupted by loss of rents, but also as the most
deprived and persecuted, and the most liable to starvation.

Both cultures, therefore, assimilated myths of persecution and martyrdom into their Famine experience. These myths may have helped to ease
the guilt of the survivor, but they further soured relations between the religions. Peter O'Leary, a priest and Gaelic Revival enthusiast who was a boy
during the Famine, recalled the difficulty faced by those who wanted to
revive the Irish language: 'There was no book in Gaelic to be had in any
place at that time—unless a person procured the Foreign Bible, but you
couldn't have anything to do with that because of the bad name the *Soupers*
had left it.'[69] The 1861 census showed that most converts had returned to
Catholicism, and funding from England for the missions dwindled away.
Articles about Nangle and the Achill colony in the *Liverpool Mercury* in
1862 caused much consternation and guilt among Evangelicals in England
as they became aware of the extent to which the sufferings of the Irish peasantry had gone unrelieved.[70] So, the Protestant opportunity arising from

[67] 'An Irishman', *Poor Paddy's Cabin; or, Slavery in Ireland. A True Representation of Facts and Characters* (London and Dublin: Wertheim & Macintosh; James M'Glashan, 1853), 12.
[68] 'An Irishman', *The Irish Widow; or, A Picture from Life of Erin and Her Children* (London: Wertheim & Macintosh, 1855).
[69] Peter O'Leary, *My Story* (*Mo Scéal Féin*), trans. Cyril O Céirín (1915; Oxford and New York: Oxford University Press, 1987), 96.
[70] Bowen, *Souperism*, 102–3.

the Famine had failed, but, ironically, it proved a Catholic opportunity instead. As Larkin has argued, the loss by death and emigration of a sizeable proportion of the population boosted an already increasing priest–people ratio, and provided a more respectable and wealthy devotional nucleus.[71] The Roman Catholic Church in Ireland emerged stronger, and with a sense of martyrdom not even the Penal Laws had provided.

It would appear that the Young Ireland movement had much less claim to appropriate the Famine than even the soupers, yet many novels link the Famine and the Young Ireland rebellion. Historians tend to agree that the two were separate: 'The splits, regroupings and new departures, the intense debate over points of administrative or legal detail, the passionate conflicts of issues of abstract principle: all seem equally set apart, as if by a wall of glass, from the unprecedented disaster unfolding in the Irish countryside.'[72] The timing of the rising had much more to do with the French Revolution than the sufferings of fellow Irishmen, and the Irish confederation was hopelessly elitist, crassly blind to the physical and mental exhaustion of the people it sought to command. Yet, as with the Easter Rising (retrospectively, at least), the leaders—William Smith O'Brien, Charles Gavan Duffy, Thomas Francis Meagher, and especially John Mitchel—were idealized in literature and politics as men who tried and failed to save their country. In the context of Fenianism in the 1860s and the Land League in the 1880s, it may have been attractive and expedient to link reactionary predecessors to issues of land and starvation. W. C. Upton's novel *Uncle Pat's Cabin* (obviously modelled on Harriet Beecher Stowe's *Uncle Tom's Cabin*), set in Fenian times, involving characters who had lived through the Famine, and dedicated to the Land League leader Michael Davitt, was praised by the historian W. E. H. Lecky as 'one of the truest and most vivid pictures of the present condition of the Irish labourer'.[73] It sets out clearly the relevance of the Famine for the labourers of the 1860s, who had been farmers and farmers' sons ruined in 1848.[74] Young Irelanders John O'Mahony and James Stephens went on to found the Fenian movement, while their former comrades turned to 'less daring forms of nationalist politics',[75] so the

[71] Larkin, 'The Devotional Revolution', 639.

[72] S. J. Connolly, 'The Great Famine and Irish Politics', in Cathal Póirtéir (ed.), *The Great Irish Famine* (Cork and Dublin: Mercier Press, 1995), 34.

[73] Quoted in Brown, *Ireland in Fiction*, 413–14n.

[74] W. C. Upton, *Uncle Pat's Cabin: or Life among the Agricultural Labourers of Ireland* (Dublin: Gill, 1882), 73.

[75] Samuel Clark, *Social Origins of the Irish Land War* (Princeton: Princeton University Press, 1979), 201.

positive representation of Young Ireland in novels in the second half of the century would presumably have been acceptable to both the hawks and the doves of Irish nationalism. The leading Irish Parliamentary Party MPs Justin McCarthy and his son Justin Huntly McCarthy even wrote elegiac novels about Young Ireland themselves. With such supporters on all sides, it may have been impolitic to be anything but enthusiastic about Young Ireland. The only voice of dissent in the literature of the early decades after the Famine was that of the painter, dramatist, and novelist William Wills. Wills's protagonist in *The Love That Kills*, the Catholic land-agent Clayton, is brought into Young Ireland by his confessor, and is at first seduced by the rhetoric of the movement, but quickly loses trust in the leaders, especially J. M. [Mitchel], T. F. M. [Meagher], and O'B. [Smith O'Brien]. In his diary, Clayton records: 'They rant about Ireland's miseries from the platform, and then sup upon spatch-cocks and champagne. They talk of her rags and her pauperism, and strut about in kid gloves and fine cloth: subscriptions flow in to them. I cannot trace this money further than their pockets. The people ask for bread, and they offer them blood.'[76] Later, Clayton attends a monster meeting to denounce Young Ireland, and narrowly escapes with his life. The novel was published in 1867, the year of Fenian insurrection, and Wills takes care to dissociate himself from Clayton's view of Young Ireland in the preface to the novel. Clayton has been acting irrationally after a blow to the head, and this madness, it appears, clouds his judgement about the politicians. But Wills's ambiguity about the true basis for Clayton's accusations against the Young Ireland leaders implies that there is no smoke without fire.

As Roy Foster has noted, Young Ireland was 'far more influential in how it was interpreted than in what it did'.[77] The autobiographical 'histories' of Duffy, Doheny, and especially Mitchel were much more important than the Ballingarry fracas. This is reflected in the literature by the elision of the rebellion from texts generally sympathetic to the movement. Justin McCarthy's *Mononia*, for example, dismisses the matter in a sentence: 'There is no need to go more fully into all this melancholy story just now, and its memory is here recalled only because of the effect it had upon the fortunes of the men and women who are the principal figures in this narrative.'[78] 'We were all very young in those days,' sighs the narrator, admitting

---

[76] W. G. Wills, *The Love That Kills: A Novel*, 3 vols. (London: Tinsley Brothers, 1867), iii. 53.

[77] Foster, *Modern Ireland*, 316.

[78] Justin McCarthy, *Mononia: A Love Story of 'Forty-Eight'* (London: Chatto & Windus, 1901), 109.

1848 was hopeless in hindsight. Even Conyngham, who took part in the rebellion with his kinsman and fellow novelist Charles Kickham, excludes Young Ireland from all but the most scathing references in *Frank O'Donnell*:

We do not mean to take up our reader's time with that ebullition that ended in the partial outbreak of '48. It was an unexpected result to the great things promised by that national party that had with it the feelings of the majority of the people. We do not mean to analyze the past; but this we say, that never was a country riper for revolution, and never were the feelings of an aggrieved people more warm in its behalf, and yet it failed miserably.[79]

Conyngham's disappointment is palpable, but despite his avoidance of the actual details of the Rising, he is siting (and perhaps mitigating) this miserable failure in the context of a genocidal famine.

Young Ireland is also important in Famine novels as a source of narrative structure and characterization. Given the number of heroes who write for *The Nation* in these novels, it is a wonder Mitchel and Duffy had any work to do. Like Trollope's *The Kellys and the O'Kellys*, which uses the trial of O'Connell as frame and background, Louise Field's *Denis* opens with the trial of *The Nation* for seditious libel, and ends with the disastrous rising and the pathetic inscription of its fatuity: 'we have not wrought any deliverance in the earth'.[80] Mitchel's transportation without any attempt at a rescue is the turning point towards failure in both *Mononia* and *Lily Lass*. In *Castle Daly*, the failure of the rising and the exile of their Young Irelander brother Connor leads both the impetuous nationalist Ellen and the rational unionist Pelham towards the centre ground of Home Rule. Louis J. Walsh's *The Next Time* is most heavily influenced by the rise and fall of Young Ireland. Walsh, a solicitor and strenuous politician who contested South Derry for Sinn Féin in the 1918 elections, later wrote a biography of Mitchel, and his novel is infused with the ideas and rhetoric of his hero. In his foreword, Walsh half-jokingly admitted that he 'plagiarised right, left and centre, and all through the book I have stolen descriptions, phrases and observations with the most unblushing effrontery', most evident in his borrowings from *Jail Journal*.[81] The novel opens with the news of Catholic Emancipation reaching Gortnanan, and the tale of the growth to adulthood of the politically opposed brothers Art and Hugh O'Donnell is punctuated by the events that changed Ireland: the founding of *The Nation*, the Repeal Year, the proscribed Clontarf monster-meeting,

[79] Conyngham, *Frank O'Donnell*, 286.   [80] Field, *Denis*, 414.
[81] Walsh, *The Next Time*, 6.

Young Ireland, the Famine, the *United Irishman*, the rising (in which Art dies), and finally Mitchel's election for Tipperary in 1875.

Morash argues that *The Next Time* marks the end of the nationalist Famine novel: 'To take this tradition of Famine narratives beyond Walsh's text to, for instance, Liam O'Flaherty's or Tom Murphy's *Famine* would be to move outside a nationalism that is formulated on a posture of yearning, to what can be termed a post-nationalist condition.'[82] But Walsh's novel could also be read as a post-nationalist text. The novel's insistence on a chronological progression from Emancipation through the Famine to prospective liberty is undermined by a vein of profound scepticism, as in the passage describing Father Hugh's joy at O'Connell's victory:

> He had lived with sorrow all his days and had seen the fever and famine and injustice stalk through the land, with ceaseless energy, and strike down in countless numbers the people whom he loved. But the sun would now shine for ever as it was doing that blessed spring day, and the birds would perpetually carol their sweet lays, and men would cease from sinning, and peace reign in every heart.[83]

Father Hugh's absurd idealism is answered by the Famine, in which he dies. Walsh continues his description of the Emancipation celebrations with a blow to O'Connell and his cronies, who would be the main beneficiaries: 'O'Connell, their beloved "Counsellor," could now sit in the London Parliament, and a Catholic judge might preside on the King's Bench or in the Court of Common Pleas and even have the privilege of sentencing Irish patriots to imprisonment or death.'[84] In other words, no change for the better. The unfortunate side-effects of emancipation are hinted at when the grocer Andy Bradley breaks his temperance pledge to celebrate—and ends up drinking steadily for a month.[85]

The Young Irelanders are certainly idealized out of all proportion in *The Next Time*; Mitchel is described romantically during the 'Peace Resolutions' debate: 'He looked very handsome as he faced the huge assembly with his well-built figure and his thoughtful and comely face surmounted by masses of soft brown hair, a stray ringlet of which he kept twining round his finger as he waited for the cheering to subside.'[86] The rising fails in this novel due to the 'slavish habits' of the people, or due to their reluctance to wait for orders—contradictory accusations that exonerate the leadership.[87] But Art's dying certitude that they would succeed 'the next time' cannot be fulfilled. By 1919 many next times had come and

[82] Christopher Morash, 'Imagining the Famine: Literary Representations of the Great Irish Famine', D.Phil. thesis (Trinity College, Dublin, 1990), 185n.
[83] Walsh, *The Next Time*, 10.   [84] Ibid., 13.   [85] Ibid., 10–11.
[86] Ibid., 129.   [87] Ibid., 212, 216.

gone—the Fenians, Home Rule, the Easter Rising—and by ending with Mitchel's election in 1875, Walsh highlights the fatuity of such aspirations: Mitchel died within a few days of winning. Young Ireland was less important for what it did than for what was written about it—and what was left out. But perhaps these novels placing Young Ireland in the context of the Great Famine are only other ways of saying the Rebellion failed: the retrospective link of Young Ireland and the victims of 'genocide' reveals not only its romantic idealization by the next generation, but also its redundancy in a new age.

Unlike travel-books of the period, which record the devastation but see the Famine as an indispensable factor in Ireland's progress into full fellowship with England, Famine novels deeply regret the loss of all that made pre-Famine Ireland distinctive. There are vague hints at a progress of sorts: in *Castle Cloyne*, Oonagh's foster son grows up to become a priest, a career that would have been barred to him before the Famine due to his poverty. This was Peter O'Leary's own experience; since childhood, it had been his ambition to be a priest, but his father would probably have been unable to afford the education: 'If it were not for the blight coming on the potatoes and the bad times that came afterwards, I don't say that he would not have been able to give me the necessary amount of schooling. But the bad times turned everything upside down.'[88] But the general feeling was one of loss. In the 'Preface' to his *Tales and Sketches* in 1845, Carleton had sounded the note of transition: 'Many of the characters contained in the following volume have already ceased to exist, and are, consequently, the property of history.'[89] Post-Famine novels portray a disjointed society, changed utterly. Julia and Edmund O'Ryan picked up the theme from Carleton, subtitling *In re Garland*, the story of an aristocrat brought so low by the Famine that he has to be supported by his illegitimate peasant daughter, 'A Tale of a Transition Time'.[90] In the wake of the Famine, pre-famine existence seemed Utopian, prelapsarian; even the vilified potato was vindicated. For Canon Sheehan, 'the great wonder is, not that so many perished in the famine, but that so many lived, and lived in comfort, in the years previous to that dread visitation'.[91] Of course, the idea that there was plenty of food in Ireland before the Famine was appropriated as

[88] O'Leary, *My Story*, 46.

[89] William Carleton, 'Preface', *Tales and Sketches Illustrating the Character, Usages, Traditions, Sports and Pastimes of the Irish Peasantry* (Dublin: James Duffy, 1845), p. viii.

[90] Julia and Edmund O'Ryan, *In re Garland: A Tale of a Transition Time* (London, Dublin, New York, and Derby: Thomas Richardson & Son; Henry H. Richardson & Co., 1870).

[91] Sheehan, *Glenanaar*, 197.

a nationalist myth of genocide, as in *Dick Massey*: 'Any one standing on the quays of a seaport, and seeing the immense quantity of food that was daily shipped off to England and elsewhere, could never have imagined that multitudes in the country in which that food was raised were wasted to skeletons, and yielding their last breath for want of a morsel to eat.'[92] The genocide theory did not begin with Mitchel and the Famine, and was being used by Carleton as early as 1833; but condemnation of exports occurs in one form or another in almost all Famine novels, even when written by those who might be implicated by such a suggestion. Mildred Darby recorded that the conviction that the government tried to destroy the whole race existed 'not only in the hearts of the actual victims of the famine, but quite as strongly in the breasts of their descendants'.[93] She affirmed that the grain harvests could have sustained twice the population, while instead they were 'exported and imported again three and four times over; each time bearing more profits and expenses, before they were bought at a purely fictitious value for the perishing people who had originally grown them!'[94] In the face of such misrule, she suggested, food riots and murders were no surprise; but it is a surprise that a novel that acknowledged the iniquity of this system should end with a strident defence of the Union.

Of course, the loss of a supposedly abundant food supply is not the only change Famine novels lament. Loss of culture and identity was fiercely mourned, and was perhaps, as Larkin suggests, *more* important: 'There may indeed be something worse than the simple fear of being destroyed—the mounting terror in the growing awareness that one is being destroyed.'[95] Field ended her novel elegiacally, mourning the loss of a way of life: 'Something was gone for ever from the heart of the Irish people, something of gaiety and fun which never quite revived after the Black Forty-seven . . . Dance and song and story were forgotten; the old harps were mouldering among the rafters of roofs; the old hand looms and spinning wheels stood still, and by degrees were broken up for firewood.'[96] The Irish language was already on the decline, but death and emigration reduced Irish-speakers to such a level that by 1854 Protestant missionaries ceased using the Irish language to proselytize. Famine novelists were resolutely against the emigration that was robbing the country not only of her people but of her language and traditions. *Dick Massey* follows the adventures of Tom Nolan and the Conroys on their way to America: passengers are starved and deprived of water, thrown overboard and treated

[92] Russell, *Dick Massey*, 284–5.   [93] Darby, *The Hunger*, 7.   [94] Ibid., 13.
[95] Larkin, 'The Devotional Revolution', 639.   [96] Field, *Denis*, 413.

brutally, and only survive at all because Tom leads a mutiny. Only 300 of
the 800 passengers arrive at New York. The sickly hue of Americans is
contrasted to the blooming cheeks of Irish emigrants, and after the death
of Mrs Conroy from fever, Tom and Norah prefer to take their chances in
Famine Ireland rather than prosperous America, and return.[97] The lot of
the emigrant, Russell asserted, was worse than anything one could face at
home:

> And the people are still flying; flying away from the beauteous isle as though it
> were the hot-bed, the birth-place of some cursed plague that fastened with deadly
> gripe upon its victims. Multitudes greater than ever shall be known have whitened
> the great floor of the Atlantic with their bleached bones. Multitudes as great have
> laid them down in their long sleep by the far off fever and ague-stricken shores of
> the St. Lawrence and Mississippi; or lingered out a miserable existence as the
> dross of humanity amongst those who hated, pitied, feared, or wondered at them.[98]

Emigrant ships are regretfully described in *Frank O'Donnell* as 'Ireland in
miniature'.[99] Ironically, both Conyngham and Russell later emigrated to
America, the former to fight in the American Civil War, the latter under
suspicion of Fenian involvement. Despite Irish indignation that men were
being forced to emigrate when half the land was uncultivated, the recurring motif of the prosperous emigrant returning just in time to save his
starving family indicates the utter prostration of the country, and the
shame of being sustained by foreign money.

   After the Famine, the 'Irish self-picture' was 'deeply suffused with
shame, resentment, and a sense of loss'.[100] Even if Famine authors could
not be implicated with the government and landlords in the state of society that could allow such a catastrophe, they were, as they claimed, impotent witnesses to unbearable suffering. Stout Mrs Meehan, the driver's
wife in *The Hunger*, is ashamed to meet her skeletal neighbours, and no
doubt well-nourished authors felt the same.[101] In this novel, the pleasure-
loving absentee landlord is temporarily shaken out of his composure by the
sight of his starving tenants gobbling free food at the races:

> Everywhere men, women and children stood eating in the pouring rain, with fear-
> ful voracity—so savage as to be more bestial than human—half choking in their
> eagerness to seize and swallow their share. Some of the children were sobbing with
> mingled hunger and longing for the food they were ramming with both hands
> down their little throats. Like a sleeping giant roused from his lair, hunger had

[97] Russell, *Dick Massey*, 162 ff.   [98] Ibid., 66.
[99] Conyngham, *Frank O'Donnell*, 345.
[100] McCormack, *A New History of Ireland*, v, p. lviii.   [101] Darby, *The Hunger*, 203.

suddenly awakened in every heart at the sight and smell of the viands provided
. . . The fear that there would not be enough to go round set hundreds snarling
and snapping like starving dogs, in their anxiety to get near the tent. . .[102]

Lord Torrabegh is horrified, and quickly orders more food for them: 'I
feel as if I could never eat another morsel myself in comfort after seeing
these famishing beasts gorging for dear life.'[103] Ironically, he recovers
quickly, and is soon discussing the Famine with his dinner guests, 'with
many head-shakings upon the prevailing scarcity of food, while great
dishes filled by smoking joints and artistic entrées provided them with a
pleasant contrast to their topic of conversation'.[104] In *Patricia of the Hills*,
Lord Clogher is devastated when he finds the child of one of his father's
tenants dead, and its mother dying: 'He seemed helpless, completely at a
loss; his hanging hands opened and closed jerkily, and his parted lips let
the breath through with a murmur that was almost a hiss.'[105] Like the
travel-writers, the novelists appear to have felt that it was worse to have to
watch the suffering: Clayton in *The Love That Kills*, driven mad by a blow
to the head and his obsession with Ellen Rae, is actually driven *sane* by the
horrors he witnesses, events the author claimed as his own experience:
'When sometimes as I walked the roads by night I have met an object
propped against the fence like a grim milestone, and found it to be a
corpse, still and stern. May the memory of those sickening times soon perish with them!'[106] Wills's experience of Famine may have been bifurcated
by his position in Irish society. The son of an impoverished Irish clergyman, he was intimate with the peasantry in his father's parish, and no
doubt did see many of them die during the Famine. And, as a bohemian
painter and playwright in London, he was often hungry and penniless. But
Wills was also related to eminent Irish families such as the Bushes,
Oranmores, the de la Poers of Gurteen, Somervilles, and Martins, and,
much to his father's regret, the ancestral house, Willsgrove in County
Roscommon, was converted during the Famine into a temporary workhouse.[107] The scenes Clayton witnesses, therefore, took place not only
under Wills's eyes, but perhaps at the instigation of his landlord kinsmen,
and in his ancestral home.

---

[102] Ibid., 66.   [103] Ibid., 66.   [104] Ibid., 139.
[105] Charles Kennett Burrow, *Patricia of the Hills* (London: Lawrence & Bullen, Ltd.,
1902), 50.
[106] Wills, *The Love That Kills*, ii. 266.
[107] Freeman Wills, *W. G. Wills: Dramatist and Painter* (London, New York, and Bombay:
Longmans, Green, & Co., 1898), 11, 22, 26–7, 47.

In his *History*, O'Rourke dwelt on stories of generosity and self-sacrifice in the midst of the more usual *unnatural* acts of the Famine.[108] This is a time of transition, when it is more natural to be unnatural, and the novels are full of gruesome deaths, cannibalism, dogs and rats devouring not only the dead but the dying, and the unnatural silence of the starving. But the starving are nameless and faceless, distanced from the author, buried in mass graves, apart. To admit that people one knows could stoop to cannibalism or abandonment is to admit that society, as Carlyle claimed, is at an end. Those who commit 'unnatural acts' are like the crowd gathered for food in *Denis*: 'a crowd that seemed in the white light and dark shadows as though composed of goblins . . . a strange procession of beings so misshapen and so fantastically clad as to seem hardly human'.[109] This is not consistent with the 'Irish self-picture' of fortitude and martyrdom projected by so many of these late-nineteenth-century Famine novels: 'All honor to our Irish race, and rare honor and sovereign glory it is, that we can boldly challenge the whole history of the most terrible famine with which it has pleased the Almighty ever to afflict a people—and from end to end the record glows red, indeed, with the blood of a martyred people, yet without the black stain of ungrateful or unnatural crime!'[110] This barefaced denial of the unnatural cannot be sustained by other authors, and the fabric of society is seen to disintegrate at its most important level, the family. In *The Love That Kills*, Clayton finds a man and his little daughter, previously a picture of industry and affection, starving to death; the man has dragged the girl outside to die so he can enjoy the morsel of food left in peace.[111] Even more disturbing is the scene in *Denis* when Mr O'Hara gives a sandwich to an emaciated child:

But never did any of those who saw that scene forget the horror of the next moment, and the agonised shriek that came from the child's blue lips. For with a bound that was like the spring of some famished wild beast upon its prey the mother had leaped upon the little one, had snatched the food from its bony fingers, and crammed it into her own mouth. The men who looked upon her face, as her eyes turned again to the child she had robbed, shuddered with a chill horror, as if they had gazed upon the face of a Medusa.[112]

Society is at an end when parents sacrifice their children to their own hunger. But, as ever, the political allegory is lurking; authors could not fail to have remembered the accusation that England had stolen Ireland's food

---

[108] O'Rourke, *History of the Great Irish Famine*, 402.   [109] Field, *Denis*, 75–6.
[110] O'Brien, *The D'Altons of Crag*, 32.   [111] Wills, *The Love That Kills*, ii. 273–4.
[112] Field, *Denis*, 392.

when they wrote such scenes. It is hardly surprising that in the face of such chaos, the survivors should be changed forever. Famine survivors are seen as dejected, melancholy, even deranged: the kindly agent Gavin Guffy is murdered by a semi-idiotic Famine survivor in *The Hunger*. Above all, they want to forget. First-generation survivors and authors were haunted by what they had seen. Peter O'Leary vividly recalled a boy he had seen once, when he was about 8 years old:

I saw the face that was on him and the terror that was in his two eyes the terror of hunger. That face and those two eyes are before my mind now, as clear and as unclouded as the day I gave them the one and only look. Somebody gave him a lump of bread. He snatched the bread and turned his back to us and his face to the wall and he started right into eating it so ravenously that you would think he would choke himself. At the time I did not realize that I was so amazed by him or by his voracity, but that sight has stayed in my mind, and will stay as long as I live.[113]

Dick Considine in *Castle Cloyne*, having watched his wife and baby starve to death, sends back money from his new home in America to buy a tombstone: 'and when it was erected, no one who saw it could ever imagine that they who slept beneath it were the victims of famine'.[114] It would be generations before this sense of shame could be effaced. Perhaps, for first-generation Famine authors, the writing was cathartic, a sort of tomb to place over their guilt in order to belie its existence.

The Famine continued to inspire Irish writers because the concerns raised by the disaster—religious conflict, armed struggle, the need for self-government, loss of identity—remained relevant to Irish readers. Yet perhaps the fact they were published at all proves their growing irrelevance for *English* audiences: the colonial implications of the representation of the Great Famine, that so disturbed Trollope that he sought to suppress them, that forced *The Times* to mimic *The Nation*, no longer raised even a tremor. In 1847 the *Athenaeum* strenuously objected to Carleton's representation of a mealmonger in *The Black Prophet*, protesting facetiously: 'There is no class of men that suffer more severely, and in general more undeservedly, than provision-dealers in a season of scarcity.'[115] But by 1910 the *Times Literary Supplement* was praising *The Hunger*—a novel that claims two million people died of starvation and disease largely due to mishandling by the government—by dispassionately praising the gifts of the author, and quoting the fact that 'the horrors . . . were such that even many of the incidents here selected had to be modified in their details to become

[113] O'Leary, *My Story*, 47.   [114] Brew, *Castle Cloyne*, iii. 60.
[115] *Athenaeum*, 1011 (13 Mar. 1847), 279.

publishable'.[116] Worst of all, in 1917 the Religious Tract Society repub-
lished Elizabeth Hely Walsh's 1865 novel *Golden Hills: A Tale of the Irish
Famine* under the completely un-Irish sounding *Kingston's Revenge: A
Story of Bravery and Single-hearted Endeavour*, making it clear that the
Famine was to remain a secondary issue. The event that had shaken Irish
society to its roots no longer held literary currency, even as melodrama.

[116] *Times Literary Supplement* (14 Apr. 1910), 135.

Conclusion

Men and women, still alive who remember the famine, look back across it as we all look back across some personal grief, some catastrophe which has shattered our lives and made havoc of everything we cared for. We, too, go on again after a while as if nothing had happened, yet we know perfectly well all the while that matters are not the least as they were before; that on the contrary they never can or will be.

> (Emily Lawless, *The Story of the Nations: Ireland* (London and New York: T. Fisher Unwin; G. P. Putnam's Sons, 1887), 402.)

The Irish famine of 1847 had results, social and political, that constitute it one of the most important events in Irish history for more than two hundred years. It is impossible for any one who knew the country previous to that period, and who has thoughtfully studied it since, to avoid the conclusion that so much has been destroyed, or so greatly changed, that the Ireland of old times will be seen no more.

> (A. M. Sullivan, *New Ireland: Political Sketches and Personal Reminiscences of Thirty Years of Irish Public Life* (Glasgow and London: Cameron & Ferguson; Fleet Street, 1877), 67.)

The 'silence' of the Great Famine was in fact broken by many. Despite the problems faced by authors such as Anthony Trollope and Mildred Darby in persuading English audiences to buy novels about an Irish famine, they persisted in writing about it, refusing to allow it to fade into silence. They may seem unlikely propagators of this story, but in the end there were few others willing or able to keep the Famine alive in the imagination: 'While there is a vast amount of written evidence, little or none of it comes from the perspective of the ordinary people. The communities who suffered worst during the Famine were, by and large, not those which had the opportunity of leaving a written testament of what had happened to their district and their people.'[1] In the absence of a large body of first-hand accounts of the Famine by its victims, the histories, travel-narratives, journalism, poetry, and novels of those who witnessed it are the next best thing. They may have been detached from the tragedy by their social

---

[1] Cathal Póirtéir, *Famine Echoes* (Dublin: Gill & Macmillan, 1995), 3.

status, disturbed by their role as voyeurs of starvation, burdened by their responsibility to report the truth about Ireland, and torn by their allegiances, either to Repeal or to the Union. But they were able to respond and leave written records, and it would be irresponsible to dismiss them. This study has attempted to unpick the assumptions behind these records and the strategies underlying their publication. But the sheer volume of material surveyed also has its own importance.

It should be evident that the dismissal of this literature as 'a handful of novels and a body of poems' is a drastic underestimation, even if one takes only the period covered by this work, 1845–1919.[2] Indeed, given William Carleton's observation in 1847 that the principal interest of a novel should never be 'so gloomy a topic as famine', but rather 'the workings of those passions and feelings which usually agitate human life, and constitute the character of those who act in it', it could be argued that it is astonishing how many authors have been and continue to be fascinated by the Famine, especially once the immediate after-shocks of starvation, disease, and emigration had been dissipated.[3] In the twentieth century, it has been used as a setting for Liam O'Flaherty's *Famine* (1937), Walter Macken's *The Silent People* (1962), Tom Murphy's play *Famine* (1968), William Trevor's short story 'The News from Ireland' (1986) and Michael Mullen's *The Hungry Land* (1986), and as a recurrent metaphor or allusion in many other novels and poems, including Patrick Kavanagh's 'The Great Hunger' (1942) and John Banville's *Birchwood* (1973). While researching this book, I at times found it difficult to escape this pervasive theme: my attempts at 'light' reading included Iris Murdoch's *The Red and the Green* (1965), Margaret Atwood's *Alias Grace* (1996), and Frank McCourt's *Angela's Ashes* (1996), none of which I expected to contain references to or scenes about the Famine, and all of which did. In 1995, Wolfhound Press, which had already issued an edition of Liam O'Flaherty's *Famine* in 1979, published Seán Kenny's *The Hungry Earth*, a back-to-the-future yarn in which a Dublin accountant bumps his head in a rural cottage and finds himself back in the Famine. It is hard to think of a greater contrast than that between O'Flaherty's consummate novel *Famine* and this laboured attempt at a morality play, but it is surely significant that Wolfhound Press chose to mark the 150th anniversary of the Famine by publishing another novel about it, indicating that the audience

[2] Terry Eagleton, *Heathcliff and the Great Hunger: Studies in Irish Culture* (London and New York: Verso, 1995), 13.
[3] William Carleton, *The Black Prophet: A Tale of Irish Famine* (London and Belfast: Simms & M'Intyre, 1847), p. iv.

for this literature has not gone away. It is also significant that the novel was the result of Kenny's involvement in a Los Angeles workshop entitled 'Return to Innocence: A Healing Journey for Irish Catholics', which Kenny described as having convinced him of 'the connectedness between past and present'.[4] This novel is an attempt to absorb the trauma of the Famine by re-creating it as race memory; we can no longer experience the Famine as victims, but it is available to us as a lesson in the value of human life. How much more present must it have been to the first and second generations of writers about the Famine, to whom the tragedy was not race memory but memory?

The Great Famine is a recurrent theme, metaphor, and allusion because of its enormous impact, not just on the Irish psyche, economy, language, culture, and society, but on the literature also. The period 1845–1919 saw many changes: the movement away from the Irish to the English language, mass emigration, consolidation of holdings, Home Rule agitation, war. Throughout this transition time, the Famine retained its grip on the imagination, producing not just 'a handful of novels' but a substantial body of literature. If we accept that the Famine left a silence behind, it must be that of the victims, and those who were too ashamed of their experiences to speak of them. But there are many other voices, clamouring for recognition of their testimony, and they must be acknowledged. The value of this literature lies in its very detachment: these witnesses, often outsiders and foreigners, watched a society disintegrate, and in their attempt to be objective proved that there was no escape from subjectivity in the midst of famine. The historians craved the emotion of fiction, the novelists sought the clarity of history; journalists from opposite ends of the political spectrum swapped positions; travellers, self-acknowledged voyeurs, prayed for the power not to see; poets assumed positions antagonistic to their social status and became men and women of action, the acknowledged—if often illegitimate—legislators of their world. William Carleton, inured from childhood to the destructive force of famine, almost overlooked the singularity of the Great Famine that he had in essence prophesied, and was devastated by its impact—the loss of his revival and his chosen audience. Anthony Trollope, honorary Irishman, found himself excluded by a catastrophe in which the country of his birth was potentially implicated; through the fractures in his justifications of government policy in the *Six Letters* and *Castle Richmond*, his powerlessness, anger, guilt, and alienation can be discerned. The Great Famine was an enormously transformative

---

[4] Seán Kenny, *The Hungry Earth* (Dublin: Wolfhound Press, 1995), 5.

experience, not just for those whose lives were destroyed by it, but also for those who witnessed, and tried to make sense of it. By deconstructing the subtextual strategies and agendas of those who actually left a written record, fiction or non-fiction, we come as close as we can to recapturing an essential aspect of the experience of the Great Famine.

BIBLIOGRAPHY

PRIMARY SOURCES

Books and Articles

'A Lady', *Christmas 1846, and the New Year 1847, in Ireland, Letters From a Lady*, ed. W. S. Gilly (Durham: G. Andrews, 1847).

ALLINGHAM, WILLIAM, *Poems* (London: Chapman & Hall, 1850).

—— *Laurence Bloomfield in Ireland: A Modern Poem* (London and Cambridge: Macmillan & Co., 1864).

—— *A Diary*, ed. Helen Allingham (Harmondsworth: Penguin, 1985).

'An Irishman', *Poor Paddy's Cabin; or, Slavery in Ireland: A True Representation of Facts and Characters* (London and Dublin: Wertheim & Macintosh; James M'Glashan, 1853).

—— *The Irish Widow; or, A Picture from Life of Erin and Her Children* (London: Wertheim & Macintosh, 1855).

'An Old Traveller', *A Week in the South of Ireland* (Dublin: James M'Glashan, 1849).

ANON., 'The Famine as Yet In Its Infancy; or, 1847 Compared With The Prospects of 1848, 1849, &c. Addressed to Every-body' (London: Hamilton, Adams & Co., 1847).

ANON., *Description of the Lakes of Killarney, and the Surrounding Scenery* (London: W. H. Smith & Son, 1849).

ANON., *A Three Days' Tour in the County of Wicklow* (London: W. H. Smith & Son, 1849).

ARMSTRONG, REVD THOMAS, *My Life in Connaught, With Sketches of Mission Work in the West* (London: Eliot Stock, 1906).

ASHWORTH, JOHN, *The Saxon in Ireland: or, The Rambles of an Englishman in Search of a Settlement in the West of Ireland* (London: John Murray, 1851).

BALCH, WILLIAM, *Ireland, As I Saw It: The Character, Condition, and Prospects of the People* (New York and London: Hallock & Lyon; H. K. Lewis, 1850).

BARRETT, J. G. ['Erigena'], *Evelyn Clare; or, The Wrecked Homesteads: An Irish Story of Love and Landlordism* (London and New York: Thomas Richardson & Son; Henry H. Richardson & Co., 1870).

BARROW, JOHN, *A Tour Round Ireland, Through the Sea-Coast Counties, in the Autumn of 1835* (London: John Murray, 1836).

BARRY, WILLIAM, *The Wizard's Knot* (London: T. Fisher Unwin, 1901).

BENNET, WILLIAM, *Narrative of a Recent Journey of Six Weeks in Ireland* (London and Dublin: Charles Gilpin; William Curry Jr. & Co., 1847).

BERENS, MRS E. M., *Steadfast Unto Death: A Tale of the Irish Famine of To-Day* (London: Remington & Co., 1880).

BOWLES, EMILY, *Irish Diamonds: or, A Chronicle of Peterstown* (London: Thomas Richardson & Son, 1864).

BREW, MARGARET, *The Chronicles of Castle Cloyne; or, Pictures of the Munster People* (London: Chapman & Hall, 1885), 3 vols.

BURRITT, ELIHU, *A Journal of a Visit of Three Days to Skibbereen, and its Neighbourhood* (London and Birmingham: Charles Gilpin; John Whitehouse Showell, 1847).

—— *The Mission of Great Suffering* (London: Sampson Low, Son & Marston, 1867).

BURROW, CHARLES KENNETT, *Patricia of the Hills* (London: Lawrence & Bullen, Ltd., 1902).

BUTT, ISAAC, 'The Famine in the Land. What Has Been Done, And What Is To Be Done', *Dublin University Magazine*, 29 (Apr. 1847), 501–40.

CARLETON, WILLIAM, 'The Retrospect', *Dublin Family Magazine*, 1/5 (Aug. 1829), 293–4.

—— 'Dick Magrath, A Sketch of Living Character', *Dublin Family Magazine*, 1/5 (Aug. 1829), 336–43.

—— *Fardorougha the Miser, or the Convicts of Lisnamona* (1838) (Belfast: Appletree Press, 1992).

—— *Father Butler. The Lough Dearg Pilgrim* (Dublin: William Curry Jr. & Co., 1839).

—— *The Fawn of Springvale, The Clarionet, and Other Tales* (Dublin: William Curry Jr. & Co., 1841), 3 vols.

—— *Traits and Stories of the Irish Peasantry* (Dublin and London: William Curry Jr. & Co.; Orr, 1843–4), 3 vols.

—— *Valentine M'Clutchy, The Irish Agent; Or, Chronicles of the Castle Cumber Property* (Dublin: James Duffy, 1845), 3 vols.

—— *Rody the Rover; or, The Ribbonman* (Dublin: James Duffy, 1845).

—— *Parra Sastha; or, The History of Paddy Go-Easy And His Wife Nancy* (Dublin: James Duffy, 1845).

—— *Tales and Sketches Illustrating the Character, Usages, Traditions, Sports and Pastimes of the Irish Peasantry* (Dublin: James Duffy, 1845).

—— *Art Maguire; or, The Broken Pledge. A Narrative* (Dublin and London: Simpkin, Marshall & Co., 1847).

—— *The Black Prophet: A Tale of Irish Famine* (London and Belfast: Simms & M'Intyre, 1847).

—— *The Emigrants of Ahadarra* (London and Belfast: Simms & M'Intyre, 1848).

—— *The Tithe Proctor* (London and Belfast: Simms & M'Intyre, 1849).

—— *The Squanders of Castle Squander* (London: Illustrated London Library, 1852), 2 vols.

—— *Red Hall: or, The Baronet's Daughter* (London: Saunders & Otley, 1852), 3 vols.

—— 'Fair Gurtha; or, The Hungry Grass. A Legend of the Dumb Hill', *Dublin University Magazine*, 47 (Apr. 1856), 414–35.

—— *The Black Baronet; or, The Chronicles of Ballytrain* (Dublin: James Duffy & Sons, 1875).

—— *The Autobiography of William Carleton* (London: MacGibbon & Kee, 1968).

CARLYLE, THOMAS, 'Chartism', *Thomas Carlyle: Selected Writings*, ed. Alan Shelston (Harmondsworth: Penguin, 1980).

—— *Reminiscences of My Irish Journey in 1849* (London: Sampson Low & Co., 1882).

CHATTERTON, LADY, *Rambles in the South of Ireland During the Year 1838* (London: Saunders & Otley, 1839), 2 vols.

CONYNGHAM, DAVID POWER ['Allen Clington'], *Frank O'Donnell: A Tale of Irish Life* (Dublin and London: James Duffy, 1861).

DALLAS, REVD ALEXANDER, *Incidents in the Life and Ministry of the Rev. Alex. R. C. Dallas, A. M., by his Widow* (London: James Nisbit & Co., 1873).

DARBY, MILDRED ['Andrew Merry'], *The Hunger, Being Realities of the Famine Years in Ireland 1845 to 1849* (London: Andrew Melrose, 1910).

DAVITT, MICHAEL, *The Fall of Feudalism in Ireland; or The Story of The Land League Revolution* (London and New York: Harper & Brothers, 1904).

DE BEAUMONT, GUSTAVE, *Ireland: Social, Political, and Religious* (Dublin & London: Richard Bentley, 1839), 2 vols.

DE TOCQUEVILLE, ALEXIS, *Journey in Ireland July–August, 1835*, ed. Emmet Larkin (Washington, DC: The Catholic University of America Press, 1990).

DE VERE, AUBREY, *English Misrule and Irish Misdeeds: Four Letters From Ireland, Addressed to an English Member of Parliament* (London: John Murray, 1848).

—— *Irish Odes and Other Poems* (New York: The Catholic Publications Society, 1869).

—— *Recollections of Aubrey De Vere* (New York and London: Edward Arnold, 1897).

DOHENY, MICHAEL, *The Felon's Track: A Narrative of '48, Embracing the Leading Events in the Irish Struggle from the Year 1843 to the Close of 1848* (London and Glasgow: Cameron & Ferguson, 1875).

DUFFERIN, LORD and BOYLE, G. F. the HON., *Narrative of a Journey from Oxford to Skibbereen During the Year of the Irish Famine* (Oxford: John Henry Parker, 1847).

DUFFY, SIR CHARLES GAVAN, *Four Years of Irish History 1845–1849* (London, Paris, and New York: Cassell, Petter, Galpin & Co., 1883).

—— *Conversations With Carlyle* (London: Sampson Low, Marston, & Co., 1892).

—— *My Life in Two Hemispheres* (London: T. Fisher Unwin, 1898), 2 vols.

EAST, REVD JOHN, *Glimpses of Ireland in 1847* (London, Bath, Bristol, and Dublin: Hamilton, Adams & Co.; C. Godwin, Binns & Goodwin, T. Noyes; J. Chilcot; J. M'Glashan, 1847).

ELGEE, JANE FRANCESCA ['Speranza'], *Poems by Speranza* (Dublin: James Duffy, 1864).

FERGUSON, LADY MARY, *Sir Samuel Ferguson in the Ireland of his Day* (Edinburgh and London: William Blackwood & Sons, 1896), 2 vols.

FERGUSON, SAMUEL., 'Inheritor and Economist—A Poem', *Dublin University Magazine*, 33 (May 1849), 638–49.

—— 'Dublin: A Poem. In Imitation of the Third Satire of Juvenal', *Dublin University Magazine*, 34 (July 1849), 102–9.

—— *Poems of Sir Samuel Ferguson*, with introduction by Alfred Perceval (Dublin and London: Talbot Press; T. Fisher Unwin Ltd., 1916).

—— *The Poems of Samuel Ferguson*, ed. Padraic Colum (Dublin: Allen Figgis, 1962).

FIELD, LOUISE, *Denis, A Study in Black and White* (London and New York: Macmillan & Co., 1896).

FORBES, JOHN, *Memorandums Made in Ireland in the Autumn of 1852* (London: Smith, Elder & Co., 1853), 2 vols.

FOSTER, THOMAS CAMPBELL, *Letters on the Condition of the People of Ireland* (London: Chapman & Hall, 1846).

FOX, EMILY ['Toler King'], *Rose O'Connor: A Story of the Day* (Chicago: Henry A. Sumner & Co., 1881).

FRASER, JAMES, *Guide Through Ireland Descriptive of its Scenery, Towns, Seats, Antiquities, etc.* (Dublin, London, and Edinburgh: William Curry Jr. & Co.; Samuel Holdsworth; Fraser & Co., 1838).

HALL, SAMUEL CARTER and ANNA MARIA, *Ireland: Its Scenery, Character, &c.* (London: Jeremiah How, 1846), 3 vols.

HALL, SPENCER T., *Life and Death in Ireland, as Witnessed in 1849* (Manchester and London: J. T. Parkes; Simpkin, Marshall, & Co., 1850).

HAMILTON, CHARLES, *Leigh's New Pocket Road-Book of Ireland* (London: Leigh, 1835).

HEAD, SIR FRANCIS B., *A Fortnight in Ireland* (London: John Murray, 1852).

HILL, LORD GEORGE, *Facts From Gweedore: With Useful Hints to Donegal Tourists* (Dublin: Philip Dixon Hardy & Sons, 1845).

—— (ed.), *Hints to Donegal Tourists; with a Brief Notice of Rathlin Island. A Sequel to Facts From Gweedore* (Dublin and London: Philip Dixon Hardy & Sons; Hatchard & Sons, 1847).

HOARE, MRS, *Shamrock Leaves; or, Tales and Sketches of Ireland* (Dublin and London: J. M'Glashan; Partridge & Oakey, 1851).

HOLE, SAMUEL, *A Little Tour in Ireland, by an Oxonian* (London: Bradbury & Evans, 1859).

INGLIS, HENRY, *Ireland in 1834* (London: Whittaker & Co., 1835), 2 vols.

IRVINE, ALEXANDER, *My Lady of the Chimney-Corner* (London: Eveleigh Nash, 1913).

JOHNSON, JAMES, *A Tour in Ireland; with Meditations and Reflections* (London: S. Highley, 1844).

KEARY, ANNIE, *Castle Daly: The Story of an Irish Home Thirty Years Ago* (London: Macmillan & Co., 1875), 3 vols.

KEEGAN, JOHN, *Legends and Poems by John Keegan*, ed. Very Revd J. Canon O'Hanlon (Dublin: Sealy, Bryers & Walker, 1907).

KELLY, MARY ['Eva'], *Poems by 'Eva' of 'The Nation'* (Dublin: M. H. Gill & Son Ltd., 1909).

KNOX, REVD JAMES SPENSER, *Pastoral Annals* (London: R. B. Seeley & W. Burnside, 1840).

KOHL, J. G., *Ireland, Scotland, and England* (London: Chapman & Hall, 1844).

MACCARTHY, DENIS FLORENCE, *Poems by Denis Florence MacCarthy* (Dublin: M. H. Gill & Son, 1884).

MCCARTHY, JUSTIN, *Mononia: A Love Story of 'Forty-Eight'* (London: Chatto & Windus, 1901).

MCCARTHY, JUSTIN HUNTLY, *Lily Lass* (London: Chatto & Windus, 1889).

MCGEE, THOMAS D'ARCY, *The Poems of Thomas D'Arcy McGee* (London, New York, and Montreal: D. & J. Sadlier & Co., 1869).

MCNEILE, REVD HUGH, *The Famine A Rod of God: Its Provoking Cause—Its Merciful Design* (London and Liverpool: Seeley, Burnside, & Seeley; Arthur Newling, 1847).

MANGAN, JAMES CLARENCE, *The Collected Works of James Clarence Mangan*, Volume I: *Poems 1818–1837*, ed. Jacques Chuto, Rudolf Patrick Holzapfel, Peter Mac Mahon, Pádraig Ó Snodaigh, Ellen Shannon-Mangan, Peter Van De Kamp (Dublin and Portland, Oreg.: Irish Academic Press, 1996).

—— *The Collected Works of James Clarence Mangan*, Volume II: *Poems: 1838–1844*, ed. Jacques Chuto, Rudolf Patrick Holzapfel, Peter Mac Mahon, Ellen Shannon-Mangan (Dublin and Portland, Oreg.: Irish Academic Press, 1996).

—— *The Collected Works of James Clarence Mangan*, Volume III: *Poems: 1845–1847*, ed. Jacques Chuto, Rudolf Patrick Holzapfel, Ellen Shannon-Mangan (Dublin and Portland, Oreg.: Irish Academic Press, 1997)

—— *The Collected Works of James Clarence Mangan*, Volume IV: *Poems: 1848–1912*, ed. Jacques Chuto, Tadhg Ó Dúshláine, Peter Van De Kamp (Dublin and Portland, Oreg.: Irish Academic Press, 1999).

—— *Poems by James Clarence Mangan; with Biographical Introduction by John Mitchel* (New York: P. M. Haverty, 1859).

—— *James Clarence Mangan: His Selected Poems*, ed. Louise Guiney (London, Boston, and New York: John Lane; Larsson, Wolffe & Co., 1897).

—— *Poems of James Clarence Mangan*, ed. D. J. O'Donoghue (Dublin and London: O'Donoghue & Co.; A. H. Bullen, 1903).

—— *The Prose Writings of James Clarence Mangan*, ed. D. J. O'Donoghue (Dublin and London: O'Donoghue & Co.; M. H. Gill & Son; A. H. Bullen, 1904).

—— *Autobiography*, ed. James Kilroy (Dublin: Dolmen Press, 1968).

MANNERS, LORD JOHN, *Notes of an Irish Tour* (London: J. Ollivier, 1849).

MARTINEAU, HARRIET, *Letters From Ireland* (London: John Chapman, 1852).

MARTINEAU, JAMES, *Ireland and her Famine: A Discourse* (London: John Chapman, 1847).

MASON, MISS, *Kate Gearey; or, Irish Life in London. A Tale of 1849* (London: Charles Dolman, 1853).

MATHISON, G. F. G., *Journal of a Tour in Ireland, During the Months of October and November 1835* (London: Samuel Bentley, 1836).

MITCHEL, JOHN, *Jail Journal; or, Five Years in British Prisons* (1854) (Washington: Woodstock Books, 1996).

—— *The History of Ireland, From The Treaty of Limerick to the Present Time* (1868) (Dublin: James Duffy, 1869), 2 vols.

—— *The Last Conquest of Ireland (Perhaps)* (1861) (Glasgow and London: Cameron & Ferguson; Stationer's Hall Court, 1876).

NEAVE, SIR DIGBY, *Four Days in Connaught* (London: Bentley, 1852).

NICHOLSON, ASENATH, *Ireland's Welcome to the Stranger: Or, Excursions Through Ireland in 1844 and 1845 for the Purpose of Personally Investigating the Condition of the Poor* (London and Dublin: Charles Gilpin; Webb & Chapman , 1847).

—— *A Treatise on Vegetable Diet with Practical Results; or, a Leaf from Nature's Own Book* (Glasgow and London: John M'Combe; Simpkin, Marshall, & Co., 1848).

—— *Lights and Shades of Ireland* (London: Charles Gilpin, 1850).

O'BRIEN, SIR LUCIUS, *Ireland: The Late Famine, and the Poor Laws* (London: Hatchard & Son, 1848).

O'BRIEN, RICHARD BAPTIST, *Ailey Moore, A Tale of the Times* (London and Baltimore: Charles Dolman; J. Murphy & Co., 1856).

—— *The D'Altons of Crag: A Story of '48 & '49* (Dublin: James Duffy & Sons, 1882).

O'BRIEN, W. P., *The Great Famine in Ireland and a Retrospect of the Fifty Years 1845–95* (London: Downey & Co., Ltd., 1896).

O'CONNELL, CATHERINE, *Excursions in Ireland During 1844 and 1850* (London: Bentley, 1852).

O'MEARA, KATHLEEN, *The Battle of Connemara* (London: R. Washbourne, 1878).

O'ROURKE, REVD JOHN, *The History of the Great Irish Famine of 1847* (Dublin and London: M'Glashan & Gill; James Duffy, Sons, & Co., 1875).

—— *The Battle of the Faith in Ireland* (Dublin: James Duffy & Sons, 1887).

O'RYAN, JULIA and EDMUND, *In re Garland: A Tale of a Transition Time* (London, Dublin, New York, and Derby: Thomas Richardson & Son; Henry H. Richardson & Co., 1870).

OSBORNE, LORD SIDNEY GODOLPHIN, *Gleanings in the West of Ireland* (London: T. & W. Boone, 1850).

—— *The Letters of S.G.O.: A Series of Letters on Public Affairs Written by the Rev Lord Sidney Godolphin Osborne and Published in 'The Times' 1844–1888*, ed. Arnold White (London and Sydney: Griffith & Farren, 1890), 2 vols.

OTWAY, CAESAR, *A Tour in Connaught* (Dublin: William Curry Jr. & Co., 1839).

—— *Sketches in Erris and Tyrawly* (Dublin and London: William Curry Jr. & Co.; Longman, Orme, & Co., 1841).

PERCIVAL, MARGARET, *The Irish Dove; or, Faults on Both Sides. A Tale* (Dublin and London: John Robertson; Simpkin, Marshall, & Co., 1849).

PÜCKLER-MUSKAU, PRINCE HERMANN VON, *Tour in England, Ireland, and France, in the Years 1828 & 1829* (London: Effingham Wilson, 1832), 4 vols.

RUSSELL, THOMAS O'NEILL ['Reginald Tierney'], *The Struggles of Dick Massey; or, The Battles of a Boy* (Dublin: James Duffy, 1860).

SCOTT, THOMAS COLVILLE, *Connemara After the Famine: Journal of a Survey of the Martin Estate (1853)*, ed. with introduction by Tim Robinson (Dublin: Lilliput Press, 1995).

SENIOR, NASSAU WILLIAM, *Journals, Conversations and Essays Relating to Ireland* (London: Longmans, Green, & Co., 1868), 2 vols.

SHEEHAN, CANON PATRICK, *Glenanaar: A Story of Irish Life* (London, New York, and Bombay: Longmans, Green & Co., 1905).

SMITH, ELIZABETH, *The Irish Journals of Elizabeth Smith 1840–1850*, ed. David Thomson and Moyra McGusty (Oxford: Clarendon Press, 1980).

SMITH, WILLIAM, *A Twelve Months' Residence in Ireland, during the Famine and the Public Works, 1846 and 1847* (London and Dublin: Longman, Brown, Green, & Longman; Hodges & Smith, 1848).

Society of Friends, *Transactions of the Central Relief Committee of the Society of Friends During the Famine in Ireland, in 1846 and 1847* (Dublin and London: Hodges & Smith; W. & F. G. Cash, 1852).

SOMERS, ROBERT, *Letters From The Highlands; or, The Famine of 1847* (London, Edinburgh, and Glasgow: Simpkin, Marshall, & Co.; Sutherland & Knox; J. R. McNair, 1848).

SOMERVILLE, ALEXANDER, *Letters From Ireland During the Famine of 1847*, ed. K. D. M. Snell (Dublin: Irish Academic Press, 1994).

THACKERAY, WILLIAM MAKEPEACE, *The Irish Sketch Book* (London: Chapman & Hall, 1843), 2 vols.

—— *The Letters and Private Papers of W. M. Thackeray*, ed. Gordon N. Ray (London: Oxford University Press, 1945), 4 vols.

—— *The History of Pendennis*, ed. John Sutherland (Oxford: Oxford University Press, 1994).

TRENCH, WILLIAM STEUART, *Realities of Irish Life* (London: Longmans, Green, & Co., 1868).

TREVELYAN, CHARLES, *The Irish Crisis* (London: Longman, Brown, Green & Longmans, 1848).

TROLLOPE, ANTHONY, *The Macdermots of Ballycloran* (London: T. C. Newby, 1847), 3 vols.

—— *The Kellys and the O'Kellys, or Landlords and Tenants, A Tale of Irish Life* (London: Henry Colburn, 1848), 3 vols.

—— *Six Letters to the Examiner 1849–50*, ed. Lance O. Tingay (London: Silverbridge Press, 1987).

—— *Castle Richmond* (London: Chapman & Hall, 1860), 3 vols.

—— *Lotta Schmidt and Other Stories* (London: Alexander Strahan, 1867).

—— *Tales of All Countries* (London: Chapman & Hall, 1867).

TROLLOPE, ANTHONY, *The Landleaguers* (London: Chatto & Windus, 1883), 3 vols.
—— *An Autobiography* (London: Oxford University Press, 1883), 2 vols.
—— *The Letters of Anthony Trollope*, Volume 1: *1835–1870*, ed. N. John Hall (Stanford: Stanford University Press, 1983).
TUKE, JAMES, *A Visit to Connaught in the Autumn of 1847* (London and York: Charles Gilpin; John Linney, 1848).
UPTON, W. C., *Uncle Pat's Cabin: or Life among the Agricultural Labourers of Ireland* (Dublin: Gill, 1882).
WALSH, LOUIS J., *The Next Time: A Story of 'Forty-Eight* (Dublin: M. H. Gill & Son, Ltd., 1919).
WALSHE, ELIZABETH HELY, *Kingston's Revenge: A Story of Bravery and Single-Hearted Endeavour* (London: The Religious Tract Society, 1917) (first published in 1865 as *Golden Hills: A Tale of the Irish Famine*).
—— *The Manuscript Man, or The Bible in Ireland* (London: The Religious Tract Society, 1889).
WEST, T. C. I. (MRS FREDERICK), *A Summer's Visit to Ireland in 1846* (London: Richard Bentley, 1847).
WHITE, GEORGE PRESTON, *A Tour in Connamara, With Remarks on its Great Physical Capabilities* (London: W. H. Smith & Son, 1849).
WHITTOCK, NATHANIEL, *A Picturesque Guide Through Dublin* (Dublin and Liverpool: J. Cornish, 1846).
WILDE, WILLIAM, *The Beauties of the Boyne, and its Tributary, the Blackwater* (Dublin, London, and Liverpool: James M'Glashan; William S. Orr, 1849).
WILLIAMS, RICHARD D'ALTON, *The Poems of Richard Dalton Williams* (Dublin: T. D. Sullivan, 1883).
WILLS, W. G., *The Love That Kills: A Novel* (London: Tinsley Brothers, 1867), 3 vols.

Contemporary Newspapers and Journals

Athenaeum
Cork Southern Reporter
Dublin Review
Edinburgh Review
Howitt's Journal
Illustrated Dublin Journal
Illustrated London News
Irish Felon
Irish Monthly Magazine
Irish Tribune
The Nation
Punch
Quarterly Review

Saturday Review
The Times
Times Literary Supplement
United Irishman

Other Contemporary Texts

ANON., *Poverty Before the Famine: County Clare 1835, First Report From His Majesty's Commissioners For Inquiring into the Condition of the Poorer Classes in Ireland* (Ennis: Clasp Press, 1996).

Athenaeum, 'Review of *Black Prophet*, Earl of Rosse's *Letters on the State of Ireland*, and G. L. Smyth's *Ireland, Historical and Statistical*', 1011 (13 Mar. 1847), 278–9.

BIRMINGHAM, GEORGE [pseudonym of CANON JAMES OWEN HANNAY], 'For the Famine of Your Houses', *Minnie's Bishop, and Other Stories of Ireland* (London, New York, and Toronto: Hodder & Stoughton, 1915).

BLANCHARD, LAMAN, '*The Irish Sketch-Book*. By Mr Michael Angelo Titmarsh', *Ainsworth's Magazine*, 3 (May 1843), 435–8.

BROWN, REVD STEPHEN, *Ireland in Fiction: A Guide to Irish Novels, Tales, Romances and Folklore* (1916) (Shannon: Irish University Press, 1969).

CROKER, JOHN W., 'Tours in Ireland', *Quarterly Review*, 85 (Sept. 1849), 491–562.

DICKENS, CHARLES, *The Pickwick Papers* (London: Chapman & Hall, 1837).

—— *Bleak House* (London: Bradbury and Evans, 1853).

DILLON, WILLIAM, *Life of John Mitchel* (London: Kegan Paul, Trench & Co., 1888).

Dublin University Magazine, 'Ireland, Social, Political, And Religious', 14 (July 1839), 107–20.

—— 'Our Portrait Gallery.—no xv. William Carleton', 17 (Jan. 1841), 66–72.

—— 'Sir F. B. Head', 40 (Dec. 1852), 735–43.

DYER, A. S., *A Hero From the Forge: A Biographical Sketch of Elihu Burritt* (London: Dyer Brothers, 1880).

EDGEWORTH, MARIA, *Castle Rackrent* (1800) (Harmondsworth: Penguin), 1992.

—— *The Absentee* (1812), (Harmondsworth: Penguin, 1999).

ELLIS, HERCULES, *Romances and Ballads of Ireland* (Dublin: James Duffy, 1850).

FIGGES, DARRELL, 'Introduction' to *Carleton's Stories of Irish Life* (Dublin: Talbot Press, 1918).

GASKELL, ELIZABETH, *Mary Barton: A Tale of Manchester Life* (London: Chapman & Hall, 1848), 2 vols.

GOTTHELF, JEREMIAS, *The Story of an Alpine Valley or, Katie the Grandmother*, trans. L. G. Smith (London: Gibbings & Co. Ltd., 1896).

HALL, SAMUEL CARTER, *'Ireland For the Irish!'* (London: *The Echo*, 1886)

HANNIGAN, KEN (ed.), *The Famine: Ireland 1845–51: Facsimile Documents* (Dublin: Public Records Office of Ireland, 1982).

H.D., *The Spectre: Stanzas with Illustrations* (London: Thomas M'Lean, 1851).

Howitt's Journal, 'Review of *The Black Prophet*', 1/17 (24 Apr. 1847), 236–7.

Irish Monthly, 'Review of Margaret Brew's *The Chronicles of Castle Cloyne*', 14/158 (Aug. 1886), 455–6.

KEARY, ELIZA, *Memoir of Annie Keary* (London: Macmillan, 1882).

KRANS, HORATIO SHEAFE, *Irish Life in Irish Fiction* (New York and London: Columbia University Press; Macmillan, 1903).

LAWLESS, EMILY, *The Story of the Nations: Ireland* (London and New York: T. Fisher Unwin; G. P. Putnam's Sons, 1887).

LEECH, H. BROUGHAM, *1848 and 1887: The Continuity of the Irish Revolutionary Movement* (London and Dublin: William Ridgway; Hodges, Figgis & Co., 1887).

LE FANU, WILLIAM, *Seventy Years of Irish Life: Being Anecdotes and Reminiscences* (London: Edward Arnold, 1893).

LEIGH, PERCIVAL, 'Titmarsh's Travels in Ireland', *Fraser's Magazine*, 27 (June 1843), 678–86.

LEVER, CHARLES, 'The Irish Sketch-Book', *Dublin University Magazine*, 21 (June 1843), 647–56.

—— 'Travels and Travellers', *Dublin University Magazine*, 22 (August 1843), 154–76.

—— 'Twaddling Tourists in Ireland', *Dublin University Magazine*, 24 (Nov 1844), 505–26.

—— 'Twaddling Tourists in Ireland—No. II', *Dublin University Magazine*, 24 (Dec 1844), 740–8.

LEWIS, GEORGE CORNEWALL, *On Local Disturbances in Ireland; and on the Irish Church Question* (London: B. Fellowes, 1836).

MACDERMOTT, MARTIN, 'Introduction', *Songs and Ballads of Young Ireland* (London: Downey & Co. Ltd., 1896).

MACDONAGH, THOMAS, *Literature in Ireland: Studies Irish and Anglo-Irish* (Dublin: Talbot Press, 1916).

MELVILLE, LEWIS, *The Life of William Makepeace Thackeray* (London: Hutchinson & Co., 1890).

MILTON, JOHN, *Paradise Lost* (1667), ed. Alastair Fowler (London: Longman, 1971).

MORGAN, LADY SYDNEY, *St Clair, or the Heiress of Desmond* (London: E. Harding, 1803), 3 vols.

—— *The Wild Irish Girl* (London: Richard Phillips, 1806), 3 vols.

—— *O'Donnel: A National Tale* (London: Henry Colburn, 1814), 3 vols.

—— *The O'Briens and the O'Flahertys* (London: Henry Colburn, 1827), 3 vols.

—— 'The Irish Sketch-Book', *Athenaeum*, 811 (13 May 1843), 455–7.

MURRAY, PATRICK, 'Carleton', *Edinburgh Review*, 96 (Oct. 1852), 384–403.

Nation, The Spirit of the Nation (Dublin and London: James Duffy & Sons, 1882).

—— *Penny Readings for the Irish People, Conducted by the Editors of the Nation* (Dublin: A. M. & T. D. Sullivan, 1870–86), 4 vols.

O'CONNELL, MRS MORGAN JOHN, *Charles Bianconi: A Biography 1786–1875* (London: Chapman & Hall, 1878).

O'DONOGHUE, D. J., *The Life of William Carleton: Being His Autobiography And Letters: And An Account Of His Life And Writings, From The Point At Which The Autobiography Breaks Off* (London: Downey & Co., 1896), 2 vols.

—— 'Introduction', *Traits and Stories of the Irish Peasantry by William Carleton*, ed., D. J. O'Donoghue (London and New York: J. M. Dent & Co.; Macmillan & Co., 1896), 4 vols.

—— *The Life and Writings of James Clarence Mangan* (Edinburgh, Dublin, Chicago, and Peabody: Patrick Geddes & Co.; M. H. Gill & Son; T. G. O'Donoghue; P. V. Fitzpatrick; Nugent Bros., 1897).

O'HEGARTY, P. S., *John Mitchel, An Appreciation, With Some Account of Young Ireland* (Dublin and London: Maunsell & Co., 1917).

O'LEARY, PETER, *My Story (Mo Scéal Féin)*, trans. Cyril O Céirín (1915) (Oxford and New York: Oxford University Press, 1987).

Public Records Office of Northern Ireland, *The Great Famine in Antrim, Randalstown and Districts: Extracts from the Minute Books of the Board of Guardians of Antrim Poor Law Union 1844–1846, 1851–1853*.

SAINTSBURY, GEORGE, 'Introduction', *The Irish Sketch Book and Contributions to the Foreign Quarterly Review 1842–4, by William Makepeace Thackeray* (London, New York, and Toronto: Oxford University Press, 1908).

SAVAGE, MARMION, *The Falcon Family; or, Young Ireland* (London: Chapman & Hall, 1845).

SHEEHY-SKEFFINGTON, FRANCIS, *Michael Davitt: Revolutionary, Agitator and Labour Leader* (London and Leipzig: T. Fisher Unwin, 1908)

Spectator, 'Carleton's *Squanders of Castle Squander*', 25/1253 (3 July 1852), 638–9.

SPENSER, EDMUND, *A View of the State of Ireland* (1633), ed. Andrew Hadfield and Willy Maley (Oxford: Blackwell, 1997).

SULLIVAN, ALEXANDER M., *New Ireland: Political Sketches and Personal Reminiscences of Thirty Years of Irish Public Life* (Glasgow and London: Cameron & Ferguson; Fleet Street, 1877).

—— *The Story of Ireland; a Narrative of Irish History from the Earliest Ages to the Present Time; Written for the Youth of Ireland* (Dublin: T. D. Sullivan, 1887).

TAYLOR, FENNINGS, *Thomas D'Arcy McGee: Sketch of his Life and Death* (Montreal: John Lovell, 1868).

TENNYSON, HALLAM, *Alfred Lord Tennyson: A Memoir* (London: Macmillan & Co. Ltd., 1897), 2 vols.

WALLER, J. F., 'Our Queen', *Dublin University Magazine*, 34 (Sept. 1849), 253–60.

WALMESLEY, CHARLES [PASTORINI], *The General History of the Christian Church, From Her Birth To Her Final Triumphant State In Heaven: Chiefly Deduced From The Apocalypse of St John, The Apostle and Evangelist* (Dublin: J. Mehain, 1790).

WARD, WILFRID, *Aubrey De Vere: A Memoir Based on his Unpublished Diaries and Correspondence* (London, New York, and Bombay: Longmans, Green, & Co., 1904).

WILLS, FREEMAN, *W. G. Wills: Dramatist and Painter* (London, New York, and Bombay: Longmans, Green, & Co., 1898).

YEATS, W. B., 'Introduction', *Stories from Carleton* (London, New York, and Toronto: Walter Scott; W. J. Gage & Co., 1889).

—— *The Variorum Edition of the Plays of W. B. Yeats*, ed. Russell K. Alspach (London and Basingstoke: Macmillan, 1966).

—— *Uncollected Prose by W. B. Yeats*, Volume I, ed. John P. Frayne (London: Macmillan, 1970).

—— *Uncollected Prose by W. B. Yeats*, Volume II, ed. John P. Frayne & Colton Johnson (London and Basingstoke: Macmillan, 1975).

SECONDARY SOURCES

ACKROYD, PETER, *Dickens* (London: Minerva, 1991).

AHERN, JAMES, *Young Ireland: Its Founder and his Circle* (Waterford: Carthage Press, 1945).

AKENSON, DONALD HARMAN, 'A Midrash on "Galut", "Exile" and "Diaspora" Rhetoric', in E. Margaret Crawford (ed.), *The Hungry Stream: Essays on Emigration and Famine* (Belfast: Institute of Irish Studies, Queen's University Belfast, 1997).

ARNOLD, DAVID, *Famine: Social Crisis and Historical Change*, (Oxford: Basil Blackwell, 1988).

BALDICK, CHRIS, *The Concise Oxford Dictionary of Literary Terms* (Oxford: Clarendon Press, 1990).

BAREHAM, TONY (ed.), *Anthony Trollope* (Plymouth and London: Vision, 1980).

BARRELL, JOHN, *The Dark Side of the Landscape: The Rural Poor in English Painting 1730–1840* (Cambridge: Cambridge University Press, 1980).

BEAMES, MICHAEL, 'Rural Conflict in Pre-Famine Ireland: Peasant Assassinations in Tipperary 1837–1847', *Past and Present*, 81 (Nov. 1978), 75–91.

BEGLEY, ANTHONY and LALLY, SOINBHE, 'The Famine in County Donegal', in Christine Kinealy and Trevor Parkhill (eds.), *The Famine in Ulster: The Regional Impact* (Belfast: Ulster Historical Foundation, 1997).

BENSON, CHARLES, 'Printers and Booksellers in Dublin 1800–1850', in Robin Myers and Michael Harris (eds.), *Spreading the Word: The Distribution Networks of Print 1550–1850* (Winchester: St Paul's Bibliographies, 1990), 47–59.

BERNSTEIN, GEORGE L., 'Liberals, the Irish Famine and the Role of the State', *Irish Historical Studies*, 29/116 (Nov. 1995), 513–36.

BERNSTEIN, MICHAEL A., 'Homage to the Extreme: The Shoah and the Rhetoric of Catastrophe', *Times Literary Supplement* (6 Mar. 1998), 6–8.

BEW, PAUL, 'A Case of Compassion Fatigue', *Spectator* (13 Mar. 1999), 37–8.

BLACK, R. D. COLLINSON, *Economic Thought and the Irish Question 1817–1870* (Cambridge: Cambridge University Press, 1960).

BOLAND, EAVAN, *In a Time Of Violence* (Manchester: Carcanet, 1994).

BOUÉ, ANDRÉ, *William Carleton, romancier irlandais (1794–1869)* (Paris: Publications de la Sorbonne, 1978).

BOURKE, AUSTIN, *'The Visitation of God'? The Potato and the Great Irish Famine* (Dublin: Lilliput Press, 1993).

BOURKE, MARIE, 'Rural Life in Pre-Famine Connacht: A Visual Document', in Raymond Gillespie and Brian P. Kennedy (eds.), *Ireland: Art into History* (Dublin and Niwot, Colo.: Town House and Roberts Rinehart, 1994), 61–74.

BOWEN, DESMOND, *Souperism: Myth or Reality: A Study in Souperism* (Cork: Mercier Press, 1970).

—— *The Protestant Crusade in Ireland, 1800–70: A Study of Protestant–Catholic Relations Between the Act of Union and Disestablishment* (Dublin: Gill and Macmillan, 1978).

BOYCE, D. GEORGE and O'DAY, ALAN (eds.), *The Making of Modern Irish Historiography: Revisionism and the Revisionist Controversy* (London and New York: Routledge, 1996).

BOYLAN, HENRY (ed.), *A Dictionary of Irish Biography* (Dublin: Gill & Macmillan, 1988).

BRADLEY, WILLIAM, '*The Tithe Proctor*—A Revaluation', *Carleton Newsletter*, 3/4 (4 Apr. 1973).

BRADY, ALEXANDER, *Thomas D'Arcy McGee* (Toronto: Macmillan, 1925).

BRADY, ANNE, and CLEEVE, BRIAN (eds.), *A Biographical Dictionary of Irish Writers* (Mullingar: Lilliput Press, 1985).

BRADY, CIARAN (ed.), *Interpreting Irish History: The Debate on Historical Revisionism 1938–1994* (Dublin: Irish Academic Press, 1994).

BROWN, MALCOLM, *The Politics of Irish Literature From Thomas Davis to W. B. Yeats* (London: Allen & Unwin, 1972).

—— *Sir Samuel Ferguson* (Lewisburg, Pa.: Bucknell University Press, 1973).

BROWN, TERENCE, 'The Death of William Carleton 1869', *Carleton Newsletter*, 2/2 (4 Oct. 1971).

BURN, W. L., 'Free Trade in Land: An Aspect of the Irish Question', *Transactions of the Royal Historical Society*, 4th ser. 31 (1949), 61–70.

CAHALAN, JAMES, *Great Hatred, Little Room: The Irish Historical Novel* (Syracuse, NY: Syracuse University Press, 1983).

—— *The Irish Novel: A Critical History* (Dublin: Gill & Macmillan, 1988).

CAIRNS, DAVID, and RICHARDS, SHAUN, *Writing Ireland: Colonialism, Nationalism and Culture* (Manchester: Manchester University Press, 1988).

CAMPBELL, STEPHEN J., *The Great Irish Famine: Words and Images from the Famine Museum, Strokestown Park, County Roscommon* (Strokestown: Famine Museum, 1994).

CANNY, NICHOLAS, 'Upper Ireland: *Modern Ireland 1600–1972*', *London Review of Books* 11/6 (16 Mar. 1989) 8–9.

CARBERY, MARY, *The Farm by Lough Gur: The Story of Mary Fogarty (Sissy O'Brien)* (London, New York, and Toronto: Longmans, Green & Co., 1937).

CARDWELL, EVELYN, 'Interpreting Famine Emigration with Children at the Ulster-American Folk Park', in E. Margaret Crawford (ed.), *The Hungry Stream: Essays on Emigration and Famine* (Belfast: Institute of Irish Studies, Queen's University Belfast, 1997).

CARROLL, JAMES, 'A Shawl of Grief', in Tom Hayden (ed.), *Irish Hunger: Personal Reflections on the Legacy of the Famine* (Boulder, Colo. and Dublin: Roberts Rinehart; Wolfhound Press).

CASEY, DANIEL J., 'Lough Derg's Infamous Pilgrim', *Carleton Newsletter*, 3/1 (4 July 1972).

—— 'Three Roads Out of Clogher: A Study of Early-Nineteenth-Century Ireland in the Life of William Carleton', *Clogher Record*, 10/3 (1981), 392–404.

CHANG, HSIEN-LIANG, *Grass Soup*, trans. Martha Avery (London: Minerva, 1995).

CLARK, SAMUEL, *Social Origins of the Irish Land War* (Princeton: Princeton University Press, 1979).

—— and DONNELLY, JAMES S. Jr. (eds.), *Irish Peasants: Violence and Political Unrest 1780–1914* (Manchester: Manchester University Press, 1983).

CLEEVE, BRIAN, *Dictionary of Irish Writers* (Cork: Mercier Press, 1971).

CLIFFORD, Brendan, *The Dubliner: The Lives, Times and Writings of James Clarence Mangan* (Belfast: Athol Press, 1988).

COCKSHUT, ANTHONY O. J., *Anthony Trollope: A Critical Study* (London: Collins, 1955).

COLLINS, BRENDA, 'The Linen Industry and Emigration to Britain During the Mid-Nineteenth Century', in E. Margaret Crawford (ed.), *The Hungry Stream: Essays on Emigration and Famine* (Belfast: Institute of Irish Studies, Queen's University Belfast, 1997).

COMERFORD, R. V., 'Churchmen, Tenants, and Independent Opposition, 1850–56', in W. E. Vaughan (ed.), *A New History of Ireland*, V: *Ireland Under the Union I 1801–70* (Oxford: Clarendon Press, 1989).

—— 'Ireland 1850–70: Post-Famine and Mid-Victorian', in W. E. Vaughan (ed.), *A New History of Ireland*, V: *Ireland Under the Union I 1801–70* (Oxford: Clarendon Press, 1989).

CONNOLLY, PETER (ed.), *Literature and the Changing Ireland* (Gerrards Cross and Totowa, NJ: Colin Smythe and Barnes & Noble, 1982).

CONNOLLY, S. J. 'The Great Famine and Irish Politics', in Cathal Póirtéir (ed.), *The Great Irish Famine* (Cork and Dublin: Mercier Press, 1995).

—— (ed.), *The Oxford Companion to Irish History* (Oxford: Clarendon Press, 1998).

COOKE, JIM (ed.), *Charles Dickens's Ireland: An Anthology* (Dublin: Woodfield Press, 1999).

COSTELLO, FRANCIS, 'The Deer Island Graves, Boston: The Irish Famine and Irish-American tradition', in Patrick O'Sullivan (ed.), *The Irish World Wide: History, Heritage, Identity*, Volume 6: *The Meaning of the Famine* (London and Washington, DC: Leicester University Press, 1997).

CRAWFORD, E. MARGARET 'Food and Famine', in Cathal Póirtéir (ed.), *The Great Irish Famine* (Cork and Dublin: Mercier Press, 1995).

—— (ed.), *The Hungry Stream: Essays on Emigration and Famine* (Belfast: Institute of Irish Studies, Queen's University Belfast, 1997).

—— 'Ireland's Haemorrhage', in E. Margaret Crawford (ed.), *The Hungry Stream: Essays on Emigration and Famine* (Belfast: Institute of Irish Studies, Queen's University Belfast, 1997).

—— 'Migrant Maladies: Unseen Lethal Baggage', in E. Margaret Crawford (ed.), *The Hungry Stream: Essays on Emigration and Famine* (Belfast: Institute of Irish Studies, Queen's University Belfast, 1997).

CRAWFORD, MARGARET, 'The Great Irish Famine 1845–9: Image Versus Reality', in Raymond Gillespie and Brian P. Kennedy (eds.), *Ireland: Art into History* (Dublin and Niwot, Colo.: Town House and Roberts Rinehart, 1994), 75–88.

CRONIN, JOHN, 'Trollope and the Matter of Ireland', in Tony Bareham (ed.), *Anthony Trollope* (Plymouth and London: Vision, 1980), 13–35.

CUNNINGHAM, JOHN, 'The Famine in County Fermanagh', in Christine Kinealy and Trevor Parkhill (eds.), *The Famine in Ulster: The Regional Impact* (Belfast: Ulster Historical Foundation, 1997).

CURTIS, L. PERRY, Jr., *Apes and Angels: The Irishman in Victorian Caricature* (Washington, DC and London: Smithsonian Institution Press, 1997).

DALLAT, CAHAL, 'The Famine in County Antrim', in Christine Kinealy and Trevor Parkhill (eds.), *The Famine in Ulster: The Regional Impact* (Belfast: Ulster Historical Foundation, 1997).

D'ALTON, LOUIS, *The Man in the Cloak: A Play on James Clarence Mangan* (Dublin: P. J. Bourke, 1971).

DALY, MARY, *The Famine in Ireland* (Dublin: Dublin Historical Association, 1986).

—— 'The Operations of Famine Relief, 1845–47', in Cathal Póirtéir (ed.), *The Great Irish Famine* (Cork and Dublin: Mercier Press, 1995).

—— 'Revisionism and Irish History: The Great Famine', in D. George Boyce and Alan O'Day (eds.), *The Making of Modern Irish Historiography: Revisionism and the Revisionist Controversy* (London and New York: Routledge, 1996).

—— 'Farming and the Famine', in Cormac Ó Gráda (ed.), *Famine 150: Commemorative Lecture Series* (Dublin: Teagasc: University College Dublin, 1997).

DAVIS, GRAHAM, 'The Historiography of the Irish Famine', in Patrick O'Sullivan (ed.), *The Irish World Wide: History, Heritage, Identity*, Volume 6: *The Meaning of the Famine* (London and Washington, DC: Leicester University Press, 1997).

DAVIS, THOMAS, 'Carleton: Novelist of the Folk', *Thomas Davis: Essays and Poems With a Centenary Memoir, 1845–1945* (Dublin: M. H. Gill & Son Ltd., 1945).

DEANE, SEAMUS, 'Irish National Character 1790–1900', in Tom Dunne (ed.), *The Writer as Witness: Literature as Historical Evidence* (Cork: Cork University Press, 1987).

DE NIE, MICHAEL, 'The Famine, Irish Identity, and the British Press', *Irish Studies Review*, 6/1 (1998), 27–35.

DEVINE, THOMAS M., *The Great Highland Famine: Hunger, Emigration and the Scottish Highlands in the Nineteenth Century* (Edinburgh: Donald, 1988).

DICKSON, DAVID, 'The Other Great Irish Famine', in Cathal Póirtéir (ed.), *The Great Irish Famine* (Cork and Dublin: Mercier Press, 1995).

—— 'The Potato and Irish Diet Before the Great Famine', in Cormac Ó Gráda (ed.), *Famine 150: Commemorative Lecture Series* (Dublin: Teagasc: University College Dublin, 1997).

DONNELLY, JAMES S., Jr., *The Land and the People of Nineteenth-Century Cork: The Rural Economy and the Land Question* (London and Boston: Routledge & Kegan Paul, 1975).

—— 'Pastorini and Captain Rock: Millenarianism and Sectarianism in the Rockite Movement of 1821–4', in Samuel Clark and James S. Donnelly, Jr. (eds.), *Irish Peasants: Violence and Political Unrest 1780–1914* (Manchester: Manchester University Press, 1983), 102–39.

—— 'The Administration of Relief, 1846–7', in W. E. Vaughan (ed.), *A New History of Ireland*, V: *Ireland Under the Union I 1801–70* (Oxford: Clarendon Press, 1989).

—— 'The Administration of Relief, 1847–51', in W. E. Vaughan (ed.), *A New History of Ireland*, V: *Ireland Under the Union I 1801–70* (Oxford: Clarendon Press, 1989).

—— 'Excess Mortality and Emigration', in W. E. Vaughan (ed.), *A New History of Ireland*, V: *Ireland Under the Union I 1801–70* (Oxford: Clarendon Press, 1989).

—— 'Famine and Government Response, 1845–6', in W. E. Vaughan (ed.), *A New History of Ireland*, V: *Ireland Under the Union I 1801–70* (Oxford: Clarendon Press, 1989).

—— 'A Famine in Irish Politics', in W. E. Vaughan (ed.), *A New History of Ireland*, V: *Ireland Under the Union I 1801–70* (Oxford: Clarendon Press, 1989).

—— 'Landlords and Tenants', in W. E. Vaughan (ed.), *A New History of Ireland* V: *Ireland Under the Union I 1801–70* (Oxford: Clarendon Press, 1989).

—— 'Production, Prices and Exports, 1846–51', in W. E. Vaughan (ed.), *A New History of Ireland*, V: *Ireland Under the Union I 1801–70* (Oxford: Clarendon Press, 1989).

—— 'The Soup Kitchens', in W. E. Vaughan (ed.), *A New History of Ireland*, V: *Ireland Under the Union I 1801–70* (Oxford: Clarendon Press, 1989).

—— 'Mass Eviction and the Great Famine: The Clearances Revisited', in Cathal Póirtéir (ed.), *The Great Irish Famine* (Cork and Dublin: Mercier Press, 1995).

—— 'The Construction of the Memory of the Famine in Ireland and the Irish Diaspora, 1850–1900', *Éire-Ireland*, 31 (Spring/Summer 1996), 26–61.

DOWLEY, LESLIE J., 'The Potato and Late Blight in Ireland', in Cormac Ó Gráda (ed.), *Famine 150: Commemorative Lecture Series* (Dublin: Teagasc: University College Dublin, 1997).

DRABBLE, MARGARET (ed.), *The Oxford Companion to English Literature* (Oxford: Oxford University Press, 1995).

DUFF, DAVID, *Victoria Travels: Journeys of Queen Victoria Between 1830 and 1900; with Extracts from her Journal* (London: Muller, 1970).

DUFFY, PATRICK, 'Emigrants and the Estate Office in the Mid-Nineteenth Century: A Compassionate Relationship?', in E. Margaret Crawford (ed.), *The Hungry Stream: Essays on Emigration and Famine* (Belfast: Institute of Irish Studies, Queen's University Belfast, 1997).

—— 'The Famine in County Monaghan', in Christine Kinealy and Trevor Parkhill (eds.), *The Famine in Ulster: The Regional Impact* (Belfast: Ulster Historical Foundation, 1997).

DUFFY, P. J., 'The Changing Rural Landscape 1750–1850: Pictorial Evidence', in Raymond Gillespie and Brian P. Kennedy (eds.), *Ireland: Art into History* (Dublin and Niwot, Colo.: Town House and Roberts Rinehart, 1994), 26–42.

DUNNE, TOM, 'Fiction as "the best history of nations": Lady Morgan's Irish Novels', in Tom Dunne (ed.), *The Writer as Witness: Literature as Historical Evidence* (Cork: Cork University Press, 1987).

—— 'A Polemical Introduction: Literature, Literary Theory and the Historian', in Tom Dunne (ed.), *The Writer as Witness: Literature as Historical Evidence* (Cork: Cork University Press, 1987).

—— (ed.), *The Writer as Witness: Literature as Historical Evidence* (Cork: Cork University Press, 1987).

—— 'Haunted by History: Irish Romantic Writing 1800–50', in Roy Porter and Mikulas Teich (eds.) *Romanticism in National Context* (Cambridge: Cambridge University Press, 1988).

EAGLETON, TERRY, 'Form and Ideology in the Anglo-Irish Novel', *Bullán: An Irish Studies Journal*, 1/1 (Spring 1994), 17–26.

—— *Heathcliff and the Great Hunger: Studies in Irish Culture* (London and New York: Verso, 1995).

—— *Scholars and Rebels in Nineteenth-Century Ireland* (Oxford: Blackwell, 1999).

ECKLEY, GRACE, 'Paddy's Ruse and Anna's Revenge: Carleton's "Essay of Irish Swearing" ', *Carleton Newsletter*, 1/1 (4 July 1970).

EDWARDS, OWEN DUDLEY, 'Introduction' to Trollope Society edition of *The Macdermots of Ballycloran* (London: Folio Society, 1991).

EDWARDS, P. D., *Anthony Trollope: His Art and Scope* (Sussex: Harvester, 1978).

EDWARDS, R. DUDLEY and WILLIAMS, T. DESMOND (eds.), *The Great Famine: Studies in Irish History 1845–52* (Dublin: Browne & Nolan, 1956).

EIRÍKSSON, ANDRÉS and Ó GRÁDA, CORMAC, *Irish Landlords and the Great Irish Famine* (Dublin: Dept of Economics, University College Dublin, 1996).

—— 'Food Supply and Food Riots', in Cormac Ó Gráda (ed.), *Famine 150: Commemorative Lecture Series* (Dublin: Teagasc: University College Dublin, 1997).

ELLIOTT-BINNS, L. E., *Religion in the Victorian Era* (London: Lutterworth Press, 1936).

EMERY, STEPHEN, 'Influence of Old Irish Beliefs on Carleton', *Carleton Newsletter*, 2/4 (4 Apr. 1972).

FITZGERALD, PATRICK, ' "The Great Hunger?" Irish Famine: Changing Patterns of Crisis', in E. Margaret Crawford (ed.), *The Hungry Stream: Essays on Emigration and Famine* (Belfast: Institute of Irish Studies, Queen's University Belfast, 1997).

FITZPATRICK, DAVID, 'Emigration, 1801–70', in W. E. Vaughan (ed.), *A New History of Ireland*, V: *Ireland Under the Union I 1801–70* (Oxford: Clarendon Press, 1989).

—— *Oceans of Consolation: Personal Accounts of Irish Migration to Australia* (Cork: Cork University Press, 1994).

—— 'Flight From Famine', in Cathal Póirtéir (ed.), *The Great Irish Famine* (Cork and Dublin: Mercier Press, 1995).

—— 'The Failure: Representations of the Irish Famine in Letters to Australia', in E. Margaret Crawford (ed.), *The Hungry Stream: Essays on Emigration and Famine* (Belfast: Institute of Irish Studies, Queen's University Belfast, 1997).

FLANAGAN, THOMAS, *The Irish Novelists 1800–1850* (New York: Columbia University Press, 1959).

—— 'Rebellion and Style: John Mitchel and the *Jail Journal*', *Irish University Review*, 1/1 (Autumn 1970), 1–29.

—— 'Literature in English, 1801–91', in W. E. Vaughan (ed.), *A New History of Ireland*, V: *Ireland Under the Union I 1801–70* (Oxford: Clarendon Press, 1989).

FOLEY, KIERAN, 'The Killarney Poor Law Guardians and the Famine, 1845–52', MA thesis (University College Dublin, 1987).

FOSTER, JOHN WILSON, *Colonial Consequences: Essays in Irish Literature and Culture* (Dublin: Lilliput Press, 1991).

FOSTER, R. F., *Modern Ireland 1600–1972* (London: Penguin, 1988).

—— 'Ascendancy and Union', in R. F. Foster (ed.), *The Oxford History of Ireland* (Oxford and New York: Oxford University Press, 1992), 134–73.

—— (ed.), *The Oxford History of Ireland* (Oxford and New York: Oxford University Press, 1992).

—— *Paddy and Mr Punch: Connections in Irish and English History* (London: Penguin, 1993).

—— *The Story of Ireland: An Inaugural Lecture delivered before the University of Oxford on 1 December 1994* (Oxford: Clarendon Press, 1995).

FREEMAN, T. W., 'Land and People, *c*.1841', in W. E. Vaughan (ed.), *A New History of Ireland*, V: *Ireland Under the Union I 1801–70* (Oxford: Clarendon Press, 1989).

GACQUIN, WILLIAM, *Roscommon Before the Famine: The Parishes of Kiltoom and Cam 1749–1845* (Dublin: Irish Academic Press, 1996).

GALLOGLY, FR DAN, 'The Famine in County Cavan', in Christine Kinealy and Trevor Parkhill (eds.), *The Famine in Ulster: The Regional Impact* (Belfast: Ulster Historical Foundation, 1997).

GARNER, EDWARD, *To Die By Inches: The Famine in North East Cork* (Cork: Eigse, 1988).

GARVIN, TOM, 'Defenders, Ribbonmen and Others: Underground Political Networks in Pre-Famine Ireland', in C. H. E. Philpin (ed.), *Nationalism and Popular Protest in Ireland* (Cambridge: Cambridge University Press, 1987).

GATES, HENRY LOUIS, Jr. (ed.), *'Race', Writing, and Difference* (Chicago: University of Chicago Press, 1986).

GEARY, LAURENCE M., 'Famine, Fever and the Bloody Flux', in Cathal Póirtéir (ed.), *The Great Irish Famine* (Cork and Dublin: Mercier Press, 1995).

—— 'What People Died of During the Famine', in Cormac Ó Gráda (ed.), *Famine 150: Commemorative Lecture Series* (Dublin: Teagasc: University College Dublin, 1997).

GILEAD, SARAH, 'Trollope's Ground of Meaning: *The Macdermots of Ballycloran*', *Victorian Newsletter*, 69 (Spring 1986), 23–9.

GILLESPIE, RAYMOND, and KENNEDY, BRIAN P. (eds.), *Ireland: Art into History* (Dublin and Niwot, Colo.: Town House and Roberts Rinehart, 1994).

GLENDINNING, VICTORIA, *Trollope* (London: Pimlico, 1992).

GOODBODY, ROB, *A Suitable Channel: Quaker Relief in the Great Famine* (Bray: Pale Publishing, 1995).

GRANT, JIM, 'The Famine in County Tyrone', in Christine Kinealy and Trevor Parkhill (eds.), *The Famine in Ulster: The Regional Impact* (Belfast: Ulster Historical Foundation, 1997)

GRAY, PETER, 'British Politics and the Irish Land Question 1843–1850', Ph.D. thesis (University of Cambridge, 1992).

—— ' "Potatoes and Providence": British Government Responses to the Great Famine', *Bullán: An Irish Studies Journal*, 1/1 (Spring 1994), 75–87.

—— 'Ideology and the Famine', in Cathal Póirtéir (ed.), *The Great Irish Famine* (Cork and Dublin: Mercier Press, 1995).

—— *Famine, Land and Politics: British Government and Irish Society 1843–1850* (Dublin and Portland, Oreg.: Irish Academic Press, 1999).

GREEN, E. R. R., 'Agriculture', in R. Dudley Edwards and T. Desmond Williams (eds.), *The Great Famine: Studies in Irish History 1845–52* (Dublin: Browne & Nolan, 1956).

HADFIELD, ANDREW, and MCVEAGH, JOHN (eds.), *Strangers To That Land: British Perceptions of Ireland from the Reformation to the Famine* (Gerrards Cross: Colin Smythe, 1994).

HALL, N. JOHN, *Trollope: A Biography* (Oxford: Clarendon Press, 1991).

HALPERIN, JOHN, *Trollope and Politics: A Study of the Pallisers and Others* (London and Basingstoke: Macmillan, 1977).

HAMER, MARY, 'Introduction' to *Castle Richmond* (Oxford: Oxford University Press, 1989).

—— 'Introduction' to *The Landleaguers* (Oxford: Oxford University Press, 1993).

HARMON, MAURICE, *Modern Irish Literature 1800–1967: A Reader's Guide* (Dublin: Dolmen Press, 1967).

HARRIS, RUTH-ANN M., ' "Where the poor man is not crushed down to exalt the aristocrat": Vere Foster's Programmes of Assisted Emigration in the Aftermath of the Irish Famine', in Patrick O'Sullivan (ed.), *The Irish World Wide: History, Heritage, Identity*, Vol 6: *The Meaning of the Famine* (London and Washington, DC: Leicester University Press, 1997).

HART, JENIFER, 'Sir Charles Trevelyan at the Treasury', *English Historical Review*, 75 (1960), 92–110.

HATTON, HELEN E., *The Largest Amount of Good: Quaker Relief in Ireland 1654–1921* (Kingston, Montreal, London, and Buffalo: McGill-Queen's University Press, 1993).

HAYDEN, TOM (ed.), *Irish Hunger: Personal Reflections on the Legacy of the Famine* (Boulder, Colo. and Dublin: Roberts Rinehart; Wolfhound Press, 1997).

HAYLEY, BARBARA, *Carleton's Traits and Stories and the 19th Century Anglo-Irish Tradition* (Gerrards Cross and Totowa, NJ: Colin Smythe, 1983).

—— *A Bibliography of the Writings of William Carleton* (Gerrards Cross: Colin Smythe, 1985).

—— and McKAY, ENDA (eds.), *Three Hundred Years of Irish Periodicals* (Dublin and Mullingar: Lilliput Press; Association of Irish Learned Journals, 1987).

HAYS, MICHAEL and NIKOLOPOULOU, ANASTASIA (eds.), *Melodrama: The Cultural Emergence of a Genre* (Basingstoke and London: Macmillan, 1996).

HEANEY, SEAMUS, 'A Tale of Two Islands: Reflections on the Irish Literary Revival', in P. J. Drudy (ed.), *Irish Studies I* (London: Cambridge University Press, 1980).

—— *New Selected Poems 1966–87* (London: Faber & Faber, 1990).

HEFFER, SIMON, *Moral Desperado: A Life of Thomas Carlyle* (London: Phoenix Giants, 1996).

HENNEDY, HUGH L., 'Love and Famine, Family & Country in Trollope's *Castle Richmond*', *Éire-Ireland*, 7 (Winter 1972), 48–66.

HICKEY, PATRICK, 'The Famine in the Skibbereen Union (1845–51)', in Cathal Póirtéir (ed.), *The Great Irish Famine* (Cork and Dublin: Mercier Press, 1995).

HILTON, BOYD, *The Age of Atonement: The Influence of Evangelicalism on Social and Economic Thought 1785–1865* (Oxford: Clarendon Press, 1991).

HORTIN, HOWARD, 'Universal Human Values in Irish Literature', *Carleton Newsletter*, 4/1 (4 July 1973).

HUTCHINSON, JOHN, *The Dynamics of Cultural Nationalism: The Gaelic Revival and the Creation of the Irish Nation State* (London: Allen & Unwin, 1987).

HYDE, RALPH W., 'Review of *Tubber Derg; Denis O'Shaughnessy; Phelim O'Toole's Courtship; and Neal Malone*', *Carleton Newsletter*, 5/2 (4 Apr. 1975).

HYNES, JOHN, 'Anthony Trollope's Creative "Culture-Shock": Banagher 1841', *Éire-Ireland*, 21 (Fall 1986), 124–31.

IBARRA, EILEEN S. (see also EILEEN SULLIVAN), 'William Carleton: An Introduction', *Éire-Ireland*, 5/1 (Spring 1970), 81–6.

—— 'Review of Carleton's *The Black Prophet*', *Carleton Newsletter*, 4/1 (4 July 1973).

Irish Famine Curriculum Committee, 'The Great Famine', submitted to the New Jersey Commission on Holocaust Education on 11 January 1996, for inclusion in the Holocaust and Genocide Curriculum at the secondary level.

JACKSON, JIM, 'Famine Diary—The Making of a Best Seller', *Irish Review*, 11 (Winter 1991–2), 1–8.

KAVANAGH, PATRICK, 'Preface' to *The Autobiography of William Carleton* (London: MacGibbon & Kee, 1968).

—— 'The Great Hunger' (1942), *Collected Poems* (London: Martin Brian & O'Keefe, 1972).

KELLEHER, MARGARET, 'The Feminisation of Famine: Narrative Representations of Irish and Bengali Famines', Ph.D. thesis (Boston College, 1992).

—— 'Irish Famine in Literature', in Cathal Póirtéir (ed.), *The Great Irish Famine* (Cork and Dublin: Mercier Press, 1995).

—— *The Feminization of Famine: Expressions of the Inexpressible?* (Cork: Cork University Press, 1997).

KELLY, EDWARD, 'William Carleton: Ascendancy Novelist', MA thesis (University College Cork, 1988).

KENNY, SEÁN, *The Hungry Earth* (Dublin: Wolfhound Press, 1995).

KERR, DONAL A., *'A Nation of Beggars'? Priests, People, and Politics in Famine Ireland, 1846–1852* (Oxford: Clarendon Press, 1994).

KIBERD, DECLAN, 'Irish Literature and Irish History', in R. F. Foster (ed.), *The Oxford History of Ireland* (Oxford and New York: Oxford University Press, 1992), 230–81.

—— *Inventing Ireland: The Literature of the Modern Nation* (London: Vintage, 1996).

—— *Irish Classics* (London: Granta, 2000).

KIELY, BENEDICT, *Poor Scholar: A Study of the Works and Days of William Carleton (1794–1869)* (Dublin: Talbot Press, 1972).

KIERSE, SEAN, *The Famine Years in the Parish of Killaloe 1845–51* (Killaloe: Boru Books, 1984).

KILROY, JAMES F. (ed.), *The Irish Short Story: A Critical History* (Boston: Twayne Publishers, 1984).

KINCAID, JAMES R., *The Novels of Anthony Trollope* (Oxford: Clarendon Press, 1977).

KINEALY, CHRISTINE, *This Great Calamity: The Irish Famine 1845–52* (Dublin: Gill & Macmillan, 1994).

—— 'Beyond Revisionism: Reassessing the Great Irish Famine', *History Ireland*, 3/4 (Winter 1995), 28–34.

—— 'The Role of the Poor Law During the Famine', in Cathal Póirtéir (ed.), *The Great Irish Famine* (Cork and Dublin: Mercier Press, 1995).

KINEALY, CHRISTINE, *A Death-Dealing Famine: The Great Hunger in Ireland* (London and Chicago: Pluto Press, 1997).

—— 'Potatoes, Providence and Philanthropy: The Role of Private Charity during the Irish Famine', in Patrick O'Sullivan (ed.), *The Irish World Wide: History, Heritage, Identity*, Volume 6: *The Meaning of the Famine* (London and Washington, DC: Leicester University Press, 1997).

—— and PARKHILL, TREVOR (eds.), *The Famine in Ulster: The Regional Impact* (Belfast: Ulster Historical Foundation, 1997).

KING, SOPHIA HILLAN, ' "Pictures Drawn From Memory": William Carleton's Experience of Famine', *Irish Review* (Winter 1995), 80–9.

—— ' "The Condition of Our People": William Carleton and the Social Issues of the Mid–1840s', in E. Margaret Crawford (ed.), *The Hungry Stream: Essays on Emigration and Famine* (Belfast: Institute of Irish Studies, Queen's University Belfast, 1997).

KINSELLA, ANNA, *County Wexford in the Famine Years 1845–1849* (Enniscorthy: Duffry Press, 1995).

KISSANE, NOEL, *The Irish Famine: A Documentary History* (Dublin: National Library of Ireland, 1995).

KLOTZ, GÜNTHER, 'Thackeray's Ireland: Image and Attitude in *The Irish Sketch Book* and *Barry Lyndon*', in Wolfgang Zach and Heinz Kosok (eds.), *Literary Interrelations: Ireland, England and the World*, Volume III: *National Images and Stereotypes* (Tübingen: Narr, 1987), 95–102.

KORNBLUM, JACQUELINE, 'Mixing History and Fiction', *Irish Literary Supplement*, 11/1 (Spring 1992), 10.

KRAUSE, DAVID, 'William Carleton, Demiurge of Irish Carnival: *Fardorougha the Miser*, 1839', *Éire-Ireland*, 29/4 (Winter 1994), 24–46.

—— *William Carleton the Novelist: His Carvival and Pastoral World of Tragicomedy* (Lanham, Md.: University Press of America, 2000).

LANSBURY, CORAL, *The Reasonable Man: Trollope's Legal Fiction* (Princeton: Princeton University Press, 1981).

LARKIN, EMMET, 'The Devotional Revolution in Ireland, 1850–75', *American Historical Review*, 77/3 (June 1972), 625–52.

LEE, JOSEPH, 'Irish Economic History Since 1500', in Joseph Lee (ed.), *Irish Historiography 1970–79* (Cork: Cork University Press, 1981).

—— (ed.), *Irish Historiography 1970–79* (Cork: Cork University Press, 1981).

—— (ed.), *Ireland: Towards a Sense of Place* (Cork: Cork University Press, 1985).

—— 'The Famine as History', in Cormac Ó Gráda (ed.), *Famine 150: Commemorative Lecture Series* (Dublin: Teagasc: University College Dublin, 1997).

LEERSSEN, JOEP, *Remembrance and Imagination: Patterns in the Historical and Literary Representation of Ireland in the Nineteenth Century* (Cork: Cork University Press, 1996).

LEGG, MARIE-LOUISE, *Newspapers and Nationalism: The Irish Provincial Press 1850–1892* (Dublin: Four Courts Press, 1999).

LLOYD, DAVID, *Nationalism and Minor Literature: James Clarence Mangan and the Emergence of Irish Cultural Nationalism* (Berkeley and London: University of California Press, 1987).

LONGLEY, EDNA, *From Cathleen to Anorexia: The Breakdown of Ireland* (Dublin: Attic Press, 1990).

LOWE-EVANS, MARY, *Crimes Against Fecundity: Joyce and Population Control* (Syracuse, NY: Syracuse University Press, 1989).

LUBBERS, KLAUS, 'Author and Audience in the Early Nineteenth Century', in Peter Connolly (ed.), *Literature and the Changing Ireland* (Gerrards Cross and Totowa, NJ: Colin Smythe and Barnes & Noble, 1982), 25–36.

—— 'Continuity and Change in Irish Fiction: The Case of the Big-House Novel', in Otto Rauchbauer (ed.), *Ancestral Voices: The Big House in Anglo-Irish Literature* (Dublin and Hildesheim: Lilliput Press and Georg Olms Verlag, 1992).

LYONS, F. S. L., *Ireland Since the Famine* (London: Fontana, 1973).

MACARTHUR, SIR WILLIAM P., 'Medical History of the Famine', in R. Dudley Edwards and T. Desmond Williams (eds.), *The Great Famine: Studies in Irish History 1845–52* (Dublin: Browne & Nolan, 1956).

MAC ATASNEY, GERARD, *'This Dreadful Visitation': The Famine in Lurgan/Portadown* (Belfast: Beyond the Pale, 1997).

—— 'The Famine in County Armagh', in Christine Kinealy and Trevor Parkhill (eds.), *The Famine in Ulster: The Regional Impact* (Belfast: Ulster Historical Foundation, 1997).

MCBRIDE, DOREEN, *When Hunger Stalked the North* (Banbridge: Adare, 1994).

MCCALL, JOHN, *The Life of James Clarence Mangan* (Dublin: Carraig Books, 1975).

MACCALL, SEAMUS, *Irish Mitchel: A Biography* (London, Edinburgh, Paris, Melbourne, Toronto, and New York: T. Nelson & Sons Ltd., 1938).

MCCAVERY, TREVOR, 'The Famine in Co. Down', in Christine Kinealy and Trevor Parkhill (eds.), *The Famine in Ulster: The Regional Impact* (Belfast: Ulster Historical Foundation, 1997).

MCCORMACK, W. J., *From Burke to Beckett: Ascendancy, Tradition and Betrayal in Literary History* (Cork: Cork University Press, 1994).

MCCRACKEN, DONAL P., 'The Land the Famine Irish Forgot', in E. Margaret Crawford (ed.), *The Hungry Stream: Essays on Emigration and Famine* (Belfast: Institute of Irish Studies, Queen's University Belfast, 1997).

MACDONAGH, OLIVER, 'Irish Emigration to the USA and the British Colonies During the Famine', in R. Dudley Edwards and T. Desmond Williams (eds.), *The Great Famine: Studies in Irish History 1845–52* (Dublin: Browne & Nolan, 1956).

—— 'The Nineteenth-Century Revolution in Government: A Reappraisal', *Historical Journal*, 1/1 (1958), 52–67.

MACDONAGH, OLIVER, *The Nineteenth Century Novel and Irish Social History: Some Aspects* (Dublin: National University of Ireland, 1970).

—— 'The Age of O'Connell, 1830–45', in W. E. Vaughan (ed.), *A New History of Ireland*, V: *Ireland Under the Union I 1801–70* (Oxford: Clarendon Press, 1989).

—— 'The Economy and Society, 1830–45', in W. E. Vaughan (ed.), *A New History of Ireland*, V: *Ireland Under the Union I 1801–70* (Oxford: Clarendon Press, 1989).

—— 'Ideas and Institutions, 1830–45', in W. E. Vaughan (ed.), *A New History of Ireland*, V: *Ireland Under the Union I 1801–70* (Oxford: Clarendon Press, 1989).

—— 'Introduction', in W. E. Vaughan (ed.), *A New History of Ireland*, V: *Ireland Under the Union I, 1801–70* (Oxford: Clarendon Press, 1989).

—— 'Politics, 1830–45', in W. E. Vaughan (ed.), *A New History of Ireland*, V: *Ireland Under the Union I 1801–70* (Oxford: Clarendon Press, 1989).

MCDOWELL, R. B., *Public Opinion and Government Policy in Ireland 1801–1846* (London: Faber & Faber, 1952).

—— 'Ireland on the Eve of the Famine', in R. Dudley Edwards and T. Desmond Williams (eds.), *The Great Famine: Studies in Irish History 1845–52* (Dublin: Browne & Nolan, 1956).

MCHUGH, ROGER, 'The Famine in Irish Oral Tradition', in R. Dudley Edwards and T. Desmond Williams (eds.), *The Great Famine: Studies in Irish History 1845–52* (Dublin: Browne & Nolan, 1956).

MCKELVEY, R. S. J. HOUSTON, *The Chimney Corner* (Belfast: *The Northern Whig*, 1967).

MACKEN, WALTER, *The Silent People* (1962) (London: Pan Books, 1988).

MARSHALL, CATHERINE, 'Painting Irish History: The Famine', *History Ireland*, 4/3 (Autumn 1996), 46–50.

MARTIN, ROBERT BERNARD, *Tennyson: The Unquiet Heart* (Oxford: Oxford University Press and Faber & Faber, 1980).

MAXWELL, CONSTANTIA, *The Stranger in Ireland from the Reign of Elizabeth to the Great Famine* (London: Cape, 1954).

MELVILLE, JOY, *Mother of Oscar: The Life of Jane Francesca Wilde* (London: John Murray, 1994).

MERCIER, VIVIAN, *Modern Irish Literature: Sources and Founders* (Oxford: Clarendon Press, 1994).

MILLER, KERBY A., *Emigrants and Exiles: Ireland and the Irish Exodus to North America* (New York and Oxford: Oxford University Press, 1985).

MIMNAGH, JOHN and SEAMUS, '*To the Four Winds': Famine Times in North Longford* (Mullingar: *The Westmeath Examiner*, 1997).

MOKYR, JOEL, *Why Ireland Starved: A Quantitative and Analytical History of the Irish Economy, 1800–1850* (London and Boston: Allen & Unwin, 1985).

MOODY, T. W., *Davitt and Irish Revolution 1846–82* (Oxford: Clarendon Press, 1982).

—— 'Irish History and Irish Mythology', reprinted in Ciaran Brady (ed.), *Interpreting Irish History: The Debate on Historical Revisionism 1938–1994* (Dublin: Irish Academic Press, 1994).

MOORE, BRIAN, *The Mangan Inheritance* (1979) (London: Flamingo, 1995).

MORASH, CHRISTOPHER, (ed.), *The Hungry Voice: The Poetry of the Irish Famine* (Dublin: Irish Academic Press, 1989).

—— 'Imagining the Famine: Literary Representations of the Great Irish Famine', D.Phil. thesis (Trinity College, Dublin, 1990).

—— 'Spectres of the Famine', *Irish Review* (Winter 1995), 74–9.

—— *Writing the Irish Famine* (Oxford: Clarendon Press, 1995).

—— 'Making Memories: The Literature of the Irish Famine', in Patrick O'Sullivan (ed.), *The Irish World Wide: History, Heritage, Identity*, Volume 6: *The Meaning of the Famine* (London and Washington, DC: Leicester University Press, 1997).

—— 'Sinking Down into the Dark: The Famine on Stage', *Bullán: An Irish Studies Journal*, 3/1 (Spring 1997), 75–86.

—— and Richard Hayes (eds.), *'Fearful Realities': New Perspectives on the Famine* (Dublin: Irish Academic Press, 1996).

MULLEN, MICHAEL, *The Hungry Land* (New York, London, Toronto, Sydney, and Auckland: Bantam, 1986).

—— *The Darkest Years—A Famine Story* (Castlebar: Cavendish House, 1997).

MULLEN, RICHARD, *Anthony Trollope: A Victorian in His World* (London: Duckworth, 1990).

MURPHY, IGNATIUS, *The Diocese of Killaloe 1800–1850* (Dublin: Four Courts Press, 1992).

—— *Before the Famine Struck: Life in West Clare, 1834–1845* (Dublin and Portland, Oreg.: Irish Academic Press, 1996).

—— *A Starving People: Life and Death in West Clare, 1845–1851* (Dublin: Irish Academic Press, 1996).

MURPHY, MAUREEN O'ROURKE, 'Carleton & Columcille', *Carleton Newsletter*, 2/3 (4 Jan. 1972).

NEAL, FRANK, 'Black '47: Liverpool and the Irish Famine', in E. Margaret Crawford (ed.), *The Hungry Stream: Essays on Emigration and Famine* (Belfast: Institute of Irish Studies, Queen's University Belfast, 1997).

—— 'The Famine Irish in England and Wales', in Patrick O'Sullivan (ed.), *The Irish World Wide: History, Heritage, Identity*, Volume 6: *The Meaning of the Famine* (London and Washington, DC: Leicester University Press, 1997).

—— *Black '47: Britain and the Famine Irish* (Basingstoke and London: Macmillan, 1998).

NOLAN, JANET, 'The Great Famine and Women's Emigration from Ireland', in E. Margaret Crawford (ed.), *The Hungry Stream: Essays on Emigration and Famine* (Belfast: Institute of Irish Studies, Queen's University Belfast, 1997).

NOWLAN, KEVIN, 'The Political Background', in R. Dudley Edwards and T. Desmond Williams (eds.), *The Great Famine: Studies in Irish History 1845–52* (Dublin: Browne & Nolan, 1956).

O'BRIEN, BRENDAN, *Athlone Workhouse and the Famine* (Athlone: The Old Athlone Society, 1995).

Ó CORRÁIN, DONNCHADH, 'Legend as Critic', in Tom Dunne (ed.), *The Writer as Witness: Literature as Historical Evidence* (Cork: Cork University Press, 1987).

O DÁLAIGH, PÁDRAIG (ed.), *A Ballad History of Ireland for Schools* (Dublin and Cork: The Educational Company of Ireland, 1929).

O'DAY, ALAN and STEVENSON, JOHN (eds.), *Irish Historical Documents Since 1800* (Maryland: Barnes & Noble, 1992).

O'DONNELL, EDWARD, ' "The Scattered Debris of the Irish Nation": The Famine Irish and New York City, 1845–55', in E. Margaret Crawford (ed.), *The Hungry Stream: Essays on Emigration and Famine* (Belfast: Institute of Irish Studies, Queen's University Belfast, 1997).

Ó DUIGNEÁIN, PROINNSÍOS, *North Leitrim in Famine Times 1840–50* (Manorhamilton: Drumlin Publications, 1992).

O'FARRELL, PATRICK, 'Whose Reality?: The Irish Famine in History and Literature', *Historical Studies*, 20/78–81 (Apr. 1982–Oct. 1983), 1–13.

—— 'Lost in Transit: Australian Reaction to the Irish and Scots Famines, 1845–50', in Patrick O'Sullivan (ed.), *The Irish World Wide: History, Heritage, Identity*, Volume 6: *The Meaning of the Famine* (London and Washington, DC: Leicester University Press, 1997).

O'FERRALL, FERGUS, 'Daniel O'Connell, the 'Liberator', 1775–1847: Changing Images', in Raymond Gillespie and Brian P. Kennedy (eds.), *Ireland: Art into History* (Dublin and Niwot, Colo.: Town House and Roberts Rinehart, 1994), 91–102.

O'FLAHERTY, LIAM, *Famine* (1937) (Dublin: Wolfhound Press, 1992).

O'GALLAGHER, MARIANNA, 'The Orphans of Grosse Île: Canada and the Adoption of Irish Famine Orphans, 1847–48', in Patrick O'Sullivan (ed.), *The Irish World Wide: History, Heritage, Identity*, Volume 6: *The Meaning of the Famine* (London and Washington, DC: Leicester University Press, 1997).

O'GORMAN, MICHAEL, *A Pride of Paper Tigers: A History of the Great Hunger in the Scariff Workhouse Union from 1839 to 1853* (Tuamgraney, Co. Clare: East Clare Heritage, 1994).

Ó GRÁDA, CORMAC, ' "For Irishmen to Forget?" Recent Research on the Great Irish Famine' (Dublin: Centre for Economic Research, University College Dublin, 1988).

—— *Ireland Before and After the Famine: Explorations in Economic History, 1800–1925* (Manchester: Manchester University Press, 1988).

—— 'Industry & Communications, 1801–45', in W.E. Vaughan (ed.), *A New History of Ireland*, V: *Ireland Under the Union I 1801–70* (Oxford: Clarendon Press, 1989).

—— 'Poverty, Population and Agriculture, 1801–45', in W. E. Vaughan (ed.), *A New History of Ireland*, V: *Ireland Under the Union I 1801–70* (Oxford: Clarendon Press, 1989).

—— *Studies in Economic and Social History: The Great Irish Famine* (London and Basingstoke: Macmillan, 1989).

—— 'Making History in Ireland in the 1940s and 1950s: The Saga of the Great Famine', *Irish Review*, 12 (Spring/Summer 1992), 87–107.

—— *Ireland: A New Economic History 1780–1939* (Oxford: Clarendon Press, 1994).

—— 'The Great Famine and Today's Famines', in Cathal Póirtéir (ed.), *The Great Irish Famine* (Cork and Dublin: Mercier Press, 1995).

—— (ed.), *Famine 150: Commemorative Lecture Series* (Dublin: Teagasc: University College Dublin, 1997).

—— 'The Great Famine and Other Famines', in Cormac Ó Gráda (ed.), *Famine 150: Commemorative Lecture Series* (Dublin: Teagasc: University College Dublin, 1997).

—— 'The Great Irish Famine: Winners and Losers' (Dublin: Dept. of Economics, University College Dublin, Apr. 1997).

—— *Black '47 and Beyond: The Great Irish Famine in History, Economy, and Memory* (Princeton: Princeton University Press, 1999).

Ó HÁINLE, CATHAL G., 'The Gaelic Background of Carleton's Traits and Stories', *Éire-Ireland*, 18/1 (Spring 1983), 6–19.

O'HERLIHY, TIMOTHY, *The Famine 1845–1847: A Survey of its Ravages and Causes* (Drogheda: Drogheda Independent Co., 1947).

Ó MUIRITHE, DIARMAID, *A Seat Behind the Coachman: Travellers in Ireland 1800–1900* (Dublin and London: Gill and Macmillan, 1972).

O'NEILL, THOMAS, 'Sidelights on Souperism', *Irish Ecclesiastical Record*, 71 (Jan.–June 1949), 50–64.

—— 'The Organisation and Administration of Relief, 1845–52', in R. Dudley Edwards and T. Desmond Williams (eds.), *The Great Famine: Studies in Irish History 1845–52* (Dublin: Browne & Nolan, 1956).

O'NEILL, TIM P., 'The Persistence of Famine in Ireland', in Cathal Póirtéir (ed.), *The Great Irish Famine* (Cork and Dublin: Mercier Press, 1995).

O'SULLIVAN, PATRICK (ed.), *The Irish World Wide: History, Heritage, Identity*, Volume 6: *The Meaning of the Famine* (London and Washington,DC: Leicester University Press, 1997).

—— and LUCKING, RICHARD, 'The Famine World Wide: the Irish Famine and the Development of Famine Policy and Famine Theory', in Patrick O'Sullivan (ed.), *The Irish World Wide: History, Heritage, Identity*, Volume 6: *The Meaning of the Famine* (London and Washington, DC: Leicester University Press, 1997).

OKRI, BEN, 'Ken Saro-Wiwa', *The Guardian* (1 Nov. 1995), 19.

OREL, HAROLD, 'Colored Photographs: William Carleton's Contribution to the Short Story Tradition', *Éire-Ireland*, 19/2 (Summer 1984), 75–97.

OVERTON, BILL, *The Unofficial Trollope* (Brighton and Totowa, NJ: Harvester and Barnes & Noble, 1982).

PARKHILL, TREVOR, 'The Famine in County Londonderry', in Christine Kinealy and Trevor Parkhill (eds.), *The Famine in Ulster: The Regional Impact* (Belfast: Ulster Historical Foundation, 1997).

—— ' "Permanent Deadweight": Emigration from Ulster Workhouses during the Famine', in E. Margaret Crawford (ed.), *The Hungry Stream: Essays on Emigration and Famine* (Belfast: Institute of Irish Studies, Queen's University Belfast, 1997).

PHELAN, JOSEPHINE, *The Ardent Exile: The Life and Times of Thomas D'Arcy McGee* (Toronto: Macmillan, 1951).

PHILPIN, C. H. E. (ed.), *Nationalism and Popular Protest in Ireland* (Cambridge: Cambridge University Press, 1987).

PÓIRTÉIR, CATHAL, *Famine Echoes* (Dublin: Gill & Macmillan, 1995).

—— 'Folk Memory and the Famine', in Cathal Póirtéir (ed.), *The Great Irish Famine* (Cork and Dublin: Mercier Press, 1995).

—— (ed.), *The Great Irish Famine* (Cork and Dublin: Mercier Press, 1995).

POLHEMUS, ROBERT M., *The Changing World of Anthony Trollope* (Berkeley: University of California Press, 1968).

POLLARD, ARTHUR, *Anthony Trollope* (London, Henley, and Boston: Routledge & Kegan Paul, 1978).

PORTER, ROY and TEICH, MIKULAS (eds.), *Romanticism in National Context* (Cambridge: Cambridge University Press, 1988).

PRATT, MARY LOUISE, 'Scratches on the Face of the Country; or, What Mr. Barrow Saw in the Land of the Bushmen', in Henry Louis Gates, Jr. (ed.), *'Race', Writing, and Difference* (Chicago and London: University of Chicago Press, 1986).

QUIGLEY, MICHAEL, 'Grosse Île: "The most important and evocative Great Famine site outside of Ireland" ', in E. Margaret Crawford (ed.), *The Hungry Stream: Essays on Emigration and Famine* (Belfast: Institute of Irish Studies, Queen's University Belfast, 1997).

RAUCHBAUER, OTTO (ed.), *Ancestral Voices: The Big House in Anglo-Irish Literature* (Dublin and Hildesheim: Lilliput Press and Georg Olms Verlag, 1992).

REILLY, A. J., *Father John Murphy, Famine Priest* (Dublin and London: Clonmore & Reynolds; Burns & Oates Ltd., 1963).

RYDER, SEAN, 'Reading Lessons: Famine and the *Nation*, 1845–1849', in Christopher Morash and Richard Hayes (eds.), *'Fearful Realities': New Perspectives on the Famine* (Dublin: Irish Academic Press, 1996).

RYLE, MARTIN, *Journeys in Ireland: Literary Travellers, Rural Landscapes, Cultural Relations* (Aldershot: Ashgate, 1999).

SADLEIR, MICHAEL, *Trollope: A Commentary* (London: Constable & Co., 1933).

SAID, EDWARD W., *Nationalism, Colonialism and Literature: Yeats and Decolonization* (Derry: Field Day Theatre Company, 1988).

—— *Culture and Imperialism* (London: Chatto & Windus, 1993).

SALMON, LUCY MAYNARD, *The Newspaper and the Historian* (New York, London, Toronto, Melbourne, and Bombay: Oxford University Press, 1923).

SCALLY, ROBERT, *The End of Hidden Ireland: Rebellion, Famine, and Emigration* (New York and Oxford: Oxford University Press, 1995).

—— 'External Forces in the Famine Emigration from Ireland', in E. Margaret Crawford (ed.), *The Hungry Stream: Essays on Emigration and Famine* (Belfast: Institute of Irish Studies, Queen's University Belfast, 1997).

SCHIRMER, GREGORY A., 'Tales From Big House and Cabin: The Nineteenth Century', in James F. Kilroy (ed.), *The Irish Short Story: A Critical History* (Boston: Twayne Publishers, 1984), 21–44.

SEN, AMARTYA, *Poverty and Famines: An Essay on Entitlement and Deprivation* (Oxford: Clarendon Press, 1981).

SHANNON-MANGAN, ELLEN, *James Clarence Mangan: A Biography* (Dublin: Irish Academic Press, 1996).

SHATTOCK, JOANNE, 'Travel Writing Victorian and Modern: A Review of Recent Research', in Philip Dodd (ed.), *The Art of Travel: Essays on Travel Writing* (London and Totowa, NJ: Frank Cass, 1982).

SHEEHY, JEANNE, *The Rediscovery of Ireland's Past: The Celtic Revival 1830–1930* (London: Thames & Hudson, 1980).

SHERIDAN, JOHN DESMOND, *James Clarence Mangan* (Dublin and London: Talbot Press and G. Duckworth & Co. Ltd., 1937).

SHILLINGSBURG, PETER L., *Pegasus in Harness: Victorian Publishing and W. M. Thackeray* (Charlottesville, Va. and London: University Press of Virginia, 1992).

SKELTON, ISABEL, *The Life of Thomas D'Arcy McGee* (Gardenvale, Canada: Garden City Press, 1925).

SLOAN, BARRY, 'Mrs Hall's Ireland', *Éire-Ireland*, 19/3 (Autumn 1984), 18–30.

—— *The Pioneers of Anglo-Irish Fiction 1800–1850* (Gerrards Cross: Colin Smythe, 1986).

SMALLEY, DONALD (ed.), *Trollope: The Critical Heritage* (London and New York: Routledge & Kegan Paul, 1969).

SMITH, SHEILA M., *The Other Nation: The Poor in English Novels of the 1840s and 1850s* (Oxford and New York: Clarendon Press and Oxford University Press, 1980).

SMYTH, ALFRED P., *Faith, Famine and Fatherland in the Irish Midlands: Perceptions of a Priest and Historian: Anthony Cogan 1826–1872* (Dublin: Four Courts Press, 1992).

SOLAR, PETER M., 'The Potato Famine in Europe', in Cormac Ó Gráda (ed.), *Famine 150: Commemorative Lecture Series* (Dublin: Teagasc: University College Dublin, 1997).

Bibliography

SPENCE, JOSEPH, 'The Philosophy of Irish Toryism, 1833–52: a Study of Reactions to Liberal Reformism in Ireland in the Generation between the First Reform Act and the Famine, with Especial Reference to Expressions of National Feeling among the Protestant Ascendancy', Ph.D. thesis (Birkbeck College, University of London, 1991).

SULLIVAN, EILEEN, 'Yeats and Carleton', *Carleton Newsletter*, 5/2 (4 Apr. 1975).

—— Carleton: Artist of Reality', *Éire-Ireland*, 12/1 (Spring 1977), 130–40.

—— *William Carleton* (Boston: Twayne Publishers, 1983).

SUTHERLAND, JOHN, *The Longman Companion to Victorian Fiction* (London: Longman, 1990).

TERRY, R. C., 'Three Last Chapters of Trollope's First Novel', *Nineteenth-Century Fiction*, 27 (June 1972), 71–80.

—— *The Artist in Hiding* (London and Basingstoke: Macmillan, 1977).

The Times, The History of The Times, Volume II: *The Tradition Established: 1841–1884* (London: The Times, 1939).

TINGAY, LANCE O., 'The Reception of Trollope's First Novel', *Nineteenth-Century Fiction*, 6 (1951), 195–200.

TÓIBÍN, COLM, 'Erasures: Colm Tóibín on the Great Irish Famine', *London Review of Books*, 20/15 (30 July 1998), 17–23.

—— *The Irish Famine* (London: Profile Books, 1999).

TRACY, ROBERT, ' "The Unnatural Ruin": Trollope and Nineteenth-Century Irish Fiction', *Nineteenth-Century Fiction*, 37 (Dec. 1982), 358–82.

—— 'Introduction' to *The Macdermots of Ballycloran* (Oxford: Oxford University Press, 1989).

TREVOR, WILLIAM, 'Introduction' to *The Kellys and the O'Kellys* (Oxford: Oxford University Press, 1982).

—— 'The News from Ireland', *Ireland: Selected Stories* (Harmondsworth: Penguin, 1995).

VANCE, NORMAN, *Irish Literature: A Social History: Tradition, Identity and Difference* (Oxford: Basil Blackwell, 1990).

VAUGHAN, W. E. (ed.), *A New History of Ireland*, V: *Ireland Under the Union I 1801–70* (Oxford: Clarendon Press, 1989).

VEYNE, PAUL, *Writing History: Essay on Epistemology*, trans. Mina Moore-Rinvolucri (Manchester: Manchester University Press, 1984).

VICKERS, BRIAN, *In Defence of Rhetoric* (Oxford: Clarendon Press, 1990).

VINCENT, JOAN, 'A Political Orchestration of the Irish Famine: County Fermanagh, May 1847', in Marian Silverman and P. H. Gulliver (eds.), *Approaching the Past: Historical Anthropology Through Irish Case Studies* (New York: Columbia University Press, 1992), 75–98.

WALKER, LINUS H., *One Man's Famine* (Galway: Linus H. Walker, 1978).

WALSH, LOUIS J., *John Mitchel* (Dublin and Cork: Talbot Press, 1934).

WALSH, RITA, ' "A terrestrial paradise": The Development of Tourism in Killarney, c. 1750–1860', MA thesis (University College Galway, Oct. 1994).

WATERS, MAUREEN, 'William Carleton, The Writer as Witness', *Études Irlandaises: Revue Française D'Histoire, Civilisation et Littérature de L'Irlande*, 11, nouvelle série (Dec. 1986), 51–63.

WEBB, TIMOTHY, 'Introduction', *The Black Prophet: A Tale of Irish Famine, by William Carleton* (Shannon: Irish University Press, 1972).

WELCH, ROBERT (ed.), *Oxford Companion to Irish Literature* (Oxford: Clarendon Press, 1996).

WHELAN, IRENE, 'The Stigma of Souperism', in Cathal Póirtéir (ed.), *The Great Irish Famine* (Cork and Dublin: Mercier Press, 1995).

WHELAN, KEVIN, 'Pre and Post Famine Landscape Change', in Cathal Póirtéir (ed.), *The Great Irish Famine* (Cork and Dublin: Mercier Press, 1995).

WHITE, HAYDEN, *Metahistory: The Historical Imagination in Nineteenth-Century Europe* (Baltimore and London: Johns Hopkins University Press, 1993).

WHITE, TERENCE DE VERE, 'Introduction' to Trollope Society edition of *The Kellys and the O'Kellys* (London: Folio Society, 1992).

WILLIAMS, JULIA and WATT, STEPHEN, 'Representing a "Great Distress": Melodrama, Gender, and the Irish Famine', in Michael Hays and Anastasia Nikolopoulou (eds.), *Melodrama: The Cultural Emergence of a Genre* (Basingstoke and London: Macmillan, 1996), 245–62.

WITTIG, E. W., 'Trollope's Irish Fiction', *Éire-Ireland*, 9 (Autumn 1974), 97–118.

WOLFE, ROBERT LEE, *William Carleton: Irish Peasant Novelist; A Preface to his Fiction* (New York and London: Garland Publications, 1980).

WOODHAM-SMITH, CECIL, *The Great Hunger: Ireland 1845–9* (London: Hamish Hamilton, 1962).

WOODS, CHRISTOPHER, 'American Travellers in Ireland before and during the Great Famine: A Case of Culture-Shock', in Wolfgang Zach and Heinz Kosok (eds.), *Literary Interrelations: Ireland, England and the World*, Volume III: *National Images and Stereotypes* (Tübingen: Narr, 1987), 77–84.

—— 'Irish Travel Writing as Source Material', *Irish Historical Studies*, 28/110 (Nov. 1992), 171–83.

ZACH, WOLFGANG and KOSOK, HEINZ (eds.), *Literary Interrelations: Ireland, England and the World*, Volume III: *National Images and Stereotypes* (Tübingen: Narr, 1987).

INDEX